HUMAN MACHINE INTERACTION – GETTING CLOSER

Edited by **Maurtua Inaki**

Human Machine Interaction – Getting Closer
Edited by Maurtua Inaki

Published by InTech
Janeza Trdine 9, 51000 Rijeka, Croatia

Publishing Process Manager Bojan Rafaj

Technical Editor Teodora Smiljanic

Cover Designer InTech Design Team

Additional hard copies can be obtained from orders@intechopen.com

Human Machine Interaction – Getting Closer, Edited by Maurtua Inaki
p. cm.
ISBN 978-953-307-890-8

For EU product safety concerns:
IN TECH d.o.o., Prolaz Marije Krucifikse Kozulić 3, 51000 Rijeka, Croatia,
info@intechopen.com or visit our website at intechopen.com.

Meet the editor

Iñaki Maurtua, an Electrical Engineer, has built his entire professional career in TEKNIKER since the mid eighties, taking part in many projects in the field of robotics, automation, monitoring and wearable computing. Among those projects, we can mention the development of six flexible manufacturing systems (FMS) and the coordination of the usability aspects in the wearit@work project, in particular in the production scenario developed with SKODA. He is currently the head of the Smart and Autonomous System Unit, working mainly in different aspects of robotics, including the Human-Robot Interaction. Machine vision and body-worn sensors are the core technologies used for such interaction. Nowadays, he coordinates two EU funded (FP7) projects in this field: "ROBOFOOT: Smart robotics for high added value footwear industry" and "MAINBOT: Mobile robots for inspection and maintenance activities in extensive industrial plants". He has published more than 30 papers in magazines, congress and book chapters.

Contents

Preface XI

Part 1 HCI Development Process 1

Chapter 1 **Automated Generation of User Interfaces - A Comparison of Models and Future Prospects** 3
Helmut Horacek, Roman Popp and David Raneburger

Chapter 2 **Human-Machine Interaction and Agility in the Process of Developing Usable Software: A Client-User Oriented Synergy** 17
Benigni Gladys and Gervasi Osvaldo

Chapter 3 **Affect Interpretation in Metaphorical and Simile Phenomena and Multithreading Dialogue Context** 51
Li Zhang

Chapter 4 **Learning Physically Grounded Lexicons from Spoken Utterances** 69
Ryo Taguchi, Naoto Iwahashi, Kotaro Funakoshi, Mikio Nakano, Takashi Nose and Tsuneo Nitta

Chapter 5 **New Frontiers for WebGIS Platforms Generation** 85
Davide Di Pasquale, Giuseppe Fresta, Nicola Maiellaro, Marco Padula and Paolo Luigi Scala

Chapter 6 **Ergonomic Design of Human-CNC Machine Interface** 115
Imtiaz Ali Khan

Part 2 Human Robot Interaction 137

Chapter 7 **Risk Assessment and Functional Safety Analysis to Design Safety Function of a Human-Cooperative Robot** 155
Suwoong Lee and Yoji Yamada

Chapter 8 **Improving Safety of Human-Robot Interaction Through Energy Regulation Control and Passive Compliant Design 155**
Matteo Laffranchi, Nikos G. Tsagarakis and Darwin G. Caldwell

Chapter 9 **Monitoring Activities with Lower-Limb Exoskeletons 171**
Juan C. Moreno and José L. Pons

Chapter 10 **Sensori-Motor Appropriation of an Artefact: A Neuroscientific Approach 187**
Yves Rybarczyk, Philippe Hoppenot, Etienne Colle and Daniel R. Mestre

Chapter 11 **Cognitive Robotics in Industrial Environments 213**
Stephan Puls, Jürgen Graf and Heinz Wörn

Chapter 12 **Intelligent Object Exploration 235**
Robert Gaschler, Dov Katz, Martin Grund, Peter A. Frensch and Oliver Brock

Preface

The way in which humans and the devices that surround them interact is changing fast. The gaming business is pushing the trend towards more natural ways of interaction; the WII and KINNECT are good examples of this. Children are becoming familiar with these new interaction approaches, guaranteeing that we will use them in more "serious" applications in the future.

Human-robot interaction is one of those applications that have attracted the attention of the research community. Here, the space sharing between robots and humans introduces an additional challenge, the risk management.

In this book, the reader will find a set of papers divided into two sections. The first one presents different proposals focused on the development process itself. The second one is devoted to different aspects of the interaction, with special emphasis on the physical interaction.

I would like to thank all of the authors for their contribution, my colleagues of the Smart and Autonomous System in TEKNIKER for their collaboration in the revision process and, of course, InTech for making the publication of this book possible.

Maurtua Inaki,
Autonomous and Smart Systems Unit,
Fundación Tekniker Eibar, Gipuzkoa,
Spain

Part 1

HCI Development Process

1

Automated Generation of User Interfaces – A Comparison of Models and Future Prospects

Helmut Horacek, Roman Popp and David Raneburger
Institute of Computer Technology, Technical University of Vienna
Austria

1. Introduction

In the past decade, demands on interfaces for human-computer interaction (HCI) as well as efforts invested in building these components of software systems have increased substantially. This development has essentially two sources: Existing tools do not well support the designer, so that building these components is time-consuming, error-prone, and requires substantial programming skills. Moreover, the increasing variety of devices with different presentation profiles, variations on media uses and combinations of several media points to a necessity of designing some sort of interface shells so that one such shell can be adapted to a set of partially divergent needs of varying presentation forms.

Especially the second factor, as also argued by Meixner & Seissler (2011), makes it advisable to specify interfaces on some sort of *abstract* level, from which operational code can be generated automatically, or at least in some semi-automated way. This aim is quite in contrast to traditional, mostly syntactic specification levels. Abstract level interfaces should not only be better understandable, especially by non-programmers, but they would also allow for a systematic adaptation to varying presentation demands, as advocated for above. Apart from the ambitious goal to define an appropriate design language and tools for building interfaces in this language, a major difficulty with such models lies in the operationalization of specifications built on the basis of these models, both in terms of degrees of automation and in terms of quality of the resulting interface appearance and functionality. Since semantic interaction specifications can abstract away plenty of details that need to be worked out for building a running system, we can expect that there is a fundamental tension between ease and intuitiveness of the design on the one hand, and coverage and usage quality of the resulting interface on the other hand.

To date, a limited set of development models for interface design have been proposed, which are in line with the motivations as outlined above: discourse-based communication models (Falb et al. (2006)), task models (Paternò et al. (1997), Limbourg & Vanderdonckt (2003)), and models in the OO method (Pastor et al. (2008)). Moreover, abstract models of interface design bear some similarities to natural language dialog systems and techniques underlying their response facilities, including reasoning about content specifications based on forces of underlying dialog concepts, as well as measures to achieve conformance to requirements of form. Therefore, we elaborate some essential, relevant properties of natural language dialog systems, which help us to develop a catalog of desirable properties of abstract models for interface design. In order to assess achievements and prospects of abstract models for interface design, we compare some of the leading approaches. We elaborate their relative strengths and weaknesses, in terms of differences across models, and we discuss to what extent they can or cannot fulfill factors we consider relevant for a successful interface design. Based on this comparison, we characterize the current position of state-of-the-art systems on a road map to building competitive interfaces based on abstract specifications.

This paper is organized as follows. We first introduce models of natural language dialog systems, from the perspective of their relevance for designing HCI components. Then we present a catalog of criteria that models for designing interfaces should fulfill to a certain extent, in order to exhibit a degree of quality competitive to traditionally built interfaces. In the main sections, we present some of the leading models for designing interfaces on abstract levels, including assessments as to what extent they fulfill the criteria from this catalog. Next, we summarize these assessments, in terms of relative strengths and weaknesses of these models, and in terms of where models in general are competent or fall short. We conclude by discussing future prospects.

2. Linguistic models

Two categories of linguistic models bear relevance for the purposes of handling discourse issues within HCIs:

- Methods for *dialog modeling*, notably those based on information states. This is the modern approach to dialog modeling that has significantly improved the capabilities of dialog systems in comparison to traditional approaches, which are based on explicit, but generally too rigid dialog grammars.
- Methods for *natural language generation*, which cover major factors in the process of expressing abstract specifications in adequate surface forms. They comprise techniques to concretize possibly quite abstract specifications, putting this content material in an adequate structure and order, choosing adequate lexical items to express these specifications in the target language, and composing these items according to the constraints of the language.

Apparently, major simplifications can be made prior to elaborating relations to the task of building HCIs: no interpretation of linguistic content and form is needed, and ambiguities about the scope of newly presented information also do not exist. Nevertheless, we will see that there are a variety of concepts relevant to HCIs, which makes it quite worth to study potential correspondences and relations.

Dialog models with information states have been introduced by Traum & Larsson (2003). According to them, the purpose of this method includes the following functionalities:

- updating the dialog context on the basis of interpreted utterances
- providing context-dependent expectations for interpreting observed signals
- interfacing with task processing, to coordinate dialog and non-dialog behavior and reasoning
- deciding what content to express next and when to express it

When it comes down to more details, there are not many standards about the information state, and its use for acting as a system in a conversation needs to be elaborated – recent approaches try to employ empirically based learning methods, such as Heeman (2007).

Semantically motivated approaches typically address certain text sorts or phenomena such as some classes of speech acts, in abstract semantics. Elaborations have been made for typical situations in information-seeking and task-oriented dialogs, including grounding and obligations, such as Matheson et al. (2000), and Kreutel & Matheson (2003). Altogether, information state-based techniques regulate locally possible dialog continuations, as well as some overarching contextual factors.

For purposes of HCI development, a few of these underlying concepts pertain:

- Sets of interaction types that regulate the coherence of the discourse continuation in dependency of the category of the immediately preceding interaction. For instance, questions must normally be answered, and requests confirmed, prior to executing an action that satisfies the request.
- Changes in the joint knowledge of the conversants according to the state of the discourse (*grounding*). For example, specifications made about properties of a discourse object should be maintained – e.g., an article to be selected eventually, as long as the interaction remains within the scope of the task to which this discourse object is associated.
- Holding evident *commitments* introduced in the course of the interaction, which essentially means that a communicative action that requires a reaction of some sort from the other conversant must eventually be addressed unless the force of this action is canceled through another communicative action. For example, a user is expected to answer a set of questions displayed by a GUI to proceed normally in this dialog, unless he decides to change the course of actions by clicking a 'back' or 'home' button or he chooses another topic in the application which terminates the subdialog to which the set of questions belongs.

The other category of linguistic models, methods for natural language generation, are characterized by a stratified architecture, especially used in application-oriented approaches (see Reiter (1994)). There are three phases, concerned with issues of *what* to say, *when* and *how* to say it, mediating between four strata:

1. A *communicative intention* constitutes the first stratum, which consists of some sort of abstract, typically non-linguistic specifications. Through the first phase called *text planning*, which comprises selecting and organizing content specifications that implement the communicative intention,
2. a *text plan*, the second stratum is built. This representation level is conceived as *language-independent*. Through operations that fall in the second phase, including the choice of lexical items and building referring expressions,
3. a *functional description* of some sort, the third stratum, is built. This representation level is generally conceived as *form-independent*, that is, neither surface word forms nor their order is given at this stage. However, details of this representation level differ considerably according to the underlying linguistic theory. Through accessing information from grammar and lexicon knowledge sources
4. a *surface form* is built, which constitutes the fourth stratum, the final representation level.

Especially the criterion of language independence of the text plan is frequently challenged on theoretical grounds, since the desirable (and practically necessary) guarantee of *expressibility* (as argued by Meteer (1992)) demands knowledge about the available expressive means in the target language. The repertoire of available linguistic means bears some influence on how content specifications may or may not be structured prior to expressing them lexically. Since transformations are typically defined in an easily manageable, widely structure-preserving manner, a high degree of structural similarity across representations from adjacent strata is essential. In order to address this problem in a principled manner, several proposals with interactive architectures have been made, to enable a text planner to revise some of its tentative choices, on the basis of results reported by later phases of processing. These approaches, however, were all computationally expensive and hard to control. In practical systems, a clever design of concrete operations on text planning and subsequent levels of processing, as well as care with the ontological design of the text plan level stratum proved to be sufficient to circumvent problems of expressibility.

It is quite remarkable, that these four strata in architectural models of natural language generation have a strong correspondence in the area of GUI development, in terms of Model Driven Approaches. In both models, higher level strata are increasingly independent of properties of the categories of proper expressive means, which are language and form in the case of natural language, and platform and code in the case of GUI development. The connection between these models becomes even tighter when we take into account multi-modal extensions to natural language generation approaches, where components in a text plan can be realized either by textual or by graphical means, including their coordination.

When it comes to examining the relevance of concrete methods originating from natural language generation for HCI purposes, several measures offer themselves, which are all neutral with respect to the proper features of natural language:

- Techniques for organizing bits and pieces of content in ontological and structural terms, following concepts of coherence, as encapsulated in a number of theories, such as Rhetorical Structure Theory, see Mann & Thompson (1988). Dominating relations on this level are hierarchical dependencies, while form and order are expressed in terms of constraints, which come to play not before concrete realizations are chosen.
- Choices between expressive means, primarily between alternative media, according to their suitability to express certain categories of content. For example, causal relations or negation elements can be presented much better in a textual rather than in a graphical form, whereas the opposite is the case for local relations.
- Structural and ontological relations may also drive the suitability of form and layout design. For example, groupings of items need to be presented in a uniform, aligned manner. Moreover, background information should be presented in moderately salient forms, quite in contrast to warnings and alert messages.

In addition, it is conceived that automated approaches to natural language generation are generally good in producing texts that are conform to norms of several sorts, such as the use of a specific vocabulary and limited syntactic forms, but also non lexically dependent conventions.

In the following sections, we refer to various aspects of linguistic models, when comparisons between models of GUI construction and transformations between representation levels are discussed.

3. Criteria

The goal of building interfaces on some level of abstract specifications is ambitious, and implementations of conceptual approaches comprise a variety of measures and the adequate orchestration of their ingredients. Consequently, assessments made about competing approaches can be broken down into a set of dimensions, where elaborations in individual approaches can be expected to address some of these dimensions in partially compensative degrees. Within this section, we apply the term 'user' to refer to an essentially untrained person who *uses* such an approach to develop an interface.

As for any software system to be built automatically or at least semi-automatically on the basis of abstract, user-provided specifications, three orthogonal criteria offer themselves:

- The *ease of use*,
  that is, the amount of training needed, prior knowledge required, and degree of effort demanded to generate adequate specifications for some piece of application.
- The *degree of operationalization*,
  that is, where the position of an approach resides on the typically long scale ranging from moderately semi-automated to fully-automated systems.
- The *coverage*,
  that is, to what extent and in what ways an approach can bring about the ingredients needed for the system to be built, hence, what kind of situations it can handle and for which ones it falls short for some reason.

In addition to these in some sense basic criteria, there are two further ones, which go beyond the development of a single system in complementary ways:

- *Adaptability in the realization*,
  that is, using the system ultimately generated in different contexts, thereby taking into account specific needs of each of these contexts, and making use of a large portion of the specifications in all contexts considered.
- *Reuse of (partial) specifications*,
  that is, the use of specifications or of some of their parts in several components of a model specified by an approach, or across different versions.

In the following, we flesh out these criteria for the specific task at hand.

As for the *ease of use*, the user should be discharged of technical details of interface development as much as possible. Ideally, the user does not need to have any technical experience in building interfaces, and only some limited teaching is required, so that the user becomes acquainted with operations the development system offers and with the conventions it adopts. In order to make this possible, the implementation of an interface development model should foresee some language that provides the building blocks of the model, and effective ways to compose them. In addition to that, certain features aiming at the support in maintaining correctness and/or completeness of specifications made can prove quite useful. While correctness proofs for programs are expensive and carried out for safety-critical tasks, if at all, measures to check completeness or correctness in some local context are much easier to realize, and they can still prove quite valuable. For example, the system might remind the user of missing specifications for some of the possible dialog continuations, according to contextually suitable combinations of communicative acts. We have filed these measures under the item *ease of use* because they primarily support a user in verifying completion and correcting errors of specifications if pointed to them, although these features can also be conceived as contributions to *degrees of operationalization*.

The *degree of operationalization* itself constitutes methods and procedures which regulate how the interpretation of a model specified by a user is transduced into executable modules, especially what activities involved in these procedures need to be carried out by hand. These measures manifest themselves in three components complementing each other:

- The *discourse structure*
- The *incorporation of references to business logic components*
- Invoking *rendering techniques*

The *discourse structure* per se constitutes the proper model which the user has to build in terms of abstract specifications. The major challenge from the perspective of the operationalization lies in providing an automated procedure for transducing the abstract specifications made into a workable system. Since setting up such a procedure is normally associated with plenty of details that go beyond of what is represented in the abstract specifications made by the user, it is particularly important to automate the derivation of all necessary details as much as possible.

The *incorporation of references to business logic components* is, strictly speaking, a subcategory of activities concerning specifications of the discourse structure. Since this particular activity is so prominent – it occurs in absolutely all models, in a significant number of instances, and is potentially associated with quite detailed specifications – we have given it a first class citizen state for our considerations. Moreover, handling this connection is also a primary task supported by the information state in linguistic models. As for linguistic models, it is generally assumed that the business logic underlying an application is properly and completely defined when interface specifications are to be made, in particular for establishing references to business logic components. However, when developing a software system, it is conceivable that some functionality originating from the discourse model may point to a demand on the business logic which has not been foreseen when this component has been designed; this situation is similar to the building of discourse models in computational linguistics, where discourse objects are introduced in the course of a conversation, which exist within the scope of this conversation only, and are related to, but not identical to some real world objects. For example, in a flight booking application, one has to distinguish between the proper flights in the database, completed flight specifications made by a customer built in the course of some customer-system subdialog, and partial, potentially inconsistent flight specifications incrementally made by the customer in the course of this dialog. Since it is generally unrealistic to assume perfect business logic design in all details, some sort of an interplay between the definition of the business logic and the design of the discourse structure may eventually be desirable. Finally, access to business logic components for reference purposes can also vary significantly in their *ease of use* across approaches, so that we have to consider this issue from the usability perspective as well.

Invoking *rendering techniques* is somehow converse to the other categories of handling specifications. It comprises how and where information can be specified that rendering methods additionally require in order to produce compositions of concrete interaction elements in an appropriate form. There are similarities between the role of rendering and components in the production of text out of internal specifications, as pursued in computational linguistics. The production of text comprises measures to assemble content specifications followed by methods to put these into an adequate linguistic form. Rendering techniques essentially have relations to the second part of this process. These techniques comprise mappings for the elements of the abstract specifications, transducing them into elements of a GUI or of some other dedicated presentation device, as well as constraints on how the results of these mappings are to be composed to meet form requirements of the device addressed. The overall task is most suitably accomplished by automating mapping specifications and device constraints as much as possible, and by providing a search procedure that picks a mapping combination in accordance with the given constraints, thereby obeying preference criteria, if available. In most natural language generation system architectures, especially those of practical systems, locally optimal choices are made in a systematic order, thus featuring computational effectiveness and simplicity of control, at the cost of sacrificing some degree of potentially achievable quality. A few clever search procedures exist, improving that quality with limited extra effort. In an elaborate version, one can expect that this process is characterized by compensative effects between search effort and quality achievement. A useful property of automated rendering techniques, similar to some natural language generation applications, is the conformance to style conventions and preference constraints, which can be ensured by the automation of form choice and composition.

The *coverage* of a discourse model in terms of discourse situations addressed may vary significantly across individual approaches. For elaborate versions, a considerably large repertoire of discourse situations and their flexible handling can prove to be important, following the experience from natural language dialog systems. For these systems, much effort has been invested in expanding the kind of discourse situations covered, which proved to be valuable, since the increased flexibility improved the effectiveness of dialog task achievement considerably.

We distinguish discourse situations according to structural relations between components of such situations. The more involved these relations are, the more challenging is it to provide the user with tools to make abstract specifications of the underlying discourse situation in an effective manner. We consider the following situations, in ascending order of complexity:

- *Groupings*
  This structural pattern constitutes a limited set of items of the same kind, which have to be addressed in the same fashion. Unlike in human spoken dialogs, they can be treated in one go in many HCI devices, such as a GUI. A typical example is a pair of questions concerning source and destination of a trip, and the associated answers.
- *Embeddings, such as subdialogs*
  In many discourse situations, an elaboration of the item currently addressed may be required. This may concern supplementary information, such as a property of some airport chosen as destination, or, most frequently, a clarification dialog, asking, for example, to disambiguate between two airports that are in accordance with some specification made so far.
- *Conditional branching*
  The appropriate continuation in a discourse situation may depend on some specific condition that arose during the preceding course of the dialog, for example through unexpected or faulty specifications. In many cases, this condition manifests itself in the category of the immediately preceding utterance or of its content, such as an invalid date specification, but it may also be the value of some recently computed state variable, such as one which makes an incompatibility between a set of query specifications explicit. The continuation after the branching may completely diverge into independent continuations, or a subdialog may be started in one or several of these branches, after the completion of which control may return to the point where the branching is invoked.

- *Repetitions and related control patterns*

  In many situations, certain discourse patterns are invoked repeatedly, mostly in case of a failure to bring about the goal underlying the fragment which conforms to this pattern. Repetitions may be unlimited, if the human conversant is supposed to provide a suitable combination of specifications within this discourse fragment, and he can retry until he succeeds or he may decide to continue the dialog in some other way. Repetition may also be constrained, for example by a fixed number of trials, such as when filling out a login mask, or when specifying details of some payment action.
- *Simultaneous and parallel structures*

  Most dialogs simply evolve as sequences of utterances over time. In some situations, however, the proper dialog can reasonably continue in parallel to executing some time-consuming system action. One class of examples concerns processing of computationally heavy transactions, such as a database request, during which the proper dialog can continue, with the result of the database request being asynchronously reported when available. Another class of examples concerns the play of a video or of a slide show, which can be accompanied by a dialog local to the context where the video respectively slide show is displayed.
- *Topic shifts, including implicit subdialog closing*

  This kind of discourse situation is the most advanced one, and it can also be expected to be the most difficult one to handle. In human conversations, topic shifts are signaled by discourse cues, thereby implicitly closing discourse segments unrelated to the newly introduced topic, which makes these shifts concise and communicatively so effective. Within a GUI, similar situations exist. They comprise structurally controlled jumps into previous contexts, frequently implemented by *Back* and *Home/Start* keys, as well as explicit shifts to another topic which is out of the scope of the current discourse segment. An example is a customer request to enter a dialog about car rental, leaving a yet uncompleted dialog about booking a flight. As opposed to human dialogs, where the precise scope of the initiated subdialog with the new topic needs to be contextually inferred, these circumstances are precisely defined within a GUI. However, providing mechanisms for specifying these options in terms of abstract discourse specifications in an intuitive manner and with limited amount of effort appears to be very challenging.

Adaptability in the realization may concern a set of contextual constraints. One of them comprises specificities of the device used, such as the available screen size, which may be significantly different for a laptop and for a PDA. Another distinction lies in the use of media, if multiple media are available, or if versions for several ones are to be produced. For example, a warning must be rendered differently whether it comes within a GUI or whether it is to be expressed in speech. Finally, the ultimate appearance of an interface may be varied according to different conventions or styles.

Reuse of partial specifications also may concern a number of issues. To start with, partial or completed specifications of some discourse situation, including specifications for rendering, may be modified according to demands of other styles or conventions – the purpose is identical to the one described in the previous paragraph, but with a different timing and organization. Moreover, the incorporation of subdialog patterns is a very important feature, useful in some variants. One possible use is the provision of skeletons that cover subdialog patterns, so that they can be instantiated according to the present discourse situation. Another possible use is the reoccurrence of an already instantiated subdialog pattern, which may be reused in another context, possibly after some modifications or adaptations to the concrete instantiations are made. Finally, versioning may be an issue, either to maintain several versions for different uses, or to keep them during the design phase, to explore the differences among them and to pick a preferred one later. Most of these reuses of partial specifications can be found in natural language generation systems, but this is hardly surprising, since almost all of them are fully automated systems.

This catalog of criteria is quite large, and some of the items in this catalog are quite advanced, so that few of the present approaches if any at all can be expected to address one or another of these advanced items, even to a limited degree. Most items in this catalog do not constitute black-or-white criteria, which makes assessing competing approaches along these criteria not an easy job. Moreover, approaches to design interfaces on some abstract specification level are not yet far enough developed and documented so that detailed, metric-based comparisons make sense. For example, the *ease of use*, in terms of the amount of details to be specified and the intuitiveness of use have to be assessed largely for each model separately, on the basis of its specificities, since experimental results about these user-related issues are largely missing. Altogether, we aim at a characterization of the current position of state-of-the-art systems, in terms of their relative strengths and weaknesses, as well as in terms of how far the state-of-the-art is in the ambitious goal of producing competitive interfaces out of abstract specifications that users can produce with reasonable effort.

4. Models in user interface development

The use of models and their automated transformation to executable UI source code are a promising approach to ease the process of UI development for several reasons. One reason is that modeling is on a higher level of abstraction than writing program code. This allows the designer to concentrate on high-level aspects of the interaction instead of low-level representation/programming details and supposedly makes modeling more affordable than writing program code. Another reason is that the difference in the level of abstraction makes models reusable and a suitable means for multi-platform applications, as one model can be transformed into several concrete implementations. This transformation is ideally even fully automatic. One further reason is that models, if automatically transformable, facilitate system modifications after the first development cycle. Changes on the requirements can be satisfied through changes on the models which are subsequently automatically propagated to the final UI through performing the transformations anew. A good overview of current state-of-the-art models, approaches and their use in the domain of UI development is given in Van den Bergh et al. (2010). It is notable that most approaches in the field of automated UI generation are based on the Model Driven Architecture[1] (MDA) paradigm. Such approaches use a set of models to capture the different aspects involved and apply model transformations while refining the input models to the source code for the final UI. In this section we will introduce and discuss model-driven UI development approaches that support the automated transformation of high-level interaction models to UI source code. We will highlight some of their strong points and shortcomings based on the criteria that we defined in section 3.

The primary focus of our criteria is the comparison of high-level models that are used as input for automated generation of user interfaces. Such models are typically tightly linked to a dedicated transformation approach to increase the *degree of operationalization* and the *adaptability in realization*. This tight coupling requires not only the comparison of the models, but also of the corresponding transformation approaches. We will use the Cameleon Reference

[1] `http://www.omg.org/mda/`

Framework by Calvary et al. (2003), a widely applied classification scheme for models used in UI generation processes, to determine the level of abstraction for the models to compare. The Cameleon Reference Framework defines four different levels of abstraction. These levels are from abstract to concrete:

1. *Tasks & Concepts*. This level accommodates high-level interaction specifications.
2. *Abstract UI*. This level accommodates a modality and toolkit-independent UI specification.
3. *Concrete UI*. This level accommodates a modality-dependent but still toolkit-independent UI specification.
4. *Final UI*. This level accommodates the final source code representation of the UI.

We apply our criteria to models on the tasks & concepts level and their transformation approaches.

Let us introduce a small excerpt from a flight booking scenario, which we will use to illustrate the presented approaches. First, the *System* asks the *User* to select a departure and a destination airport. Next the System provides a list of flights between the selected airports to the User. The User selects a flight and the System checks whether there are seats available on this flight or not (i.e., already overbooked). Finally, the System either asks the User to select a seat or informs him that the flight is already overbooked.

4.1 Discourse-based Communication Models

Discourse-based *Communication Models* provide a powerful means to specify the interaction between two parties on the tasks & concepts level. They integrate three different models to capture the aspects required for automated transformations (i.e., source code generation). Communication Models use a *Domain-of-Discourse Model* to capture the required aspects of the application domain. Moreover, they use an *Action-Notification Model* to specify actions that can be performed by either of the interacting parties and notifications that can be exchanged between them. The core part of the Communication Model is the *Discourse Model* that models the flow of interaction between two parties as well as the exchanged information (i.e., message content). The Discourse Model is based on human language theories and provides an intuitive way for interaction designers to specify the interaction between a user and a system. Discourse Models use Communicative Acts as basic communication units and relate them to capture the flow of interaction. The Communicative Acts are based on Speech Acts as introduced by Searle (1969). Typical turn takings like question-answer are modeled through Adjacency Pairs, derived from Conversation Analysis by Luff et al. (1990). Rhetorical Structure Theory (RST) by Mann & Thompson (1988) together with Procedural Relations are used to relate the Adjacency Pairs and provide the means to capture more complex flows of interaction. Discourse Models specify two interaction parties. Each Communicative Act is assigned to one of the two interacting parties and specifies the content of the exchanged messaged via its *Propositional Content*. The Propositional Content refers to concepts specified in the Domain-of-Discourse and the Action-Notification Model and is important for the operationalization of Communication Models (see Popp & Raneburger (2011) for details). Thus, the Discourse, the Domain-of-Discourse and the Action-Notification Model form the Communication Model which provides the basis for automated source code generation.

Let us use our small flight selection scenario to illustrate the discourse-based approach. Figure 1 shows the graphical representation of the Discourse Model for our scenario. This Discourse Model defines two interaction parties - the Customer (green or dark) and the

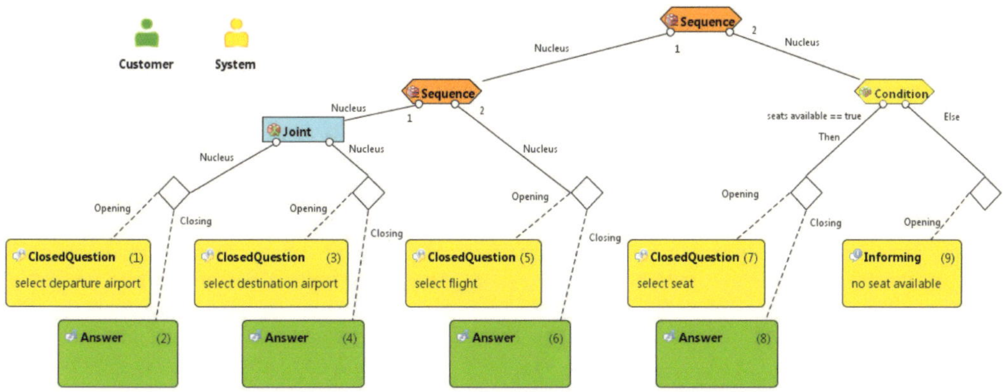

Fig. 1. Flight Booking Discourse Model from Raneburger, Popp, Kaindl & Falb (2011)

System (yellow or light). The Communicative Acts that are exchanged are represented by rounded boxes and the corresponding Adjacency Pairs by diamonds. The Adjacency Pairs are connected via RST or Procedural Relations. The green (or dark) and yellow (or light) fill color of the elements indicates the assigned interaction party.

Ease of Use — A graphical representation of Discourse Models eases their use for the designer. Various tutorials indicate that Discourse Models are intuitive to use during an informal design phase due to their human language theory basis. They support easy modeling of typical turn-takings in a conversation through the Adjacency Pairs and the specification of a more complex interaction through their Relations.

A high degree of operationalization for Communication Models is provided by the Unified Communication Platform (UCP) and the corresponding UI generation framework (UCP:UI). The aim during the development of UCP and UCP:UI was to stay compliant or apply well-established specification techniques so that only limited teaching is required. Therefore, an SQL-like syntax is used to specify the Propositional Content of each Communicative Act. Cascading Style Sheets[2] are used for style and layout specifications.

Degree of Operationalization — Discourse-based Communication Models can be operationalized with UCP and UCP:UI. A high degree of operationalization, however, requires more detailed specifications in the input models. Communication Models use the Propositional Content of each Communicative Act and the additional specification of conditions for Relations to provide the needed information for their operationalization and to specify the interface between UI and application logic. The Propositional Content specifies the content of the exchanged messages (i.e., Communicative Acts) and how they shall be processed by the corresponding interaction party. Popp & Raneburger (2011) show that the Propositional Content provides an unambiguous specification of the interface between the two interacting agents. In case of UI generation, the Propositional Content specifies the references to business logic components.

Additionally to the Propositional Content, Popp et al. (2009) include UML-state machines[3] in UCP to clearly define the procedural semantics of each Discourse Model element. Hence, each Discourse Model can be mapped to a finite-state machine. This composite state machine

[2] `http://www.w3.org/Style/CSS/`
[3] `http://uml.org`

is used to derive and define the corresponding UI behavior in case of UI generation (see Raneburger, Popp, Kaindl & Falb (2011)).

The runtime environment uses a Service-oriented Architecture and is provided by UCP Popp (2009). Figure 2 illustrates the operationalization of the Communication Model. The upper part depicts the integration of the Discourse, the Domain-of-Discourse and the Action-Notification Model into the Communication Model. The lower part shows that the Communication Model provides an interface that supports the distribution of the application and the generated UI on different machines. The *System* and the *Customer* communicate through the exchange of Communicative Acts over the Internet.

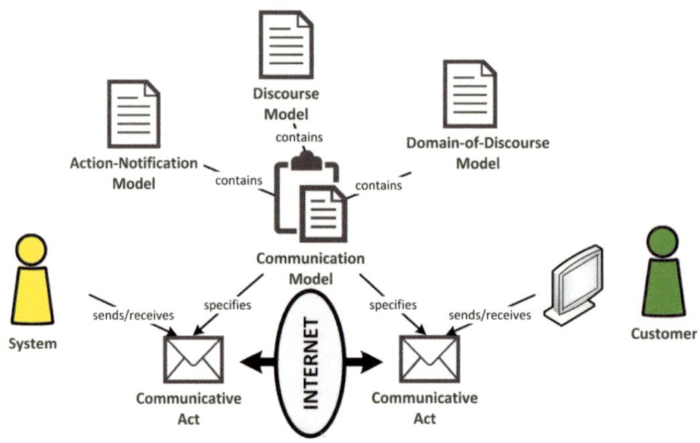

Fig. 2. The Communication Model as Runtime Interface

Coverage — Discourse Models define two abstract interaction parties. This makes them suitable to model not only human-machine but also machine-machine interaction as stated by Falb et al. (2006). Interaction Parties can be assigned to Communicative Acts as well as to Relations. Therefore, Communication Models provide a means to explicitly specify the interaction party on which the progress of the interaction depends at a certain time.

As mentioned above, each Propositional Content is defined for a certain Communicative Act, which form the basic communication units. This implies that Communicative Acts and their corresponding values cannot be updated after they have been sent to the other interaction party. For example, let's consider the selection of a departure and a destination airport in a flight selection scenario. It would be sensible to limit the list of destination airports according to the selected departure airport. If the selection of both airports is concurrently available this cannot be done, because no Communicative Acts are exchanged between the UI and the business logic between the selection.

Adaptability in Realization — Discourse-based Communication Models are device- and platform-independent. For a device-specific UI generation however, additional information about the target device, style and layout must be provided. UCP provides this information in form of default templates that can be selected and modified by the designer.

UCP:UI incorporates a methodology to transform Communication Models into WIMP-UIs for different devices and platforms at compile time. It uses automated optimization to generate UIs for different devices as presented in Raneburger, Popp, Kavaldjian, Kaindl & Falb (2011). Because of this optimization there is no user interface model on abstract UI level. However, we create a consistent screen-based UI representation on concrete UI level — the Screen Model.

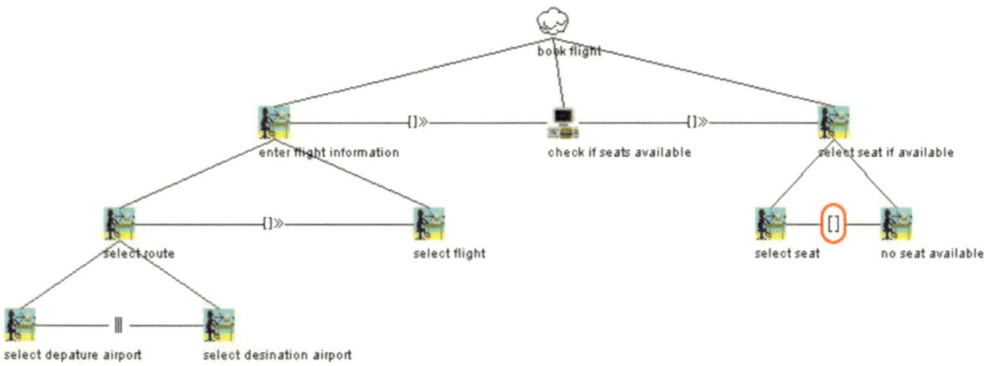

Fig. 3. Flight Booking Concur Task Tree Model

Raneburger (2010) argues that the adaptability during the UI generation process is important in order to generate a satisfying UI for the end user. This is due to the reason that high-level models for UI generation per se do not provide the appropriate means to specify non-functional requirements like layout or style issues. UCP:UI provides the possibility to specify layout and style issues either in the transformation rules used to transform the Communication Model into a Structural Screen Model, or via CSS.

Reuse of Partial Specification — So far there is no support for reuse of partial specifications.

4.2 Task models

Task models provide designers with a means to model a user's tasks to reach a specific goal. A thorough review of task models can be found in Limbourg & Vanderdonckt (2003) and a taxonomy for the comparison of task models has been developed by Meixner & Seissler (2011). In our chapter we focus on task models using the Concur Task Tree (CTT) notation as defined by Paternò et al. (1997). This notation is the de-facto standard today.

Each CTT model specifies its goal as an abstract root task. In order to achieve this goal the root task is decomposed into sub-tasks during the model creation phase. The leaf nodes of the CTT model are concrete *User*, *Interaction* or *Machine Tasks*. The subtasks on each level are related through *Temporal Operators*. These operators are used to specify the order in which the tasks have to be performed to reach the specific goal.

Figure 3 depicts the CTT Model for our running example. The abstract root task *bookflight* is decomposed into several concrete Interaction or Machine tasks that are required to reach the specific goal (i.e., to select a flight ticket). These concrete tasks are either performed by a human user (Interaction Tasks) or the system (Machine Tasks). Interaction Tasks are depicted as a human user in front of a computer and Machine Tasks as a small computer. Tasks on the same level in a CTT diagram are related via a Temporal Operator. The tasks *select departure airport* and *select destination airport* are on the same level and shall be enabled at the same time. This is expressed by the *interleaving* Temporal Operator that relates them. The *select flight* task requires the information of the airports selected in the *select route* task. Therefore, the *enabling with information passing* Temporal Operator is used to relate these tasks. Our scenario states that the machine shall check whether seats are available or not after a certain flight has been selected (i.e., after the *enter flight information* task is finished) and either offer a list of seats or inform the user that no seats are available. We modeled this decision with the *choice* Temporal Operator that relates the *select seat* and *no seat available* interaction tasks.

Task Models, just like Communication Models, have been designed in order to support automated UI generation. In this chapter we use our criteria to compare two major task-based UI development frameworks: the MARIA-Environment (MARIAE) and the USer Interface eXtensible Markup Language[4] (UsiXML) framework.

MARIAE is based on the MARIA user interface specification language developed by Paternò et al. (2009) and provides tool-based design support on all four levels of the Cameleon Reference Framework.

The UsiXML language forms the basis of the UI development framework presented in Vanderdonckt (2008). UsiXML is a XML-compliant markup language that describes the UI for multiple contexts of use such as Character User Interfaces (CUIs), Graphical User Interfaces (GUIs), Auditory User Interfaces, and Multimodal User Interfaces. The UsiXML framework uses CTT models on the tasks & concepts level and supports the designer with tools during the UI generation. The interoperability between the tools is accomplished through the common use of UsiXML. The focus of UsiXML development team is not the development of UI models and a generation approach but the creation of a UI specification language that supports the specification of all needed models with one language.

Ease of Use — A graphical representation for all CTT elements together with tool support through the CTT-Environment (CTTE) developed by Mori et al. (2002) makes the creation of task models affordable for designers. MARIAE as well as the UsiXML framework provide tool support on all four levels of the Cameleon Reference Framework.

Degree of Operationalization — The degree of operationalization for fully specified task models is high. Both approaches use device-specific, but platform and modality independent CTT models on the tasks & concepts level. They provide tool support for the transformation into UIs for multiple modalities.

References to the application logic can be specified through the definition of modified objects for each task or Web service calls. However, it faces the same UI update problem as Communication Model.

Coverage — Task models are primarily used to model user-driven applications. User-driven in this context means that the user decides which tasks to execute next and not the system. CTT models in principle support the specification of preconditions in order to model scenarios in which the system decides what task to execute next. CTT does not support the unambiguous specification of such preconditions. Therefore, these preconditions are not considered during the course of the UI generation in MARIAE. This leads to the derivation of wrong Presentation Task Sets and the corresponding Navigators in the end and poses therefore a limitation of the coverage. The consideration of the following two aspects would solve this problem. First, a clear syntax for the specification of the preconditions is required. Second, these preconditions must be considered and evaluated during the UI generation process.

Figure 3 shows the CTT model that we created after having failed using the preconditions. The *choice* Temporal Operator, marked with a red (or gray) ellipse, represents the check for available seats. Figure 3 is not a true model of our scenario as CTT does not specify the user and the system explicitly as roles. Therefore, it does not support the assignment of

[4] `http://www.usixml.org/`

Temporal Operators to the machine or the system. Even our small scenario shows that there is an expressiveness problem if CTT models shall be used to model machine decisions. This problem could be solved if it would be possible to assign roles and specify conditions for Temporal Operators.

Apart from specifying the interaction between a user and a system, CTT models can also be used to specify the collaborative interaction between more than two users. Such Cooperative Task Models define an arbitrary number of interaction parties and the flow of interaction between them. The interaction between each interaction party and the system is specified through CTT models.

Adaptability in Realization — CTT models are device-specific. However, both approaches provide tools to adapt the CTT for different devices and contexts of use and to generate the corresponding UI at design time. Based on these UIs, both frameworks support the migration of an application's UI through migratory UIs (see Bandelloni & Paternò (2004) and Collignon et al. (2008)) that adapt to various contexts of use (i.e., device, environment, etc.) during runtime.

Reuse of Partial Specifications — To the best of our knowledge there is no support for reuse of partial specifications so far.

4.3 Models in the OO-Method

The *OO-Method* has been developed by Pastor et al. (2008) and introduces a so-called *Conceptual Model* to define all aspects that are needed to generate information system applications. The Conceptual Model consists of an *Object Model*, a *Dynamic Model*, a *Functional Model* and a *Presentation Model*. This method uses a model compiler to transform these four models into a UI for an application fully automatically. CTT models are only used on Computational Independent Level. They are not processed fully automatically, but rather define a basis for the creation of the four models mentioned above.

The OO-method has been tailored for the creation of information system applications. Therefore, it is *not easy to use* for untrained users. Furthermore, its focus on information systems limits the *coverage* of the corresponding models on the one hand, but increases their *degree of operationalization* on the other hand. Tool support for the OO-Method on an industrial scale is provided by the Olivanova transformation engine[5]. *Adaptability* for the resulting UI is considered as important and constitutes a current field of research (see Pederiva et al. (2007)). Their current approach is to provide additional rendering information in so called transformation templates developed by Aquino et al. (2008). This approach has been chosen as not all parts of the rendering engines and the corresponding models are accessible for alterations. To the best of our knowledge there is no support for reuse of partial specifications so far.

5. Assessment

In this section, we compare the models introduced in the previous section, according to the criteria defined before. Since neither their state of elaboration, nor the details of documentation available are such that an in depth comparison appears to be sensible, we summarize some of the criteria in our comparison. We characterize the state of all models

[5] `http://www.care-t.com`

with respect to single or related sets of criteria, and we contrast discourse-based with task models respectively OO models where appropriate.

Concerning the ease of use, there is sufficient evidence that both models behave reasonable. The discourse-based model has been presented in various tutorials, and participants were able to build simple models already after short training. Tasks models are well known and commonly used, which makes it plausible that they are even easier to use than the discourse-based model, since no training is required to get acquainted with idiosyncrasies of the model. Both models support the user in building models according to syntactic conventions, but they fail to provide means of repair semantic errors in user specifications. Graphical CTT models use a different icon for each temporal operator that represents its meaning. Compared to Communication Models such operators are more easy to read. However, RST-based Communication Model Relation provide additional semantic information that can be exploited to derive the layout of a resulting graphical UI or the emphasis of different parts in a speech UI. The OO-Method uses task models only during an informal design phase. The creation of the Conceptual Model requires detailed knowledge of the models involved. Therefore, such a model cannot be created by untrained users. Altogether, concretely assessing the ease of use depends on the particular user. If you are familiar with established modeling concepts the use of all models will be affordable, the Discourse Models even with less amount of training due to their natural language basis.

The operationalization is quite differently organized across models and approaches. In the discourse-based model, the abstract user specifications are operationalized and, by the aid of schematic patterns for rendering purposes, successively transduced into executable code. For the task model, operationalization depends on a suitable orchestration of transformation processes that mediate between the layers of representation. A weak point in both models is the reference to business logic. While the discourse-based model offers an admittedly rudimentary way to handle references to business logic elements, this part seems not well supported formally in the task model. The OO-Method focuses on the creation of UIs for information systems. Information systems require only a limited set of business logic functionality. The OO-Method's Dynamic Model together with its Functional Model provide an explicit specification of the objects managed by the business logic and the events changing their states.

Discourse Models and CTT Models are both on the tasks & concepts level of the Cameleon Reference Framework. One could argue however that Discourse Models are on a slightly higher level of abstraction as their Relations introduce an additional semantic layer and are decoupled from their procedural semantics through an explicit state machine representation. Hence, Discourse Models have a greater coverage but per se a lesser degree of operationalization than CTT models.

The coverage can be assessed easier for the discourse-based model, since its building blocks have close relations to the categories of coverage, as they appear in our list of criteria. This model can handle quite well various sorts of conditionally determined discourse continuations, as well as groupings of semantically-related discourse acts. Simultaneous actions, though in principle expressible, are not yet fully supported by the operationalization method. Finally, advanced discourse continuations, that is, topic changes involving the implicit leave of open subdialogs is not elaborated yet. Assessing the coverage for task models is a bit speculative, since this cannot be done on the level of tasks per se. It depends on how the task model specifications are mapped onto compositions of interactions, by transformations between these layers of representation. This transformation is quite challenging, including a

Criterion	Discourse-based	Task-based	OO-method
Ease of use	reasonable, some experimental evidence	best known approach	detailed specifications needed
Operational-ization	systematic process, clear application logic interface	good tool support on all abstraction levels	direct model compilation
Coverage	good repertoire, but no advanced discourse continuation patterns	user-driven applications	tailored to information systems
Adaptation	explicit support, some degree of elaboration	device specific input model	device specific input model
Reuse	not yet developed	not yet developed	not yet developed

Table 1. Comparing Discourse-based, task-based and OO approach

variety of choices with substantial differences in effectiveness. Intuitively, the coverage of the OO-Method seems smaller as its focus is on information systems only.

The attitude towards adaptation is quite divergent between the competing approaches. While discourse-based models explicitly support the adaptation to multiple devices from the same abstract representation, the task model requires the designer to take into account properties of the intended device already from the beginning. Thus, this part of the philosophy behind the task model makes the generation process a bit easier, but it may turn out to be quite awkward, if changes of the intended device or extension in their variation prove necessary or at least desirable. Elaborations of the discourse-based model have already demonstrated some success in producing structural variations driven by device constraints from the same abstract specifications, it remains to be seen how far the repertoire of device variants and associated rendering alternations can be extended. The OO-Method uses a device-specific Presentation Model and does not support adaptability for different devices during its compilation process.

Concerning the last category of criteria, reuse, it is not surprising that neither of the two approaches has to offer something yet. Reuse of partial specifications is quite an advanced issue in the context of HCI, since it is a priori not clear how portions suitable for reuse can be precisely defined, and how they need to be adapted to the context in which they are reused. For the design of larger interfaces, however, such a feature will eventually be indispensable.

Major differences between the models are summarized in Table 1. Some of the major problems are shared by all approaches: missing user support for handling semantic errors, reference to business logic elements, and reuse of partial specifications.

Altogether, the competing models turn out to exhibit complementary properties in several factors, which has its source in fundamental differences of the underlying philosophy. The task model treats the interface design as an integral part of the overall software design. Specifications to be made are decoupled into a primary, highly abstract design at the task level, and subsequent transformations, which gradually concretize the task model into a working interface. Success of this model widely depends on the suitability of the intermediate representation levels and on the skill of the designer in finding effective optimizations when building transformations mapping between adjacent representation levels. The discourse-based model has quite different priorities. The proper design resides on the level of discourse interactions, which is a level deeper than the primary design level of the task model. Consequently, the designer can concentrate his efforts on precisely this level, which makes his task quite uniform. It is assumed that he is able to structure the design of the interaction specifications in a suitable manner, without an abstracting task model, but supported by the underlying linguistic concept. Moreover, user interface production and adaptation for one or several devices is automated, guided by declarative representations of device constraints.

Table 1 indicates that each modeling and transformation approach has its own limitations. Therefore, it is important to have a set of criteria as provided in our chapter, to compare them in order to find the most appropriate model and approach for a given problem.

6. Conclusion and future work

In this paper, we have described and compared three models for HCI design which operate on some abstract, semantically-oriented levels - a discourse-based, a task model, and an OO model. We have made this comparison along an advanced set of criteria, which has demonstrated achievements and shortcomings of these approaches, but also complementary strengths and weaknesses grounded in the different nature of these approaches.

When expanding the coverage in these models, difficulties are expected to be complementary, according to the differences in the architectural design of the models. In the discourse-based model, additional representation elements must be defined to enable the user to built specifications for more advanced discourse situations. Since these elements are likely to be associated with relatively complex semantics, similar to the procedural relations, much care must be devoted to this task - users must get a handle on understanding how to use these elements, in order to achieve a desired system behavior. Moreover, modules responsible for operationalization must be enhanced accordingly, which may be challenging for some complex representation elements. In contrast to that, additional representation elements in task and OO models probably need not to be semantically complex, but several such elements from different representation levels are likely to contribute to specific coverage extensions. In such a setting, the challenge is to define complementing expressive means adequately. For the user, it is important to understand, on which level he needs to make partial specifications, and how they interact to obtain a desired system behavior.

In order to strengthen these models, they should address several factors that became apparent through our comparison: the discourse-based model may profit from some sort of relations between discourse fragments and tasks, inspired by the task model, but different from the use there. The task model may allow for some degrees of adaptation to device variants, although not in the principled manner as the discourse-based model does. The OO model may adapt some of the information encapsulated in discourse relations to support adaptation in the rendering process, and it may put some emphasis on making the task of the designer less dependent on knowledge and training. Finally, all models should take the incorporation to business logic more serious, and try to address some more advanced and effective patterns of communication as well as measure to support some degree of reuse of partial specifications.

7. References

Aquino, N., Vanderdonckt, J., Valverde, F. & Pastor, O. (2008). Using profiles to support transformations in the model-driven development of user interfaces, *Proceedings of the 7th International Conference on Computer-Aided Design of User Interfaces (CADUI 2008)*, Springer.

Bandelloni, R. & Paternò, F. (2004). Migratory user interfaces able to adapt to various interaction platforms, *International Journal of Human-Computer Studies* 60(5-6): pp. 621–639. HCI Issues in Mobile Computing.

Calvary, G., Coutaz, J., Thevenin, D., Limbourg, Q., Bouillon, L. & Vanderdonckt, J. (2003). A unifying reference framework for multi-target user interfaces, *Interacting with Computers* 15(3): pp. 289–308. Computer-Aided Design of User Interface. URL: *http://www.sciencedirect.com/science/article/pii/S0953543803000109*

Collignon, B., Vanderdonckt, J. & Calvary, G. (2008). Model-driven engineering of multi-target plastic user interfaces, *Proceedings of the Fourth International Conference on Autonomic and Autonomous Systems (ICAS 2008)*, IEEE Computer Society, Washington, DC, USA, pp. 7–14.

Falb, J., Kaindl, H., Horacek, H., Bogdan, C., Popp, R. & Arnautovic, E. (2006). A discourse model for interaction design based on theories of human communication, *Extended Abstracts on Human Factors in Computing Systems (CHI '06)*, ACM Press: New York, NY, pp. 754–759.

Heeman, P. (2007). Combining reinforcement learning with information-state update rules, *Proceedings of the North American Chapter of the Association for Computational Linguistics Annual Meeting*, pp. 268–275.

Kreutel, J. & Matheson, C. (2003). Incremental information state updates in an obligation-driven dialogue model, *Logic Journal of the IGPL* 11(4): pp. 485–511.

Limbourg, Q. & Vanderdonckt, J. (2003). Comparing task models for user interface design, *in* D. Diaper & N. Stanton (eds), *The Handbook of Task Analysis for Human-Computer Interaction*, Lawrence Erlbaum Associates, Mahwah, NJ, USA, chapter 6.

Luff, P., Frohlich, D. & Gilbert, N. (1990). *Computers and Conversation*, Academic Press, London, UK.

Mann, W. C. & Thompson, S. (1988). Rhetorical Structure Theory: Toward a functional theory of text organization, *Text* 8(3): pp. 243–281.

Matheson, C., Poesio, M. & Traum, D. (2000). Modelling grounding and discourse obligations using update rules, *Proceedings of the 1st Annual Meeting of the North American Association for Computational Linguistics (NAACL2000)*, pp. 1–8.

Meixner, G. & Seissler, M. (2011). Selecting the right task model for model-based user interface development, *ACHI 2011, The Fourth International Conference on Advances in Computer-Human Interactions*, pp. 5–11.

Meteer, M. (1992). *Expressibility and the problem of efficient text planning*, St. Martin's Press, Inc. New York, NY, USA.

Mori, G., Paternò, F. & Santoro, C. (2002). Ctte: Support for developing and analyzing task models for interactive system design, *IEEE Transactions on Software Engineering* 28: pp. 797–813.

Pastor, O., España, S., Panach, J. I. & Aquino, N. (2008). Model-driven development, *Informatik Spektrum* 31(5): pp. 394–407.

Paternò, F., Mancini, C. & Meniconi, S. (1997). ConcurTaskTrees: A diagrammatic notation for specifying task models, *Proceedings of the IFIP TC13 Sixth International Conference on Human-Computer Interaction*, pp. 362–369.

Paternò, F., Santoro, C. & Spano, L. D. (2009). Maria: A universal, declarative, multiple abstraction-level language for service-oriented applications in ubiquitous environments, *ACM Trans. Comput.-Hum. Interact.* 16: pp. 19:1–19:30. URL: *http://doi.acm.org/10.1145/1614390.1614394*

Pederiva, I., Vanderdonckt, J., España, S., Panach, I. & Pastor, O. (2007). The beautification process in model-driven engineering of user interfaces, *Proceedings of the 11th IFIP TC*

13 International Conference on Human-Computer Interaction — INTERACT 2007, Part I, LNCS 4662, Springer Berlin / Heidelberg, Rio de Janeiro, Brazil, pp. 411–425. URL: *http://dx.doi.org/10.1007/978-3-540-74796-3_39*

Popp, R. (2009). Defining communication in SOA based on discourse models, *Proceeding of the 24th ACM SIGPLAN Conference Companion on Object Oriented Programming Systems Languages and Applications (OOPSLA '09)*, ACM Press: New York, NY, pp. 829–830.

Popp, R., Falb, J., Arnautovic, E., Kaindl, H., Kavaldjian, S., Ertl, D., Horacek, H. & Bogdan, C. (2009). Automatic generation of the behavior of a user interface from a high-level discourse model, *Proceedings of the 42nd Annual Hawaii International Conference on System Sciences (HICSS-42)*, IEEE Computer Society Press, Piscataway, NJ, USA.

Popp, R. & Raneburger, D. (2011). A high-level agent interaction protocol based on a communication ontology, *in* C. Huemer & T. Setzer (eds), *EC-Web 2011*, Vol. 85 of *Lecture Notes in Business Information Processing*, Springer Berlin Heidelberg, pp. 233–245.

Raneburger, D. (2010). Interactive model driven graphical user interface generation, *Proceedings of the 2nd ACM SIGCHI Symposium on Engineering Interactive Computing Systems (EICS '10)*, ACM, New York, NY, USA, pp. 321–324. URL: *http://doi.acm.org/10.1145/1822018.1822071*

Raneburger, D., Popp, R., Kaindl, H. & Falb, J. (2011). Automated WIMP-UI behavior generation: Parallelism and granularity of communication units, *Proceedings of the 2011 IEEE International Conference on Systems, Man and Cybernetics (SMC 2011)*.

Raneburger, D., Popp, R., Kavaldjian, S., Kaindl, H. & Falb, J. (2011). Optimized GUI generation for small screens, *in* H. Hussmann, G. Meixner & D. Zuehlke (eds), *Model-Driven Development of Advanced User Interfaces*, Vol. 340 of *Studies in Computational Intelligence*, Springer Berlin / Heidelberg, pp. 107–122. URL: *http://dx.doi.org/10.1007/978-3-642-14562-9_6*

Reiter, E. (1994). Has a consensus nl generation architecture appeared, and is it psycholinguistically plausible?, *Proceeding INLG '94 Proceedings of the Seventh International Workshop on Natural Language Generation*, Association for Computational Linguistics.

Searle, J. R. (1969). *Speech Acts: An Essay in the Philosophy of Language*, Cambridge University Press, Cambridge, England.

Traum, D. & Larsson, S. (2003). The information state approach to dialogue management, *in* R. Smith & J. van Kuppevelt (eds), *Current and New Directions in Discourse and Dialogue*, Kluwer Academic Publishers, Dordrecht, pp. 325–353.

Van den Bergh, J., Meixner, G., Breiner, K., Pleuss, A., Sauer, S. & Hussmann, H. (2010). Model-driven development of advanced user interfaces, *Proceedings of the 28th of the international conference extended abstracts on Human factors in computing systems*, CHI EA '10, ACM, New York, NY, USA, pp. 4429–4432. URL: *http://doi.acm.org/10.1145/1753846.1754166*

Vanderdonckt, J. M. (2008). Model-driven engineering of user interfaces: Promises, successes, and failures, *Proceedings of 5th Annual Romanian Conf. on Human-Computer Interaction*, Matrix ROM, Bucaresti, pp. 1–10.

2

Human-Machine Interaction and Agility in the Process of Developing Usable Software: A Client-User Oriented Synergy

Benigni Gladys[1] and Gervasi Osvaldo[2]
[1]*University of Oriente*
[2]*University of Perugia*
[1]*Venezuela*
[2]*Italy*

1. Introduction

The human-machine interaction model, in its simplest meaning, describes the issues related to an individual who interacts with a machine in a given context. At the level of information processing, each input and output, and each related process is modelled on the behaviour of the machine and of the human being. It is worth noticing that the inputs of a person (defined as the actors) are her/his sensorial organs (e.g. sight, hearing, smell, etc.) and the outputs (defined as the effectors) are the fingers and the voice. On the other hand, the inputs of a machine are represented by the interactive devices (focused on controlling the execution of the program) such as the keyboard and the mouse, which are classified as non-immersive virtual reality devices, while the outputs are represented by the presentation devices (focused on the display of the information) such as the screen, the sounds and the alarms.

These inputs originate from the interface of a computer application, which provides a series of actions (e.g. a click) in which the main actor in the human-machine interaction is *the user*. We have to take into account that in the production of web or desktop applications the final product must conform to the highest standard in quality considering the high competitiveness of the information society. Nowadays the progress made in Software Engineering, Usability and Object-Oriented Software Engineering has often made available usable agile products, thanks also to the invaluable contributions of gurus like Nielsen and Norman. Agile usability is a recent concept developed by Nielsen & Norman (dateless), and the term *agile* is a paradigm in software production.

The term *agile development process* substitutes the classical waterfall model in the production of software as stated by Grezzi (2004) who considers the final user as the key element for success in the design of any software application. We fully agree with the assertion of the authors of the Manifesto for Agile Software Development: *the contribution of people is more relevant than the processes or the technology used*. Ultimately we feel that a synergy or symbiosis among different disciplines characterized by usability engineering, agility, software quality and the human factor exists.

The aim of the present paper is to emphasize the importance of agile software development for releasing software products based on the Human Machine Interaction paradigms and centred on user needs and expectations. The agile usability and the object-oriented software engineering perspectives are at the centre of the process to achieve agile methods and to release products centred on users. To reach this goal, the model based on the Human-Machine Interaction principles is proposed, and conceptual models related to each one of the actors (user-client, designer-programmer) who take part in the different stages of software development are presented.

To show the importance of agile usability, the ISO standards quality and the agile method are used to propose some development methodology (USABAGILE Web, SCRUM, among others) which would be the starting point of the process of delivering high quality products centred on the needs and expectations of the *user*, the entity on which all activities are orientated.

2. Human machine interaction and its development through technical Interaction

The Human Machine Interaction (HMI) is related to the study of the interaction between the human and the machine (represented in our case by the computer) and the tasks the users are routinely carrying out using software interfaces. The important aspect of HMI is the knowledge of how machines and humans interact in order to carry out the users tasks in their context.

The HMI found the solution for several problems in computational science, by combining several disciplines like social and physical sciences, engineering and art [Martinez 2007]. The HMI takes advantage of the advances in computational science, psychology, mathematics, graphic arts, sociology, artificial intelligence, linguistics, anthropology and ergonomics. Therefore, a software developer has to take into account the four main components of a human-machine system:

a. the user;
b. the machine and its system;
c. the task;
d. the environment.

The main issue is to comprehend the user in the environment in which she/he carries out her/his tasks, in order to design applications suited to her/his needs. Furthermore, the implemented software has to respond to a request specified through an input device and it has to receive all the necessary information through a device (e.g.: a computer). It is hard to know when the interfaces were introduced, since the human being has interacted with machines from the prehistoric age. What is really clear is that interfaces evolved in order to make human life more comfortable and easy, according to a design centred on human being.

The interfaces' evolution depends on the devices, the operating systems, the programming languages and the ways users approach computers and mobile devices. In particular the most important driving factor of the interfaces' evolution was the advent of operating systems based on a Graphical User Interface (GUI), combined with the evolution of Smart

Phones and mobile devices, which make information available in a ubiquitous and very intuitive way. The future evolution of computer technologies will be driven by the concept of ubiquitous computing and natural languages and interfaces.

3. The human processor as a reference point in the processing of information: user conceptual model, designer conceptual model and programmer conceptual model

To study the human factor designing interactive systems we take into account the cognitive psychology, which according to the Manning definition [Manning 1992] is *the study of those mental processes which make easily possible the recognition of familiar objects, known people, the management of our surrounding world, including the skills of reading, writing, programming, plans execution, thinking, decision-making and memorizing what one has learnt.*

To understand and to take advantage of the human-machine interaction concepts, it is necessary to understand the human memory and cognitive processes. The model of the human processor is shown in Figure 1. This model has been included in the model of multiple memories to achieve a better comprehension of the global process of learning. In the field of Human Machine Interaction there are various research areas which are devoted to the understanding of the various processors, in order to define principles and guidelines for designing good and efficient interfaces.

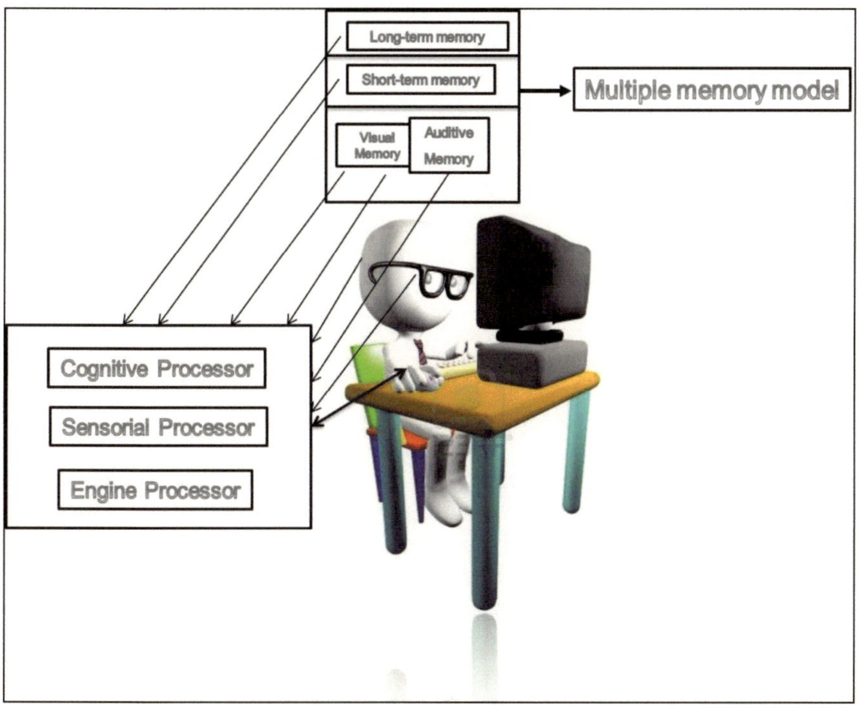

Fig. 1. Model of the Human Processor.

The learning research area involves the comprehension of the human processor model, under the assumption that taking advantage of the capabilities of gathering information, we are facilitating the process of a more efficient and faster learning process. The Engine Processor is responsible for efficiently managing all interactive mechanisms suitable for a given interface affecting the learning process. The Sensorial Processor captures the information after having received some stimulus from the environment through the human senses, transforms it in a concept and then transfers the concept to the Cognitive Processor.

The Sensorial Processor uses a memory area (buffer) for each sensorial organ (sight, hearing, smell, taste and touch). Finally, the Cognitive Processor is of utmost importance in the learning process. We can consider a learning process as fast in all cases in which we achieve a rapid transfer of information between the short and the long term memory, assuming that the transfer between the sensorial memory and the short term memory has been done properly.

Considering that the model of the human processor is able to receive and process information in response to a sensorial stimulus, we have to know the users and their contexts in order to design and implement suitable interfaces centred on users. For this reason the main aim of the involved parties in the development of an agile and usable product shown in Figure 2 is to cooperate, in order to achieve the goal of releasing agile and usable products.

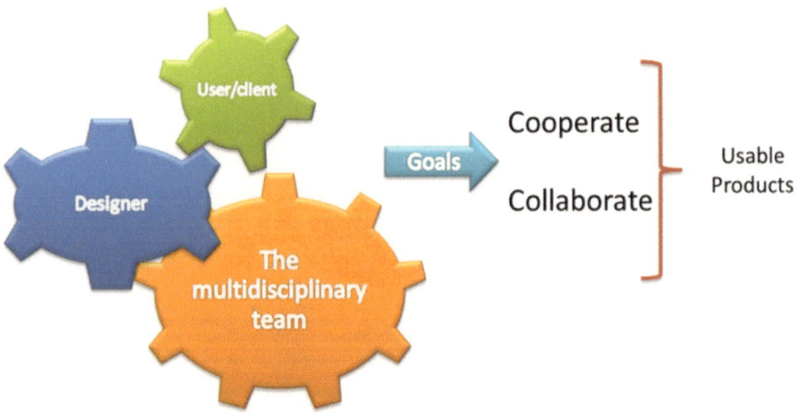

Fig. 2. Aims of the actors of usable agile products development.

When modelling the application, one has to consider the user perspective together with the designer and the programmer perspectives. It is important to emphasize that, even though the user is the key element on which the application has to be focused, being the buyers of the product and the final users of the interface for performing various tasks (user perspective), other actors are crucial too. In fact, the designer outlines usable interfaces, providing the user with all the necessary facilities, the comfort and the ability to complete a given set of tasks easily (designer perspective). Finally, the programmer implements the application following all specifications provided by the designer (programmer perspective).

In Figure 3, considering the relative importance of the actors described above, we can show the metaphor corresponding to the mental models of each of them playing a role in the process of building a user centred application.

3.1 The user model

To be able to create the user model it is fundamental to know the user's experience, her/his knowledge and expectations. We can become acquainted with such issues by carrying out usability tests (observing, polling, asking, etc). Such tests have to be carried out with the final users of the product.

If the interface is implemented in the wrong way, the user may have a strange behaviour in the future, while trying to counteract the weakness of the application.

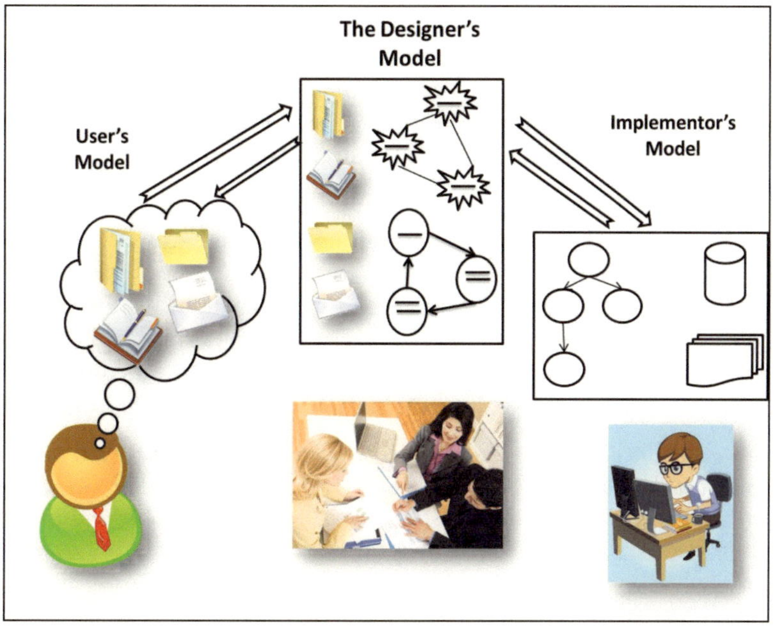

Fig. 3. Mental models from the actors.

3.2 The programmer model

The programmer knows which are the software developing platforms, the operating systems, the developing tools, the programming language and the specifications required to deliver the application. Such knowledge does not necessarily allows the programmer to produce suitable interfaces. The programmer implements the interfaces according to the specifications received from the designer model.

3.3 The designer model

The designer has to figure out what the user will perceive and see using the application. The designer translates into the computer domain the comprehension and the analysis of the User Model. In Figure 3 the interaction of the designers with the other actors is stressed, since if we want to plan properly the correct model of a given software product, we have to consider that: a) the designers have their own system model; b) the image of the system is implemented according to a given plan; c) the User Model is built through the interaction with the system.

The designer hopes that the User Model fits her/his own model. In any case, the communication is performed through the system. The system has to reflect a model of a clear and consistent design between the User and the Designer Models.

4. Object-oriented software engineering and its interrelationship with usability engineering

In section 2 we stressed the importance of user-centred design and once again we refer to this concept in order to link Object-Oriented Software engineering (OOSI) with Usability Engineering (UE); to this end it is relevant to mention the characteristics of the User-centred Design (UCD) based on the standard ISO 13407, whose role is: (a) to actively involve users and clearly understand the requirements of the user and the task; (b) to define an appropriate distribution of responsibilities between the users and technology; (c) to highlight the iteration of design solutions and multidisciplinary design.

We need to be involved in each phase of the software development to understand and define the context of use, the tasks and the way in which users work and how they work with the developed product. Let us remember that the success of the development and subsequent use of the software can be achieved involving the users and the customers in each stage of the development process. The user-centred design leads to an interactive design, where in particular the feedback offered by users and customers is a source of fundamental information to achieve the goal. Martínez la Teja said: (Martínez la Teja, 2007)

> *It requires combining a variety of skills and knowledge depending on the nature of the system to be developed, which is why the multidisciplinary team may include members of the management, experts on the application, end users, system designers, experts in marketing, graphic designers, specialists in human factors and training staff. It is possible that one person represents several of these areas, but something important to consider is that the designer can never represent the user, unless the design is developed for her/his personal use.*

For this reason today in each of the phases of the development of a software product, there is a pool of users, customers, designers and programmers who interact and obtain an incremental and iterative design of the application to be launched into the market. Currently all actors work jointly in the various phases of the cycle of traditional development systems (starting from the most known and used: the "waterfall model"), combining the Software Engineering principles updated with the Object Oriented ones, with their different phases, tools, techniques, and models available through the Unified Modeling Language (UML). Furthermore, the software development has to be carried out in parallel with the life cycle of the Usability Engineering.

4.1 In the software development life cycle

One of the most basic structured models (Lorés & Granollers, s.d.), serving as a block construction for other models of systems development life cycle, is the waterfall model (see Figure 4). Currently, the waterfall model is being replaced by iterative and incremental models associated with the latest technology of the object oriented programming, although the waterfall model is still the basis of all implemented models (see for instance the USABAGILE Web model described in section 7).

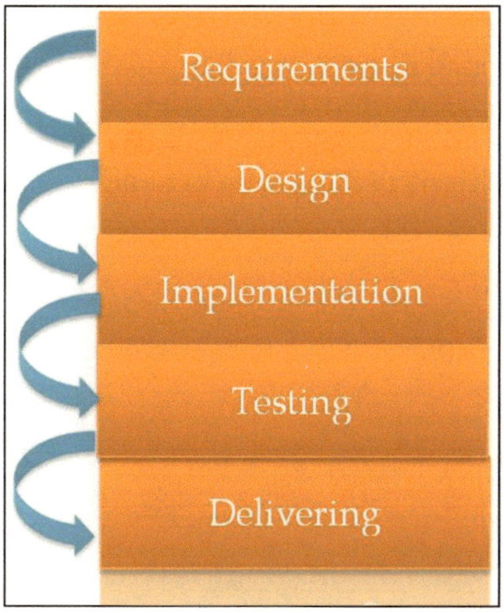

Fig. 4. Waterfall model.

As you can infer from Figure 4, the waterfall model starts from the collection of information culminating with the release of the software product. No feedback is present between the various stages, which was one of the failures of the method.

4.2 Software engineering

Zavala's definition of a software product (Zavala, 2000), "*a software product is a product designed for a user*", is useful to understand how Software Engineering represents an important systematic approach to the development, operation, maintenance and removal of software, which allows cost-effective and usable software products to be released. The process of software engineering is defined as a set of stages partially ordered with the intention of achieving a goal, in this case, a software quality (Jacobson, 1998) output. In the process of software development the needs of the user are translated into software requirements, transformed into design requirements and then the design is implemented in a code. Finally, the code is tested, documented and certified for operational use. Specifically, it defines who is doing what, when to do it, and how to achieve a certain objective (Jacobson, op. cit.). The process of software development requires a set of concepts, a methodology and its own language. This process is also called the *software life cycle*, which is composed by four major phases: design, development, construction and transition. The design phase defines the scope of the project and develops a business case study. The development phase defines a plan of the project, specifying the characteristics and the underlying architecture. In the building phase the product is implemented and in the transition phase the product is transferred to users.

Taking into account the drawbacks of the waterfall model (mainly the lack of feedbacks from the users after the software development process was started) software engineering released a new development model, called spiral (see Figure 5), in which it is possible to move backward and forward between the various phases, as a consequence of user feedbacks.

This model encourages the incremental development (see Figure 6) in the software life cycle, and prototyping. In fact through the prototype it is possible to provide the user with an idea of how to run the application, and which functions are possible, so that it will be possible to cycle the development phases, introducing high level of flexibility and being able to change the initial requirements, as a result of the feedbacks received from the users.

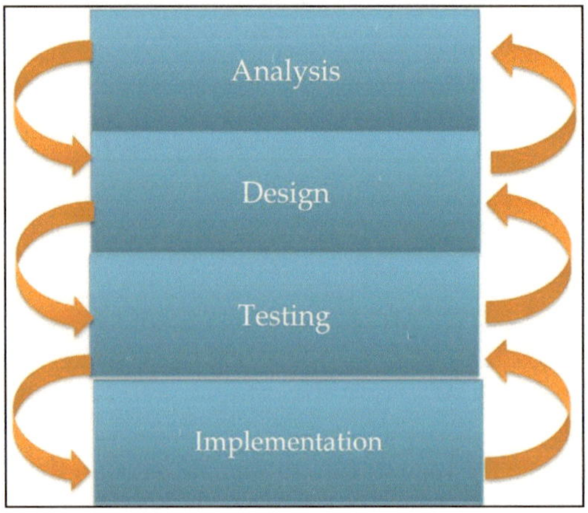

Fig. 5. Spiral Development Model.

These new paradigms adopted in the models related to the software development processes, as pointed out by Lorés & Granollers (op. cit.), also impose a change in the model of the user-application interaction, which forces the adoption of a new methodology in which the interaction with users is more natural, and more efficiently implemented, and which facilitates the comprehension of the system by new users and eliminates the inconsistencies in the interaction model.

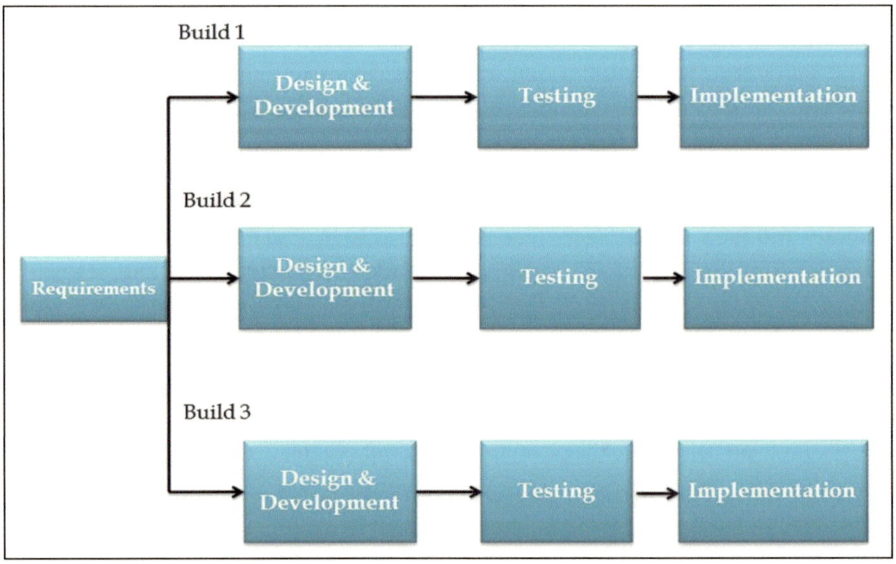

Fig. 6. Incremental Life Cycle Model.

4.3 The usability and the user centred design

The usability of software applications is an important branch of software engineering called usability engineering, which spans the "Human Machine Interaction" that helps the designers and the developers to release applications which are easy to use and understand, whose tasks may be carried out easily by the users, according to the principles introduced by cognitive psychologists (Norman, 1998).

Nielsen (1993), who was considered the "father" of usability, defines it as *a support to user tasks* (i.e.: it makes easier for people to do what they want to do). Merkovich (1999) expressed the needs of usability as a measure of its usefulness, its simplicity, its ease of learning and an assessment of a task, and a given context. Floría (2000) defines usability as the measure of how a product can be used by the users to achieve specific goals with effectiveness, efficiency and satisfaction in the context of a given use. The three authors agreed that usability has the purpose of facilitating the tasks of a user in a given context, which represents the user and the system in the environment in which she/he operates.

Usability, according to Floría (op. cit.), refers to the speed and ease with which people carry out their tasks through the use of the product, and involves the following concepts: (a) *an approach focused on the user:* to develop a usable product, designers and developers have to interact with people who represent the current or potential users of the product. (b) *develop a comprehensive knowledge of the context of use:* people use products to increase their own productivity. A product is considered easy to learn and use when the time required to the user to carry out her/his tasks is short, when the number of required steps is small, and when the probability of successfully carrying out the appropriate action is high; to develop usable products one has to understand the objectives of the user, and the type of work and tasks the product automates, modifies or embellishes. (c) the product has to meet the needs of the user: users are busy people trying to carry out a task. They will relate usability with productivity and quality. The hardware and software are tools that help busy people to carry out their tasks and to enjoy their leisure.

The International Organization for Standardization (ISO) provided two definitions of usability: the ISO/IEC 9241-11 (1998), defined the concept of usability as "*the extent to which a product can be used by certain users to achieve specific goals with effectiveness, efficiency and satisfaction in a context of specified use*". This definition is focused on the concept of usage quality, i.e.: refers to how effectively the user carries out specific tasks in specific scenarios. The ISO/IEC 9126-1 (2001) provided the following definition : "*usability refers to the ability of a software being understood, learnt, used and being attractive to the user, under specific conditions of use*". Manchón (2003) noted that this definition emphasizes the internal and external attributes of the product, which contribute to its usability, functionality and efficiency. He also noted that the usability depends not only on the product but also on the fundamental actor, the "user". The usability cannot be evaluated on an isolated product (Bevan (1994) quoted by Manchón, op. cit.).

The usability of a software application must be one of the driving criteria of the software quality assessment, and one of the main characteristics determining the user satisfaction using a new product.

Considering these issues related to the software development, the main target of a software developer is to implement software products very intuitively, inducing in the final user only a small cognitive load to perform the required tasks. In fact, if an agile approach is adopted and if the user is involved from the beginning of the project, the various tasks the user has to carry out will be considered in all phases of the software development, and consequently the agility will become the integrating process for the user involvement and her/his satisfaction will be guaranteed independently from the specific technique, method or tool adopted. The requirement is to develop an agile and usable product.

4.3.1 Characteristics of usability

Nielsen (op. cit.) argued that usability is not a simple one-dimensional property of a user interface. Usability has multiple components and is associated with five (5) basic characteristics: learning ability, efficiency of use, capacity for memorization, bug tracking and user satisfaction. In some ways the learning capacity is the main attribute of usability. A system should be easy to learn so that the user can start any task using the system quickly.

It is also important that the various tasks have to be organized and documented so that they should be easy to remember, in this way even an occasional user can be productive relatively quickly. The system should also have a low error rate, so that the users can solve errors easily. Above all, it is important to prevent the system from catastrophic errors. And finally, the satisfaction of the user has to be taken into account.

The above mentioned features imply indirectly a reduction and a general optimization of production costs, as well as an increase in productivity. Usability allows the users to perform tasks faster. On the other hand, Merkovich (op. cit.) explained how the usability concept involves the usefulness, the ease of use, the ease of learning and the user's appreciation of the product.

The utility is the ability of a tool to help meet specific tasks and it is important to note that a tool which is very usable for one task, can be less usable for another, even though it is a task which is similar but not identical. The ease of use is related to the efficiency, measured as the rate of possible errors. A very easy to use tool will allow the user to carry out more operations per unit of time (or shortest time for the same operation) and will decrease the likelihood of errors occurring.

The ease of learning is a measure of the time required to carry out a task with a given degree of efficiency, achieving a degree of knowledge, even if the system will not be used for a while. While the ease of learning is usually directly related to the usability, this is not necessarily true. The ease of learning is a relative measure, as there are very complex systems that cannot be learned quickly.

Commercial software producers are implementing their own techniques for the design and the implementation of software. In some cases the usability principles are included, and even considered unavoidable. Floría (op. cit.) summarizes the main benefits originated from the adoption of the usability techniques in the design and implementation of software systems: a) *a reduction of the production costs*: such costs, in fact, can be reduced avoiding the over-design and the modifications required by the customers after the product has been released; b) *a reduction of the maintenance and support costs*: the usable systems require less training, a reduced support and maintenance actions; c) *a reduction of the usage costs*: the systems fitting the user needs increase the productivity and the quality of the actions and of the decisions; the systems hard to use diminish the wellness and the motivation of the user, and may contribute to the increase of absenteeism from work. Furthermore the users waste more time using the system and they are not pushed to explore the advanced facilities of the system, which may not be used in the routinary actions; d) *improve the quality of the product*: the user-centred design turns out products with high quality and more easy to use, more competitive in a scenario were simple products are preferred.

4.3.2 Products usable on the basis of the principles of user-centred design

After having stressed the importance of the usability concept, particularly designing products, our attention is focused now on the importance of the user-centred design. Floría (op. cit.) stated that to achieve a high level of usability it is necessary to adapt the design process to the user-centred design principles, which represent a reformulation of the principles of classical ergonomics from which the accessibility guidelines are derived. The author presents the principles of user-centred design: 1) the control of the situation must be handled by the user; 2) it must be a direct approach; 3) the consistency is essential in the design part; 4) we have to enable the solution of errors; 5) we have to catch appropriate feedbacks from the users; 6) the aesthetics cannot be neglected; 7) the design should be characterized by simplicity; 8) it is essential to follow a rigorous design methodology; 9) the design team must be balanced in term of competencies; 10) there are four parts in the design process (analysis, design, implementation and test); 11) the usability concepts have to be taken into account during the design process; 12) the design has to be understood by users; 13) if the user pool is not enough satisfied by the design, the process has to be restarted from the beginning.

It should be noted that some of the principles of user-centred design are related to the principles of the heuristic evaluation, and both are directed to foster the usability of the systems. However, they clearly differ, since the user-centred design principles are used, despite the redundancy, in the design phase of a system, while the heuristic evaluation is used to measure the system's degree of usability, and to verify that it complies with the principles of user-centred design. The adoption of usability principles as driving concepts of a methodology for designing agile and usable software, may sort out a powerful tool for implementing an high quality product focused on user needs.

4.4 Standard ISO 9000-3: quality

Nowadays the major concern in software development is related to the quality of products. The users are expecting software products which have to be easy to learn and use, able to solve their needs and face their problems. Unfortunately, the software industry is often affected by huge problems like the high costs related to the refinement and the optimization of the released code, the time wasted correcting bugs, and the presumption of knowing all users needs. The agile software development process combined with the usability principles allow to prevent such problems by adopting good design and implementation strategies, and helping the designers and the code developers to fulfil the schedule and the budget constraints.

The software industry is adopting models to improve the quality of their operations and correct their failures. It is desirable they will implement a statistical analysis of the software development process to monitor the activities, ensuring they are able to produce the same results. The adoption of an agile and usable approach and the quality control techniques will guarantee the successful planning of future projects, the costs optimization, the increase of the efficiency and the productivity, allowing to develop best quality products and to generate more benefits for the company.

The most popular quality control standard, the ISO 9000-3 released by the International Standards Organization (ISO), defines the guidelines for quality control, governing the implementation of the standard ISO 9001 to the development, provision and maintenance of software. It provides to both developers and customers, a set of guidelines for assessing the quality of software development processes.

The adoption by software companies of the standard ISO 9000-3 allows to: a) increase the competencies to afford the European market; (b) enable them to meet the client expectations; (c) obtain quality benefits and competitive advantages in the market; (d) adopt a clear market strategy; (e) reduce production costs. The benefits of obtaining the ISO 9000-3 certification, include the: a) increasing quality of the documentation systems; (b) positive cultural change induced in the employees; (c) increased efficiency and productivity; (d) increased perception of quality; (e) increased client satisfaction; (f) reduced customer quality audit; (g) time reduction of the system development.

The standard ISO 9000-3 is based on the assumption that following a well-defined software engineering strategy the company will be able to release higher quality software products, meeting the deadlines. The Software Engineering provides development models, methods and techniques to specify requirements, to establish the development plan, and to design, code, test, and document software products. In other words, it provides the instruments to release a software product according to the standard ISO 9000-3.

4.5 The usability engineering

The complexity of IT applications has stimulated the research on usability engineering, which in particular profits of the achievements of the human-machine interaction discipline. The usability engineering is a multidisciplinary field, combining expertise on computer science, psychology, linguistics, sociology, anthropology and industrial design. This term has been used since the mid of 1980s, to identify a new discipline which provides "*systematic methods and tools for the complex task of designing user interfaces easily understandable, quickly learnable and reliably operable*" (Buttle, 1996).

The importance of the user interface of a software application is known from the origin of the computer science, since the user is experiencing through it the benefits and the services of a software application. Most of the technical quality of the application appears through the user interface. If it is not effective, the functionality of the application and its usefulness are limited: the users are confused, frustrated and angry; the developers lose credibility and the company has to bear high costs and low productivity. The usability engineering aims to minimize the cognitive and perceptual overload of the user using an application. It uses a method of iterative design with rapid prototyping (support tools are essential), whose skeleton is represented by the cycle "analysis - design – implementation - evaluation" (see Figure 7), which is repeated several time, increasing progressively the system quality and its functions. The stage of evaluating the prototype, comparing its functions with the user expectations and needs, is a crucial phase for the success of the proposed approach.

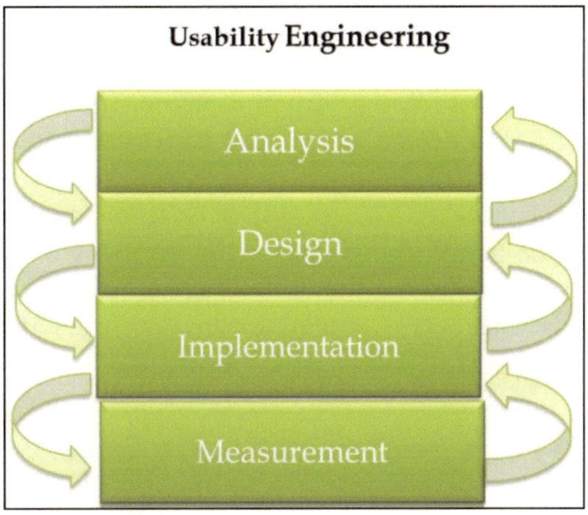

Fig. 7. Usability Engineering method.

In a proper usability engineering process the following steps should be carried out: a) define the goals of usability; (b) establish the planned usability levels to be achieved; (c) analyse the impact of different design solutions; (d) take into account the feedbacks from the users to design the product; (e) iterate through the cycle design-evaluation-redesign to achieve the planned user consensus and quality. Finally, in Figure 8 we summarize the evolution of the three methods and their interrelations respect to the traditional software development cycle, trying to include for the first time the usability engineering in the software development process.

5. Usability and the new engineering paradigm: agile usability

The usability is an attribute of software systems assessing their quality, which can be expressed as a sum of the ease of learning, the efficiency, the error recovery, and the satisfaction of the user (Nielsen, 1994). On the other hand, the user-centred design is a highly structured process, which is focused on the interpretation of needs and objectives of the user of a product. Therefore, if we consider the end user, the goal of the interaction design is to provide her/him useful features. This is why, when designing applications usable agile, we should consider that the interaction designers are focusing their attention on what is desirable for the user in terms of user interface functions, the interface developers are interested on what they are able to build for the application, and stakeholders (companies or users) on what is feasible starting from the experience of the user. The user experience in agile usable software development is important since: a) the end users make emphasis on the necessary functions which enable them to achieve their goals; (b) they facilitate the interface design, identifying its behaviour; (c) the experience of the users allow to define the formalism, using of the agile method. Such aspects, that are crucial for the group of designers and developers, are determining the success of the final product having included the users and their experiences in the application development cycle.

Agile usability is a recent concept developed by Nielsen & Norman (s. d.), who stated that the *agile* term is a new paradigm of software production. The *agile* term identifies a software development process which replaces in the software production the above mentioned classical cascade model (waterfall), as pointed out by Grezzi (2004). The agile model divides into several cycles the typical cycle of a software development process. Therefore, the phases related to the analysis, the design, the implementation, the testing and the release of the software product are applied to a small group of functions (phase) and repeated for each of the subsequent phases. Each of these small and incremental phases, is called in agile terminology "sprint", as for the SCRUM method, by which we will assume the same term to describe the incremental aspects of the development team in each stage of the software development process. If the result of each particular sprint is not considered functionally "complete", it has to be included in the following sprints in order to fulfil the user expectations. Once a sprint has been completed, the development team has to reconsider the priorities of the project.

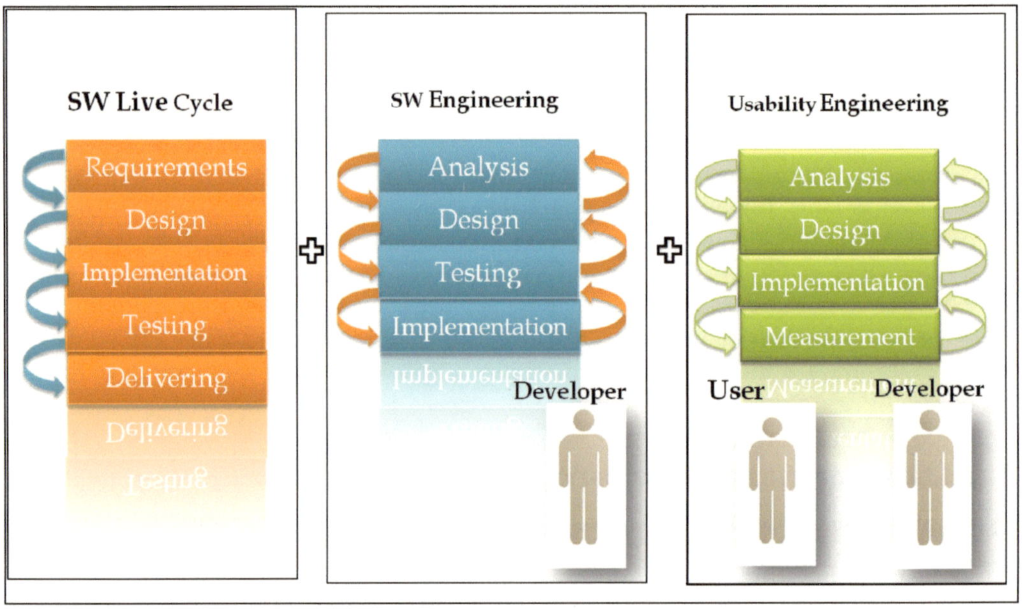

Fig. 8. The integration of the three models (Software life cycle, Software engineering and Usability engineering) to reach an optimal design and implementation of a software product.

Agile methods privileged the communication in real time, preferably face to face, respect to the written documentation. As described by Canós, Letelier & Penadés (s. d.), the agile development team is composed by those persons who are necessary for carrying out the software project. This team should at least include the designers and their customers. The aim is the customer satisfaction, not only the fulfilment of a contract. The use of agile methodologies, and in particular of the usable-agile method, has the purpose of minimizing the costs of software development. The most important principles of the agile methodology are expressed in the *Agile Manifesto* (Beck, Beedle, Cockburn et al., 2001): a) individuals and their interactions are more important than processes and tools: the relationships and communications between the actors of a software project are the principal resources of the project; (b) it is more important to have a working software respect to an excellent documentation: new versions of the software have to be released at frequent intervals, maintaining a simple and technically advanced code, minimizing the documentation; (c) it is more important the collaboration with customers than the contract negotiation; (d) Responding to change is more important than following a plan: the development group has to be ready to find new solutions as soon as a change in the project occurs.

The term agile indicates all those development methodologies that transformed the old paradigms of Software Engineering (waterfall model, spiral model, etc.) based on a set of specifications and in a sequential structure of software development. This is common to a set of methodologies we can group together, such as eXtreme Programming (XP), SCRUM, Feature Driven Development, DSDM, Crystal, Lean Software Development, Agile Usability Engineering (AUE). Such methodologies are called agile because they allow to review and modify the set of specifications during the development phase, activating a strong exchange of information between the designers, the developers, and the users.

A group of developers who is using an agile approach must understand that the user-centred design and usability are explicit development methodologies and should therefore be included in the software production process.

Agile usability is a system for the evaluation of the usability of a software product to be carried out during the agile development of any application (also Web sites), performing usability tests as soon as each development phase has been completed (Nielsen, op. cit.). This makes a breakthrough in the quality of software, since the usability of a product is tested from the beginning of the development cycle, reducing the risk of releasing a product the users will not appreciate and use.

6. Methodology AGILUSAB

We present a methodology for developing usable and agile applications, which takes into account the quality of software standards, the usability engineering and considers the interaction of the development team with the users a fundamental phase for a successful development of any software application. AGILUSAB is an incremental and iterative methodology proposed to develop software, with a particular attention to web applications.

6.1 Steps of the method

AGILUSAB, shown in Figure 9, is the methodology presented as a series of steps of comprehensive development phases, starting from the analysis, the design, the development of the user interface, the testing and the release of the application. AGILUSAB is an agile methodology for the development of interfaces and for the usability evaluation of the final products, in which the users and the customers play a crucial role being included in all phases of the development cycle.

AGILUSAB is an iterative Software Engineering method (Grezzi, 2004), it works mainly on simple interfaces (like a Web page) and provides for each development cycle the usability evaluation of each module, allowing the redesign of the proposed interface if considered necessary as a consequence of the assessment made.

The component of the method related to the usability is divided into three well known phases, which can be precisely evaluated: inspection, inquiry and testing. During the inspection the interface is analysed using empirical methods, like the heuristics of Nielsen, the cognitive paths (cognitive walkthrough), or other techniques the team of designers, developers and usability experts are considering convenient to use. The inquiry phase uses techniques to assess the usability of the operations the user or the customer may carry out using the interface; these techniques might include: questionnaires, observation, focus group, thinking aloud, among others. In the testing phase potential representative users are considered to analyse how they carry out their tasks using the system (or a prototype of it), and the comments of the usability evaluators are taken into account; among the most commonly used techniques are: measures of performance, protocols of expression of the user, remote testing, retrospective testing, and alternatives to the classic usability testing, such as: coaching method, shadowing method, teaching method, Co-discovery method, retrospective testing. Finally, the results obtained in the various phases of the usability evaluation process are discussed with the panel of evaluators to obtain an overview of the assessment made. The part of the method that refers to the development of a given implementation, forms a cycle consisting of six phases: analysis, design, prototyping, implementation, testing and release.

Analysis: The agile development methodology starts with the analysis phase, whose objective is to show the behaviour of the interface through the use of case diagrams (see Figure 10), a very popular technique of Software Engineering, introduced by the Unified Modelling Language (UML). Once having shown the behaviour of the interface to the users, a dialogue with them is established. On the basis of the decisions taken by the developer team, a (low, medium or high-fidelity) prototype in paper or software is shown to the user, showing the behaviour of the new component. It is initially recommended to show a low-fidelity prototype. If no modifications are necessary, the user is informed that on the basis of her/his observations this phase can be closed, otherwise the phase is repeated from the beginning. The implemented prototype is then passed to the design phase.

Design: in the analysis phase the behaviour of the interface is analysed, while in the design phase the coherence of the various possible operations is carried out. At the beginning of this phase the logical structure of the interface has to be defined, sketching the various actions a potential user can carry out when interacting with it. To represent these actions, we use the sequence diagram technique provided by UML. To have an idea of the logical structure of the interface, the logical representation in term of the present classes (tables, objects…) is added to the sequence diagram. To explore all possible connections the navigation tree will be used, which consists on a highly connected graph having as root the considered interface and as sons the various reachable interfaces, as shown in Figure 11. Once the analysis of the behaviour of the interface have been carried out, the team will meet again with the pool of users and customers in order to asses the obtained results, evaluating the opportunity of redesigning the interface. In this case a new prototype will be defined, according to the users comments and requirements.

Prototyping: The prototype has to be designed during the analysis and design phases, as described in the previous two paragraphs. Once the prototype behaviour has been defined, it has to be implemented according to the principle of the "Agile Manifesto". Once the implemented prototype is approved by the users, the customers and the development group, the implementation phase can be started.

Implementation: this phase runs as the implementation phase of the classical Software Engineering approach, since it is not necessary the dialogue with the customers and the users (they are not supposed to be expert programmers and therefore their contribution is useless).

Testing: during this phase, the team of developers has to select a community of potential typical users and test the functionality of the interface. The test is useful to assess the improvements made by the different usability evaluation methods adopted in each stage of the development. A good approach could be to select users involved in some of the usability tests carried out in the previous phases, to observe her/his reaction acting on an already operational interface. Once an interface has been tested, there are three possible actions: a) if the test was not satisfactory, the cycle is repeated taking into account the users observations and fixing the errors; (b) if the test was successful and if a new interface has to be implemented, a new cycle will be started; (c) If all components have been implemented and tested, the release phase will be started.

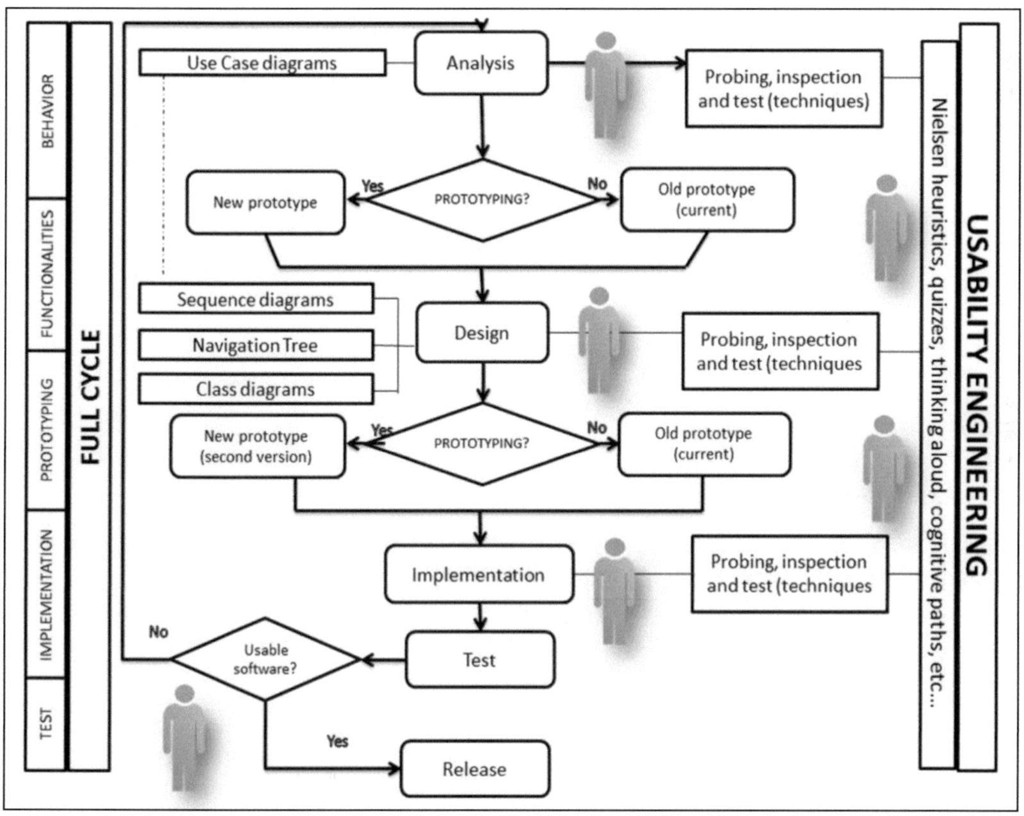

Fig. 9. Method AGILUSAB.

Release: the last phase of AGILUSAB is done only once, after all necessary cycles and iterations have been completed successfully. With the release phase the software is finally validated by the development team, the users and the customers, and is released for production.

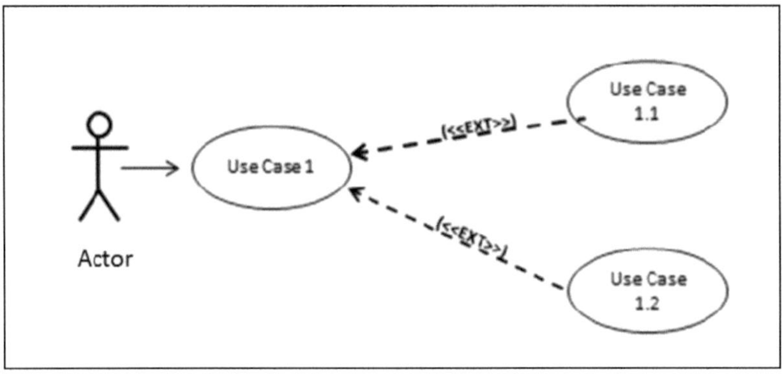

Fig. 10. Sample use case with an actor.

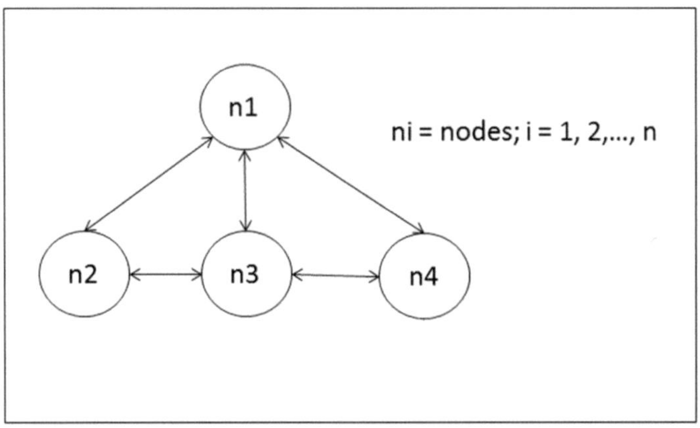

Fig. 11. Navigation tree.

7. Results: AGILUSAB used to restructure a web application

In order to test the AGILUSAB approach we evaluated the usability of the software product related to the web site of the travel agency MAVITUR (http://www.maviturviaggi.com), analyzing the XHTML pages and evaluating the usability of the software product. We applied our techniques and models (mainly the use case diagram and the sequence diagram) to identify, if applicable, the components with lack of usability and applying in such case the agile usability approach to restore its expected behaviour and functionality.

At the end of the evaluation process the team (composed by usability experts, final users and customers) expressed the evaluation of each interface. We are summarizing the results considering for each cycle only one interface of the software application.

HOME PAGE (index.html)

The inspection and the evaluation results are summarized in Table 1. The priority of the action required are expressed in the following way: 1= high, 2 = medium, 3 = low.

In Figure 12 the use case diagram of the home page is presented, related to the *analysis* phase. In Figure 13 the sequence diagram is presented and in Figure 14 the navigation tree of the same page is shown; both figures are related to the *design* phase. In conclusion, the team, considered the high number of usability problems detected in the current version, decided to design a new prototype according to the agile usability approach. In particular, new functions were planned in order to facilitate the navigation of the web site.

7.1 Web site evaluation using the closed questionnaire technique

We defined a questionnaire containing 32 general questions related to the web site. The responses were collected and evaluated using the open source package LimeSurvey, a very efficient tool for facilitating the collection of a suitable statistical sample and able to perform the descriptive statistics over the collected responses. The statistical sample were made by 95 users of the site, selected among customers and potential users. In Figure 15 an excerpt of the questionnaire is shown and in Figure 16 the summary of responses to a given question processed by LimeSurvey is shown.

The questionnaire responses made by the users were highly considered by the team, since they allow to catch wishes and expectations of the potential users of the web site. If a given problem were experienced by the 70% or more of the users, the assigned priority were 1, while if only few of them noticed a problem, this was rated with priority 3 and in the remaining cases the assigned priority were 2.

FAMILY (CATEGORY)	PROBLEM	COMMENT	PRIORITY
Design (graphic)	*Click* unknown	The user does not quickly understood that the photo gallery is located at the top right and she/he can click on it.	1
Design (layout)	*Frozen layout*	Small schemes that require horizontal scrolling	2
Design (scrolling)	*Scrolling*	The displacement was hiding significant areas of the page	1
availability *(navigation)*	*Advanced technologies and Plugin*	The lack of Flash Player damaged the graphic aspect of the site and prevented the access to the gallery.	2
Information (content)	*bums contents*	Missing text explaining the nature of the site and the agency.	1
Support (flow problems)	*User guide*	The sections "News" and "Events" are not important.	1
Design (graphic)	*Violation of the Web rules*	The hyperlink structure do not follow the Web rules	3
Information (content)	*Arrangement of contents*	The navigation menu is not arranged properly: it highlighted the external appearance of the agency and not what the user really is looking for.	1
Information (content)	*Fulfilment of the user needs*	The organization of the content is not suitable for fulfilling the user expectations visiting a travel agency website.	1
Design (typography)	*Font colour and background*	The colours are not appropriate and do not motivate the user to visit the offered services.	1

Table 1. Evaluation results related to the home page of the inspected site.

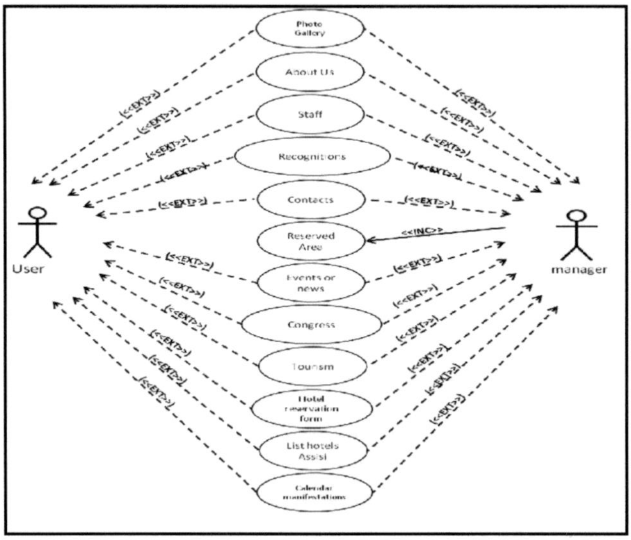

Fig. 12. Use case of the home page of Mavitur travel agency.

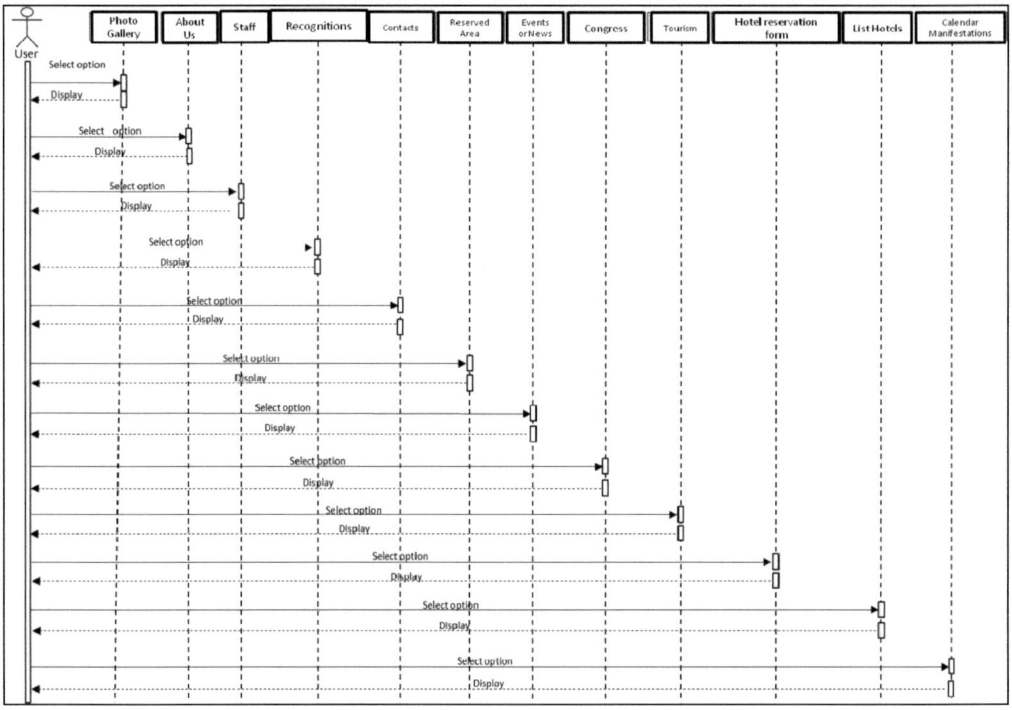

Fig. 13. Sequence diagram of the home page of Mavitur travel agency.

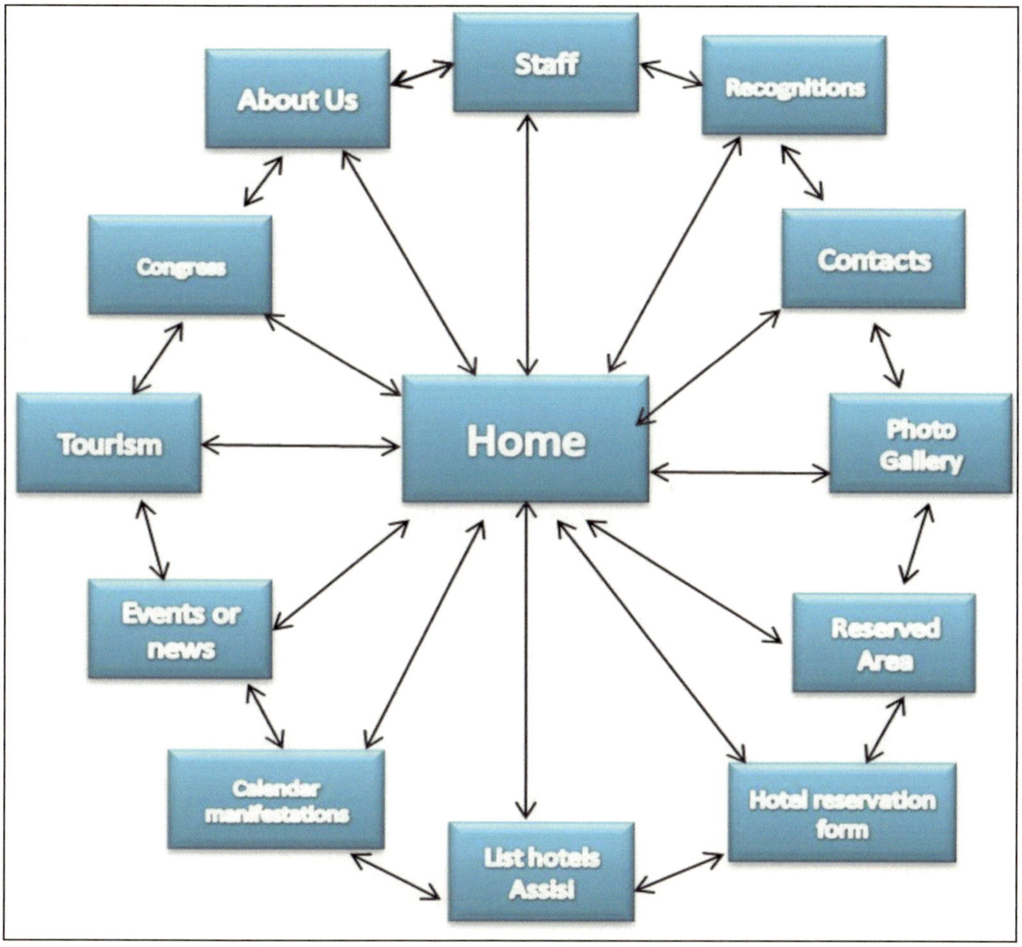

Fig. 14. Navigation tree of the interface version 1.0 of the home page of Mavitur travel agency.

Some responses provided by users were useful to identify a few usability problems not detected previously by the team. In Table 2 the detected problems are shown. The assigned priority was proportional to the frequency of the response among users.

The final decision of the team, at the end of the usability tests of the web site, were to redesign the site from scratch, considering the serious usability problems detected. In the following paragraphs the various milestones of the project will be analysed considering the implementation issues and the tests made with the users according to the agile methodology.

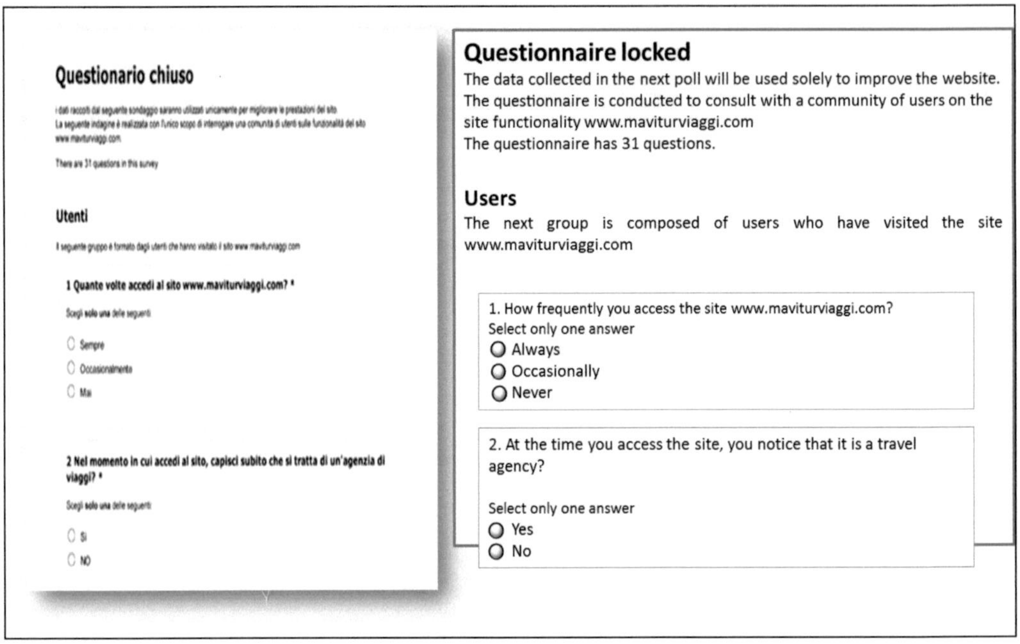

Fig. 15. Questions in the questionnaire (Original in Italian, English translation).

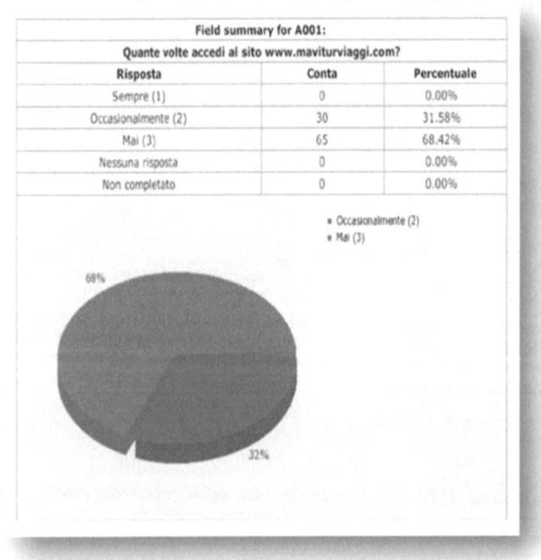

Answer	Total	percentage(%)
Always (1)	0	0,00
Occasionally (2)	30	31,58
Never (3)	65	68,42
Unanswered	0	0,00
No complete	0	0,00

Fig. 16. Results of the questionnaire obtained through the application LimeSurvey.

In order to present the results of the research made by our team we will describe the behaviour of the web site, its functions and the resulting graphical interface. In particular our attention will be focused on the home page of the web site. This page has been completely redesigned, optimizing its behaviour and increasing its functions, as a consequence of the performed usability tests. The team introduced a hierarchical menu, structured with submenus in order to improve the usability of the web site.

FAMILY (CATEGORY)	PROBLEM	COMMENT	PRIORITY
Design (graphic)	*Click* unknown	The buttons on the home page does not invite the user to click; this fact does not help the user to comprehend the functionality of the site.	**2**
Availability (Information Architecture (IA))	*Specificity of the link, labels and buttons*	The buttons on the site do not represent the assigned function.	**3**
Information (content)	*Satisfying customer needs*	The map does not show the location of the agency nor the hotels of Assisi.	**1**
Design (Writing)	*Poor wording*	The texts on the site will not attract customers to usufruct of the services offered by the agency.	**3**
Support (flow problems)	Guide users	The arrangement of the contents can confuse users and prevent run some actions.	**3**
Search	*Irrelevant the search site*	Missing search function on the site.	**3**
Information (content)	*Satisfying customer needs*	The site design is not consonant with what users expect from a travel agency.	**1**
Information (content)	*Satisfying customer needs*	Reservation cards do not have a validation application to filter bad data.	**1**

Table 2. Report of the concerns expressed by the users after having accessed the original web site.

In Figure 17 the use case resulting from the new design is shown. Figure 18 is describing the functions of the web site through the sequence diagram. In Figure 19 the resulting navigation tree is shown. The class diagram is not applicable in the present case, since a database is not necessary.

In Figure 20 the graphical interface resulting from the application of the usability guidelines and taking into account the suggestions made by the users after having accessed the original web site, is shown. In particular all colours have been changed in order to match the colours of the company logo. The contrast between the text and the background has been optimized taking into account users with visibility problems. We maintained the graphic design of the original version of the web site.

After having defined the prototype of the home page we afforded the implementation and testing phases. Since the implementation cannot be described here, we detail the testing phase, to prove that the usability guidelines allowed to implement a convenient web site, more usable and accessible.

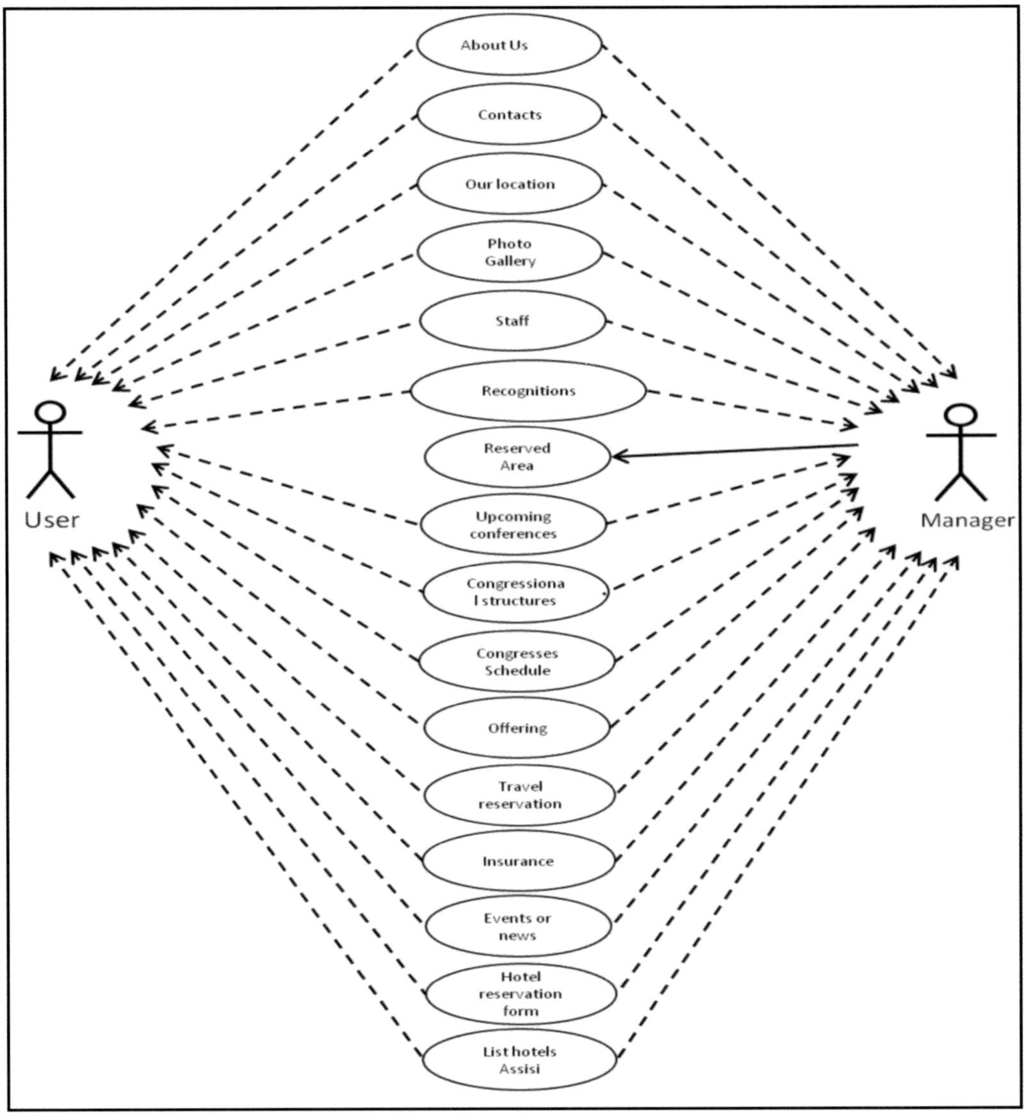

Fig. 17. Use Case diagram of section Home Page v 2.0.

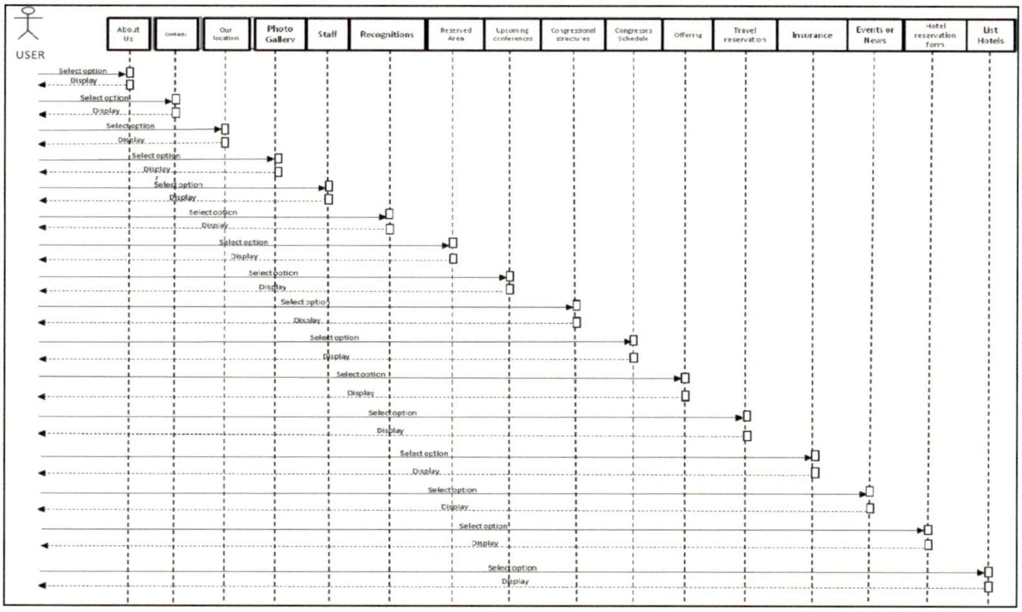

Fig. 18. Sequence Diagram Home Page v2.0.

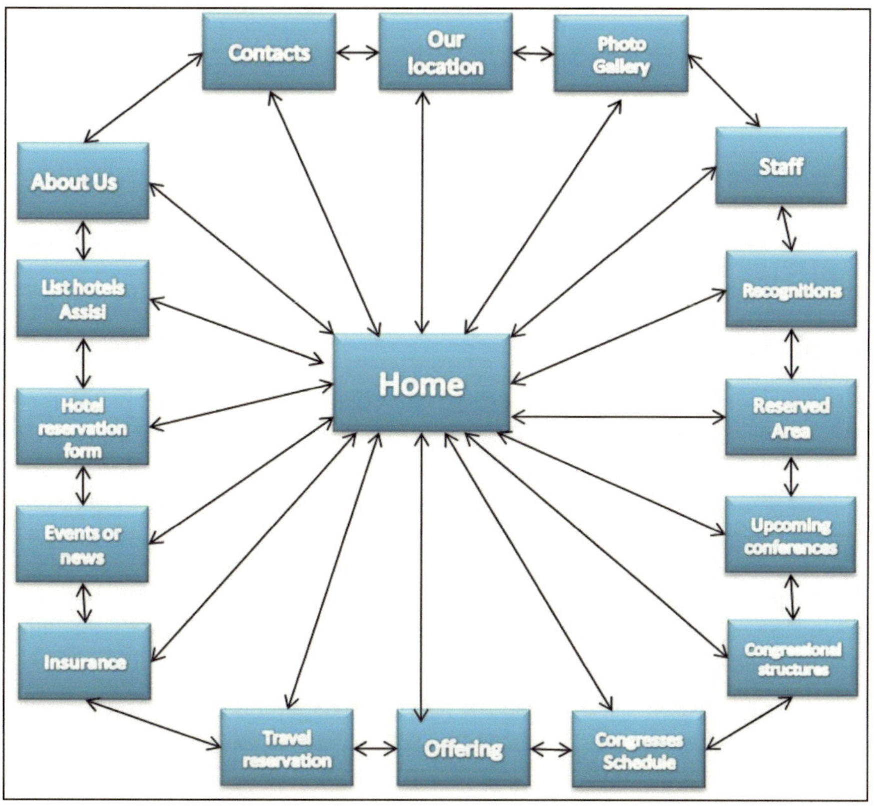

Fig. 19. Navigation Tree Home Page v 2.0.

To this purpose we repeated the usability test on the new graphical interface. The new test were run on a set of 10 users, 5 of them were aware of the features of the original web site. The results were really good, since all users appreciated the usability and the ease of use of the new graphical interface, proving that our method, based on the agile usability approach, is efficient and helps the developers to implement usable and simple software products.

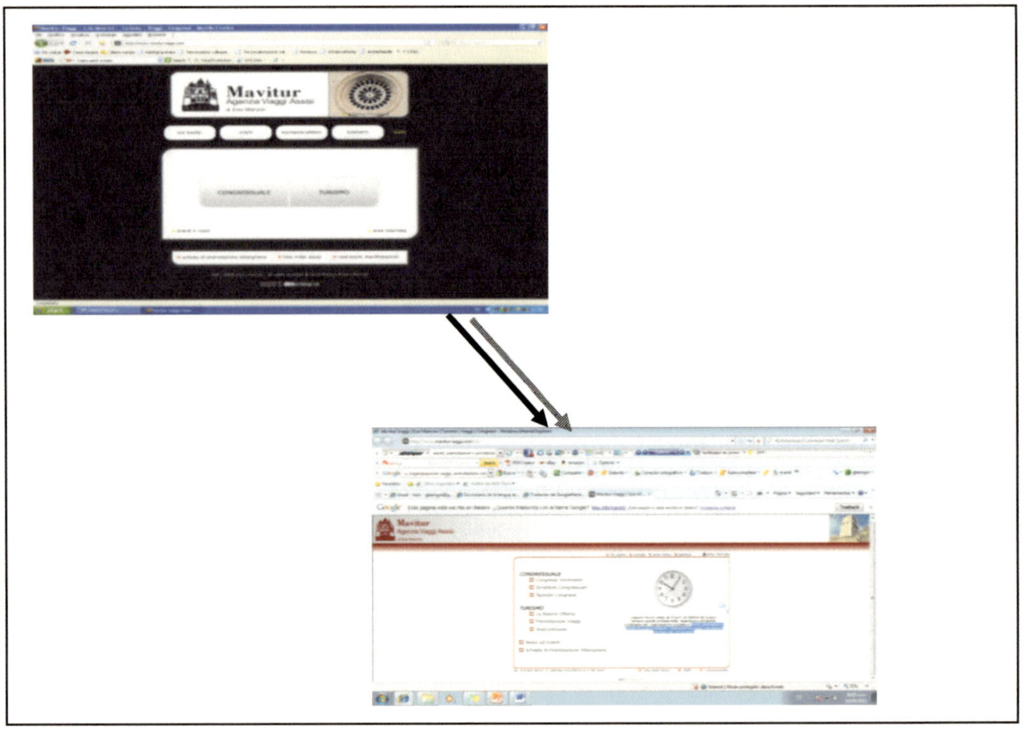

Fig. 20. GUI Home Page v 2.0.

8. Conclusions

At the present time the Human Machine Interaction has taken a central role in computer science, since it is focused on the importance of users and their experiences in all phases of software development.

We presented our AGILUSAB method, based on the agile and the usable methodologies and we presented the results obtained applying our method to a web site of a travel agency located in Assisi (PG), Italy. The AGILUSAB method allowed to redesign the web site solving all issues related to the lack of usability and the poor access to the relevant information. The coherence introduced in the navigation tree, the harmony of colours, make the user interaction easier and more effective.

Software products released according to the AGILUSAB method will minimize the cognitive load of the user, will minimize the errors and stimulate the user to interact with the site, successfully profiting of the information available. The collaboration between the stakeholders (end-users, customers, project managers, designers, architects, analysts, developers) allows to release products highly competitive and adaptable to their needs.

We want to add another important benefit related to the AGILUSAB method, which is related to social and economical issues. As per the social issues we would note that the constant evolution of the Internet, the inclusion of social networks and increasingly cheaper prices of computer products, enabled a large number of people to use the computer and access the global network. The diffusion of agile and usable products will enable people to use the technology in a more productive and efficient way. As per the economic issues, the diffusion of agile and usable methods will optimize the software life cycle, reducing the time required for releasing the final product and reducing the development costs, since the final users are deeply involved in all phases of the software production.

For computer science professionals it is crucial to approach the psychology of customers and users, increasing the capability of establishing a dialogue with them. The strong competition we are observing nowadays is claiming new approaches and innovative strategies to catch the user expectations and wishes. The usability of the released software represents an important criterion for a positive evaluation of a company and its employees.

9. References

Benigni, G., Gervasi, O., Ordaz, J., Pallottelli, S. *Usabilidad ágil y reingeniería de sitios web: Usableweb.* Saber. Volume 3 - 2011, in press, Venezuela.

Benigni, G., Gervasi, O., Passeri, L., Tai-Hoon, K. (2010). *USABAGILE Web: A Web Agile Usability Approach for Web Site Design.* Lecture Notes in Computer Science, Volume: 6017, Publisher: Springer Berlin Heidelberg, pages 422-431, March 2010, Germany.

Beck, K., Beedle, M., Cockburn, A. et. al. (2001). *Manifesto for agile software development.* Date of access [April, 2011]. Available from: <http://www.agilemanifesto.org/principles.html>.

Butler K.A. *Usability Engineering turns 10.* Interactions, June 1996.

Canós, J., Letelier, P. y Penadés, Mª. (s. f.). *Metodologías ágiles en el desarrollo de software.* Date of access [February, 2011]. Available from: http://www.willydev.net/descargas/prev/TodoAgil.pdf.

Floría, A. (2000). *Recopilación de Métodos de Usabilidad.* Date of access [March, 2011]. Available from: <http://www.sidar.org/visitable/Herramientas.htm>.

Grezzi, C. (2004) *"Ingegneria del software, fondamenti e principi"*, Editorial Pearson.

ISO/IEC 9241-11. (1998). *Guidance on usability.*

ISO/IEC 9126-1(2001). *Software engineering – Product quality -- Part 1: Quality model.*

Jakob Nielsen, (2003). *Usability Engineering*, Academic Press, USA.

Jacobson, I. (1998). *Object-Oriented Software Engineering.* USA: Addison Wesley.

Lorés, J., Granollers, T. (s. f.). *La Ingeniería de la Usabilidad y de la Accesibilidad aplicada al diseño y desarrollo de sitios web.* Date of access [February, 2011]. Available from: <http://es.scribd.com/usabilidad-y-diseno/d/19452307>

Manchón, E. (2003).*¿Qué es la usabilidad? Definición de Usabilidad.* Date of access [February, 2010]. Available from: <http://www.alzado.org/articulo.php?id_art=39>

Manning, L. (1992). *Introducción a la neuropsicología clásica y cognitiva del lenguaje.* Madrid: Trotta.

Martínez de la Teja, G. (2007). *Ergonomía e interfases de interacción humano-computadora.* IX Congreso Internacional de Ergonomía. Date of access [April, 2011]. Available from: http://www.semac.org.mx/archivos/9-6.pdf.

Merkovich, E. (1999). *La Intersección entre Factores Humanos, Diseño Gráfico, Interacción y Comunicación.* Date of access [March, 2011]. Available from: <http://fractal.gaiasur.com.ar/infoteca/siggraph99/diseno-de-interfaces-y-usabilidad.html>.

Nielsen, J. (1993). *Usability Engineering.* Academic Press, Inc. Boston.

Nielsen, J. (2008). *Agile Development Projects and Usability.* Date of access [February, 2011]. Available from: <http://www.useit.com/alertbox/agile-methods.html>

Nielsen, J. & Norman, D. (s. f.). *Agile Usability: Best Practices for User Experience on Agile Development Projects.* 2nd edition. Nielsen Norman Group Report.

Norman, D. A. (1988). *The psychology of everyday things,* ISBN-13 978-0-465-06710-7 Basic Books, New York, NY

Pressman, R. (2005). *Software Engineering: A Practitioner's Approach.* 5th edition. McGraw-Hill Higher Education.

Rodríguez, L. (n. d.). *Scrum, una metodología Ágil (I).* Date of access [February 19, 2011], Available from: http://es.debugmodeon.com/articulo/scrum-una-metodologia-agil-i.

Schwaber, K. & Beedle, K. (2002). Agile Software Development with Scrum. 1st Edition. ISBN: 0130676349, ISBN-13: 9780130676344. Prentice Hall.

Wittawat, Ch. (2010). *Software engineering, Software Document, Software Process.* Date of access [February, 2011]. Available from: *http://software-document.blogspot.com/2010/06/spiral-model.html*

Zavala, R. (2000). *Diseño de un Sistema de Información Geográfica sobre internet.* Date of access [Mach, 2011]. Available from: <http://www.angelfire.com/scifi/jzavalar/apuntes/IngSoftware.html>.

3

Affect Interpretation in Metaphorical and Simile Phenomena and Multithreading Dialogue Context

Li Zhang
School of Computing, Engineering and Information Sciences, University of Northumbria, Newcastle, UK

1. Introduction

The detection of complex emotions and value judgments from open-ended text-based multi-threaded dialogue and diverse figurative expressions is a challenging but inspiring research topic. In order to explore this line of research, previously we have developed an affect inspired AI agent embedded in an improvisational virtual environment interacting with human users. The human players are encouraged to be creative at their role-play under the improvisation of loose scenarios. The AI agent is capable of detecting 25 affective states from users' open-ended improvisational input and proposing appropriate responses to stimulate the improvisation.

We notice in the collected transcripts, metaphors and similes are used extensively to convey emotions such as "mum rocks", "u r an old waiter with a smelly attitude", "I was flamed on a message board", "u stink like rotten meat", "a teenage acts like a 4 year old" etc. Such figurative expressions describe emotions vividly. Fainsilber and Ortony (1987) commented that "an important function of metaphorical language is to permit the expression of that which is difficult to express using literal language alone". There is also study on general linguistic cues on affect implication in figurative expressions as theoretical inspiration to our research (Kövecses, 1998; Barnden, 2007; Zhang et al., 2009). Thus affect detection from metaphorical and simile phenomena draws our research attention. In this chapter, we particularly focus on affect interpretation of a few metaphors including cooking and sensory metaphors, and simile expressions with the usage of comparative 'like' prepositional phrases.

Moreover, our previous affect sensing is conducted purely based on the analysis of each turn-taking input itself without using any contextual inference. However, most relevant contextual information may produce a shared cognitive environment between speakers and audience to help inference affect embedded in emotionally ambiguous input and facilitate effective communication. As Sperber & Wilson (1995) stated in Relevance theory "communication aims at maximizing relevance and speakers presume that their communicative acts are indeed relevant". Such relevant contextual profiles have also been employed in our present work to model cognitive aspect of personal and social emotion and assist affect sensing from literal and figurative input. Also we only focus on 'neutral' and 9 most commonly used emotions (disapproving, approving, grateful, happy, sad, threatening, regretful, angry, and caring) out of the 25 affective states on contextual emotion analysis and prediction. We used a school bullying[1] and a crohn's disease[2] scenario in our previous user testing and the AI agent played a minor role in the improvisation of both scenarios. In this chapter, we mainly use the collected transcripts of both scenarios for the illustration of metaphor and simile phenomena recognition and contextual affect analysis.

2. Related work

Much research has been done on creating affective virtual characters. Indeed, emotion theories, particularly that of Ortony et al. (1988) (OCC), are used widely in such research. Egges et al. (2003) provided virtual characters with conversational emotional responsiveness. Aylett et al. (2006) also focused on the development of affective behaviour planning for their synthetic characters.

Text-based affect detection becomes a rising research branch recently (Shaikh et al., 2007; Zhang, 2010; Liu & Singh, 2004). Façade (Mateas, 2002) included shallow natural language processing for characters' open-ended input. But the detection of major emotions, rudeness and value judgements was not mentioned. Zhe and Boucouvalas (2002) demonstrated an emotion extraction module embedded in an Internet chatting environment. However the emotion detection focused only on emotional adjectives, and did not address deep issues such as figurative expression of emotion. Also, the concentration purely on first-person emotions is narrow. Context-sensitive research is also employed to detect affect. Ptaszynski et al. (2009) developed an affect detection component with the integration of a web-mining technique to detect affect from users' input and verify the contextual appropriateness of the detected emotions. However, their system targeted conversations only between an AI agent and one human user in non-role-playing situations, which greatly reduced the complexity of the modeling of the interaction context. Moreover, the metaphorical description of emotional states is common in literature and has been extensively studied (Fussell and Moss, 1998), for example, "he nearly exploded" and "joy ran through me," where anger and joy are being viewed in vivid physical terms. In the work of Zhang & Barnden (2010), a few other metaphorical affective expressions (such as animal metaphor ("X is a rat") and food metaphor ("X is walking meat")) were intensively studied and affect was derived from such simple metaphorical expressions.

There are also well-known cognitive theories on emotion modeling. The OCC model provided cognitive appraisal theories for 22 emotional states, while Gratch and Marsella (2004) also presented an integrated emotion model of appraisal and coping, in order to reason about emotions and to provide emotional responses, facial expressions and potential social intelligence for virtual agents. However, there is very limited research on contextual

[1] It is mainly about the bully, Mayid, is picking on a new schoolmate, Lisa. Elise and Dave (Lisa's friends) and Mrs Parton (the school teacher) are trying to stop the bullying.

[2] Peter has Crohn's disease and has the option to undergo a life-changing but dangerous surgery. He needs to discuss the pros and cons with friends and family. Janet (Mum) wants Peter to have the operation. Matthew (younger brother) is against it. Arnold (Dad) is not able to face the situation. Dave (the best friend) mediates the discussion.

emotion modeling in cognitive science to guide our practical development on contextual affect analysis. Lopez et al. (2008) have proposed an emotion topology integrated with the consideration of contextual and multimodal elements to facilitate computerization.

Our work thus distinguishes on the following aspects: (1) affect detection from metaphorical and simile expressions; (2) affect sensing for basic and complex emotions in improvisational role-play situations; (3) affect detection for second and third person cases (e.g. 'you', 'she'); and (4) affect interpretation based on contextual profiles.

3. The original affect detection processing and the system architecture

As mentioned earlier, our original system has been developed for secondary school students to engage in role-play situations in virtual social environments. Without pre-defined constrained scripts, the human users could be creative in their role-play within the highly emotionally charged scenarios. After an inspection of the recorded improvisational transcripts, we noticed that the language used for improvisation is complex and idiosyncratic, e.g. often ungrammatical and full of abbreviations, mis-spellings, etc. Several pre-processing procedures have been developed in our application previously to deal with misspellings, abbreviations, letter repetitions, interjections and onomatopoeia etc. Moreover, the language contains a large number of weak cues to the affect that is being expressed. These cues may be contradictory or they may work together to enable a stronger interpretation of the affective state. In order to build a reliable and robust analyser of affect it is necessary to undertake several diverse forms of analysis and to enable these to work together to build stronger interpretations. Also our previous affect detection has been performed solely based on the analysis of individual turn-taking user input without any contextual inference. Overall, we have adopted rule-based reasoning, robust parsing, pattern matching, semantic and sentimental profiles (e.g. WordNet (Fellbaum, 1998) and WordNet-Affect (Strapparava and Valitutti, 2004)) for affect detection analysis. Jess, the rule engine for Java platform, has been used to implement the rule-based reasoning while Java has been used to implement other algorithms and processing with the integration of the off-the-shelf language processing tools, such as WordNet.

In our turn-taking based affect interpretation, we have considered the following affective expressions. We found that one useful pointer to affect was the use of imperative mood, especially when used without softeners such as 'please' or 'would you'. Strong emotions and/or rude attitudes were often expressed in this case. Expression of the imperative mood in English is surprisingly various and ambiguity-prone. We have used the syntactic output from the Rasp parser (Briscoe and Carroll, 2002) and a semantic resource (Esuli and Sebastiani, 2006) to deal with certain types of imperatives. In an initial stage of our work, affect detection was based purely on textual pattern-matching rules that looked for simple grammatical patterns or templates partially involving specific words or sets of specific alternative words. As mentioned above, Jess is used to implement the pattern/template-matching rules in the AI agent allowing the system to cope with more general wording and ungrammatical fragmented sentences. The rules conjectured the character's emotions, evaluation dimension (negative or positive), politeness (rude or polite) and what response the automated actor should make. However, it lacked other types of generality and could be fooled when the phrases were suitably embedded as subcomponents of other grammatical structures.

In order to go beyond certain such limitations, sentence type information obtained from Rasp was also adopted in the rule sets. Such information not only helped the agent to detect affective states from the input (such as the detection of imperatives), and to decide if the detected affective states should be counted (e.g. affects detected in conditional sentences were not valued), but also contributed to proposing appropriate responses.

The results of this affective analysis were then used to (see Figure 1):

1. Control the automated actor (EMMA) that operates a character in the improvisation. I.e. the detected affective states enable the AI agent to make appropriate responses to stimulate the improvisation.
2. Additionally, drive the animations of the avatars in the user interface so that they react bodily in ways that is consistent with the affect that they are expressing, for instance by changing posture or facial expressions.

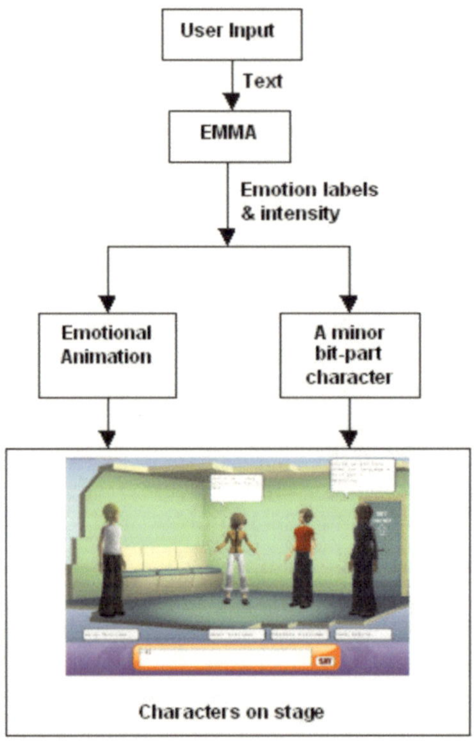

Fig. 1. Affect detection and the control of characters.

We have also developed responding regimes for the AI actor. EMMA normally responds to, on average, every Nth speech by another character in one improvisational session, where N is a changeable parameter (currently usually set to 3). However, it also responds when EMMA's character's name is mentioned, and makes no response if it cannot detect anything useful in the utterance it is responding to. The one-in-N average is achieved by sampling a random variable every time another character says something. We also have N dynamically adjustable according to how confident EMMA is about what it has discerned in the utterance at hand so that it is less likely to respond if it has less confidence. EMMA makes a random response from several stored response candidates that are suitable for the affective quality it has discerned in the utterance it is responding to.

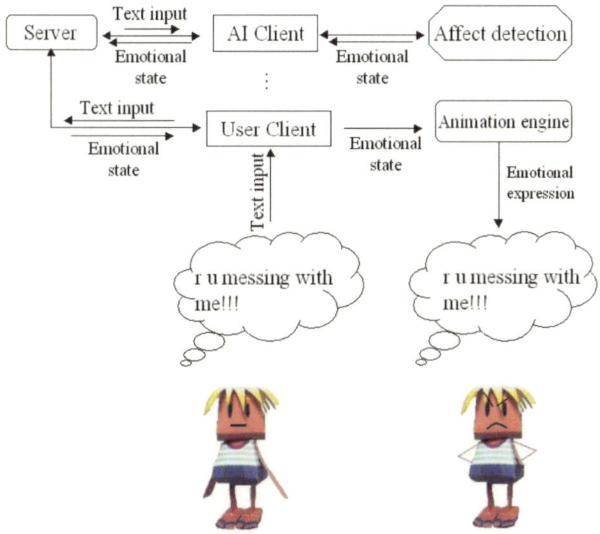

Fig. 2. An example of real-time interaction.

Moreover, our system employs a client/server architecture for implementation. The conversational AI agent and other human-controlled characters consist of clients. The server broadcasts messages sent by one client to all the other clients. Thus user's text input from normal user client is sent to the AI agent client via the server. Then the AI agent, who plays a minor role in the improvisation with other human-controlled characters, analyzes the user's text input and derives the affective implication out of the text. Then the AI agent also searches its knowledge base to provide a suitable response to the human players using the detected affective states. We have particularly created the AI agent's responses in a way which could stimulate the improvisation by generating sensitive topics of the storyline. Then an XML stream composed of the detected affective state from one user input and the AI agent's response is dynamically created and broadcasted to all other clients by the server. The users' clients parse the XML stream to obtain the information of the previous "speaker's" emotional state and the current AI character's response. An animation engine has embedded in each user client which updates the user avatars' emotional facial and gesture animation on each user's terminal. Therefore, if the previous human-controlled character expresses 'anger' affective state by saying "r u messing with me!!!", the animation engine in each user client updates emotional animation of that character on each terminal using cross behavior via simple facial and gesture animation (see Figure 2). In each session, up to five characters are engaged in.

4. Metaphorical affect interpretation

Metaphorical language can be used to convey emotions implicitly and explicitly, which also inspires cognitive semanticists (Kövecses, 1998). Examples such as, "he is boiling mad" and "Lisa fired up straightaway", describe emotional states in a relatively explicit if metaphorical way. But affect is also often conveyed more implicitly via metaphor, as in "his room is a cesspit": affect (such as 'disgust') associated with a source item (cesspit) gets carried over to the corresponding target item (the room). There are also cooking metaphor examples implying emotions implicitly, such as "he is grilled by the teacher", "he knew he was going to be toast when he got home". In these examples, the suffering agents have been figuratively conceptualized as food. They bear the results of intensive or slow cooking. Thus, these agents who suffer from such cooking actions tend to feel pain and sadness, while the cooking performing agents may take advantage of such actions to achieve their intentions, such as persuasion, punishment or even enjoyment. We detected affect from such metaphorical expressions previously and used the AI agent as a useful application of theoretical inspiration for figurative language processing generally.

Especially we notice sensory and another type of cooking metaphors not only implying emotions but also sharing similar linguistic syntactical cues. The sensory metaphor we are interested in includes temperature, smell, taste, and light metaphors. We gather the following examples for the study of the semantic and syntactical structures of such metaphorical expressions, including cooking metaphor: "the news inflamed her temper", "he dishes out more criticism than one can take", "she was burned by a shady deal"; light metaphor: "you lighted up my life"; temperature metaphor: "they are kindling a new romance"; taste metaphor: "bittersweet memories" and smell metaphor: "love stinks", "the stench of failure" etc.

In the above cooking metaphor examples, the cooking actions are performed on cognitive abstract entities ('temper', 'criticism') or human agents ('she') [physical cooking actions + abstract entities/human agents]. Sometimes, human agents are also the objects of cooking actions performed by abstract subject entities ("she was burned by a shady deal"), which may lead to human agents' negative emotional experience. Similarly in the sensory metaphor examples, the light and temperature metaphors show similar syntactical structures with actions conducting respectively on existence ('my life') or relationship abstract entities ('romance') [physical actions + abstract entities]. Emotion abstract entities are also used as subjects that are capable of performing actions such as love in smell metaphors [abstract subject entities + physical actions]. Overall, the above cooking and sensory metaphors indicate that: abstract entities are able to perform physical actions while they can also be the objects of physical actions. Also examples show cognitive abstract entities may also have characteristics of food, temperature, taste or smell ('adj. + abstract entities'). In another word, some cognitive abstract entities could be un-cooked ("a raw talent"), tasty ("bittersweet memories") or have temperature ("heated debate", "burning love") or smell ("the stench of failure"). We use such semantic preference violations to sense these metaphor phenomena and their affective states.

First, we use Rasp (Briscoe & Carroll, 2002) to indentify each subject, verb phrase and object in each sentence. Then we particularly send the main terms in these three components to WordNet (Fellbaum, 1998) to recover their hypernyms. We also focus on the analysis of phrases with a structure of 'adjective + noun' by deriving the synonyms or related nouns for the adjective and hypernyms for the noun term using WordNet. If the inputs indicate structures of 'abstract subject entities + actions', 'physical actions + abstract object entities' or 'temperature/smell/taste/cooking adjectives + abstract entities', then the inputs are recognized as metaphorical expressions. The detailed processing is also shown in Figure 3.

For example, the AI agent carries out the following processing to sense the metaphorical expression "they are kindling a new romance".

1. Rasp: the input -> 'subject PPHS2 (they) + VBR (are) + VVG (kindle + ing) + AT1 (a) + JJ (new) + object NN1 (romance)'
2. WordNet: 'kindle' -> hypernym: FLARE UP, LIGHT. 'Romance' -> relationship -> abstract entity;
3. An evaluation profile (Esuli & Sebastiani, 2006) determines: LIGHT-> positive; 'romance' -> positive.
4. The input indicates -> 'third person subject performs a 'positive' action towards an abstract entity (romance) -> it is recognised as a metaphorical input.
5. The third person human subject (they) may experience a positive emotion by boosting up a 'positive' relationship abstract entity.

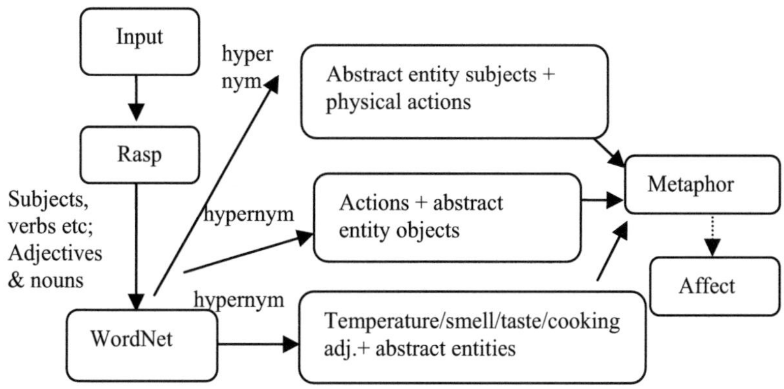

Fig. 3. Metaphor interpretation and detection.

Moreover, the AI agent conducts the following processing to sense the metaphorical expression "Mayid has a smelly attitude":

1. Rasp: 'NP1 (Mayid) + VHZ (has) + AT1 (a) + JJ (smelly) + NN1 (attitude)'
2. WordNet: 'attitude' -> hypernym: psychological feature -> abstract entity. 'smelly' -> synonyms & related nouns: ill-smell, foul, and malodorous.
3. The evaluation profile indicates: foul, malodorous -> 'negative'.
4. Part of the input is interpreted as: 'a cognitive abstract entity has negative smell (i.e. a smell adj with negative indication + an abstract cognitive entity)' -> identified as a smell metaphor with negative implication.
5. The input becomes: 'NP1 (Mayid) + VHZ (has) + a smell metaphor with negative indication' -> implies 'insulting/angry' of the speaker towards 'Mayid'.

Although the above metaphor recognition is at its initial stage, the system is capable of performing affect sensing and metaphor recognition more robustly and flexibly. It can also recognize other metaphorical input such as "a warm reception", "she is burnt by a shady deal", "deep, dark thoughts", "he stirred up all kinds of emotion" etc.

In the Crohn's disease scenario, metaphorical expressions have also been used to indicate battles between family members and Peter's stress towards his life changing operation. An example interaction taken from a recorded transcript is as follows:

Dave: what are your other options peter
Peter: im trying very hard but theres too much stuff blocking my head up
Peter: my plate is already too full.... there aint otha options dave

In the first input from Peter, 'thoughts' have been regarded as physical solid objects that can occupy physical space such as a plate or head. With the contextual inference, in Peter's second input, plate has also been metaphorically used to refer to one's head. Moreover, we can hardly consider the last input as a metaphorical expression if without any contextual inference. This also indicates directions of our future work on metaphor interpretation.

5. Affect sensing from simile expressions

In the collected transcripts from the school bullying scenario, we also notice similes are used to convey strong emotions by linking and comparing dissimilar concepts via prepositions such as 'like'. An example interaction is demonstrated as follows.

1. Mayid: you need to stop being such an ugly little girl [angry]
2. Mrs Parton: Mayid detection![threatening]
3. Mayid: the only problem with me is that lisa is so mean to me. [angry]
4. Lisa: you need to learn how to be nice and act your age. [neutral]-> [angry]
5. Mayid: look at you though [neutral] -> [angry]
6. Lisa: about what? I don't even know u. tell him miss. [neutral] -> [angry]
7. Mayid: *a teenager acts like a 4 year old* [neutral] -> [angry]
8. Mayid: I bet you still play with Barbie dolls
9. Mrs Parton: CALM DOWN NOW!
10. Elise: that crap really don't suit u mayid
11. Lisa: *a teenager acts like a heavyweight boxer*

Indicated by italics in the above example, Mayid used a simile to indicate 'insulting/angry' by comparing Lisa's behavior of calling the schoolteacher for help with that of a 4 year old, while Lisa also employed a similar simile expression to imply Mayid's inappropriate behavior such as threatening or beating other characters as if he were a heavyweight boxer. There are also other similar simile expressions implying emotions such as "you dance like an angel", "Tom ate like a pig", "she sings like a bird" etc. In our processing, we particularly focus on such similes with a syntactical structure of 'subject + verb + preposition (like) + object'. The subjective evaluation profile and WordNet are then used to further derive the affect attached with the simile input. For example, we use the following processing to interpret the simile expression "you dance like an angel":

1. Rasp: 'PPY (you) + VV0 (dance) + II (like) + AT1 (an) + NN1 (angel)'
2. WordNet: 'angel' -> good person -> physical entity.
3. The evaluation profile shows: 'angel' -> positive;
4. The input indicates: 'the performance of a second person subject is compared with that of another person with 'positive' implication'.
5. The input implies 'affectionate'.

For the example, "a teenager acts like a heavyweight boxer", the processing taken is in the following.

1. Rasp: 'subject NN1 (teenager) + VVZ (acts) + II (like) + AT1 (a) + object NN1 (heavyweight) + object NN1 (boxer)'
2. WordNet: 'heavyweight' -> 'wrestler' -> person; 'boxer' -> 'combatant', 'battler' -> person
3. The input becomes: 'the subject's action is compared with that of another person' -> recognized as a simile.
4. Since the evaluation profile cannot provide any positive/negative evaluation values for the noun terms: 'heavyweight', 'wrestler', 'boxer', 'combatant', and 'battler', the root forms of the noun terms are used to retrieve the evaluation values.
5. The evaluation profile determines: 'wrestle', 'combat', 'battle' -> 'negative'; thus 'heavyweight' and 'boxer' -> 'negative'.
6. The input implies: 'the subject's action is compared with that of another person with a negative indication' -> thus the input conveys 'insulting/angry'.

However, purely based on the analysis of the input "a teenage acts like a 4 year old" itself, the AI agent recognizes the simile expression but fails to determine the affect conveyed in it due to the following processing:

1. Rasp: 'subject NN1 (teenager) + VVZ (acts) + II (like) + AT1 (a) + MC (4) + NNT1 (year) + JJ (old)'
2. WordNet: 'old' -> age; the evaluation profile: age -> objective (i.e. non-emotional);
3. The input becomes: 'the subject's action is compared with that of a 'neutral' object' -> recognized as a simile.

Since interaction context plays important roles in discovering affect conveyed in emotionally ambiguous input, it is resorted to to further justify the affect detected from the analysis of individual turn-taking input. I.e. context-based affect detection is employed to justify the neutral expression drawn from the analysis of the input itself, such as affect justification for the above neutral simile expression. As Schnall (2005) stated that the intention of communication is to achieve the greatest possible cognitive outcome with the smallest possible processing effort, i.e. "to communicate only what is relevant". Thus in the following section, we discuss context-based affect detection and emotion modeling in personal and social interaction context to justify affect interpretation in literal and figurative expressions.

6. Context-based affect detection

Lopez et al. (2008) suggested that context profiles for affect detection included social, environmental and personal contexts. In our study, personal context may be regarded as one's own emotion inclination or improvisational mood in communication context and the social context may refer to other characters' emotional influence to the current speaker. We believe that one's own emotional states have a chain effect, i.e. the previous emotional status may influence later emotional experience. We make attempts to include such effects into emotion modelling. Bayesian networks are used to simulate such personal causal emotion context. E.g. we regard the first, second and third emotion experienced by a particular user respectively as A, B and C. We assume that the affect B is dependent on the first emotional state A. Further, we assume that the third emotion C, is dependent on both the first and second emotions, A and B. In our application, given two or more most recent emotional states a user experiences, we may predict the most probable emotion this user implies in the current input using a Bayesian network.

Briefly, a Bayesian network employs a probabilistic graphical model to represent causality relationship and conditional (in)dependencies between domain variables. It allows combining prior knowledge about (in)dependencies among variables with observed training data via a directed acyclic graph. It has a set of directed arcs linking pairs of nodes: an arc from a node X to a node Y means that X (parent emotion) has a direct influence on Y (successive child emotion). Such causal modelling between variables reflects the chain effect of emotional experience. It uses the conditional probabilities (e.g. P[B|A], P[C|A,B]) to reflect such influence between prior emotional experiences to successive emotional expressions.

In our application, any combination of the 10 most commonly used emotional states could be used as prior emotional experience of the user. Also each conditional probability for each potential emotional state given two or more prior emotional experiences (such as P[approval|A,B] etc) will be calculated. The emotional state with the highest conditional probability is selected as the most probable emotion the user conveys in the current turn-taking. Moreover, it is beneficial that the Bayesian network allows us to use the emotional states experienced by a particular character throughout one improvisation as the prior input to the network so that our system may learn about this user's emotional trend gradually for future prediction. In detail, at the training stage, two human judges (not involved in any development) marked up 3 example transcripts of the school bullying scenario, which consisted of approximately 470 turn-taking inputs. For each character, we extract three sequences of emotions from the improvisation of the 3 example transcripts to produce prior conditional probabilities. We take a frequency approach to determine the conditional probabilities for each Bayesian network. When an affect is annotated for a turn-taking input, we increment a counter for that expressed emotion given the two preceding emotions. For each character, a conditional probability table is produced based on the training data. An example conditional probability table is presented in Table 1.

		Probability of the predicted emotional state C being:			
Emotion A	Emotion B	Happy	Approval	...	Angry
Happy	Neutral	P00	P01	...	P09
Neutral	Angry	P10	P11	...	P19
Disapproval	Disapproval	P20	P21	...	P29
Angry	Angry	P30	P31	...	P39

Table 1. An example conditional probability table for emotions expressed by one character

In the above table, the predicted emotional state C could be any of the most frequently used 10 emotions. At the training stage, the frequencies of emotion combinations in a 10 * 10 * 10 ((A*B)*C) matrix are produced dynamically. This matrix represents counters (N_{CAB}) for all outcomes of C given all the combinations of A and B. A one-dimensional array is also needed to store counters (N_{AB}) for all the combinations of two prior emotions, A and B. Such a conditional probability matrix is constructed at run-time for each human-controlled character in the school bullying scenario based on the training emotional sequences.

For the prediction of an emotion state mostly likely implied in the current input by a particular character at the testing stage, the two prior recent emotional states are used to determine which row to consider in the conditional probability matrix, and select the column with the highest conditional probability as the final output. The emotional sequences used for testing expressed by each character have also been used to further update and enrich the training samples so that these testing emotional states may also help the system to cope with any new emotional inclination because of each character's creative improvisation.

An example algorithm of the Bayesian affect sensing is provided in the following. For the initial run of the algorithm, A, B and C are initialized with the most recent affects detected for each character purely based on the analysis of individual input.

Pseudo-code for affect prediction using a Bayesian network

Function Bayesian_Affect_Prediction
{
1. Verify the contextual appropriateness of the affect C predicted by the Bayesian reasoning;
2. Produce the row index, i, for any given combination of the two preceding emotional states A & B in the matrix;
3. Indicate the column index, j, for the recommended affect C;
4. Increment counters: $N_{AB}[i]$ and $N_{CAB}[i][j]$;
5. Update two preceding emotions by: Emotion A = Emotion B; Emotion B = The newly recommended affect C;
6. Produce the new row index, k, for any given combination of the updated two preceding emotional states A & B;
7. Calculate probabilities (i.e. $P[C|A,B] = N_{CAB}[k][column]/N_{AB}[k]$) for the predicted emotional state C being any of the 10 emotions;
8. Select and return the affect with the highest probability as the predicted affect C; }

At the testing stage, when an affect is predicted for a user's input using the Bayesian network, the contextual appropriateness of the detected affect will be further justified. The verification processing using neural network-based reasoning, which will be introduced at a later stage, results in a final recommended affect. Then the conditional probability table obtained from the training stage is updated with the newly recommended affect and its two preceding emotions. The above processing is iterative to predict affect throughout an improvisation for a particular character based on his/her personal emotional profiles.

Moreover social emotional context also has great potential to affect the emotional experience of the current speaking character. E.g., a recent threatening input contributed by Mayid may cause Lisa and her friends to be 'angry'. A neural network algorithm, backpropagation, is used to model such an effect, which accepts two most recent emotions contributed by two other characters as input. The neural network implementation has three layers and 2 nodes in the input layer & 10 nodes respectively in the hidden and output layers indicating 'neutral' and the most commonly used 9 emotions in our application. Since it is a supervised learning algorithm, we use emotional context gathered from transcripts across scenarios as training data. This neural network-based reasoning may discover the emotional influence of other characters towards the current speaker as output.

At the training stage, we have used 5 transcripts of the school bullying scenario collected in our previous user testing to generate the training data of the emotional contexts. Two human judges have been used to provide affect annotations of these interaction contexts. After the neural network has been trained to reach a reasonable average error rate (less than 0.05), it is used for testing to predict emotional influence of other participant characters towards the speaking character in the test interaction contexts.

For the affect analysis of the above example transcript of school bullying scenario shown at the beginning of section 5, first of all, the AI agent performs affect sensing purely based on the analysis of the input itself without any contextual reasoning to annotate each user input. Therefore we annotate the affect conveyed from the 1st input to the 4th input. Since the 4th input from Lisa indicates non-emotional and generally statement inputs with second person subjects tend to convey emotions (e.g. "u r an angel", "u aren't needed here" etc), the contextual affect analysis based on the above description is activated. However since this is Lisa's first input, we do not have any emotional profile yet to activate the improvisational mood prediction using the Bayesian approach. But we can still resort to the neural network-based social context modeling to reason the emotional influence from other characters to Lisa. With the most recent emotional context, 'threatening (2nd input)' and 'angry (3rd input), provided by Mrs Parton and Mayid, as input to the Backpropagation reasoning, it deduces that in the 4th input Lisa has the highest probability (0.985) to be 'angry'. Thus we adjust the affect implied in the 4th input to 'angry' caused by the social emotional context from other characters. Similarly for the 5th 'neutral' input from Mayid, the AI agent conducts the following processing:

1. The emotional profile of Mayid: 'angry(1st input) and angry (3rd input)' used as input to personal emotional context modeling via the Bayesian network -> 'angry' as the predicted most probable affect;
2. The social emotional context contributed by two other characters: 'threatening (2nd input) and angry (4th input)', used as input to Backpropagation reasoning -> 'angry' as Mayid's mostly likely emotional inclination, which strengthens the output obtained from personal emotion context modeling.
3. The 5th input from Mayid is adjusted to be 'angry'.

With the emotional context contributed by Mayid for the 3rd (angry) and 5th input (angry), the neural network-based social emotional context modeling also indicates 'anger' is implied in the 6th input from Lisa. For the 7th input "a teenager acts like a 4 year old", we have the following procedure taken to detect affect from the simile expression.

1. The personal emotional profile of Mayid: 'angry (1st input), angry (3rd input) and angry (5th input)', as input to the Bayesian reasoning -> Mayid is most likely to be 'angry' again in the current 7th input;
2. The related social emotional context: 'angry (4th input) and angry (6th input)', as input to the neural network reasoning -> Mayid is most probable to be influenced to become 'angry'.
3. Thus the simile input implies 'anger' other than being 'neutral'.

Our AI agent can also sense other simile phenomena with similar syntactical structures and the affective states implied in them ("he walks like a lion", "u stink like rotten meat" etc). The contextual affect detection based on personal and social cognitive emotion modeling has also been used to uncover and justify affect implied in other emotionally ambiguous metaphorical and literal input.

7. Evaluations and conclusions

As mentioned previously, the detected affective states from users' open-ended text input have also been used to produce emotional animation for human players' avatars. The emotional animation mainly includes expressive gestures and social attention (such as eye gazing). Thus, our processing has employed emotions embedded in the scenarios, dialogue and characters for expressive social animation generation without distracting users from the learning context. We also carried out user testing with 220 secondary school students from Birmingham and Darlington schools for the improvisation of school bullying and Crohn's disease scenarios. Generally, our previous statistical results based on the collected questionnaires indicate that the involvement of the AI character has not made any statistically significant difference to users' engagement and enjoyment with the emphasis of users' notice of the AI character's contribution throughout. Briefly, the methodology of the testing is that we had each testing subject have an experience of both scenarios, one including the AI minor character only and the other including the human-controlled minor character only. After the testing sessions, we obtained users' feedback via questionnaires and group debriefings. Improvisational transcripts were automatically recorded during the testing so that it allows further evaluation of the performance of the affect detection component.

We also produce a new set of results for the evaluation of the updated affect detection component with contextual and metaphorical affect interpretation based on the analysis of some recorded transcripts of the school bullying scenario. Generally two human judges marked up the affect of 400 turn-taking user input from the recorded 4 transcripts of this scenario (different from those used for the training of Bayesian and neural networks). In order to verify the efficiency of the new developments, we provide Cohen's Kappa inter-agreements for the AI agent's performance with and without the new developments for the detection of the most commonly used 10 affective states. The agreement for human judge A/B is 0.57. The inter-agreements between human judge A/B and the AI agent with the new developments are respectively 0.48 and 0.43, while the results between judge A/B and the agent without the new developments are only respectively 0.39 and 0.34.

Although future work is needed, the new developments on contextual affect sensing using both Bayesian and neural network based reasoning have improved the AI agent's performance comparing with the previous version. We have also provided evaluation results of the improvisational mood modeling using the Bayesian networks for the 3 leading characters in the school bullying scenario based on the analysis of the 4 testing transcripts. We have converted the recognized affective states into binary evaluation values and obtained the following accuracy rates shown in Table 2 by comparing with the annotation of one human judge.

	Mayid	Lisa	Elise
Positive	52%	46%	55%
Negative	94%	73%	86%
Neutral	27%	35%	33%

Table 2. Accuracy rates of improvisational mood modeling using Bayesian networks.

Generally negative emotions are well detected across testing subjects. Since in the school bullying scenario, the big bully tends to make other characters suffer, the improvisation tends to be filled with negative emotional expressions such as threatening, angry and fear. Although positive and neutral expressions are recognized less well, the percentages of the inputs indicating positive and neutral expressions based on the human judges' interpretation are respectively approximate 30% and 25%. Thus although there is room for further improvements, the performances of affect sensing from positive and neutral expressions are acceptable.

Moreover, we also provide accuracy rates for the performance of the affect sensing in social interaction context using neural networks. Approximate 100 interaction contexts taken from the selected 4 example transcripts of the school bullying scenario are used for testing. We have also converted the recognized affective states into binary evaluation values and obtained 69% accuracy rate for positive emotions and 88% for negative emotions by comparing with the annotation of one human judge. The results indicate that other characters' emotional influence to the speaking character embedded in the interaction context is well recovered in our application using neural net based inference.

From the inspection of the evaluation results, although contextual affect detection based on both personal and social interaction context is provided, there are still some cases: when the two human judges both believed that user inputs carried negative or positive affective states, the AI agent regarded them as neutral. One most obvious reason is that sometimes Bayesian networks failed to predict some of the positive affective states (e.g. grateful) due to their low frequencies presented in the training data. Also affect sensing based on the analysis of individual turn-taking input sometimes failed to uncover the affect embedded in emotionally ambiguous input due to characters' creative improvisation which may affect the performance of contextual affect sensing. We also aim to extend the evaluation of the context-based affect detection using transcripts from other scenarios.

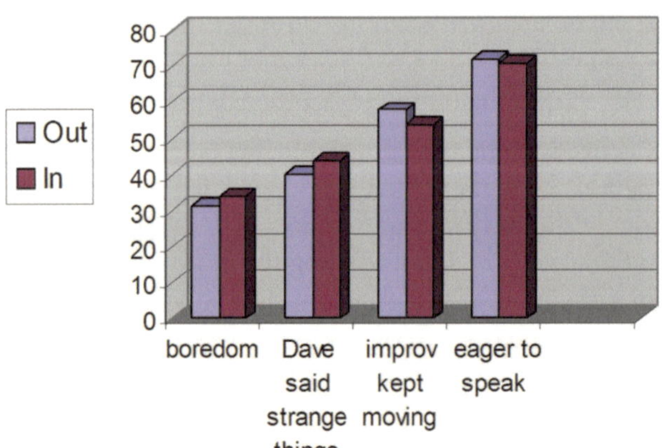

Fig. 4. Statistical results for 'boredom', 'Dave said strange things', 'improvisation kept moving' and 'eager to make own character speak' when EMMA is OUT (blue) or IN (purple) an improvisation.

Using a metaphorical resource (http://knowgramming.com), our approach for disease, cooking and sensory metaphor recognition obtains 50% average accuracy rate among the 80 testing examples. Also, we intend to use other resources (e.g. Wallstreet Journal and other metaphorical databases (e.g. ATT-Meta)) to further evaluate the metaphorical affect sensing. With a limited sample size of 40 simile examples extracted from the transcripts of school bullying and Crohn's disease scenarios, our approach for simile detection achieves 63% accuracy rate. The simile interpretation will also be further developed to accommodate more complex phenomena in future work.

Figure 4 also shows some evaluation results from a 'within-subjects' analysis looking at the difference made PER SUBJECT by having EMMA IN (= playing Dave, in either scenario) or OUT. When EMMA is out, the overall boredom is 31%. When EMMA is in, it changes to 34%. The results of 'human Dave and EMMA Dave said strange things' respectively are 40% and 44%. When EMMA changes from in to out of an improvisation, the results of 'improvisation kept moving' are respectively 54% to 58% and the results of 'the eagerness to make own character speak' are respectively 71% to 72%. Although the measures were 'worsened' by having EMMA in, in all cases the worsening was numerically fairly small and not statistically significant.

We have exploited emotion evolvement and prediction in personal and social context using the Bayesian reasoning and a supervised neural network. The conversational intelligent agent has also been equipped with the capabilities of metaphor & simile recognition and interpretation. Although the proposed approaches indicate initial exploration on context-based affect analysis and metaphor & simile inference, the implementation has enabled the AI agent to perform more effectively in affect detection tasks. In future work, we intend to employ emotion research of Hareli and Rafaeli (2008) and use Hidden Markov Models to further study and model how emotions evolve within individuals and in social communication context given various stimuli.

8. Appendix

Inspection of the transcripts collected indicates that EMMA usefully pushed the improvisation forward on various occasions. The following example transcript collected from the previous user testing shows how EMMA contributed to the drama improvisation in the Crohn's disease scenario. In the following interactions, Dave was played by EMMA.

DIRECTOR: are we ready to go to the restaurant? /*Background changes to a 3D restaurant.*/
Janet Williams: this is nice
Peter Williams: its a bit posh
Arnold Williams: no one else is here
Janet Williams: oh shut up
Dave Atkins: Could we all tone down our language a bit? ppl r watching...
Arnold Williams: dont boss me about wife
Peter Williams: so i think its a good place to tell you im going to die unless i have an operation
Janet Williams: i will thats why i married you
Arnold Williams: peter talk about it another time
Peter Williams: excuse me
Janet Williams: no

… … …
Arnold Williams: your blood pressure will get too high
Peter Williams: im confussed
Janet Williams: nobody cares what u think dad
Dave Atkins: Arnold, y u dont want 2 b involved in? Peter is ur son.
Arnold Williams: i just dont want to talk about it. i do care sbout him
DIRECTOR: remember, Peter, it's you're choice
Janet Williams: oh shut up
Peter Williams: its my choice
Arnold Williams: bossy
… … …
Peter Williams: I'M THE ILL ONE
Dave Atkins: Arnold, Peter needs ur support and u can't just ignore it.
Janet Williams: nobody cares peter
Arnold Williams: we know peter now stop talking about it
Peter Williams: yes i need your support
Dave Atkins: Hey guys, lets all calm down a bit.
Arnold Williams: we will discuss it later
Janet Williams: well you have got mien
Peter Williams: help me daddy
Arnold Williams: not now son
Peter Williams: well when
Janet Williams: he is not your daddy
Arnold Williams: another time
Peter Williams: i dont like u
Arnold Williams: wife i need your support on this
Dave Atkins: I think we all should respect Peter's decision.
Peter Williams: u should love me
Janet Williams: peter lets go home u have spolit it dad
Arnold Williams: i do son
Janet Williams: i hate u dad
Dave Atkins: wat??
Arnold Williams: lets talk about it another time
Dave Atkins: Guys, let's try 2 sort this out calmly.
Arnold Williams: thats not very nice mum
Peter Williams: yes calmly
DIRECTOR: ok 2 mins left, help peter make a decision
Peter Williams: what shall i do??
Janet Williams: ok if dad if you stop arguing then i will stop
Peter Williams: have the operation??

9. References

Aylett, A., Louchart, S. Dias, J., Paiva, A., Vala, M., Woods, S. and Hall, L.E. (2006). Unscripted Narrative for Affectively Driven Characters. *IEEE Computer Graphics and Applications.* 26(3). 42-52.

Barnden, J.A. Metaphor, semantic preferences and context-sensitivity. (2007). In K. Ahmad, C. Brewster & M. Stevenson (Eds), *Words and Intelligence II: Essays in Honor of Yorick Wilks*, 39-62.

Briscoe, E. & Carroll, J. (2002). Robust Accurate Statistical Annotation of General Text. In Proceedings of *the 3rd International Conference on Language Resources and Evaluation*, Las Palmas, Gran Canaria. 1499-1504.

Egges, A., Kshirsagar, S. & Magnenat-Thalmann, N. (2003). A Model for Personality and Emotion Simulation, In *Proceedings of Knowledge-Based Intelligent Information & Engineering Systems* (KES2003), Lecture Notes in AI. 453-461.

Esuli, A. and Sebastiani, F. (2006). Determining Term Subjectivity and Term Orientation for Opinion Mining. In *Proceedings of EACL-06*, Trento, IT. 193-200.

Fainsilber, L. and Ortony, A. (1987). Metaphorical uses of language in the expression of emotions. *Metaphor and Symbolic Activity*, 2(4):239-250.

Fellbaum, C. (1998). *WordNet, an Electronic Lexical Database*. The MIT press.

Fussell, S. and Moss, M. (1998). Figurative language in descriptions of emotional states. In *Social and Cognitive Approaches to Interpersonal Communication*, S. R. Fussell and R. J. Kreuz, Eds., Lawrence Erlbaum.

Gratch, J. and Marsella, S. (2004). A Domain-Independent Framework for Modeling Emotion. *Journal of Cognitive Systems Research*. Vol 5, Issue 4, pp.269-306.

Hareli, S. and Rafaeli, A. (2008). Emotion cycles: On the social influence of emotion in organizations. *Research in Organizational Behavior*, 28, 35-59.

Kövecses, Z. (1998). Are There Any Emotion-Specific Metaphors? In *Speaking of Emotions: Conceptualization and Expression*. Athanasiadou, A. and Tabakowska, E. (eds.), Berlin and New York: Mouton de Gruyter, 127-151.

Liu, H. & Singh, P. (2004). ConceptNet: A practical commonsense reasoning toolkit. *BT Technology Journal*, Volume 22, Kluwer Academic Publishers.

Lopez, J.M., Gil, R., Garcia, R., Cearreta, I. and Garay, N. (2008). Towards an Ontology for Describing Emotions. In *Proceedings of the 1st world summit on The Knowledge Society*: Emerging Technologies and Information Systems for the Knowledge Society.

Mateas, M. (2002). Interactive Drama, Art and Artificial Intelligence. Ph.D. Thesis. School of Computer Science, Carnegie Mellon University.

Ortony, A., Clore, G.L. & Collins, A. (1988). *The Cognitive Structure of Emotions*. Cambridge U. Press.

Ptaszynski, M., Dybala, P., Shi, W., Rzepka, R. And Araki, K. (2009). Towards Context Aware Emotional Intelligence in Machines: Computing Contextual Appropriateness of Affective States. In *Proceedings of IJCAI*.

Schnall, S. (2005). The pragmatics of emotion language. *Psychological Inquiry*, 16, 28-31.

Shaikh, M.A.M., Prendinger, H. & Mitsuru, I. (2007). Assessing sentiment of text by semantic dependency and contextual valence analysis. *In Proceedings of ACII 2007*, 191-202.

Sperber, D., & Wilson, D. (1995). *Relevance: Communication and Cognition* (2nd ed.). Oxford, UK: Blackwell.

Strapparava, C. and Valitutti, A. (2004). WordNet-Affect: An Affective Extension of WordNet. In *Proceedings of the 4th International Conference on Language Resources and Evaluation* (LREC 2004), Lisbon, Portugal, 1083-1086.

Zhang, L. (2010). Exploitation on Contextual Affect Sensing and Dynamic Relationship Interpretation. In *ACM Computers in Entertainment*. Vol.8, Issue 3.

Zhang, L. & Barnden, J.A. (2010). Affect and Metaphor Sensing in Virtual Drama. *International Journal of Computer Games Technology*. Vol. 2010.

Zhang, L., Gillies, M., Dhaliwal, K., Gower, A., Robertson, D. & Crabtree, B. (2009). E-drama: Facilitating Online Role-play using an AI Actor and Emotionally Expressive Characters. *International Journal of Artificial Intelligence in Education*. Vol 19(1).

Zhe, X. & Boucouvalas, A.C. (2002). Text-to-Emotion Engine for Real Time Internet Communication. In *Proceedings of International Symposium on Communication Systems, Networks and DSPs*, Staffordshire University, UK, 164-168.

4

Learning Physically Grounded Lexicons from Spoken Utterances

Ryo Taguchi[1], Naoto Iwahashi[2], Kotaro Funakoshi[3], Mikio Nakano[3], Takashi Nose[4] and Tsuneo Nitta[5]
[1]*Nagoya Institute of Technology,*
[2]*National Institute of Information and Communications Technology,*
[3]*Honda Research Institute Japan Co., Ltd.,*
[4]*Tokyo Institute of Technology,*
[5]*Graduate School of Engineering, Toyohashi University of Technology*
Japan

1. Introduction

Service robots must understand correspondence relationships between things in the real world and words in order to communicate with humans. For example, to understand the utterance, "Bring me an apple," the robot requires knowledge about the relationship between the word "apple" and visual features of the apple, such as color and shape. Robots perceive object features with physical sensors. However, developers of service robots cannot describe all knowledge in advance because such robots may be used in situations other than those the developers assumed. In particular, household robots have many opportunities to encounter unknown objects. Therefore, it is preferable that robots automatically learn physically grounded lexicons, which consist of phoneme sequences and meanings of words, through interactions with users.

In the field of automatic speech recognition, several methods have been proposed for extracting out-of-vocabulary (OOV) words from continuous speech by using acoustic and grammatical models of OOV word classes such as personal names or place names (Asadi 1991; Schaaf, 2001; Bazzi & Glass, 2002). However, these studies have not dealt with the learning of physically grounded meanings.

Holzapfel et al. proposed a method for learning a phoneme sequence and the meaning of each word using pre-defined utterances in which unknown words are inserted, such as "my name is <*name*>", where any name can replace <*name*> (Holzapfel et al., 2008). Methods similar to Holzapfel's method have been used with many existing robots learning the names of humans or objects. However, these methods do not solve the problem of a robot's inability to learn words from undefined utterances.

Gorin et al., Alshawi, and Roy & Pentland conducted experiments to extract semantically useful phoneme sequences from natural utterances, but they have not yet been able to acquire the correct phoneme sequences with high accuracy (Gorin et al., 1999; Alshawi, 2003; Roy & Pentland, 2002). Since phoneme sequences obtained by recognizing utterances may contain errors, it is difficult to correctly identify the word boundaries. For example, Roy and Pentalnd extracted keywords by using similarities of both acoustic features and meanings, but 70% of the extracted words contained insertion or deletion errors at either or both ends of the words. This method obtains many word candidates corresponding to each true word through learning. If robots speak words through speech synthesis, they have to select the word that has the most correct phoneme sequence from the candidates. However, this method does not have a selection mechanism because it is designed for speech recognition not for speech synthesis.

This chapter focuses on the task in which a robot learns the name of an object from a user's vocal instruction involving the use of natural expressions while showing the object to the robot. Through this learning, the robot acquires physically grounded lexicons for speech recognition and speech synthesis. User utterances for teaching may include words other than names of objects. For example, the user might say "this is James." In this paper, names of objects are called keywords, and words (or phrases) other than keywords are called non-keyword expressions. We assume that keywords and non-keyword expressions are independent of each other. Therefore, the same non-keyword expressions can be used in instruction utterances for different keywords. The robot in this task had never been given linguistic knowledge other than an acoustic model of phonemes. A robot can recognize user utterances as phoneme sequences with this model but cannot detect word boundaries. The robot must learn the correct phoneme sequences and the meanings of keywords from a set of utterance and object pairs. After learning, we estimate the learning results by investigating whether the robot can output the correct phoneme sequence corresponding to each object.

To solve this task, we propose a method for learning phoneme sequences of words and relationships between them and objects (hereafter *meanings*) from various user utterances, without any prior linguistic knowledge other than an acoustic model of phonemes. Roy and Petland's method focuses on acoustic and semantic information of each word, and ignores words other than keywords. However, we believe that insertion or deletion errors at the ends of the words can be decreased by learning and using grammatical relationships between each non-keyword expression and keywords. Therefore, we formulated the utterance-object joint probability model, which consists of three statistical models: acoustic, grammatical, and semantic. Moreover, by learning this model on the basis of the minimum description length principle (Rissanen, 1983), acoustically, grammatically, and semantically appropriate phoneme sequences can be acquired as words.

We describe the utterance-object joint probability model in Section 2 and explain how to learn and use the model in Section 3. We show and discuss the experimental results in Section 4 and conclude the paper in Section 5.

2. Utterance-object joint probability model

2.1 Joint probability model

The joint probability model of a spoken utterance and an object is formulated as follows.

Learning sample set $\mathbf{D}$ is defined in Eq. 1.

$$\mathbf{D} = \{ \mathbf{d}_i \mid 1 \le i \le M \}, \tag{1}$$

where $\mathbf{d}_i$ is the i-th learning sample and M is the number of samples. Each sample consists of a spoken utterance and an object, which are given at the same time.

$$\mathbf{d}_i = (\mathbf{a}_i, o_i), \tag{2}$$

where $\mathbf{a}_i$ is a sequence of feature vectors extracted from a spoken utterance. Each feature vector corresponds to a speech frame of tens of milliseconds. The notation o_i is an ID representing an object. In the real world, a computer vision technique is necessary for robots to identify objects. However, this chapter does not address the problem of computer vision for focusing on automatic segmentation of continuous speech into words. Therefore, we assume that objects can be visually identified without errors and a module for word acquisition can receive IDs of objects as the identification results. In the following explanation, we call $\mathbf{a}_i$ an utterance, and o_i an object, and we omit index i of each variable.

The joint probability of $\mathbf{a}$ and o is denoted by $P(A=\mathbf{a}, O=o)$, where A and O are random variables. We assume that A and O are conditionally independent given a word sequence $\mathbf{s}$. This means that an utterance is an acoustic signal made from a word sequence and that the word sequence indicates an object. Therefore, $P(A=\mathbf{a}, O=o)$ is defined as follows.

$$\begin{aligned} P(A=\mathbf{a}, O=o) &= \sum_{s} P(A=\mathbf{a}, O=o, S=\mathbf{s}) \\ &= \sum_{s} \{P(A=\mathbf{a} \mid S=\mathbf{s}) P(S=\mathbf{s}) P(O=o \mid S=\mathbf{s})\} \end{aligned} \tag{3}$$

We call $P(A=\mathbf{a}, O=o)$ utterance-object joint probability. Figure 1 shows a graphical model of $P(A,O)$. The notations S and W_j are random variables representing a word sequence and each word, respectively.

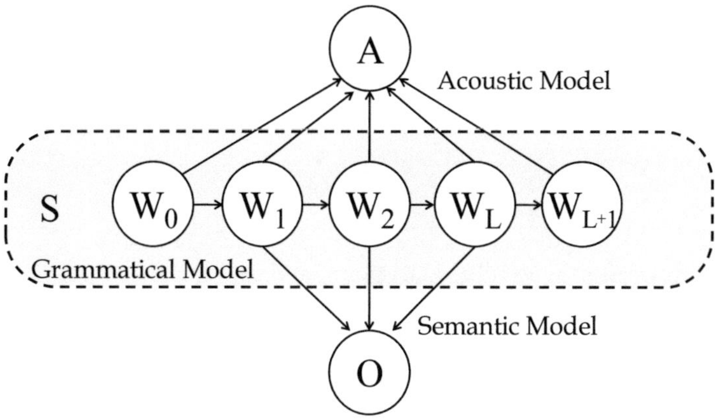

Fig. 1. Utterance-object joint probability model.

In the following explanation, we omit random variables to simplify formulas. The notation $P(\mathbf{a} \mid \mathbf{s})$ is the probability of an acoustic feature given a word sequence. $P(\mathbf{a} \mid \mathbf{s})$ is calculated from the phoneme acoustic model as usual speech recognition systems do. We use a hidden Markov model as the phoneme acoustic model. The learning of the phoneme acoustic model requires much more speech data. However the phoneme acoustic model can be learned before the lexical learning task because it does not depend on domains. $P(\mathbf{s})$ is the probability of a word sequence, which we call the grammatical model, and $P(o|\mathbf{s})$ is the probability of an object given a word sequence. It represents a meaning of an utterance. We call it the semantic model.

In general statistical speech recognition algorithms, the acoustic and grammatical models are generally used. On the other hand, in the utterance-object joint probability model, the semantic model is also used.

Equation (3) requires a large amount of calculation because there are a large number of word sequences. Therefore, we approximate the summation by maximization as expressed by Eq. (4). This approximation enables efficient probability calculation using the beam search algorithm.

$$P(\mathbf{a},o) = \max_{\mathbf{s}} \{ P(\mathbf{a}|\mathbf{s})P(\mathbf{s})P(o|\mathbf{s}) \} \tag{4}$$

The acoustic, grammatical, and semantic models differ in modeling accuracy. In statistical speech recognition algorithms, a weighting parameter is used to decrease a difference between the acoustic and grammatical models. In our method, we multiply the acoustic score by the weighting parameter α . We call α acoustic model weight.

The logarithm of utterance-object joint probability is defined as follows:

$$\log P(\mathbf{a},o) \approx \max_{s} \{ \alpha \log P(\mathbf{a}|\mathbf{s}) + \log P(\mathbf{s}) + \log P(o|\mathbf{s}) \} \tag{5}$$

We verified practical effectiveness of weighting $P(\mathbf{s})$ or $P(o|\mathbf{s})$ through preliminary experiments, but they were not effective.

2.2 Grammatical model

We use a word-bigram model as the grammatical model.

$$P(\mathbf{s}) = \prod_{i=1}^{L+1} P(w_i | w_{i-1}), \tag{6}$$

where w_i is the i-th word in $\mathbf{s}$, w_0 is the start point, and w_{L+1} is the end point. A general word-bigram model represents the relationship between two words. However, the bigram model used in our method represents the relationship between keywords and each non-keyword expression. The words that are considered as keywords are not distinguished each other and they are treated as the same word in the bigram model. Namely, this is a class bigram model in which keywords is considered as a class. A method for determining whether or not a word is a keyword is described in Section 2.4.

2.3 Semantic model

A word sequence consists of keywords and non-keyword expressions. In an ideal situation, $\mathbf{s}$ consists of a single keyword and some non-keyword expressions. However, in the initial stage of learning, some keywords can be wrongly divided into short keywords. In this case,

s can include several short keywords. Moreover, non-keyword expressions are independent of objects. Therefore, $P(o\,|\,\mathbf{s})$ is calculated from multiple keywords, as expressed by Eq. (7).

$$P(o\,|\,\mathbf{s}) = \sum_{i=1}^{L} \gamma(\mathbf{s},i)\, P(o\,|\,w_i) \tag{7}$$

where $P(o\,|\,w_i)$ represents the meaning of word w_i. Index i is from 1 to L because w_0 and w_{L+1} are independent of objects. The notation $\gamma(\mathbf{s},i)$ is the meaning weight of w_i and is calculated on the bases of the number of phonemes as follows:

$$\gamma(\mathbf{s},i) = \begin{cases} \dfrac{\mathrm{N}(w_i)}{\mathrm{N}(\mathbf{s})} & \text{if } w_i \text{ is a keyword} \\ 0 & \text{otherwise} \end{cases}, \tag{8}$$

where $N(w_i)$ is the number of phonemes of w_i, and $N(\mathbf{s})$ is the total amount of phonemes of keywords included in **s**. The meaning weight of w_i is assigned as zero when w_i is not a keyword. If **s** does not include any keyword, $P(o\,|\,\mathbf{s})$ is assigned as zero as a penalty for rejecting the recognition result.

$\gamma(\mathbf{s},i)$ is a heuristics. However, when **s** includes several keywords, the negative effects of short keywords, which are wrongly divided, are reduced by using the heuristics in which relatively long keywords are more effective for calculating $P(o\,|\,\mathbf{s})$.

2.4 Keyword determination

To determine whether or not a word is a keyword, the difference between the entropy of o and its conditional entropy given a word w is calculated as follows:

$$I(w) = -\sum_{o} P(o)\log P(o) + \sum_{o} P(o\,|\,w)\log P(o\,|\,w) \tag{9}$$

If w is a non-keyword expression, the conditional probability distribution $P(O\,|\,W{=}w)$ and probability distribution $\mathrm{P}(O)$ are approximately the same because w is independent of objects.

On the other hand, if w is a keyword, the entropy of $P(O\,|\,W{=}w)$ is lower than that of $\mathrm{P}(O)$ because $P(O\,|\,W{=}w)$ is narrower than $\mathrm{P}(O)$.

If the difference $I(w)$ is higher than the threshold T, w is considered a keyword. The threshold was manually determined on the basis of preliminary experimental results.

2.5 Keyword output

To correctly speak the name of o, the robot has to choose keyword $\tilde{w}$, the best representation of o, from many keywords acquired though learning. The formula for choosing $\tilde{w}$ is defined as Eq. (10).

$$\begin{aligned} \tilde{w} &= \underset{w \in \Omega}{\arg\max}\, P(w \mid o) \\ &= \underset{w \in \Omega}{\arg\max}\, P(w, o) \\ &= \underset{w \in \Omega}{\arg\max} \left\{ \log P(w) + \log P(o \mid w) \right\} \end{aligned} \quad , \qquad (10)$$

where Ω is the set of acquired keywords.

3. Lexical learning algorithm

Figure 2 gives an overview of lexical learning algorithm. The algorithm consists of four steps. In step 1, all user utterances are recognized as phoneme sequences. Then the initial word list is built based on statistics of sub-sequences included in the phoneme sequences. In step 2, all user utterances are recognized as word sequences using the word list. Parameters of the grammatical and semantic models are learned from the recognition results. In step 3, the word list is rebuilt using the models that have been learned. Specifically, word deletion based on the minimum description length (MDL) principle and word concatenation based on the word-bigram model are executed. By this process, unnecessary words are deleted and those wrongly divided into short words in step 1 are restored. In step 4, model parameters are re-learned using the word list, which has been rebuilt. By repeating word list rebuilding (step 3) and model parameter re-learning (step 4), more correct phoneme sequences of keywords are acquired. The details of each step are explained after the next section.

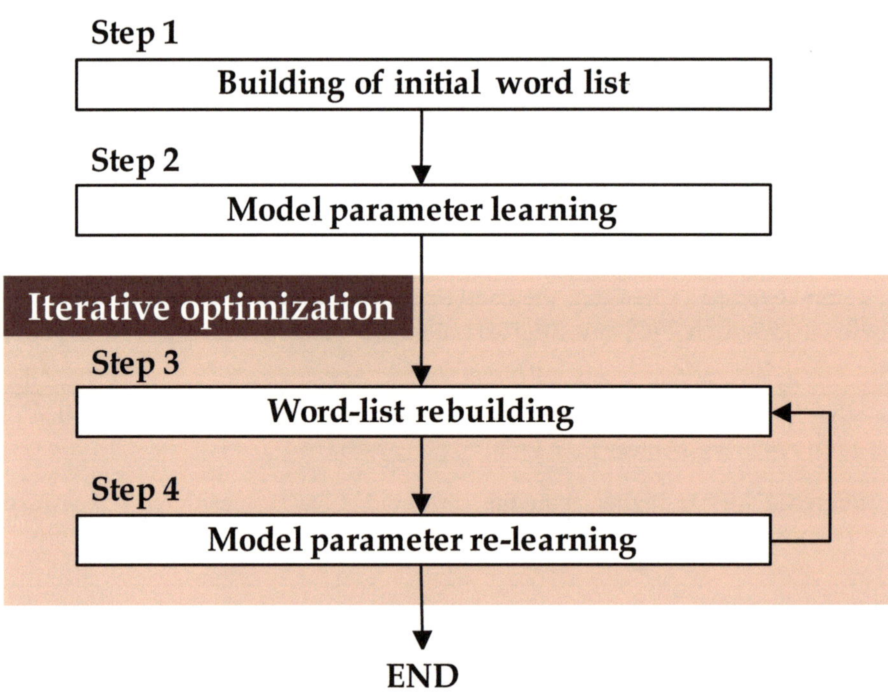

Fig. 2. Overview of lexical learning algorithm.

3.1 Step 1: building of initial word list

First, all user utterances are recognized as phoneme sequences by using the phoneme acoustic model. Next, a word list is built by extracting subsequences included in the phoneme sequences. The entropies of phonemes before or after each subsequence are calculated. If the boundary of a phoneme sequence equals the boundary of a true word, the entropies are high because varied phonemes, which are the start or end of other words, are observed before or after the sequence. If a word is divided into short sub-sequences, the entropies are low because specific phonemes, which are the start or end of the adjacent sub-sequences in the word, are observed before or after each sub-sequence. Many word candidates can be obtained with this algorithm when the entropies of a sub-sequence are not zero and its frequency is more than two, it is registered on the word list as a word candidate.

3.2 Step 2: model parameter learning

Utterances are recognized as word sequences using both the phoneme acoustic model and word list. Note that N-best hypotheses are output as a recognition result for each utterance in our algorithm. Parameters of the word-bigram and semantic models are learned from all word sequences included in the N-best hypotheses to improve the robustness of learning. Moreover, the backward bigram that predicts words before each word is also learned.

The word meaning model $P(o \mid w)$ is calculated as follows.

$$P(o \mid w) = \frac{F(o,w)}{\sum_{o} F(o,w)} \tag{11}$$

where o is an object, w is a word and $F(o, w)$ is a co-occurrence frequency of o and w. $F(o, w)$ is calculated as follows.

$$F(o,w) = \sum_{i=1}^{M} \frac{1}{N_i} \sum_{j=1}^{N_i} F(o,w,\mathbf{s}_j^i) \tag{12}$$

$$F(o,w,\mathbf{s}_j^i) = \begin{cases} 1 & \text{if } o = o_i \text{ and } w \in \mathbf{s}_j^i \\ 0 & \text{otherwise} \end{cases}, \tag{13}$$

where M is the number of learning samples, N_i is the number of hypotheses obtained by recognizing utterance $\mathbf{a}_i$ and $\mathbf{s}^i_j$ is a word sequence of j-th hypothesis. The notation $F(o, w, \mathbf{s}^i_j)$ represents the co-occurrence of o and w in $\mathbf{s}^i_j$. In this algorithm, the number of actual N-best hypotheses differs from utterance to utterance because the beam search algorithm is used. Therefore, $P(o \mid w)$ is calculated by normalizing the frequency of $F(o, w, \mathbf{s}^i_j)$ by N_i.

3.3 Step 3: word-list rebuilding

3.3.1 Word deletion using MDL

Unnecessary words in the word list are deleted based on the MDL principle (Rissanen, 1983). The sum of the description length of observed data by each model, and description length of parameters of the model is calculated in this principle. Then, the model that has the minimum sum is chosen as the best.

In this algorithm, the description length of the model parameter set $\boldsymbol{\theta}$, which consists of the word list and parameters of each probability model, and learning sample set **D** is defined as follows:

$$DL(\boldsymbol{\theta}) = -L(\mathbf{D}\,|\,\boldsymbol{\theta}) + \frac{f(\boldsymbol{\theta})}{2}\log M\,, \tag{14}$$

where $L(\mathbf{D}\,|\,\boldsymbol{\theta})$ is a log likelihood of $\boldsymbol{\theta}$, $f(\boldsymbol{\theta})$ is the degree of freedom of $\boldsymbol{\theta}$, and M is the number of learning samples. $L(\mathbf{D}\,|\,\boldsymbol{\theta})$ and $f(\boldsymbol{\theta})$ are calculated using Eqs. (15) and (16), respectively.

$$\begin{aligned} L(\mathbf{D}\,|\,\boldsymbol{\theta}) &= \sum_{i=1}^{M} \log P(\mathbf{a}_i, o_i\,|\,\boldsymbol{\theta}) \\ &= \sum_{i=1}^{M} \log\left\{ \sum_{\mathbf{s}} P(\mathbf{a}_i, o_i, \mathbf{s}\,|\,\boldsymbol{\theta}) \right\} \\ &\approx \sum_{i=1}^{M} \log\left\{ \max_{\mathbf{s}\in\boldsymbol{\Psi}_i} P(\mathbf{a}_i, o_i, \mathbf{s}\,|\,\boldsymbol{\theta}) \right\} \end{aligned} \tag{15}$$

$$f(\boldsymbol{\theta}) = K + (K^2 + 2K) + CK\,, \tag{16}$$

where $\boldsymbol{\psi}_i$ is the N-best hypotheses obtained by recognizing utterance $\mathbf{a}_i$ ($\boldsymbol{\psi}_i = \{\ \mathbf{s}_j^i\,|\,1 \le i \le N_i\ \}$), K is the number of words in the word list, and C is the number of object IDs.

The first term "K" in the right-hand side of Eq. (16) means the number of parameters of the word list, the second term "(K^2+2K)" means the number of parameters of the grammatical model, and the third term "CK" means the number of parameters of the semantic model. Note that $f(\boldsymbol{\theta})$ does not include the number of parameters of the acoustic model because it is not learned.

These definitions are not strict MDL because there are some approximations and the acoustic model weight α is used. However, we believe they work well.

The optimization of the word list requires calculating the log likelihoods in all combinations of possible word candidates. However, it is computationally expensive and not practical. Therefore, using the N-best hypotheses obtained in Step 2, we approximately calculate the difference in the description lengths of two models, one that includes w and the other that does not. This is done by computing the likelihood of the hypothesis that is the highest among those that do not include w.

The model obtained by subtracting word w from the original model $\boldsymbol{\theta}$ is denoted by $\boldsymbol{\theta}^{-w}$. The description length $DL(\boldsymbol{\theta}^{-w})$ is calculated by subtracting the difference from $DL(\boldsymbol{\theta})$. If

$DL(\boldsymbol{\theta}^{-w})$ is lower than $DL(\boldsymbol{\theta})$, w is removed from the original model $\boldsymbol{\theta}$. This word deletion is iterated in order of decreasing difference of DLs. When no w can be removed, the word deletion process finishes. A flowchart of word deletion is shown in Fig. 3.

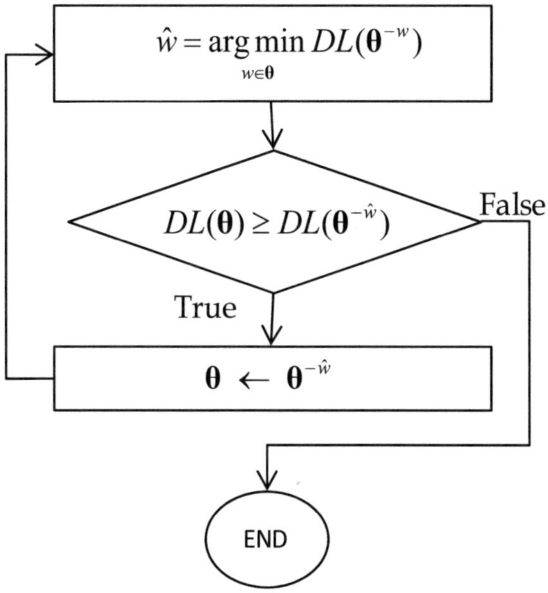

Fig. 3. Flowchart of word deletion.

3.3.2 Word concatenation using word-bigram model

If forward or backward bigram probability of two words is higher than a certain threshold (0.5 in this work), a new word candidate is generated by concatenating them into one word. This leads to recovering the erroneous dividing of words in Step 1. A new word list is built by merging the word-deletion and word-concatenation results.

3.4 Step 4: model parameter re-learning

The parameters of the word bigram and semantic models have to be re-learned because the composition of the word list changed in step 3. Therefore, they are learned using the same algorithm as in step 2.

3.5 Iterative optimization of steps 3 and 4

The new word candidates obtained by word concatenation are not based on the MDL principle because they are generated using the word-bigram model. Moreover, the words that have already been concatenated may not be removed. The necessity of each word has to be determined using the MDL principle. Therefore, word deletion and word concatenation are re-executed in step 3. Through the iteration of steps 3 and 4, acoustically, grammatically, and semantically useful words are acquired. However, word deletion in step 3 is local optimum. For this reason, after some iterations, the result that has the minimum DL is chosen as the best.

4. Experimental results

4.1 Conditions

To verify the effectiveness of the proposed method, we conducted experiments in which a navigation robot learns the names of locations in an office from Japanese utterances of a user. There were ten locations and each location had an object ID. The keywords corresponding to the locations are listed in Table 1. Six non-keyword expressions were used such as "kokowa <*keyword*> desu", which means "this is <*keyword*>" in English, and "konobasyowa <*keyword*>", which means "this place is <*keyword*>" in English, where each keyword can replace <*keyword*>. The sixty utterances, which consisted of all combinations, were recorded in a noiseless environment. Speakers of the utterances were seventeen Japanese men.

After learning from the data set of each speaker, the robot output ten keywords representing each location based on Eq. (10). The phoneme accuracy for the keywords was estimated using Eq. (17).

$$Acc = \frac{N - D - S - I}{N}, \tag{17}$$

where N is the number of the phonemes of true keywords, D is the number of deleted phonemes, S is the number of substituted phonemes, and I is the number of inserted phonemes. ATR Automatic Speech Recognition (ATRASR) (Nakamura et al., 2006) was used for phoneme recognition and connected word recognition. An acoustic model and finite-state automaton for Japanese phonemes were given, but the knowledge of words was not. By using ATRASR, the average phoneme accuracy was 81.4%, the best phoneme accuracy was 90.4%, and the worst phoneme accuracy was 71.8% for the seventeen speakers' data.

In the first experiment to determine an acoustic model weight α, we investigated the effect of the acoustic model weight using spoken utterance data from one person. In the second experiment, we investigated the effectiveness of iterative optimization using spoken utterance data of sixteen speakers.

Object ID	Keyword (in Japanese)	in English
1	/kaigishitsunomae/	the front of a meeting room
2	/tsuzinosaNnobuusu/	Tsuzino's booth
3	/furoanomaNnaka/	the center of a floor
4	/gakuseebeyanomae/	the front of a student room
5	/ochanomiba/	a lounge
6	/takeuchisaNnobuusunominami/	the south of Takeuchi's booth
7	/koosakushitsu/	a workshop
8	/ashimonoheya/	Ashimo's room
9	/sumaatoruumu/	Smart room
10	/sumaatoruumunoiriguchi/	the entrance of smart room

Table 1. Keywords used in experiments.

Non-keyword expressions (in Japanese)	in English
/kokononamaewa/ <*keyword*>	This place is called <*keyword*>.
/kokowa/ <*keyword*> /desu/	This is <*keyword*>.
/konobashowa/ <*keyword*>	<*keyword*> is here.
<*keyword*> /notokoroniiqte/	Please go to <*keyword*>.
<*keyword*> /eonegai/	Take me to <*keyword*>, please.
/imakara/ <*keyword*> /eiqte/	Go to <*keyword*> now.

Table 2. Non-keyword expressions used in experiments.

4.2 Effect of acoustic model weight

To determine an acoustic model weight α, we investigated its effect using spoken utterance data from one person picked at random. The phoneme accuracy was 86.8% for utterances of this person. After repeating word-list rebuilding (step 3) and model parameter re-learning (step 4) nine times, the model that had the minimum DL was chosen. Ten keywords corresponding to the ten objects were output using this model. We calculated the average phoneme accuracy for the output keywords. We call this accuracy output keyword phoneme accuracy.

The effect of the acoustic model weight α on output keyword phoneme accuracy is shown in Figure 4. When $\alpha = 10^{-4}$ or $\alpha = 10^{-5}$, the output keyword phoneme accuracy was the best (90.7%). If the weight was reduced too much, output keyword phoneme accuracy decreased because the acoustic adequacy of each word was ignored.

Figure 5 shows the number of words registered in the word list and the number of keywords determined using Eq. (9). In this experiment, the correct number of words was eighteen and the correct number of keywords was ten. When $\alpha = 10^{-4}$ or $\alpha = 10^{-5}$, the number of words and keywords were correct.

Figures 4 and 5 show that $\alpha = 10^{-4}$ or $\alpha = 10^{-5}$ is the best. Therefore, we set $\alpha = 10^{-5}$ in the second experiment.

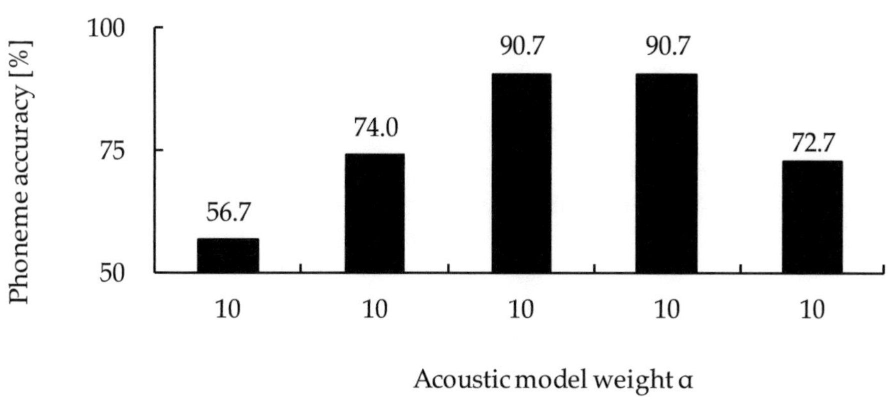

Fig. 4. Effects of acoustic model weight on optimum keyword phoneme accuracy.

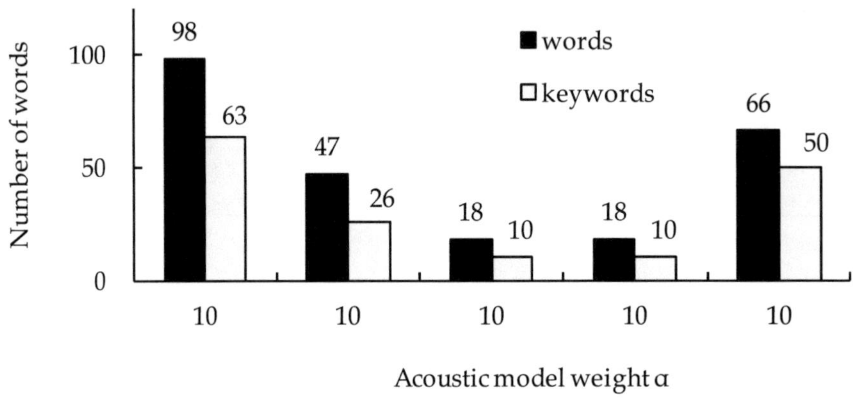

Fig. 5. Effects of acoustic model weight on number of acquired words.

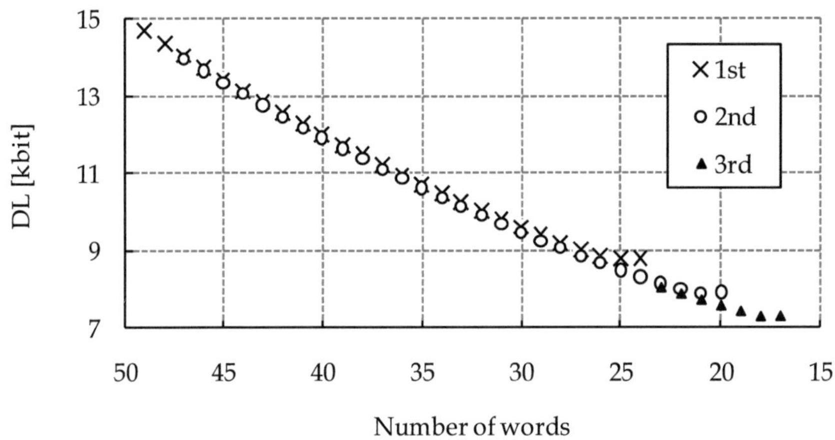

Fig. 6. Variation of description length in iterative optimization process.

4.3 Effects of iterative optimization

4.3.1 Variation in description length in iterative optimization process

To explain how the MDL principle works in iterative optimization, Figure 6 shows the variation of the DL in the above-mentioned experiment (more than 50 words were omitted). The initial word list, which consisted of 215 words, was constructed in step 1. The word-bigram and semantic models of these words were learned through step 2. Then, the first word deletion ("1st" in this figure) was executed. This word deletion was halted at 25 words because the DL of 24 words was higher than that of 25 words. A new word list consisting of 46 words was constructed by integrating the 25 words and the 22 words made by word concatenation. After model parameter re-learning, the second word deletion was executed ("2nd" in this figure). Through the iterations of steps 3 and 4, the number of newly added words gradually decreased, and the number of words was convergent.

4.3.2 Evaluation of iterative optimization process

We evaluated the effectiveness of the iterative optimization process from experiments using a sample data set of sixteen speakers other than the speaker of the above experiment. Figure 7 shows the average results among all speakers. The horizontal axis represents the number of iterations. The histogram indicates the number of acquired words and keywords included in the word list. We can see that the iterations decreased the number of words. Finally, an average of thirteen keywords was obtained. This number is close to ten, which is the correct number of keywords in the training utterance set. The dashed line in this figure represents phoneme accuracy for manually segmented keywords, which were obtained by manually segmenting phoneme sequences of all utterances into the correct word sequence. This accuracy was 81.5%. The solid line in this figure represents the output keyword phoneme accuracy of each learning result. This accuracy was 49.8% without optimization. In contrast, by iterating steps 3 and 4 accuracy increased up to 83.6%. This accuracy was slightly above the phoneme accuracy for manually segmented keywords.

Figure 8 shows the correct-segmentation, insertion error, and deletion error rates of output keywords. Correct segmentation means that there is no insertion error or deletion error at the start and end of an output keyword. The insertion and deletion error rates are the percentages of insertion errors and deletion errors occurring at the start or end of the output keywords. Many deletion errors occurred at the beginning of the iterations, but they decreased by iterative optimization. Finally, the correct-segmentation rate improved to 97%.

Table 3 lists examples of obtained keywords before and after iterative optimization. We can see that keyword segmentation errors were corrected. Table 4 lists examples of acquired non-keyword expressions after iterative optimization. We can also see that non-keyword expressions can be learned with high accuracy. These results prove that the proposed method makes it possible to appropriately determine the boundary of keywords.

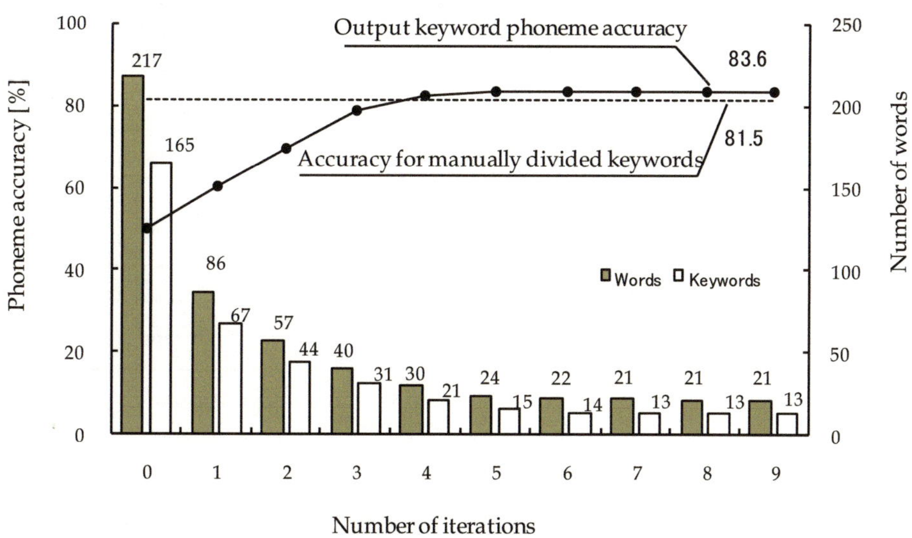

Fig. 7. Effects of iterative optimization on phoneme accuracy and number of words.

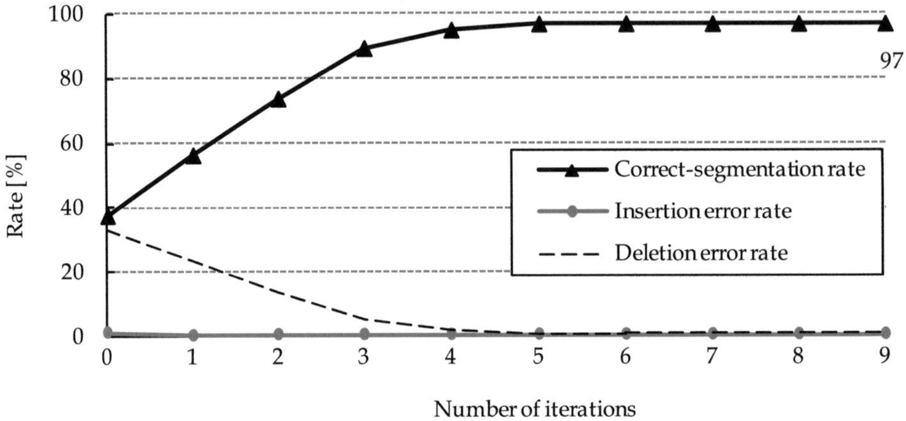

Fig. 8. Effects of iterative optimization on word segmentation.

ID	Correct keyword	Output keyword before iterative optimization	Output keyword after iterative optimization
1	/kaigishitsunomae/	/ka/	/kaigishitsugamae/
2	/tsuzinosaNnobuusu/	/tsuzinasaNnobuusu/	/tsuzinasaNnobuusu/
3	/furoanomaNnaka/	/furoanamaNnaka/	/furoanamaNnaka/
4	/gakuseebeyanomae/	/kuseebeyanamae/	/gakuseebeyanamae/
5	/ochanomiba/	/ba/	/watanamiba/
6	/takeuchisaNno buusunominami/	/taikee/	/taikeechisaNno buusunaminami/
7	/koosakushitsu/	/koosakushitsu/	/koosakushitsu/
8	/ashimonoheya/	/ashima/	/ashimanoheya/
9	/sumaatoruumu/	/mu/	/sumaatoruumu/
10	/sumaatoruumuno iriguchi/	/riguchi/	/sumaatoruguna iriguchi/

Table 3. Examples of output keywords before and after iterative optimization.

Correct non-keyword expression	Acquired non-keyword expression
/kokononamaewa/	/kokonagamaewa/
/kokowa/	/kokowa/
/desu/	/gesu/
/konobashowa/	/konabashowa/
/notokoroniiqte/	/notokoroniiqte/
/eonegai/	/eonegai/
/imakara/	/imakara/
/eiqte/	/ereiqke/

Table 4. Examples of acquired non-keyword expressions after iterative optimization.

4.4 Discussion

Experimental results show that the method acquired phoneme sequences of object names with 83.6% accuracy and a 97% correct-segmentation rate. The deletion error rate at the ends of words was 3%. These results suggest that keywords can be acquired with high accuracy. The phoneme accuracy of output keywords was slightly above the phoneme accuracy for manually segmented keywords. In manual segmentation, the average phoneme accuracy of each keyword was calculated from six keyword segments manually extracted from six utterances for learning the keyword. Therefore, the effect of variations in each utterance was included in the accuracy. For example, even if there is mispronunciation of one utterance, the average phoneme accuracy decreases. In word deletion using MDL, the acoustic score of each word was calculated from multiple utterances, and the words with high acoustic scores were kept. Keyword candidates extracted from utterances including mispronunciations were deleted because they had low acoustic scores. Therefore, such mispronunciations were corrected by word deletion, and the phoneme accuracy of output keywords improved.

In the real world, a computer vision technique is necessary for robots to identify objects. However, in our experiments, we assumed that objects can be visually identified without errors and a module for word acquisition can receive IDs of objects as the identification results. We believe that it is easy to extend the word meaning model. In fact, we proposed a method for automatically classifying continuous feature vectors of objects in parallel with lexical learning (Taguchi et al., 2011). In those experiments, a mobile robot learned ten location-names from pairs of a spoken utterance and a localization result, which represented the current location of the robot. The experimental results showed that the robot acquired phoneme sequences of location names with about 80% accuracy, which was nearly equal to the experiments in this chapter. Moreover, the area represented by each location-name was suitably learned.

5. Conclusions

We proposed a method for learning a physically grounded lexicon from spontaneous speeches. We formulated a joint probability model representing the relationship between an utterance and an object. By optimizing this model on the basis of the MDL principle, acoustically, grammatically, and semantically appropriate phoneme sequences were acquired as words. Experimental results show that, without a priori word knowledge, the method can acquire phoneme sequences of object names with 83.6% accuracy. We expect that the basic principle presented in this study will provide us with a clue to resolving the general language acquisition problem in which morphemes of spoken language are extracted using only non-linguistic semantic information related to each utterance.

6. References

Alshawi, H. (2003). *Effective utterance classification with unsupervised phonotactic models*, Proc. NAACL 2003.

Asadi, A. Schwartz, R. & Makhoul, J. (1991). *Automatic Modeling for Adding New Words to a Large Vocabulary Continuous Speech Recognition System*, Proc. ICASSP91, pp. 305--308.

Bazzi, I. & Glass, J. (2002). *A multi-class approach for modelling out-of-vocabulary words*, Proc. ICSLP02, pp. 1613--1616.

Gorin, A. L., Petrovska-Delacretaz D., Wright, J. H. & Riccardi, G. (1999). *Learning spoken language without transcription*, Proc. ASRU Workshop.

Holzapfel, H. Neubig, D. & Waibel, A. (2008). *A Dialogue Approach to Learning Object Descriptions and Semantic Categories*, Robotics and Autonomous Systems, Vol. 56, Issue 11, pp. 1004—1013.

Nakamura, S., Markov, K., Nakaiwa, H., Kikui, G., Kawai, H., Jitsuhiro, T., Zhang, J., Yamamoto, H., Sumita, E. & Yamamoto, S. (2006). *The ATR multilingual speech-to-speech translation system*, IEEE Trans. on Audio, Speech, and Language Processing, vol. 14, no. 2, pp. 365--376.

Rissanen, J. (1983). *A universal prior for integers and estimation by minimum description length*, The Annals of Stat., Vol. 11, No. 2, pp.416--431.

Roy, D. & Pentland, A. (2002). *Learning words from sights and sounds: A computational model*, Cognitive Science, 26, pp. 113--146.

Schaaf, T. (2001). *Detection of OOV Words Using Generalized Word Models And A Semantic Class Language Model*, Proc. Eurospeech 2001.

Taguchi, R., Yamada, Y., Hattoki, K., Umezaki, T., Hoguro, M., Iwahashi, N., Funakoshi, K. & Nakano, M. (2011). *Learning Place-Names from Spoken Utterances and Localization Results by Mobile Robot*, Proc. of INTERSPEECH2011, pp.1325--1328.

5

New Frontiers for WebGIS Platforms Generation

Davide Di Pasquale[1], Giuseppe Fresta[2], Nicola Maiellaro[1], Marco Padula[1] and Paolo Luigi Scala[1]
[1]*ITC-CNR, Construction Technologies Institute, Italian National Research Council*
[2]*ISTI-CNR, Institute of Information Science and Technology "Alessandro Faedo", Italian National Research Council*
Italy

1. Introduction

Information intensive applications usually involve highly collaborative activities and aspects throughout all the different stages of the information seeking and retrieval process. They are usually performed by work groups composed by heterogeneous professionals: a pervasive collaboration of diverse partners is needed to harmonize different tasks through the common objective.

Team components are usually located in different physical structures and the workflow tasks, such as data harvesting, aggregation, elaboration and presentation, need a high quality and quantity of communication to deliver a result with high standard level. Designing and implementing an integrated system able to deal with large amount of highly heterogeneous data, to allow distributed data access and to provide collaboration between partners requires a deep analysis of the diverse requirements and habits of all the operators.

Such a development environment should take into account all these requirements and should be open to real time modifications and improvements with the audit of the final users.

Target domains for such kind of information systems are environment heritage conservation and tourism promotion: these domains refer to a complex production chain where private companies and public institutions are involved with specific interests and skills.

A relevant amount of the information needed and produced in these activities are referred to the territory, therefore have to be represented as geo-referenced data and the system being set up in order to create and share each task of the knowledge workflow must support a widespread typology of data (Barricelli et al., 2008).

Two important aspects are to be stressed in the design of this kind of information systems: one is the possibility to shorten the publication cycle of the information, providing authoring tools to the information providers in order to let them quickly edit and/or update information with a minor help from the IT staff. The other is the ability of creating a customizable environment that can be adapted to the diverse professionals involved in the whole process.

Such a complex system can nowadays be developed by integrating already available components and making them inter-operable or adopting an integrated approach and developing a single integrated design environment. The latter approach has many benefits in terms of homogeneity in design and usability both for content generator actors and end users.

In this work we present a proposal for the creation of an integrated design and content management environment for a WebGIS application. The proposed system is addressed to local administrations in collaboration with diverse data providers and should be designed implementing a methodology that supports a strict cooperation between developers and end users in terms of features' design and use feedback.

To address these requirements, the Software Shaping Workshop methodology for the design and development of virtual environments has been adopted, as described in Section 3: the proposed architecture will support all the stakeholders involved in the environment heritage conservation and tourism promotion workflow by implementing information manipulation and exploitation functionalities on three levels: meta-design level, design level and use level.

The fairly extended state of the art presented in Section 2 highlights the novelty of our approach by offering an integrated environment covering the complete workflow, realized by the means of a network of specialized sub-environments where all the actors can exchange and produce information that will be stored in a shared knowledge base.

2. The state of the art

In the last decades, the diffusion of Internet access and the development of the Web is allowing easy and fast access to information for an increasing number of users. Spatial (or geographic) information is a kind of information with increasing importance nowadays: solving spatially oriented problems in order to make decisions in both public and private sector is a consolidated emerging trend in ICT. The need to combine data from various sources in a consistent and high quality way assumes readability of data and further knowledge of data origin, quality, compatibility and structure: accepting and promoting standards and norms for digital data and computer based communication processes affects the sustainability of digital content as well as the compatibility of data, software and hardware.

2.1 Standards for data exchange in geomatics applications

Developing and adopting joined approaches and standards for spatial data acquisition and exchange provides many benefits like portability, interoperability, and maintainability. Standards organizations are active at multiple levels, such as government organizations, e.g. The American National Standards Institute (ANSI), the International Organization for Standardization (ISO), and industry associations, such as the Open Geospatial Consortium (OGC, formerly known as OpenGIS) (Groot, McLaughlin, 2000). The OGC Abstract Specification, for example, defines all OGC Web Services (OWS) that follow the Service Architecture Interoperability approach and provide models for metadata documentation; the Geography Markup Language (GML) specification models spatial features and topological relationships between them and The Web Feature Service (WFS) describes a service-based supply of vector information as feature collections.

In addition to formal standards bodies and specification programs, there exist numerous de facto standards, like, for example, the file format widely used in the spatial data domain: the shapefile (by Environmental Systems Research Institute, ESRI (ESRI, a)). Other examples of de facto standards in matter of geo-data manipulation and exchange are:

- GeoRSS - Implements the approach of Really Simple Syndication (RSS) feeds. Applications such as Google Maps, Yahoo Maps and others implement GeoRSS since it has been released as an OGC White Paper in 2006 (Open Geospatial Consortium, 2006a).
- GeoJSON (GDAL) - Extends JavaScript Object Notation (JSON) to encode objects with location information expressing a variety of geographic data structures and thus JSON tools can also be used for processing GeoJSON data. Its format is human-readable and generally more compact than XML. Spatial data format types supported in GeoJSON include points, polygons, multi-polygons, features, geometry collections, and bounding boxes, which are stored along with feature information and attributes. GeoJSON is supported by numerous mapping and GIS software packages, including OpenLayers, GeoServer (GeoServer, 2008), GeoDjango (Django Software Foundation, 2005), GDAL (GDAL) and Safe Software FME (Safe Software) and also with PostGIS and Mapnik (Pavlenko, 2009) via the GDAL OGR conversion library. Yahoo! and Google also support GeoJSON in their API services.
- Tiled Maps - This approach implements a tile of small images loaded on request as the user pan the view, optimizing web traffic through cache exploitation (Open Source Geospatial Foundation, 2006). The very responsive feedback in map panning and zooming resulted in a widespread adoption of the Tiled Map Service Specification (TMSS), and WMS Tiling Client Recommendation (TCR).
- GML - The Geography Markup Language is "an XML grammar written in XML Schema for the modeling, transport, and storage of geographic information including both the spatial and non-spatial properties of geographic features" (Open Geospatial Consortium, 2006b). Following the OGC Abstract Specification data model, GML 3.2.1 models the reality in terms of features with complex, nonlinear, 3D geometry, features with 2D topology, features with temporal properties, dynamic features, coverage, and observations. It conforms to many ISO standards and, like XML, GML is only concerned with the representation of geographic data content. The representation of the geospatial features in the form of maps, can be obtained transforming GML data through Extensible Style sheet Language Transformations (XSLT).
- GDAL - Geospatial Data Abstraction Library is a translator library for geospatial raster data formats. It provides a single abstract data model to the calling application for all supported data formats (GDAL, 2011a).
- OGR Simple Feature Library is a C++ Open Source library, similar to GDAL, providing access to a variety of vector file formats. Most important supported formats are ESRI Shapefiles, SDTS, PostGIS, MapInfo mid/mif and TAB formats (GDAL, 2011b).
- SVG - Scalable Vector Graphics is an XML-based language that describes images in terms of simple elements, dots, poly-lines, elementary shapes. It is a standard developed by the W3C (World Wide Web Consortium) and uses mathematical

statements to describe the shapes and paths of an image so that can easily be made scalable. It features searchable text information and, being based on XML, this format conforms to other XML-based standards such as XML Namespace, XLink, and XPointer for linking from within SVG files to other files on the Web.

- WFS - The Web Feature Service Implementation Specification (Open Geospatial Consortium,2005) has been developed by the OGC to allow the execution of queries and the extraction of features from the geographical data to respond to user requests. Its implementation allows a client to retrieve geospatial data encoded in GML from multiple Web Feature Services. The WFS is XML compliant and can be interfaced with diverse datastore technologies, uses XML through HTTP to communicate with clients and provides data manipulation operations on GML features.

2.2 Desktop GIS

Spatial information requires for its treatment and analysis special software tools, namely geographic information systems (GIS) (Konecny, 2003), (Longley, 2001). Common applications of these tools can be found in many sectors like land management, urban planning, and public administration, as well as many personal uses like leisure planning or social experiences sharing, so that GIS approach to spatial information has become an important part of a variety of information systems used for supporting decision-making processes in business, public administration, and personal matters. Geographic information system management tools have been traditionally developed as desktop standalone applications, due to the computing intensive activity typical of their role. Among the most significant Open Source software applications, at least the following should be surveyed.

gvSIG: a local and remote map viewer (2D and 3D) with support for the OGC standards, as well as a tool for publishing maps on paper and in map servers. It has a large variety of vector and raster analysis tools and enables the viewing and editing of maps in the field using palmtops or smartphones.

GRASS: developed for Unix platform, it's a mature software and since Quantum GIS (QGis) introduced an interface for GRASS into its functionalities, the diffusion of this software has increased even among non professionals. Its renewed 3D engine with support for vector geometries and raster data introduced a better managing of volumetric pixel (voxels) in 3D rendering. Grass features APIs for Python, Perl and PHP.

MapWindow (MapWindow Open Source Team) is developed for the .Net platform for Windows and it also features an ActiveX control. It has been adopted by the United States Environmental Protection Agency as the primary GIS platform and features a number of available plug-ins to expand compatibility and functionality. Current stable release is 4.7.

Quantum GIS or QGis (Open Source Geospatial Foundation, g) is a user friendly Open Source software that runs on Linux, Unix, Mac OSX, and Windows and supports vector, raster and database formats. QGIS is licensed under the GNU Public and is coded upon the QT library by Nokia. It supports PostGIS and SpatiaLite, the OGR library, ESRI shapefiles, MapInfo, SDTS and GML, the GDAL library, GRASS locations and mapsets and can manage all OGC-compliant services like WMS , WMS-C (Tile cache), WFS and WFS-T.

The system for Automated Geoscientific Analyses, or **SAGA** (Böhner) is a GIS for Windows and Linux with analysis tools for raster data, digital elevation models and numerical simulations like prediction of soil properties, terrain dynamics and climate parameters evolution.

Open JUMP (Jump Pilot Project) is a GIS application written in Java. It supports the GML format and the WMS protocol. it's particular strength is the editing of geometry and attribute data. A growing number of vector analysis tools for topologic analysis and overlay operations is available. Current release 1.4 adds advanced raster data processing capabilities.

OSSIM (Open Source Geospatial Foundation, f) is an open source software with advanced geo-spatial image processing for remote sensing, photogrammetry, and GIS applications through a C++ library.

OrbisGIS (IRSTV) focuses on data acquisition techniques (remote sensing, modeling and simulation, site enquiries…), spatial data processing and representation (storage, modeling, multiscale 3D+t simulations) and is based on libraries such as JTS (Java Topology Suite) or ImageJ. It provides the ability to visualize or process 2D vector and/or raster data that may be stored in a flat file or remote DataBase Management System. Current version is 3.0

uDig (Refraction Research) is Java open source desktop application built with Eclipse Rich Client (RCP) technology. It can be extended with RCP "plug-ins" and vice-versa can be used as a plug-in in an existing RCP application. Version 1.2.2 is its current stable release.

Among **commercial desktop GIS** the most diffuse software are:
ArcView (ESRI, c), by ESRI; its key features are map authoring with templates, spatial query with query-building tools, basic modeling and analysis with custom reports generation, simple feature editing and data integration.

Bentley Map (Bentley Systems Inc., a) natively manages Oracle Spatial to store and edit all types of spatial data, can analyze 2D and 3D spatial data, supports many formats, features models and rule-based symbology and annotation, generates 3D scenes and animations.

ERDAS (ERDA Suite) presents a complete suite for turning acquired imagery into GIS data. It supports many source data formats, including orthos, terrain, features, maps, 3D data, land cover data and processing models.

Intergraph's **GeoMedia** (GeoMedia) products suite is a set of integrated applications that provide access to geospatial data in many formats and bring an integrated geospatial view together, along with a set of analytic and editing tools.

2.3 Web GIS

Classic GIS software packages (desktop or professional GIS) have some drawbacks which limit their diffusion among all the users who need to use spatial information: first of all, the high costs; desktop software is then accessible only from the computer on which it is installed and their user interfaces requires training. The fact that desktop GIS is still a proprietary technology limits also the possible customization of their features. These problems along with spreading of the Internet and increasing demand for spatial information have driven a rapid process of geo-enabling the Web and a rapid development of Internet GIS applications or Web GIS. Components of a typical Web GIS system include:

Data

- Spatial data - data with a positional or geographic component (maps), in some data file format (e.g. SHP, DWG, SDF, DGN) or stored in a spatial database (e.g. PostGIS, MySQL, Oracle Spatial, SDE)
- Attribute data - characteristics or properties of map features, stored as textual or tabular data, typically in a relational database

Software

- Map Server - the Web GIS core server application
- server middleware - to interpret requests from clients, interact with the web GIS application, and package the data for transfer via the web: often is integrated in the web GIS application
- web GIS Application - presentation layer application that interacts with the users and exposes the services of the Map Server. It's usually a thin or light client application that runs in the web browser and is based on client-side scripting languages.
- Web server - e.g. Apache, Internet Information Server
- Client web browser - e.g. Internet Explorer, Mozilla
- Client-side applet or plug-in - requirement depends on the technology
- Web-database application software - e.g. PHP, ASP.NET, ColdFusion

Hardware

- Central server computer
- Client computers
- Connection through the Internet or, for intranet sites, through a LAN or WAN

Some implementation examples of the main aspects of web GIS development are hereafter described.

Many **geospatial data**, and related metadata, are stored in database formats for more efficient accessing methods. With these tools the query for spatial characteristics is enabled and the ability to query them from another application is supported by the Open DataBase Communication (ODBC) standard. The most diffuse platforms are hereafter mentioned.

MySQL (SUN Microsystems, a) is the most used free (but not fully open source) database in Web applications and has recently introduced ad hoc *spatial extensions* (SUN Microsystems, b) that not yet follow the OGC Simple Features Interface Standard (SFS) (Open Geospatial Consortium)but allow to add geo-related capabilities to Structured Query Language (SQL).

PostGIS, the module for the Open Source Database PostgreSQL (PostgreSQL Global Development Group), provides storing capabilities and geographic analysis operations for geospatial information and offers a wide range of both free and proprietary tools, being also supported by ArcSDE, the of ESRI database access middleware and being fully compliant to the OGC SFS.

pgRouting extends the PostGIS / PostgreSQL geospatial database to provide geospatial routing functionality. It is the best option for network calculations and to analyse graphs; routes are processed directly in SQL, without using middleware.

Among proprietary and commercial software the most diffuse database with embedded geo-capabilities are:

Oracle 11g, with its extension Oracle Spatial (Oracle), provides tools for complex geospatial applications that require spatial analysis and processing. It includes full 3-D and Web services support to manage all geospatial data including vector and raster data, topology, and network models and is supported by the GDAL open source tool.

ArcSDE (ESRI, b), by ESRI, is a core component of ArcGIS for Server. It manages spatial data in a relational database management system (RDBMS) and enables it to be accessed by ArcGIS clients. The geodatabase is the primary data storage model for ArcGIS; it provides a single central location to access and manage spatial data.

Smallworld Technology's database technology called Version Managed Data Store (**VMDS)** has been designed and optimized for storing and analyzing complex spatial and topological data and networks typically used by enterprise utilities such as power distribution and telecommunications. The native Smallworld datastore can be stored in an Oracle Database. This allows the use of Oracle facilities for backups and recovery.

The core application in web GIS systems is the **map server** that, after having processed user requests, generates the requested map using data retrieved from spatial databases.

Due to the fact that commercial products are expensive, complex, and often not standards compliant, a number of Open Source Projects have reached high diffusion and high quality levels.

The main project is the map server of the University of Minnesota, **UMN MapServer** (University of Minnesota); born as a bunch of scripts to dynamically generate web maps from a ArcINFO GIS, it was developed by the North American Space Agency, the University of Minnesota and the Department of Natural Resources of Minnesota and is now a project of OSGeo maintained by tens of round-the-world developers. It can run as an executable Common Gateway Interface (CGI) or as a library and its main characteristics are: scale dependent feature drawing and application execution, feature labeling including label collision mediation, fully customizable template driven output, use of TrueType fonts, Map element automation (scalebar, reference map, and legend), Thematic mapping using logical or regular expression-based classes, support for popular scripting and development environments (e.g. PHP, Python, Perl, Ruby, Java, and .NET), cross-platform support, support of numerous Open Geospatial Consortium OGC standards (WMS, non-transactional WFS, WMC, WCS, Filter Encoding, SLD, GML, SOS, OM), a multitude of raster and vector data formats (TIFF/GeoTIFF, EPPL7), and many others via GDAL (ESRI shapefiles, PostGIS, ESRI ArcSDE, Oracle Spatial, MySQL) and many others via OGR.

The **deegree2** (Open Source Geospatial Foundation, a) open source map server is based on Java components and offers an high level of compliance to the OCG standards specifications (WMS, WFS-T, WCS, CSW, WPS and SOS). It is released under Lesser GNU Public License (L-GPL) and its main characteristics are: Simplified installation and configuration, Tool-based configuration (for WFS and WCS), Support of GML 3.1 with a complex Feature Model and 3D-geometries, Support of PostGIS 1.0 and Oracle spatial/locator (9i/10g), Advanced capabilities for object-relational mappings in the WFS, Multiple data sources for WMS layers, Dynamic rendering rules within SLD, High-quality and large-size print outputs through Web Map Print Service (WMPS).

GeoServer is developed on the Java 2 Enterprise Edition (J2EE) platform. This allows the applications to be deployed on any J2EE compliant application server (Apache Tomcat, RedHat JBoss and Apache Geronimo, WebLogic and IBM WebSphere. It runs also as a middleware for geographic editing applications, supporting the transactional Web Feature Service (WFS-T) OGC protocol. It natively support the integration with OpenLayers (see next paragraphs).

In 2006 Autodesk released sources of its map server, **MapGuide Open Source**.
It includes client application that support feature selection, property inspection, map tips, and operations such as buffer, select within, and measure. MapGuide includes an XML database for managing content, and supports most popular geospatial file formats, databases, and standards. It can be deployed on Linux or Windows, supports Apache and IIS web servers, and offers extensive PHP, .NET, Java, and JavaScript APIs for application development as well as tools for AutoCAD publication. MapGuide Open Source is licensed under the LGPL.

TileCache (MetaCarta) is indeed a Python-based WMS-C/TMS middleware server that caches requests to the WMS map servers boosting the efficiency of the WMS services when used with compatible client applications like those based on OpenLayers or World Wind (by NASA). A Java porting of this application is also integrated into GeoServer.

There are many **proprietary and commercial solutions** that target almost only business market due to high licensing costs: common prizes are, for example, $10,000 for 2CPUs servers (Webmap) or $7,500 for 1 CPU plus $5,000 for each extra CPU (ArcIMS) or $24,000 for 2 concurrent transactions over unlimited CPUs (GeoMedia). Most known platforms are:

ESRI's **ArcIMS:** claimed to be easy to install and set up and can be used to rapidly build a site with scalable architecture, data integration capabilities and standards-based customization, integration, and communication. It's being dismissed in favour of **ArcGIS for Server**, that integrates with ArcGIS for Desktop which is used to author geographic content. It can also be deployed on Cloud infrastructure and includes APIs in common scripting languages (JavaScript, Flex, Silverlight/WPF) to build and embed interactive maps in websites. Data is delivered in different formats, raster (JPG, PNG, or GIF, no additional client software is required) or vector (Requires a Java plug-in on the client side, using ArcXML). Its advantages are: Out-of-the-box usability, Capability of administering server software from a remote location, integration with other ESRI GIS software. Main disadvantages: needs converters for use non-ESRI data sources and depends on third party software products for being used as middleware.

Autodesk **Infrastructure Map Server** is a web-based mapping software for publishing and sharing CAD, GIS, and other infrastructure asset information via the Internet. It includes templates that enable users to quickly deliver information from AutoCAD Map 3D software to the web. It's the evolution of MapGuide (released as open source) and its main features are: Mobile viewer extension for using Infrastructure Map Server with popular touch-screen devices, GeoREST extension to repurpose existing server and Feature Data Objects (FDO) data using a RESTful web services protocol, WMS & WFS publishing fors simplify the publishing process with an OGC WMS & WFS publishing interface, QuickPlot functionality,

Pre-caching of base layer tiles for performance boost and Stylization user interface to create rich cartographic maps.

MapInfo developers provided the first tools to Microsoft that allowed them to include mapping functionality in their products and collaborated with Oracle Corporation to develop the original spatial add-on for the Oracle 8i database. The MapInfo client, desktop GIS application, can access data from any standard database supporting the Oracle, Microsoft and IBM software databases. In addition, MapInfo Professional can read and write Oracle Spatial software data types directly. MapInfo SpatialWare extends this same capability to an IBM Informix or MicrosoftSQL server.

Intergraph's **GeoMedia WebMap** delivers data both in raster and vector format: in the second case an additional plug-in must be installed in clients for decoding the ActiveCGM (computer graphics metafile) format. It offers enterprise data access, sophisticated geospatial analysis, and map generation plus powerful linear referencing and analysis capabilities (including routing and dynamic segmentation Web services) and the ability to build a Web application that writes data to Oracle Spatial or Microsoft SQL Server application.

With respect to the desktop GIS applications, also referred to as thick or fat clients, fully functional without a network connection, another type of clients is called **light clients** as they only need a web browser to interact and visualize data produced by Map Servers. This kind of web applications is generally based on Hyper Text Markup Language (HTML) documents with all logics written in client-side scripting language like Javascript or with the implementation of Java applets. These applications can interface with different Map Servers leveraging standard data exchange protocols.

OpenLayers (Open Source Geospatial Foundation, e) is an Open Source advanced Javascript library for the creation of light Web-GIS clients developed by MetaCarta. It handles WMS and WFS, has map tiling and proactive cache support and supports, among a wide set of data formats, OpenMaps, Google Maps and Yahoo Maps. According to its developers, OpenLayers is intended to separate map tools from map data so that all the tools can operate on all the data sources. Plug-ins add extra features, like the support for WMS layers with SVG as image format, for SVG enabled browsers. The current release, v. 2.11, have improved support for mobile devices, with a focus on touch interactions, and a general optimization of map rendering performances. The power and versatility of this library is one of the central aspects that make it a very diffuse choice in web GIS development, as in the the case of the implementation hereafter proposed.

Ka-Map is a JavaScript library that integrates, server side, with PHP scripts dedicated to the interface with the UMN MapServer. It supports map tiling and caching, and major features are: keyboard navigation options for zooming and panning, zooming to pre-set scales, scalebar, legend and keymap support, query layer data via point and click on the map. Currently the developing seems dismissed, with version 1.0 dated at 2007 and developers version 2.0, with the integration with OpenLayers library, stagnant at 2008.

Mapbender (Open Source Geospatial Foundation, c) is implemented in PHP, JavaScript and XML and dual licensed under GNU GPL and Simplified BSD license. It provides a data model and web based interfaces for displaying, navigating and querying OGC compliant map services. It currently supports WMS, WFS(-T) and WMC services. It features KML support, new interface platforms integrating jQueryUI (jQuery Project, a), WFS improvements, feature encoding, translucency, personalisation, catalogue interface, search module and a compressible directory tree. Current version 2.7 integrates with other Javascript library as OpenLayers (geodata management) and jQueryUI (presentation and server interaction).

MapFish (Open Source Geospatial Foundation, d) is based on the Pylons Python web framework; it provides specific tools for creating web services that allows querying and editing geographic objects. It currently offers APIs also for Ruby on Railsand PHP/Symfony via plug-ins. It makes use of OpenLayers for geographic data and of ExtJS (Sencha), the JavaScript component library devoted to user interface design for delivering rich client application experience.

GeoTools (Open Source Geospatial Foundation, b) is a Java library for geomatics applications development with functionalities for clients (both light than desktop) and servers. It can manage many data formats (Shapefiles, PostGIS, MySQL, Oracle, ArcSDE, Geomedia, GeoTIFF, ArcGrid and others), and supports many OGC standards (for example WFS, SLD, Filter Encoding). Its main features are: supports OGC Grid Coverage implementation, coordinate reference system and transformation support, symbology using OGC Styled Layer Descriptor (SLD) specification, attribute and spatial filters using OGC Filter Encoding specification, supports Java Topology Suite (see next).

The Java Topology Suite (**JTS**) is a library compliant to the OGC standard Simple Features Specification for SQL and is devoted to 2D topology functions. It offers functions like *union* or *intersection* of shapes and interpretation of topology queries on shape states (e.g. detecting the overlap of 2 or more shapes). Its last release is 1.11 (2010) and presents many portings into other languages: GEOS (C/C++), Net Topology Suite (C#), GeoTools.NET (.NET) and JSTS (JavaScript). PostGIS and GRASS are developed using this library.

2.4 Authoring tools

An authoring environment for web GIS provides a tool which is used for the creation of web based GIS applications. This environment/programming method may be based on HTML coding, a scripting language or specific programs created for web GIS applications. All types of authoring environments employ data sources (the spectrum of format depends on the support of file formats and data file standards) and result in various application formats, which either follow an open standard or a proprietary application format.

A very expectable powerful authoring language for web GIS is HTML (Hyper Text Markup Language). Its technical implementation, recommended by the W3C (WWW Consortium) lacks of specific aspects related to geomatics and the adoption of client side scripting libraries like those mentioned in the previous paragraphs, or the implementation of client-server technologies via java virtual machine or ad hoc plug-ins is needed. The presentation layer logics are served using various technologies or various aspects: CSS (Cascading Style Sheets) for styling the appearance of the application, XML (eXtensible mark-up Language) for configurations and/or data exchange between application layers, SVG (Scalable Vector Graphics) for graphic rendering, etc. The extension of HTML with client-side scripting libraries devoted to the development of user interfaces like the mentioned jQuery or ExtJs boosts the interaction with the final user and helps to make thinner the border between web application and standalone software. Server-side technologies like PHP, Perl, Python or many others are self-standing programming language that can be interfaced by client-side scripts to send and request data or invoke calculations and get results.

Many commercial suites offer authoring platforms for the creation and customization of web facilities in the field of geomatics. They are often the collation of different tools, generally desktop applications, for creating the geographical content, edit the web aspect of the site and perfect its online publication. ESRI, for example, with its **ArcGIS**, lets the user author data, maps, globes, and models on the desktop and serve them out for use on different platforms (desktop, web browser, mobile devices). It also features a set of tools for building custom applications. Bentley offers its **Geo Web Publisher** V8i (Bentley Systems Inc., b) to author and deploy web GIS applications, incorporating drawings, maps, models, aerial photography, and images within custom browser presentations: it can be defined as a desktop GIS editor with an embedded web authoring tool.

MapXtreme (Pitney Bowes Software Inc.) from Pitney Bowes is a software development kit (SDK) based on .NET (so MS Windows only) for integrating location intelligence with existing applications and is addressed mainly to business systems. It allows developers to build custom mapping applications and provide tailored views of geographic data. Also Intergraph, with the already cited **Geomedia** Suite, and Cadcorp's **GeognoSIS** (CadCorp) present some tools for the web publication of their map server output.

Also after a detailed review of the existing solutions among free and open source software as well as commercial and proprietary solutions, it seems that a fully web based authoring tool for web GIS applications, that is an authoring application completely accessible and usable simply with an internet connection for the creation of a fully customizable web GIS, seems to be an approach not yet implemented and worth to be further investigated.

	Desktop GIS	**WebGIS**	**Scripting languages**	**Authoring tools**	**Our proposal**
GeoData modification capabilities	yes	N/A	yes	some	yes
WebGIS creation/exporting capabilities	some systens	N/A	yes	yes	yes
Ease of use	medium	high	low	high	high
Extendability	some systems	no	yes	some systems	yes
Interoperability	high	N/A	high	high	not needed
Availability	low	high	N/A	low	high

Table. 1. A comparison table between the state of the art and the proposed approach to WebGIS generation.

Table 1 summarizes a comparison between our approach and the macro-areas present in the state of the art; the parameters evaluated are:

- GeoData modification capabilities: does the evaluated tool allow its users to modify and update the data used to build the final WebGIS platform?
- WebGIS creation/exporting capabilites: does the evaluated tool allow the creation of a WebGIS platform?
- Ease of use: the degree uf usability of the system by users that are not computer scientists
- Extendability: can the evaluated tool be extended with additional features?
- Interoperability: is the evaluated tool easy to be integrated into a workflow comprising other tools for the WebGIS
- creation?
- It is worth noting that being our proposal a fully integrated environment, spanning from WebGIS meta-design to its use, we consider its interoperability to be of high degree.
- Availability: can the evaluated tool be accessed from different devices or remotely?

3. The software shaping workshop methodology for WebGIS platform generation

The Software Shaping Workshop (SSW) methodology, in its general form (Costabile et al., 2006, 2007a; Fogli et al., 2005, Nielsen, 1993) allows to design and develop virtual environments that a) support the activities of users acting a specific role in their community and having a specific application domain; b) are tailorable, customizable and adaptive to the working context; c) support the exchange of information among users belonging to different communities; d) are multimodal and interactive. The methodology is evolutionary and participatory: the final user can customize and evolve his/her own virtual environment and he/she is involved in each step of the system development. The star life cycle model of the product (Hartson & Hix, 1989) is referred, that covers the entire life of the product: each prototype must be evaluated before its development.

The SSW methodology considers the development of two different kinds of workshops: the application workshop and the system workshop. The application workshop is a virtual environment customized to each member of the community, according to his/her performing task and role, to his/her abilities (physical and cognitive) and capabilities, and to his/her culture and language. The system workshop is a virtual environment that permits to customize the application workshop to users' preferences, characteristics and needs. As defined in (Costabile et al., 2007b), we consider meta-design as "a design paradigm that includes final users as active members of the design team and provides all the stakeholders in the team with suitable languages and tools to foster their personal and common reasoning about the development of interactive software systems that support final users' work" (Costabile et al., 2007b).

With this idea in mind, workshops are organized into a three level network in which each member of the design team (software engineers, HCI experts and domain experts) collaborate to design and develop virtual environments customized and tailored for their activity domain and performing tasks:

- at the top, meta-design level, software engineers use a system workshop to create other system workshops in order to permit other software engineers, HCI experts

and domain experts to collaborate to design and development of application workshops;
- at the middle, design level, designers collaborate, using their own system workshops, for designing and implementing application workshops;
- at the bottom, use level, domain experts tailor and use application workshops in order to perform their task.

Each expert is a stakeholder that evaluates the system considering it from his/her perspective biased by his/her different cultural backgrounds, experiences and standpoints of problems. Thus, a communication gap arises among the component of the design team: software engineers, HCI and domain experts adopt different approaches to abstraction and follow different reasoning strategies to model, perform and document the tasks to be carried out in a given application domain; furthermore, each expert expresses and describes such tasks adopting his/her own language and jargon (Fogli et al., 2007; Fischer, 2000).

Communication among the application and the system workshops is supported by an annotation tool. Application workshops' users can, in fact, annotate interface elements to point out to the design team problems or functionalities enhancements they need. At the use level, final users exchange data related to their current task in order to cooperate to achieve a common goal. At the design level, HCI experts and domain experts exchange programs specifying the workshops they are going to develop. HCI and domain experts also communicate with software engineers when it is necessary to develop new tools for supporting their activities. The lower levels are connected to the upper ones by communication paths, allowing final users and designers to interact with other workshops annotating their problems and communicating them to all the experts working in the same SSW network (Costabile et al., 2007a). The SSW methodology allows to design virtual environments in analogy with artisan workshops, i.e. small working environment where artisans such as blacksmiths and joiners manipulate raw materials in order to manufacture their artefacts. Artisans can adapt the environment to their needs by making available all and only the tools they need in the different specific situations. By analogy, the methodology permits to design virtual environments as virtual workshops allowing the user to access sets of virtual tools having a familiar shape and behaviour. Such workshops consent users to perform their tasks and to adapt their virtual working environment using a high-level visual language, manipulating objects in a realistic manner. Final users may act a dual role: the role of consumers when they use the tools offered by the system and they match their needs or they may act the role of designers when they need to adapt the tools to their necessities. Two personalization activities have been recognized in (Costabile et al., 2005): customization, which is carried out by the design team generating application workshops for a specific users community and tailorization, which is the activity performed by the final users adapting an application workshop to particular activities and work contexts. Each actor involved at meta-design level will use a workshop that lets him acquire data from different sources, manage and store it in a repository shared between all the software environments.

Digitization of paper-based cartographic material and data entry tasks will be speeded-up and the results optimized by functionalities such as automatic colours and levels balancing, and auto-completion of recurring data based on already stored information. Another important aspect that has to be taken into consideration at meta-design level is the creation of metadata: it will be possible for actors involved to compile sets of metadata and associate them to the data, for example pictures or maps.

Metadata and annotations will be implemented according to the W3C Annotea project (W3C, 2001), based on RDF (W3C, 2004) and XPointer (W3C, 2002) standards: RDF is used to specify metadata and annotations, while XPointer is used to locate annotations and the corresponding annotated documents, all of the stored in the shared repository. Content managers and publishers, acting at design level, will exploit their workshops to further manipulate all the information produced at meta-design level: two distinct environments constituting the workshop used at design level can be identified: the *Data Manipulation Environment* (DME), and the *WebGIS Composer Environment* (WGCE). In the DME, content managers can browse the shared repository and retrieve data (together with metadata and annotations) needed for the development of a specific WebGIS instance, that will be exploited by final users at use level. Automatic categorization of documents on the basis of metadata will ease the searching and aggregation process, supported by graphical representations of sets of data, that will be directly manipulated with drag&drop style of interaction. Finally, all the data needed for a specific WebGIS instance will be saved in a dedicated format, creating a "package" ready-to-use to Web publishers. Using the WGCE, Web publishers can interactively build a WebGis application by graphically compose the layout of the user interface by choosing from a palette HTML elements and their style; these pre-existing elements can be customized and personalized by the Web publishers, to better answer to their needs. The binding between the newly created WebGIS instance's user interface and the data pertaining to it will be automatically managed by the WGCE, exploiting the package prepared at meta-design level: information such as: points of interest, thumbnail pictures associated to them, searchable elements and other data will be automatically inserted in the proper graphical element of the WebGIS interface.

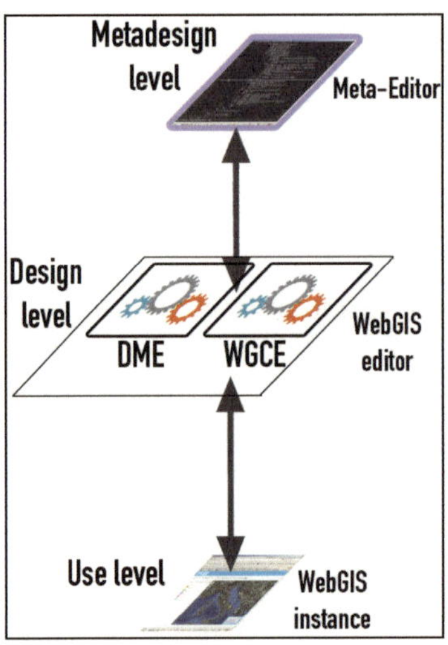

Fig. 1. The SSW methodology specified for WebGIS platform generation.

The Web publisher will then activate the functionalities needed at use level, by accessing a rich set of pre-built computational elements which implement the most popular and used WebGIS-oriented functionalities such as: searching points of interest by specifying particular parameters (e.g. address, typology, name), compute the route from a point of interest to another, and choosing different map representations. The pre-built set of functionalities will be developed using the OpenLayers Javascript API and exploiting the Web services published by Google: this hybrid approach will permit to add flexibility and extensibility to the core set of computational elements. At use level, final users will interact with the WebGIS instance implemented at design level, exploiting the information and the documents prepared at meta-design level. The adoption of the emerging HTML5 standard, and the use of jQuery-UI library for advanced interaction and animation support will allow to give final users a powerful yet easy to use environment.

4. A System's architecture proposal

Taking as a starting point the SSW methodology specialized to WebGIS platforms generation, we then propose an architecture encompassing the three levels depicted in Fig. 1. First of all, the main actors of the system and the workflow comprising all the activities they perform are identified and described. The architecture of the network of systems is presented with the help of a UML class diagram showing the main elements of the system and how they interact one with the other. Use case diagrams are then used to more clarify the roles of the various actors and the activities they are involved in.

4.1 Environment heritage conservation and tourism promotion workflow

Let us identify in some more details the four different activities constituting the work cycle (Figure 2): in the first phase, information gathering, the public local administration departments retrieve heterogeneous data about the territory and the services offered at different levels to inhabitants and tourists, their spatial distribution, the viability and all the possible information of touristic nature. Often all the data gathered by the public administration is paper-based cartographic material and needs to be converted in digital form to be subsequently manipulated by exploiting graphic editing tools and, in the case of geographic data manually aggregated using spreadsheet software. The operators of the public administrations (PA operators) are the main actors during this activity.

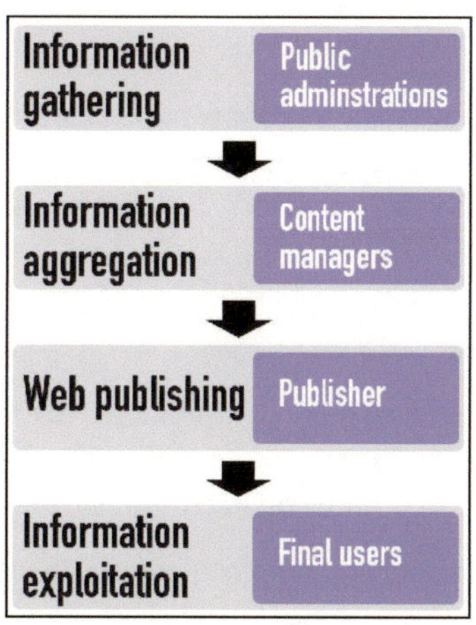

Fig. 2. The workflow for heritage conservation and tourism promotion WebGIS platforms' development.

In the second phase, information aggregation, data coming from the previous activity is retrieved and classified also on the basis of metadata attached to it by PA operators: different data sources are merged to produce a multi-layered map that comprises all the information regarding a specific resort. Content managers are acting during this phase of the work cycle; they face problems dealing with decoding and working on different data sources using various software tools not inter-operable, thus hindering the cooperation among them.

The structured information encompassed in the multilayered map is passed over the Web publishing phase, in which an environment for building spatially-enabled Internet applications is properly configured to let final users to access the maps through an interactive Web application. Web publishers, the actors involved in these activities, need to configure the Web mapping software application for proper publication of the multi-layered map built by the content managers.

This customization procedure is usually not supported by interfaces designed using a WIMP (Window, Icon, Menu and Pointing Device) interaction style: Web publishers are then forced to carry out activities not properly related to their professional skills such as editing configuration files. The last phase is information exploitation where the final users, which are the stakeholders involved, can browse the multi-layered map in order to gather specific information of their interest, characterized by a high degree of multimediality, expressing complex queries through a graphical interface.

Since Web applications have an international target, their design and development should take into consideration that they will be accessed by users with different cultural backgrounds and speaking different languages. The creation of applications that can effectively be used by an international community is called "internationalization" and is defined in (Dunne, 2006) as "the process of generalizing a product so that it can handle multiple languages and cultural conventions without the need for redesign". In the process of developing internationally usable software, the activity following the internationalization is called localization, defined in (Dunne, 2006) as "the translation and adaptation of a software or Web product, which includes the software application itself and all related product documentation".

The architecture we propose describes a system supporting all the stakeholders previously identified by giving them access to custom environments in which they interact with tools they are accustomed to, with a localized interface and offering functionalities for collaborative work.

4.2 The proposed architecture

The UML class diagram depicted in Fig. 3 represents the architecture of the network of workshops previously shown in Fig. 1; it specifies the relations between the different software components and how they relies on each other.

The fulcrum is the User Interface class, which is specialized by the three subclasses Meta-Design Environment, Design Environment and Use Environment. User Interface class manages all the aspects related to the interaction between the system and the users: in this case, giving the fact the user interface must support four different categories of users (PA operators at meta-design level, content managers and publishers at design level, and final users at use level), each one of its subclasses instantiates the different functionalities and tool each environment offers to its users.

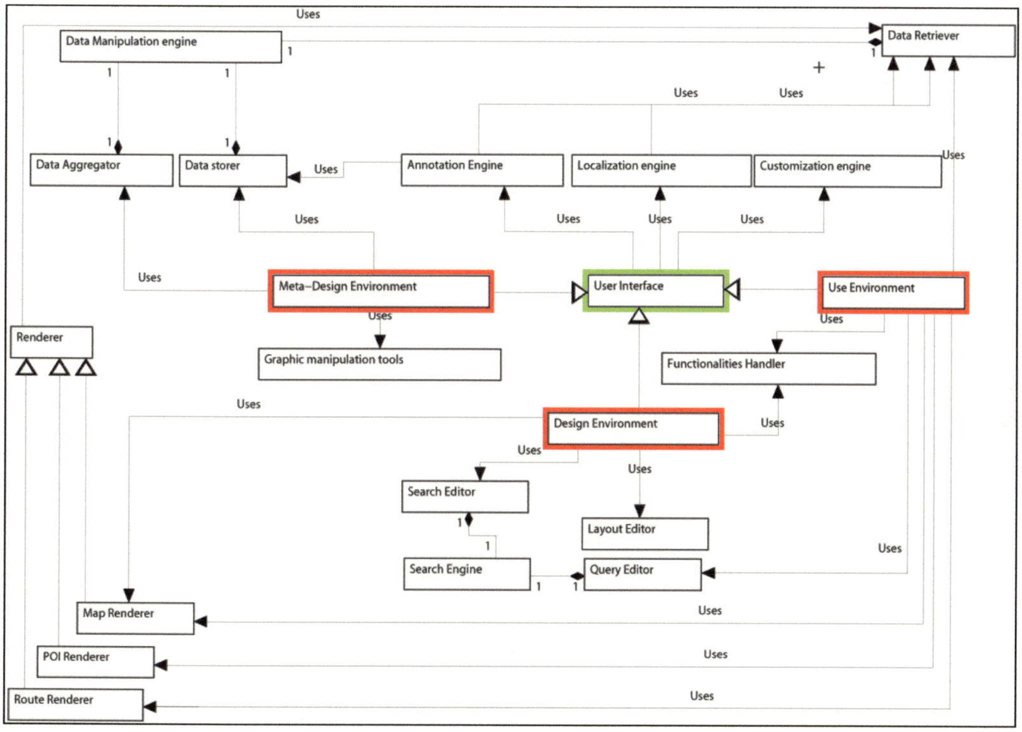

Fig. 3. UML class diagram of the proposed architecture.

All the graphical entities that will be materialized in the interfaces users can interact with, such as icons, buttons, text fields and text labels, are localized according to the preference each user indicates, and customized on the basis of the role of each user, i.e. if s/he is a PA operator, a content manager and so on. The user interface localization process is performed by the Localization engine, which lets users to decide the interface language, chosen from a list of four languages (italian, english, german and french). It relies on XML language files, and can be expanded simply by adding a new language file. Users can choose their language whenever they want by clicking on an icon representing the flag of the language's country.

In contrast, the customization engine acts automatically on the user interface: contextually to the environment invoking it, it presents widgets and data coherently to the skills and role of the user. For example, PA operators are used to work with spreadsheets, where datasets are represented in a rows-columns fashion: at meta-design level, the environment they interact with recreates this kind of organization, and all the editing operations allowed on datasets, such as add or remove data, organize and annotate data, are offered to the user as operation on rows or columns. At the same time, some of the activities performed by the PA operators involve the use of image manipulation programs: they will then be given a set of tools for image manipulation such as gamma corrections, automatic contrast adjustment and so on: all these functionalities are implemented by the Graphic manipulation tools class.

Content managers, on the other hand, acting at design level will be able to interact with the same data meta-designers have previously gathered and edited, but in terms of geo-referenced points of interest on a map, or trails comprising a subset of the data identified at meta-design level.

Web publishers will then exploit tools to let them graphically organize the representation of the data previously manipulated by content managers in terms of icons to be associated with points of interests, text labels and HTML elements concerning visual organization of information.

The Annotation Engine allows to create and recall annotations produced by the system's stakeholders: annotations are mostly used as a mean of communication between actors of different levels. At design level, content managers can annotate the data produced at meta-design level if they found errors or if they need some kind of information that has not been produced. Doing so, PA operators can retrieve these annotations and correct the problems. At use level, final users can add geo-referenced annotations to the map they are browsing, or read annotations left by other users; this allows them to share their impressions and experiences about places they have visited. Moreover, they can annotate the WebGIS instance itself, to communicate to content managers and Web publishers their needs in terms of information or functionalities available. By retrieving these annotations, actors at design level can improve the WebGIS instance, following the natural co-evolution of users and system.

The Data Manipulation Engine class implements, through the Data Aggregator, Data Storer and Data Retriever, all the functionalities needed by all the actors involved in the workflow to read, edit and write data according to their role in the system: the Data aggregator is used to manipulate datasets and create new ones; this is particularly useful to homogenize data gathered from different sources and create new ones, that will be saved in a suitable format by exploiting the Data Storer. The Data Retriever manages all the operations to access data already stored.

The Renderer class is specialized by three different subclasses, each one of them taking care of rendering, mostly in the WebGIS instance at use level, different geo-referenced graphical elements: the map, the points of interest and the routes.

The Renderer relies on the Data Retriever to get geo-referenced data and annotations to display in the WebGIS instance, and on the Data Storer to save annotations and temporary routes computed by final users.

The Functionalities Handler is a class that allows web publishers at design level to activate and configure the functionalities that will be offered to final users at use level, through the WebGIS instance. They comprise: map zoom and pan, selection of points of interest, allow or deny annotations' creation, route computation and so on.

At the same time, the Functionalities Handler is called at use level to actually implement the selected functionalities.

The Layout Editor acts as a graphical editor for the disposition of the functionalities and the information visualized by final users interacting with the WebGIS instace: content managers can build the WebGIS instance's layout by dragging and dropping widgets associated to map's browsing tools and visual elements such as page header, page layout and how final users' requested information should be displayed.

Finally the Search Engine, constituted by the Search Editor and the Query Editor, allows content managers to configure the search tool used by final users at use level.

By exploiting the Search Editor, content managers can configure which geo-referenced data can be searched by final users and the way they are allowed to build their queries. Final users can then use the Query Editor present in the WebGis instance to search the desired information.

4.3 Meta-design Level

The main actors at this level are the *Public Local Administrators,* pursuing the information gathering, mashing up different information sources provided by diverse providers. They act as the main data providers, retrieving data about the territory and the services offered at different levels to inhabitants and tourists. Data are often heterogeneous in their formats (digital, cartographic, text-based) and in the kind of contents. The Meta-Editor they use lets them manipulate data through tools resembling the ones present in spreadsheet software or image manipulation programs. The result of this operation are one or more data documents that can be saved in various formats such as DBF file format or tab delimited text files, or geo-referenced image files.

Fig. 4 (left) represents the use case diagram for the PA operator actor; as can be seen, the activities s/he can perform are:

- Aggregating data: using the Meta-Editor the PA operator can load different files In Microsoft Excel format, DBF format or tab delimited text format, and manipulate them in order to aggregate them and produce the data files used at design level by content managers
- Accessing annotations: Pa operators can access data annotated by content managers at design level in order to fulfil their requirements
- Adding metadata: metadata can be appended to data files in order to signal particular information about them to content managers, to let them better perform their activities. Metadata is also used to configure DME and WGCE
- Configuring DME and WGCE: by adding metadata at meta-design level, once the data files are sent at design level and loaded into the DME of WGCE, on the basis of the information contained in them, some aspects of these environment are automatically configured. In particular, metadata specify which column of the data files represent longitude and latitude of points of interest, or their classification (i.e. if they represent religious buildings, naturalistic attractions, and so on).

4.4 Design level

Two different actors perform their activities at design level: content managers and web publishers.

The *content managers* refine the work performed by PA operators at meta-design level and structure the data in so-called layers, that will be visualized in the WebGIS instance accessed by final users at use level. They are also responsible to associate icons or text labels to points of interest or routes that will be displayed in the WebGIS instance's map, often on the basis of some kind of classification of this geo-referenced data.

The *web publishers* set up an environment for displaying spatially-enabled information through the WGCE and provide a customization of the output layout on the basis of the user needs, eventually by mean of a set of tools directly accessible by the stakeholders. In many cases the production cycle needs to be structured in a continuous fashion, being the up to date of the information a main requirement for the global objective. In this scenario a facility for the up-to-date data entry is required in order to achieve a quick response time of the whole data production chain. One or more customized Web interfaces can be set up for the configuration and the upgrading of the system.

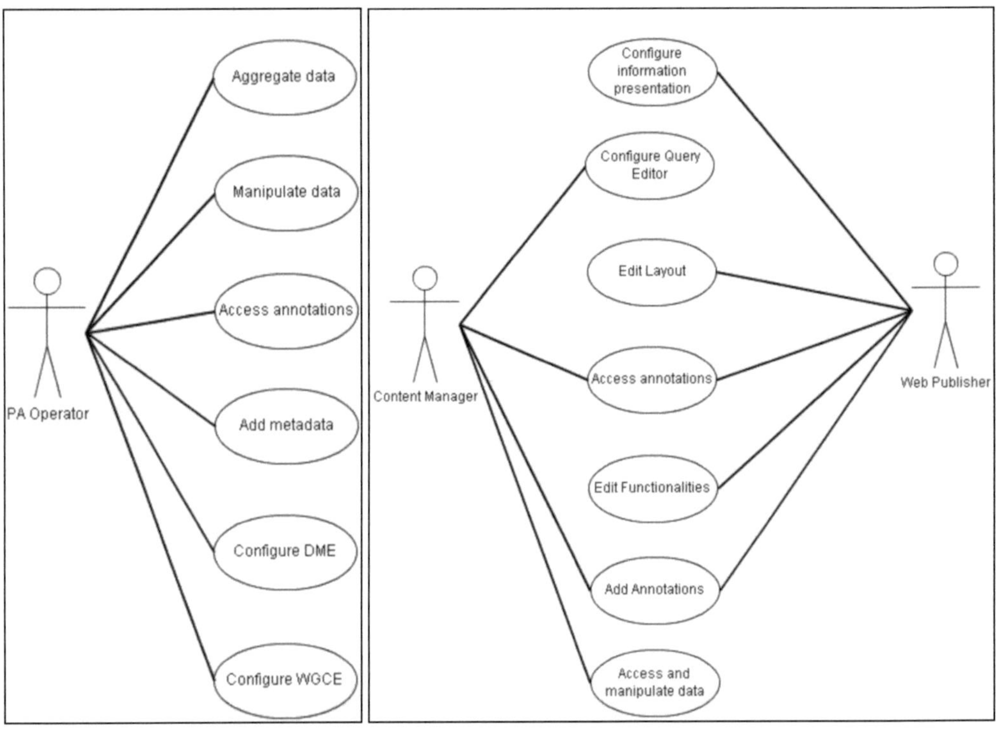

Fig. 4. Left: use case diagram for PA Operator actor. Right: use case diagram for content manager and web publisher actors.

In Fig. 4 (right) is depicted a combined use case diagram for both content managers and web publisher, both of them acting at design level.

Content mangers perform the following activities:

- Accessing and manipulating data: data coming from meta-design level must be accessed by content managers and sometimes needs to be furtherly modified; on the basis of this data they can produce all the layers needed by the WebGIS instance in order to let final users access geo-referenced data under the form of categorized points of interest and routes localizes onto a map.

- Configuring query editor: the query editor will be used by final users to search for specific points of interest or routes: content managers have to configure this functionality by specifying which kind of data can be searched and how: in fact the query editor can be configured to provide final users a search tool based on exact keyword matching, or based on wildcards. Moreover, it can help final users by suggesting possible keywords they might be interested to search for.
- Adding annotations: content managers can add annotations to data produced by PA operators in order to signal to them possible problems or incomplete data.
- Accessing annotations: content managers can read annotation appended to data by PA operators.

Web publisher can:

- Configure information presentation: information that will be displayed in the WebGIS instance must be configured and organized in order to allow an efficient consultation by final users; this is particularly true for information that has to be visualized as a result of a query that has been performed. Web publishers decide where this information will be rendered and its graphical style.
- Edit layout: by exploiting the interactive tools offered by the WGCE, content managers can graphically place into the WebGIS instance the desired functionalities, and can compose its layout by performing drag&drop of elements such as widgets and text labels.
- Adding annotations: just as content managers can do, web publishers can add annotations to data produced by PA operators in order to signal to them possible problems or incomplete data.
- Accessing annotations: content managers can read annotation appended to data by PA operators.

4.5 Use level

The *final users* are the recipients of the information flow and must be made able to gather specific information of their interest, for example browsing a multi-layered map or executing complex queries through a graphical interface, accessing data possibly characterized by a high degree of multimediality.

Once defined the actors involved in the process, a special interest is focused in finding a methodology aimed at designing software environments that allow final users to become designers of their own tools. The proposed approach for achieving this goal is the adoption of SSW methodology (Costabile2007a).

As depicted in Fig. 5, final users perform the following activities:

- search information. By exploiting the search functionality, final users can search the WebGIS instance for specific information by specifying keywords, or selecting keywords from a set of suggested ones. This allow them to locate points of interest or routes on the map that fulfil specific parameters (e.g. searching the WebGIS instance for all the points of interest which fall into the category "churches");

- visualize geo-referenced information. By browsing the map, or by browsing a list of points of interest or routes, final users can access geo-referenced data such as pictures or descriptions;
- adding annotations. Final users can annotate places they have visited in order to share with other users their experiences, or can annotate the WebGIS instance's interface to communicate to content managers and Web publisher their needs or to suggest enhancements;
- accessing annotations. Final users can access geo-referenced annotations left on the map by other users in order to read impressions and thoughts about places or attractions;
- exploit functionalities. All the functionalities that have been activated by web publishers at design level are available to use by final users; they can be map browsing functionalities or advanced search functionalities (i.e. by using wildcards to specify the keywords to search for);
- compute routes. Final users can compute routes by specifying a starting point and an ending point on the map; the WebGIS instance will automatically elaborate a route that can be the shortest one, or the one comprising more touristic attractions.

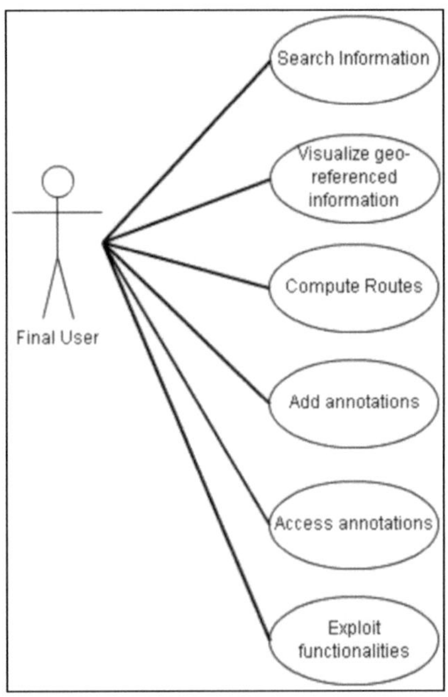

Fig. 5. Use case diagram for final user actor.

5. System's prototype description

A prototype of the system based on the architecture described in section 4 has been developed. In its actual development stage, the prototype offers data manipulation functionalities only at design level, while all the meta-design activities are still carried out using an external software. The prototype allows to produce a WebGIS instance for the search and browsing of categorized points of interest localized over a map, and the fruition of multimedia information associated to them.

At design level, content managers can exploit data coming from a dbf file automatically classify points of interest, configure the search functionality offered at use level, specify which icons should represent a particular category of points of interest, specify aliases for particular data fields to be displayed at use level, and indicate the initial state of the map in terms of central latitude and longitude coordinates and zoom factor. Web publishers can act on the overall WebGIS instance presentation by loading a graphical logotype and by inserting a page title and sub-title. Moreover, they configure the information's layout that will be shown to the final users when they select a point of interest. It is a Web-based application supporting collaborative activities among users belonging to the different communities of practice identified in section 3.1, which allow the exchange of documents, generate a shared knowledge base and allow to reach a common goal. The development of the prototype stemmed from the urge manifested by many cities located in the south of Italy to publish a WebGIS application for touristic promotion; they needed a cost effective tool they can easily use to rapidly configure deploy the application, possibly on different hardware platforms and in different places (informative kiosks, local web server, etc.). We propose a technique of interactive systems development based on AJAX (Asynchronous JavaScript and XML), while the OpenLayers API has been used for geospatial data rendering in the Web browser.

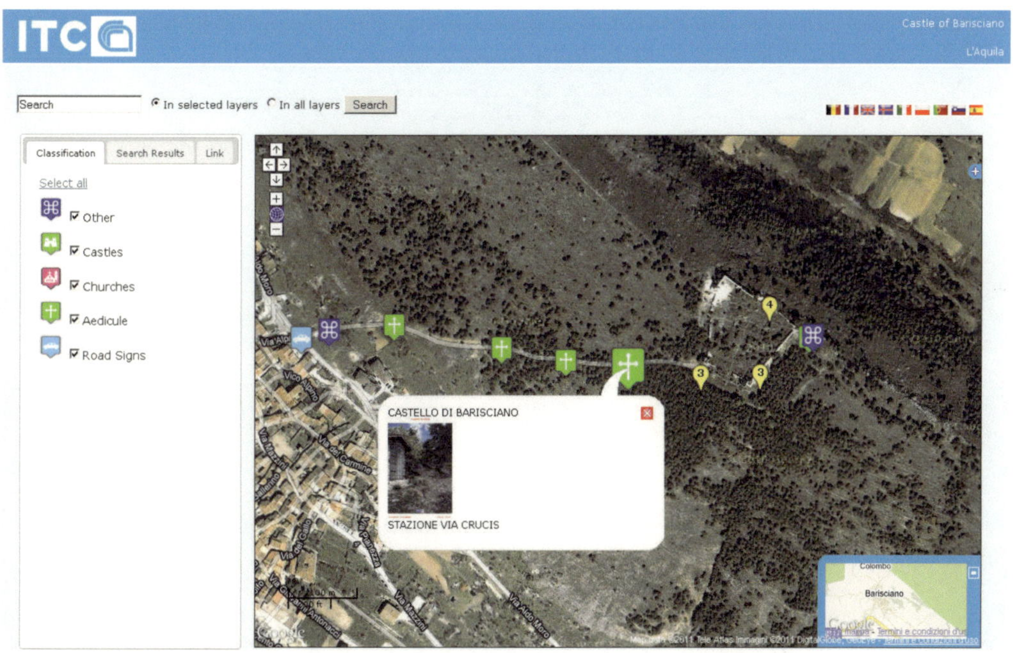

Fig. 6. The resulting WebGIS instance.

The AJAX Web application model involves several technologies: XHTML and CSS for presentation, Document Object Model (DOM) for dynamic display and interaction, XML and XSLT for data interchange and manipulation, XMLHttpRequest for asynchronous data retrieval and JavaScript. To meet the requirement of simplicity for what concerns system's deployment, data is not kept in a database (this would require the installation of a database management system if not present on the Web server) but in XML files, exception made for geo-referenced data, stored in GeoJSON (Geographic JavaScript Object Notation) format: GeoJSON represents an adaptation of the JSON data-interchange format for expressing geo-referenced data based on a subset of JavaScript language (GeoJSON).

For the realization of an editing environment characterized by a high degree of interaction JQuery UI has been used: built upon the more general JQuery library, it is a JavaScript library providing abstractions for low-level interaction and animation, advanced graphical effects and customizable event handling (jQuery Project, b).

At the same time, JQuery UI has been used for the WebGIS instance user interface (Fig. 7), to provide final users an easy to use set of tools for map browsing and information research.

At this time, the prototype consists of the DME, a limited sets of tool constituting the WGCE, and the resulting WebGIS instance that will be used by final users.

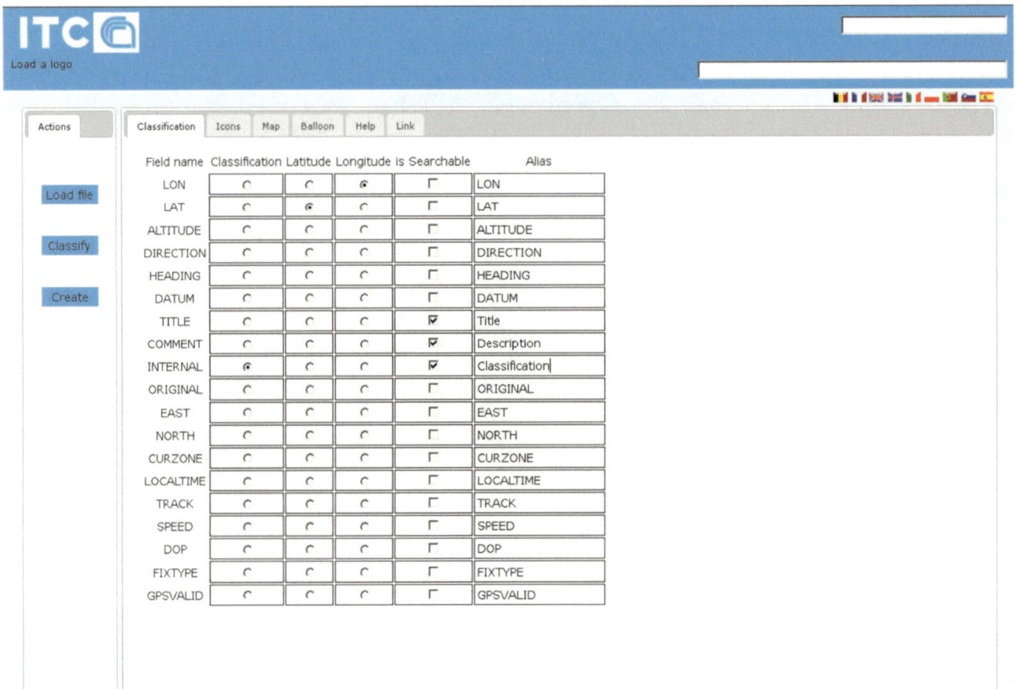

Fig. 7. One of the sub-environments of the DME.

PA Operators send data files in DBF format to the content manager who loads them in the DME by using the "Load file" button located at the far left of the interface shown in Fig. 8. As a result of this loading operation, fields names are visualized as the first column of the central matrix, while the other columns are active, and allow the content manager to define which fields should be used as classification field, longitude and latitude fields, and if a particular field is searchable by final users. Moreover, they can decide to show an alias of the actual field name in the WebGIS instance; this is particularly useful if fields name in the original DBF data file may not be clear to the final user. As an example, in Fig. 8 the content manager have inserted the alias "Description" for the field "COMMENT" which could be confusing.

Once this first activity is finished, the content manager can activate the automatic classification of the geo-referenced data present in the DBF file on the basis of the values found in the chosen classification field and associate to each class of points of interest a meaningful icon and a description by switching to the "Icons" tab (Fig. 8). Every computed class will result in a layer of points of interest of that class in the WebGIS instance.

After the choice of the icons to be associated to each class of points of interest, by switching to the "Map" tab, the content manager can, by acting on a map of the world, decide the starting zoom factor and the center of the map that will be visualized in the WebGIS instance.

Web publishers can, in contrast, decide the layout of the information shown to the final users once a point of interest is clicked on the map: the "Balloon" tab lets them graphically organize the information that will fill a balloon popping up when final users will select a point of interest in the WebGIS instance (as shown in Fig. 8).

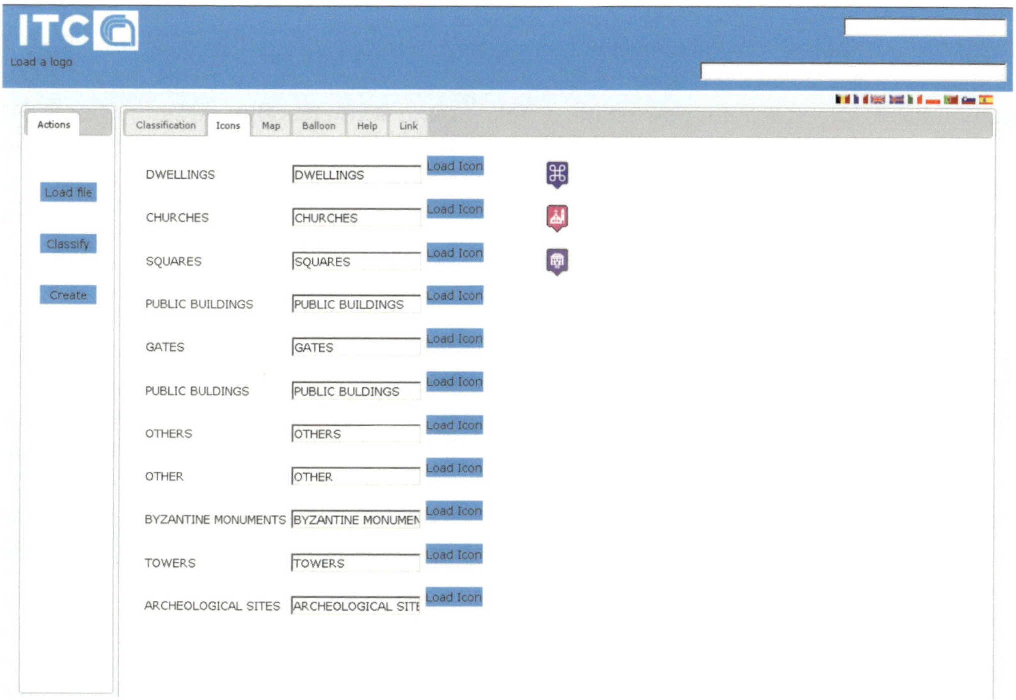

Fig. 8. Icons choice for the automatically computed classification of the points of interest.

Finally, the "Help" tab offers an online help about the functionalities of the system, while the "Link" tab lets web publishers select a set of http links that could be of some interest for final users, and they will be accessible by them by clicking on the "Link" tab in the WebGIS instance.

It is also possible for web publishers to load a logo and specify a title and a subtitle that will be displayed in the heading of the WebGIS instance, by, in turn, clicking on the "Load a logo" text in the upper left and filling the text fields in the upper right.

Once everything has been properly set up, by clicking on the "Create" button in the left column of the interface, the WebGIS instance is create under the form of a ZIP archive file: decompressing it in a Web Server directory will result in the desired WebGIS instance.

Content managers, web publishers and final users can also localize the interface they interact with by clicking the flags located in the upper right of the screen; for the prototype have been produced localization files for english and italian language.

For what concerns the WebGIS instance, final users can browse the central map and click on points of interest to display the geo-referenced information attached to them, or they can search for specific points of interest by using the search field in the upper left of the screen: they can choose to search for particular keywords in all the classes' layers or just in the selected ones by acting on the radio buttons located between the search field and the search button. By deselecting a layer (clicking on the checkbox associated to it in the left column), points of interest belonging to that layer will be hidden.

The results of the search activity will be displayed in the "Search Results" tab.

The adopted approach has some benefits compared to the existing solutions for this kind of applications (see Table 1). First of all the designed prototype offers a single development environment for each authoring phase of the project. Most of other authoring tools for Geographic applications, for example Geo Web Publisher by Bentley Systems, are desktop GIS applications for editing the map data and an embedded web editor for the customization of the presentation layer. In other cases the authoring workflow must be split and edited using several different applications of the software suite, like in the Esri suite or in MapXtreme by Pitney Bowes or again in the Geomedia Suite. It must be pointed out that all surveyed solutions use a hybrid approach consisting of a desktop application for map data editing and often (but not always) a web application for web interface authoring: a single environment completely accessible via web is a novelty and a useful approach under many points of view. In the first instance the interaction with a single user interface is more user friendly than forcing the user to make different authoring steps with different applications. A web application, moreover, is, by definition, accessible from anywhere and with almost any hardware capable of running a modern web browser: this makes the proposed solution a versatile approach for on-the-run authoring needs or in case of low computational power devices.

6. Conclusion

This chapter proposes a novel approach to the development of WebGIS platforms for tourism promotion and heritage conservation. By adopting a point of view that takes into account not only information fruition by final users, but considering the whole workflow comprising activities such as data harvesting and manipulation, their management and publishing, it is possible to provide a network of integrated environments supporting all the stakeholders involved in the process with dedicated tools. A broad state of the art underlines the large availability of technologies that can be exploited to develop this kind of system, and at the same time reveals the lack of proper authoring environments. According to the SSW design methodology a system architecture has been proposed and discussed, and the actors of the system have been described in terms of how they interact with the system. Finally, a prototype of the system offering a subset of the designed functionalities is described.

7. Acknowledgment

Giuseppe Fresta, Marco Padula and Paolo L. Scala would like to dedicate this chapter to the memory of their master and friend Piero Mussio: whithout his precious guide this work couldn't be possible.

8. References

Barricelli, B. R., Maiellaro, N., Padula, M., & Scala, P. L. (2008). A collaborative system for environment and tourism information authoring and Web publishing: an institutional case study, *Proceedings of ICIW 2008*, Athens, Greece, June 2008.

Bentley Systems Inc. n.d. Bentley Map, 18 July 2011, Available at: <http://www.bentley.com/en-US/Products/Bentley+Map/Product-Overview.htm>

Bentley Systems Inc. n.d. Bentley's Geo Web Publisher, 18 July 2011, Available at: <http://www.bentley.com/en-US/Products/Bentley+Geo+Web+Publisher/>

Böhner, j. n.d. SAGA, 18 July 2011, Available at: < http://www.saga-gis.org>

CadCorp. n.d. GeognoSIS, 18 July 2011, Available at: <http://www.cadcorp.com/products_geographical_information_systems/geognosis.htm>

Costabile, M. F., Fogli, D., Lanzilotti, R., Marcante, A., Mussio, P., Parasiliti Provenza, L., & Piccinno, A. (2007). Meta-design to Face Co-evolution and Communication Gaps Between Users and Designers. Lecture Notes in Computer Science, Vol. 4554, pp. (46-55), 9783540732785.

Costabile, M. F., Fogli, D., Lanzilotti, R., Mussio, P., & Piccinno, A. (2005). Supporting Work Practice through End User Development Environments, Technical Report, Bari, Italy: Università degli Studi di Bari, Dipartimento di Informatica, October 2005.

Costabile, M. F., Fogli, D., Mussio, P., & Piccinno, A (2006). End-user development: the software shaping workshop approach. In End User Development Empowering People to Flexibly Employ Advanced Information and Communication Technology, H. Lieberman, F. Paternò and V. Wulf (Eds.), pp. 183-205, Dordrecht: Springer, 9781402042201.

Costabile, M. F., Fogli, D., Mussio, P., & Piccinno, A. (2007). Visual interactive systems for end-user development: A modelbased design methodology. *IEEE Transactions on Systems, Man and Cybernetics - Part A: Systems and Humans*, Vol 37, No. 6, (2007), pp (029-1046).

Django Software Foundation (2005). GeoDjango, 18 July 2011, Available from: <http://geodjango.org/docs/db-api.html>

Dunne, Kieran. 2006. *Perspectives on Localization*. American Translators Association, John Benjamins Publishing Co., 9027231893.

Ellis, C. A., Gibbs, S. J., & Rein, G. L. (1991). Groupware - some issues and experiences, Communications of the ACM, Vol. 34, No. 1, pp. (39–58).

ERDA Suite, 18 July 2011, Available at: http://www.erdas.com

ESRI, 18 July 2011, Available at: http://www.esri.com/

ESRI, n.d. ArcSDE, 18 July 2011, Available at: <http://www.esri.com/software/arcgis/arcsde/>

ESRI. n.d. ArcView , 18 July 2011, Available at: <http://www.esri.com/software/arcgis/arcview>

Fischer, G. (2000). Symmetry of ignorance, social creativity, and meta-design. Knowledge-Based Systems, Vol. 13, No. 7-8, pp. (527-537), 09507051.

Fogli, D., Fresta, G., Marcante, A., Mussio, P., & Padula, M. (2005). Annotation in cooperative work: from paper-based to the web one, Proceedings of International workshop on annotation for collaboration, La Sorbonne, Paris, France, November 2005.

Fogli, D., Marcante, A., Mussio, P., & Parasiliti Provenza, L. (2007). Design of visual interactive systems: a multi-faced methodology, Peoceedings of Converging on a Science of Design through the Synthesis of Design Methodologies, San Jose, CA, USA, May 2007.

GDAL (2011). GDAL Data Model, 18 July 2011, Available at: <http://www.gdal.org/gdal_datamodel.html>

GDAL (2011). OGR, 18 July 2011, Available at: <http://www.gdal.org/ogr/>

GDAL. n.d. GeoJSon GDAL, 18 July 2011, Available at: http://gdal.org/ogr/drv_geojson.html

GeoJSON, 18 July 2011, Available at: http://geojson.org/geojson-spec.html

GeoMedia, n.d. 18 July 2011, Available at: <http://www.intergraph.com/sgi/products/productFamily.aspx?family=10&country=>

GeoServer (2008). 18 July 2011, Available from: <http://svn.codehaus.org/geoserver/tags/2.0.0-alpha1/geoserver/release/README.txt>

Groot, R. & McLaughlin, J. (2000). *Geospatial Data Infrastructure, Concepts, Cases and Good Practice*, Oxford University Press.

Hartson, H. R., & Hix, D. (1989). Human-computer interface development: concepts and systems for its management. ACM *Computing Surveys (CSUR)*, Vol. 21, No. 1, pp. (5–92).

Institut de Recherche Sciences et Techniques de la Ville (IRSTV). n.d. OrbiGIS, 18 July 2011, Available at: < http://www.orbisgis.org>

jQuery Project. n.d. jQuery, 18 July 2011, Available at: http://jquery.com/

jQuery Project. n.d. JQuery UI, 18 July 2011, Available at: http://jqueryui.com

Jump Pilot Project, n.d. OpenJUMP, 18 July 2011, Available at: < http://www.openjump.org/>

Konecny, G. (2003). *Geoinformation: Remote Sensing, Photogrammetry and Geographic Information Systems*. (1st ed.) Taylor & Francis, London

Longley, P.A. (2001). Geographic Information Systems and Science, (1st ed.), John Wiley & Sons, Chichester

MapWindow Open Source Team, n.d. MapWindow, 18 July 2011, Available at: <http://www.mapwindow.org>

MetaCarta, n.d., TileCache, 18 July 2011, Available at: <http://tilecache.org>

Nielsen, J. (1993). *Usability Engineering*. Academic Press, 0125184069, San Diego.

Open Geospatial Consortium. n.d. Simple Feature Access - Part 2: SQL Option., 18 July 2011, Available at: <http://www.opengeospatial.org/standards/sfs>
Open Geospatial Consortium (2005). WFS Web Feature Service Implementation Specification, 18 July 2011, Available At: <http://portal.opengeospatial.org/files/?artifact_id=8339>
Open Geospatial Consortium (2006) GeoRSS White Paper, 18 July 2011, Available at: <http://www.opengeospatial.org/pt/06-050r3>
Open Geospatial Consortium. (2006). OpenGIS Geography Markup Language (GML) Implementation Specification, 18 July 2011, Available at: <http://portal.opengeospatial.org/files/?artifact_id=20509>
Open Source Geospatial Foundation (2006) Tiling standard, 18 July 2011, Available at: <http://wiki.osgeo.org/index.php/TilingStandard>
Open Source Geospatial Foundation, nd. degree map server, 18 July 2011, Available at: <http://www.deegree.org/>
Open Source Geospatial Foundation, nd. GeoTools, 18 July 2011, Available at: http://www.osgeo.org/geotools
Open Source Geospatial Foundation, nd. Mapbender, 18 July 2011, Available at: <http://www.mapbender.org>
Open Source Geospatial Foundation, nd. MapFish, 18 July 2011, Available at: <http://mapfish.org/>
Open Source Geospatial Foundation, nd. OpenLayers, 18 July 2011, Available at: <http://openlayers.org/>
Open Source Geospatial Foundation, nd. OSSIM, 18 July 2011, Available at: < http://www.ossim.org>
Open Source Geospatial Foundation, nd. QuantumGIS, 18 July 2011, Available at: < http://www.qgis.org/>
Oracle, n.d. Oracle 11g Spatial 18 July 2011, Available at: <http://www.oracle.com/technetwork/database/options/spatial>
Pavlenko, A. (2009). Mapnik python module, 18 July 2011, Available at: <http://svn.mapnik.org/tags/release-0.6.0/docs/api_docs/python/mapnik-module.html>
Pitney Bowes Software Inc. n.d. MapExtreme 2008, 18 July 2011, Available at: http://www.pbinsight.com/products/location-intelligence/developer-tools/desktop-mobile-and-internet-offering/mapxtreme-2008/
PostgreSQL Global Development Group. n.d. PostgreSQL, 18 July 2011, Available at: <http://www.postgresql.org/>
Refraction Research. n.d. uDig, 18 July 2011, Available at: < http://udig.refractions.net/>
Safe Software. n.d. 18 July 2011, Available at: <http://www.safe.com/reader_writerPDF/geojson.pdf>
Sencha. n.d. ExtJs, 18 July 2011, Available at: http://www.sencha.com/products/extjs/
SUN Microsystems. n.d. MySQL, 18 July 2011, Available at: http://www.mysql.com/
SUN Microsystems. n.d. MySQL Spatial Extensions , 18 July 2011, Available at: <http://dev.mysql.com/doc/refman/5.5/en/spatial-extensions.html>
University of Minnesota, n.d. MapServer, 18 July 2011, Available at: <http://mapserver.org/>

W3C. (2001). Annotea, 18 July 2011, Available at: http://www.w3.org/2001/Annotea/ Last accessed 2011-03-01

W3C. (2002). XPointer, 18 July 2011, Available at: <XML Pointer Language, http://www.w3.org/TR/xptr/>

W3C. (2004). RDF, 18 July 2011, Available at: <Resource Description Framework, http://www.w3.org/RDF/>

6

Ergonomic Design of Human-CNC Machine Interface

Imtiaz Ali Khan
Department of Mechanical Engineering, Aligarh Muslim University, Aligarh, India

1. Introduction

Ever since the industrial revolution opened the vistas of a new age, the process of industrialization has been at the core of the economic development of all countries. In a simple sense, industrialization means replacement of human labor by machinery to manufacture goods. In this way it induces a shift from home (craft) to factory based production. In a more rational sense, it is a process whereby the share of industry in general and manufacturing in particular, in total economic activities increases.

Worldwide the machine tool industry is a small manufacturing sector, but widely regarded as a strategic industry as it improves overall industrial productivity through supplying embodied technology. The introduction of computer numerically controlled (CNC) has rejuvenated the market. The production and trade have been mostly concentrated in industrialized countries accounting for more than two-thirds of share. However, it is gaining importance among developing countries. The production of high-end machines is concentrated in the USA, Germany Switzerland and Japan. In the mid-range segment Japan is the market leader. In the low-end segment Taiwan and Korea are predominant.

Ergonomics (Human Factors Engineering) is concerned with the 'fit' between people and their technological tools and environments. It takes account of the user's capabilities and limitations in seeking to ensure that tasks, equipment, information and the environment suit each user. To assess the fit between a person and the used technology, ergonomists consider the job (activity) being done and the demands on the user; the equipment used (its size, shape, and how appropriate it is for the task), and the information used (how it is presented, accessed, and changed). The term 'ergonomics' is generally used to refer to physical ergonomics as it relates to the workplace (as in for example ergonomic chairs and keyboards). Physical ergonomics is important in the medical field, particularly to those diagnosed with physiological ailments or disorders such as arthritis (both chronic and temporary) or carpal tunnel syndrome. Ergonomics in the workplace has to do largely with the safety of employees, both long and short-term. Ergonomics can help reduce costs by improving safety. This would decrease the money paid out in workers' compensation. For example, over five million workers sustain overextension injuries per year. Through ergonomics, workplaces can be designed so that workers do not have to overextend themselves and the manufacturing industry could save billions in workers' compensation. Workplaces may either take the reactive or proactive approach when applying ergonomics practices. Reactive ergonomics is when something needs to be fixed, and corrective action is taken. Proactive ergonomics is the process of seeking areas that could be improved and fixing the issues before they become a large problem. Problems may be fixed through equipment design, task design, or environmental design. Equipment design changes the actual, physical devices used by people. Task design changes what people do with the equipment. Environmental design changes the environment in which people work, but not the physical equipment they use.

Ergonomics literature provides ample evident of many successful ergonomic interventions and their positive impact for both employees and employers of all sectors of the society. It is generally accepted that the application of ergonomics is essential for improving working conditions, system efficiency and promotion of the working-life quality. While ergonomics has shown good potential for ensuring optimum technology utilization and proper technological development in the industrialized world, interest and attention paid to the subject is very low among organizations and industrial managers in the industrially developing countries. Almost, two-thirds of the world population in these countries has little or no access to the vast knowledge base that makes ergonomics such an important tool for improving work environment and increase productivity (Shahnavaz et al. 2010). When applying the appropriate type of ergonomics, there would be improvements in quality, productivity, working conditions, occupational health and safety, reduction of rejects and increases in profit (Yeow and Sen, 2002). Ergonomics intervention and its potential to deliver benefits has been accepted and practiced worldwide. The term intervention refers to efforts made to effect change and render such change stable and permanent (Westlander et al. 1995). The objective of ergonomics intervention is to design jobs that are possible for people to do, are worth doing and which give workers job satisfaction and a sense of identity with the company and protect and promote workers' health. Ergonomics intervention should therefore result in improving both the employees' wellbeing (health, safety and satisfaction) as well as the company's wellbeing (optimal performance, productivity and high work quality) (Shahnavaz, 2009).

Companies once thought that there was a bottom-line tradeoff between safety and efficiency. Now they embrace ergonomics because they have learned that designing a safe work environment can also result in greater efficiency and productivity. Recently, U.S. laws requiring a safe work environment have stimulated great interest in Ergonomics - from ergonomic furniture to ergonomic training. But it is in the design of the workplace as a whole where the greatest impact can be seen for both safety and efficiency. The easier it is to do a job, the more likely it is to see gains in productivity due to greater efficiency. Analogously, the safer it is to do a job, the more likely it is to see gains in productivity due to reduced time off for injury. Ergonomics can address both of these issues concurrently by maximizing the workspace and equipment needed to do a job.

Today, Ergonomics commonly refers to designing work environments for maximizing safety and efficiency. Biometrics and Anthropometrics play a key role in this use of the word Ergonomics. Anthropometry refers to the measurement of the human individual for the purposes of understanding human physical variation. Today, anthropometry plays an important role in industrial design, ergonomics and architecture where statistical data about the distribution of body dimensions in the population are used to optimize products. Changes in life styles, nutrition and ethnic composition of populations lead to changes in the distribution of body dimensions and require regular updating of anthropometric data collections. Engineering Psychology often has a specialty dealing with workplace or occupational Ergonomics. While health and safety has always been a dynamic and challenging field, individuals now are being asked to demonstrate cost savings with resources that are more limited than ever. How do companies meet the expectations of "doing more with less" in the health and safety field? One approach that has proven effective in scores of manufacturing companies is to leverage the efforts of ongoing improvement initiatives to accelerate ergonomics improvements.

Recent developments in the field of information and communication technologies and specialized work requiring repetitive tasks have resulted in the need for a human factor engineering approach. Through examining, designing, testing and evaluating the workplace and how people interact in it, human factor engineering can create a productive, safe and satisfying work environment. With the high technology applications getting more widespread at the global level the problems associated with the introduction of this hi-tech have also been generating more concern. Most part of such concern is reflected in occupational stresses in the form of poor job performance, waste leisure time, low level of job satisfaction, alcohol related problems and hence forth. One most notable component of hi-tech era emerged in the shape of human-CNC machine interaction (HMI) that basically comprises of a CNC workstation and an operator. The use of CNC systems is increasing exponentially. This is accompanied with a proportionate increase in occupational stresses too in human operators. Previous studies pertaining to HMI by different researchers in the field revealed that all sorts of problems associated with the use of CNC machines could be traced in terms of physical characteristics of the CNC workstation, visual factors, psychological factors and postural factors. Present studies mainly associated to the last said factor that relates to constrained postures of the CNC operators governed by the characteristics of given workstation. It is well documented that the constrained posture is always associated with static muscular efforts that might lead subsequently to muscular fatigue in humans. If such a postural stress is allowed to persist on a prolonged basis it may adversely affect not only the muscles, but also the joint systems, tendons and other tissues.

Factors such as work environment and the work performed are crucial from the ergonomic design point of view. Preferred term for conditions that are subjectively or objectively influenced or caused by the work is musculoskeletal disorder. Many occupations are associated with a high risk of arm and neck pain. Some risk factors can be identified, but the interaction between the factors is not much understood. It is important to recognize personal characteristics and other environmental and socio-cultural factors which usually play a key role in these disorders. Working with hands at or above the shoulder level may be one determinant of rotator cuff tendinitis. Industrial workers exposed to the tasks that require working over shoulder level include panel controlled CNC machine operators, shipyard welders, car assemblers, house painters and so on. Disorder and pain in the arm have been related to the gripping an instrument and awkward posture. Several factors which are considered to influence the static activity of the shoulder muscles are horizontal distance between the worker and the working place, position of the task, height of the working table, shoulder joint flexion, abduction/adduction and the posture etc. (Westgaard et al. 1988). Disorder and visual discomfort have been related to the visual display unit (VDU) position and awkward posture. Factors which are considered to influence the activity of the eye muscles are horizontal distance between the worker and height of the VDU screen and the posture etc. (Westgaard et al., 1988). Present work is taken to develop a better understanding of the effect of angle of abduction and viewing angle in a HMI environment. The CNC-EDM interaction system was targeted keeping in-view the exponential growth of the automation nowadays and the use of CNC machines in manufacturing and design. Therefore, the need of the moment is an efficient and effective ergonomic design of the CNC-workstations. Unorganized CNC machine working environment which does not meet the human capabilities is considered as a major source of stress and errors. Review of literature suggests that the original sources of postural stresses may be traced in terms of poor CNC workstation design. In recent years, the major emphasis is on preventing musculoskeletal injuries in the workplace. These injuries create a significant cost for industry.

Many of the injuries in manufacturing are musculoskeletal disorders caused by cumulative trauma. We call these injuries that result from cumulative wear and tear, cumulative trauma disorders (CTDs). Back injuries, tendinitis and carpal tunnel syndrome are examples of common CTDs. Workplace risk factors for CTDs include repetitive motions, high forces, awkward postures and vibration exposure. CTDs in manufacturing can be associated with such activities as manual material handling, hand tool usage, awkward postures and prolonged equipment operation. One effective way to reduce the risk of CTDs such as carpal tunnel syndrome and back injuries is to establish an ergonomic process. Do not regard an ergonomic processes as separate from those intended to address other workplace hazards. Use the same approaches to address ergonomic processes issue—hazard identification, case documentation, assessment of control options and healthcare management techniques that you employ to address other safety problems. It is important to realize that you cannot combat cumulative disorders effectively with a quick-fix program. Rather, a long-term process, which relies on continuous improvement, is the preferred approach to reducing CTDs. Successful programs not only result in reduction of injuries, but they achieve quality and productivity gains, as well. For an ergonomic process to be successful, it is imperative that management is committed to the process, participates in the process and provides the necessary resources to ensure its success. Nowadays, efforts in health promotion programs have increased. Notwithstanding, work related musculoskeletal disorders (WMSDs) remain a widespread and growing issue of concern in the automated manufacturing industry. In the coming years, WMSDs leading to absence and reduced employment ability along with an aging work force with comparatively high wages will become an even greater challenge to these automated manufacturing companies facing worldwide competition. The prevention of WMSDs is achieved through improvements in the design of working conditions and tasks as well as through influencing the health promoting behavior of individuals. What is needed, nowadays, is a systematic approach, that enables automated industries to identify and control physical stress at work that leads to WMSDs in a comprehensive manner.

The most important considerations in the human-CNC machine interaction environment are the angle of abduction and viewing angle, which plays a key role in system design. Hence, their effect on human performance in a CNC-EDM environment has been explored in this work.

2. Related works

The rapid growth of automation has led to the development of research on human- machine interaction environment. The research aims at the design of human-machine interfaces presenting ergonomic properties such as friendliness, usability, transparency and so on. Recently public and private organizations have engaged themselves in the enterprise of managing more and more complex and coupled systems by means of the automation. Modern machines not only process information but also act on the dynamic situations as humans have done in the past like managing manufacturing processes, industrial plants, aircrafts etc. These dynamic situations are affected by uncertain human factors. The angle of abduction and viewing angle are considered frequently in the design of the systems like human-computer interaction, human-CNC machine interaction and so on. A review of the literature finds a relatively large number of studies on the angle of abduction and viewing angle. The influence of external factors such as arm posture, hand loading and dynamic exertion on shoulder muscle activity is needed to provide insight into the relationship between internal and external loading of the shoulder joint as explored by Antony et al. (2010). The study collected surface electromyography from 8 upper extremity muscles on 16 participants who performed isometric and dynamic shoulder exertions in three shoulder planes (flexion, mid-abduction and abduction) covering four shoulder elevation angles (30^0, 60^0 , 90^0 and 120^0). Shoulder exertions were performed under three hand load conditions: no load, holding a 0.5 kg load and 30% grip. It was found that adding a 0.5 kg load to the hand increased shoulder muscle activity by 4% maximum voluntary excitation (MVE), across all postures and velocities. Kuppuswamy et al. (2008) determined that the abduction of one arm preferentially activates erector spinae muscles on the other side to stabilize the body. The study hypothesizes that the corti cospinal drive to the arm abductors and the erector spinae may originate from the same hemisphere. Terrier et al. (2008) explored that the shoulder is one of the most complex joints of the human body, mainly because of its large range of motion but also because of its active muscular stabilization. The study presented an algorithm to solve the indeterminate problem by a feedback control of muscle activation, allowing the natural humorous translation. In this study the abduction was considered in the scapular plane, accounting for the three deltoid parts and the rotator cuff muscles. Gutierrez et al. (2008) determined the effects of prosthetic design and surgical technique of reverse shoulder implants on total abduction range of motion and impingement on the inferior scapular neck. The study concluded that the neck-shaft angle had the largest effect on inferior scapular impingement, followed by glen sphere position. Levasseur et al. (2007) explored that a joint coordinate system allows coherence between the performed movement, its mathematical representation and the clinical interpretation of the kinematics of joint motion. The results obtained revealed a difference in the interpretation of the starting angles between the International Society Biomechanics (ISB) joint coordinate system and the aligned coordinate system. No difference was found in the interpretation of the angular range of motion. Wickham et al. (2010) performed an experiment to obtain electromyography (EMG) activity from a sample of healthy shoulders to allow a reference database to be developed and used for comparison with pathological shoulders. In this study temporal and intensity shoulder muscle activation characteristics during a coral plane abduction/adduction movement were evaluated in the dominant healthy shoulder of 24 subjects. The study concluded that the most reproducible patterns of activation arose from the more prime movers muscle sites in all EMG variables analyzed and although variability was present, there emerged invariant characteristics that were considered normal for this group of non pathological shoulders. Gielo-Perczak et al. (2006) conducted a study to test whether glen humeral geometry is co-related with upper arm strength. The isometric shoulder strength of 12 subjects during one-handed arm abduction in the coronal plane in a range from 5^0 to 30^0, was correlated with the geometries of their glenoid fossas. The study concluded that the new geometric parameter named as the area of glenoid asymmetry (AGA) is a distinguished factor which influence shoulder strength when an arm is abducted in a range from 5^0 to 30^0. Mukhopadhyay et al. (2007) explored that industrial jobs involving upper arm abduction have a strong association with musculoskeletal disorders and injury. Biomechanical risk factors across different mouse positions within a computer controlled workstation were explored by Dennerlein et al. (2006). One of the two studies with 30 subjects (15 females and 15 males) examined the three mouse positions: a standard mouse (SM) position with the mouse placed to the right of the keyboard, a central mouse (CM) position with the mouse between the key board and the human body and a high mouse (HM) position using a keyboard drawer with the mouse on the primary work surface. The second study examined two mouse positions: the SM position and a more central position using a different keyboard (NM). In this work the muscle activity of the wrist and upper arm postures were recorded through the electromyography technique. The CM position was found to produce the most neutral upper extremity posture across all measures. The HM position has resulted the least neutral posture and highest level of muscle activity. The study also indicated that the NM position reduces wrist extension slightly and promote a more neutral shoulder posture as compared to the SM position. The study concluded that the HM position was least desirable whereas the CM position result the minimum awkward postures. Peter et al. (2006) determined the differences in biomechanical risk factors during the computer tasks. The study was conducted with the 30 touch-typing adults (15 females and 15 males). The subjects were asked to complete five different tasks: typing text, filling of a html form with text fields, text editing within a document, sorting and resizing objects in a graphics task and browsing and navigating a series of internet web pages. The study reported that the task completion with the help of both the mouse and the keyboard result the higher shoulder muscle activity, larger range of the motion and the larger velocities and acceleration of the upper arm. Susan et al. (2006) reported large and statistically significant reductions in muscle activity by modifying a workstation arrangement of an ultrasound system's control panel. In this study, the right suprascapular fossa activity indicated a reduction of muscle activity by 46%, between a postural stance of 75 and 30 degrees abduction. Choudhry et al. (2005) in their study compared the anthropometric dimensions of the farm youths of the north-eastern region of the India with those of China, Japan, Taiwan, Korea, Germany, Britain and USA. The study concluded that all the anthropometric dimensions of the Indian subjects were lower than those from the other parts of the world. Human laterality is considered to be one of the most important issues in human factors engineering. Hand anthropometric data have indicated differences between right and left-handed individuals and between females and males. A study was carried out by Yunis (2005) on the hand dimensions of the right and left-handed Jordanian subjects. The results indicated that there were significant differences in the hand anthropometric data between right and left-handed subjects as well as between the females and males subjects. Alan et al. (2003) explored in their study that the constant intramuscular (IMP) / EMG relationship with increased force may be extended to the dynamic contractions and to the fatigued muscles. In this study IMP and EMG patterns were recorded through shoulder muscles in the three sessions. It was found in the study that during the brief static tasks the IMP and EMG patterns increased with the shoulder torque. Jung-Yong et al. (2003) determined the upward lifting motion involved at the scapula at various shoulder angles. In particular, 90 and 120 degrees of flexion, 30 degrees of adduction, and 90 degrees of abduction were found to be the most vulnerable angles based on the measured maximum voluntary contractions (MVCs). The average root mean square value of the EMG increased most significantly at 90 to 150 degrees of flexion and at 30 and 60 degrees of abduction. The increasing demand of the anthropometric data for the design of the machines and personal protective equipments to prevent the occupational injuries has necessitated an understanding of the anthropometric differences among occupations. Hongwei et al. (2002) identified the differences in various body measurements between various occupational groups in the USA. The analysis of the data indicated that the body size or the body segment measurements of some occupational groups differ significantly. The optimum height of the table of the operating room for the laparoscopic surgery was investigated by Smith et al. (2002). The study concluded that the optimum table height should position the handles of the laparoscopic instrument close to the surgeon's elbow level to minimize discomfort. The study determined the optimum table height as 64 to 77 centimeters above the floor level. In the retail supermarket industry where the cashiers perform repetitive light manual material-handling tasks during scanning and handling products, the cases of the musculoskeletal disorders and the discomfort are high. Lehman et al. (2001) conducted a research to determine the effect of working position (sitting versus standing) and scanner type (bi-optic versus single window) on the muscle activity. Ten cashiers from a Dutch retailer environment participated in the study. Cashiers exhibited the lower muscle activity in the neck and shoulders when standing and using a bi-optic scanner. The shoulder abduction was also less for the standing conditions. Yun et al. (2001) investigated the relationship between the self-reported musculoskeletal symptoms and the related factors among visual display terminals (VDT) operators working in the banks. The subjects of the study were 950 female bank tellers. The study was carried out to specify the prevalence of the WMSDs and to identify the demographic and task-related factors associated with the WMSD symptoms. The study indicated the percentages of the subjects reported the disorders of the shoulder, lower back, neck, upper back, wrist and the fingers as 51.4, 38.3, 38.0, 31.2, 21.7 and 13.6 respectively. Another case study was conducted in an automobile assembly plant by Fine et al. (2000). There were 79 subjects who reported shoulder pain. More than one-half also had positive findings in a physical examination. Subjects who were free of shoulder pain were randomly selected. Forty-one percent of the subjects flexed or abducted the right arm "severely" (above 90 degrees) during the job cycle, and 35% did so with the left arm. Disorders were associated with severe flexion or abduction of the left (odds ratio (OR) 3.2) and the right (OR 2.3) shoulder. The risk increased as the proportion of the work cycle exposure increased. The findings concluded that, the shoulder flexion or abduction, especially for 10% or more of the work cycle, is predictive of chronic or recurrent shoulder disorders. David et al. (1988) investigated the effect of the anthropometric dimensions of the three major ethnic groups in the Singapore. The study was carried out with the help of the 94 female visual display units (VDU) operators. Few anthropometric differences were recorded among the Chinese, Malays and Indians. On comparing the data with the Americans and Germans, the three Asian cohorts were found smaller in the body size. Because of the smaller body build the Asian VDU operators preferred a sitting height of about 46 centimeters and a working height of about 74 centimeters while as the European operators preferred the sitting and working heights as 47 centimeters and 77 centimeters respectively. The position of the upper arm and head, as an indicator of load on the shoulder and risk of shoulder injury for workers performing electromechanical assembly work, was explored by Westgaard et al. (1988). In this study postural angles, in terms of flexion/extension and abduction/adduction of the right upper arm and the shoulder joint, as well as flexion/extension of head and back were measured for a group of female workers. Adopting a posture with an arm flexion of less than 15 degrees, an arm abduction of less than 10 degree and using a light (0.35 kg) hand tool, resulted in a 20% incidence of sick leaves due to shoulder injuries of workers employed between 2-5 years, and 30% incidence for those employed more than 5 years. This was significantly lower for other groups working with higher arm flexion. The study concluded that the magnitude of the postural angles of the shoulder joint influenced the shoulder load. Another study for standing, supported-standing, and sitting postures was carried out with subjects simulating assembly work in places with poor leg space by Bendix et al. (1985). The postures and the upper trapezius muscle load were examined using statometric and electromyography methods, respectively. While supported-standing or sitting, the lumbar spine moved toward kyphosis, even with no backward rotation of the pelvis. In adopting the position for anteriorly placed work, the arms were raised 30 degrees forward or more, the trunk was flexed as well. It was concluded in the study that, if leg space is poor, variation between supported-standing and standing should be encouraged, and an ordinary office chair should be avoided. Also, the working level should be arranged so that it is lower than 5 centimetres above the elbow level if no arm/wrist support is possible.

The viewing angle is considered frequently in the design of the systems like human-computer interaction, human-CNC machine interaction and so on. A review of the literature finds a relatively large number of studies on the viewing angle. Smith et al. (2010) explored that the attention mediates access of sensory events to higher cognitive systems and can be driven by either top-down voluntary mechanisms or in a bottom-up, reflexive fashion by the sensory properties of a stimulus. The study investigated the effect of an experimentally induced opthalmoplegia on voluntary and reflexive attentional orienting during visual search. The study observed that abducting the eye into the temporal hemi field elicited deficits of both voluntary and reflexive attention for targets that appeared beyond the oculomotor range. Kong-King et al., (2007) determined the viewing distance and screen angle for electronic paper (E-Paper) displays under various light sources, ambient illuminations and character sizes. Findings of this study indicate that mean viewing distance and screen angle should be 495 millimetres and 123.7 degrees (in terms of viewing angle, 29.5 degrees below the horizontal eye level), respectively. Proper visualization of the background of surgical field is essential in the laparoscopic surgery and it reduces the risk of iatrogenic injuries. One of the important factors influencing visualization is the viewing distance between surgeon and the monitor. Shallaly et al., (2006) performed an experiment with 14 surgeons. The experiment was designed to determine two working distances from a standard 34 centimeters (14 inch) diagonal cathode ray tube (CRT) monitor: one the maximum view distance permitting small prints of a near vision chart to be identified clearly by sight and second the minimum view distance (of a standard resolution chart) just short of flicker, image degradation or both. The results indicated that the maximum view distance allowing identification averaged 221 centimeters (range 166-302 centimeters). The mean minimal viewing distance short of flicker/image degradation was determined as 136 centimeters (range 102-168 centimeters). For most surgeons the extrapolated monitor viewing distances for the laparoscopic surgery ranges from 139 centimeters to 303 centimeters (57-121 inch) for the maximal distance viewing and from 90 centimeters to 182 centimeters (36-73 inch) for close-up viewing (i.e. optimal working range of 90 to 303 centimeters or 36-121 inch). It was concluded that the maximal and minimal (close-up) viewing distances are variable, but the surgeon should never be farther than 3 meters (10 ft.) or closer than 0.9 meter (3 ft.) from the monitor. Another study for visual display unit work environment was carried out by Svensson et al., (2001). In this study two viewing angles, namely 3 degrees above the horizontal and 20 degrees below the horizontal, were considered. The findings concluded that the load on the neck and shoulders was significantly lower at 3 degrees as compared to 20 degrees. Jan et al., (2003) explored that low VDU screen height increases the viewing angle and also affects the activity of the neck extensor muscles. Ayako et al., (2002) determined the effects of the tilt angle of a notebook computer on posture and muscle activities. It was concluded in the study that at 100 degree tilt angle, the subjects had relatively less neck flexion. Visual display units are widely used in the industries. The optimization of their orientation is a critical aspect of the human-machine interaction and impacts on the worker health, satisfaction and performance. Due to increase in the visual and musculoskeletal disorders related to VDU use, a number of ergonomic recommendations have been proposed in order to combat this problem. Fraser et al., (1999) observed that, the monitor position, 18 degree below eye level had no significant effect on the position of the neck relative to the trunk while, the mean flexion of the head, relative to the neck increased 5 degrees. Burgess-Limerick et al., (2000) determined optimal location of the visual targets as 15 degrees below horizontal eye level. Adjustability effect of the touch screen displays in a food service industry was investigated by Batten et al., (1998). To determine the optimal viewing angle or range of a given touch-screen display, an anthropometric analysis was carried out. The results recommended the adjustable range of the touch-screen display as 30 to 55 degrees to the horizontal. Mon-Williams et al., (1998) in their study pointed out that as vertical gaze angle is raised or lowered the 'effort' required to binocular system also changes. The results indicated that the heterophoria varies with vertical gaze angle and stress on the vergence system during the use of HMDs will depend, in part, on the vertical gaze angle. Another case study was conducted by Koroemer et al., (1986). Sixteen male and sixteen female subjects were used in the study. The findings concluded that the subject looks down steeply at an average of 29 degrees below the horizontal, when sitting with the trunk and head upright. Also this angle is steeper when the visual target is at 0.50 meter distance (-33 ±11.3 degrees) and flatter when the target is at 1.00 meter (-24 ±10.4 degrees).

The reviewed researches have clearly indicated that the musculoskeletal disorder is one of the major factors as far as human injuries in the computer controlled working environment are concerned. The above findings have been used to formulate the present studies of the effect of the angle of abduction and viewing angle in a CNC-EDM interaction environment.

3. Methodology

3.1 Study I

3.1.1 Subjects

Experimental investigation was carried out with three groups of 18 subjects each. Groups were divided according to the variation in height of the subjects; i.e. (Group1) - Subjects of height 5′ 9″, (Group2) - Subjects of height 5′ 6″ and (Group3) - Subjects of height 5′ 4″. All subjects were of same sex (i.e. male), age varied from 21-26 years with mean age of 23.72 yrs (S.D = 1.592) and mean arm length of 28.5 inch, 28 inch and 27.5 inch for 5′ 9″, 5′6″ and 5′4″ tall subjects, respectively.

3.1.2 Experimentation

In order to conduct the investigation, an experiment was designed in a controlled CNC-EDM (Computer Numerically Controlled-Electro Discharge Machine) wire cutting environment (Figure 1), at "The National Small Industries Corporation Ltd." (NSIC) Aligarh, India.

Three levels of Angle of Abduction, namely 45, 55 and 60 degrees (Figure 2), were considered on the basis of the findings discussed in the related works and comprehensive surveys conducted at various EDM centers. Before actual start of the experiment, each of the subjects was asked to go through the instruction sheet served by the experimenter. Specific time interval was allowed to perform the actual task of the data entry for one set of the experimental condition. To start and stop the task, instruction was given through prerecorded voice on a recorder. Data entry time taken by the user constituted the index of the human performance. The performance of each subject at a pre-specified time was recorded (Figure 3) through entering a specially designed coded computer program on Electra, Maxi-cut-e CNC Wire-cut EDM for performing single pass cutting of alloy steel (HCHCr) work piece. The entered (data entry) program had the following specifications:

- Work piece shape----------- rectangular
- Work piece height---------- 24 millimeters
- Wire material ---------------- brass alloy
- Wire diameter --------------- 0.25 millimeter
- Angle of cut ------------------ vertical
- Work piece hardness--------56 HRC
- Length of cut----------------- 10 millimeters

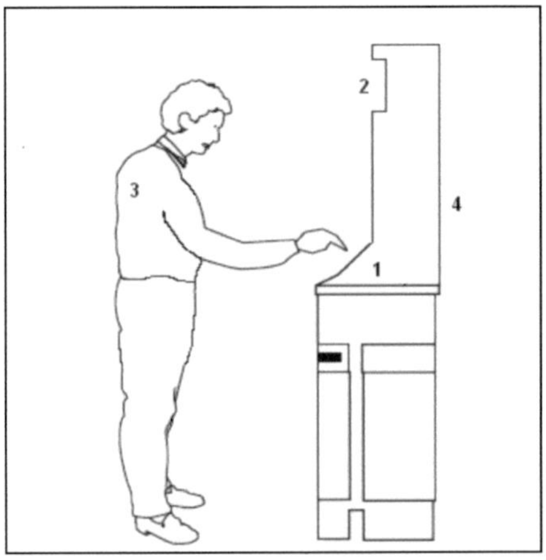

Fig. 1. Schematic representation of experimental setup: (1) Key-board (2) Visual display (3) Subject (4) CNC-EDM Control panel.

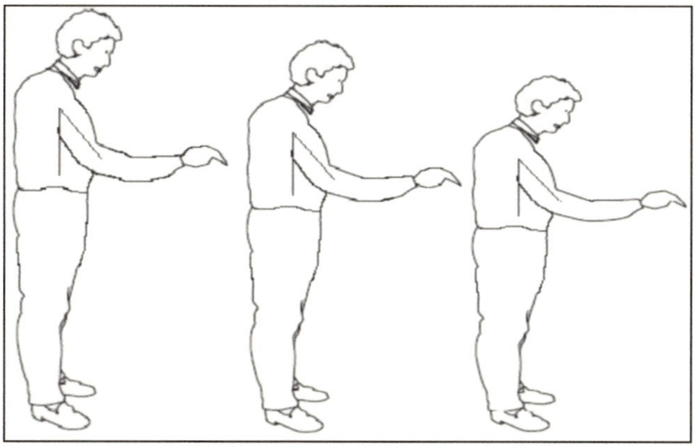

Fig. 2. Showing the abduction angles (45, 55 and 60 degrees) for 5′9″, 5′6″ and 5′4″ tall subjects, respectively.

Fig. 3. Picture showing subject performing the data entry task.

3.1.3 Statistical analysis

The experimental data collected, in terms of subject's performance in a CNC-EDM environment, was investigated using statistical analysis with repeated measures. A method of comparison of the mean was used to determine the optimum level of Angle of Abduction.

3.1.4 Results I

The analysis of variance pertaining to the single factor repeated measure type of statistical design was performed over the data collected. The result is shown in the analysis of variance (ANOVA) Table-1;

S	Type III Sum of Squares	df	Mean Square	F-value	P-value
AA	40.571	2	20.286	158.204	<0.0001
E	6.539	51	0.128		
T	2121.011	54			

Table 1. Summary of Analysis of Variance. S-Source, AA- Angle of Abduction, E-Error, T-Total, df- degree of freedom.

F-ratio was used for testing the statistical hypothesis, and the level of significance for the test was set to 0.01. It was concluded that;

(i) The null hypothesis, "Angle of Abduction does not significantly affect the operator's performance in a CNC-EDM environment", was rejected, because of the aggregate's mean time difference (performance data in terms of time). (ii) Null hypothesis rejected because the $F\text{-value}_{ov}$ = 158.204 (from Table-1) was greater than $[F_{0.01}(2, 51)]_{cv} = 5.0472$ obtained from the F-table using the values for degrees of freedom (2, 51). [*Where ov = observed value and cv = critical value*]. (iii) Null hypothesis rejected because the P-value for F-value = 158.204 was found to be less than 0.0001 i.e. ($p<0.0001$), which was less than the set significance level (α = 0.01).

Since the angle of abduction had statistically significant effect so far as the data entry task was concerned, an attempt was made to develop a mathematical model to search for the relationship between human performance and the abduction level. Then linear and non-linear regression analyses were performed. For the case of non-linear, exponential, hyperbolic and power function models were examined. The criterion fixed for selecting the best model was the value of the co-efficient of determination, R^2, i.e., the best one would have the highest value of R^2. Proceeding this way the exponential model was found to have the maximum value (0.8852) of the R^2. The best fit model had the following form:

$$Y = 0.4625 * X^2 - 1.8295 * X + 7.2525$$

Where, Y = Human performance in a CNC-EDM environment and X = Angle of abduction level.

For the above mathematical model, data were generated and a graph was drawn showing relationship between the human performance and angle of abduction level (Figure 4).

3.1.5 Statistical conclusion

The null hypothesis stated above was rejected since F_{ov} = 158.204 was greater than F_{cv} **= 5.0472**. Furthermore, the computed **probability value (p-value) i.e. [p<0.0001]** meant that the test was strongly significant at 1%; hence Ho (**null hypothesis)** must be **unequivocally rejected** at the critical value of 1% **because 0.0001 is << 0.01.** Thus the above result indicated that the null hypothesis was rejected and it was found that the angle of abduction had a significant effect on human performance in a CNC-EDM environment.

Variation in performance under different levels of angles of abduction was shown graphically in Figure 4. To establish which one out of the three considered angles of abduction was optimal, the data was further analyzed by the method of mean comparison proposed by Winer (1971).

Contrast	Contrast sum of square	df	Mean square	F-value	P-value
2 vs3	8.1225	1	8.1225	63.46	<0.0001
1 vs (2,3)	32.4723	1	32.4723	253.69	<0.0001

Table 2. Summary of the analysis.

Where; 1: First treatment mean (at an angle of abduction of 45 degrees), 2: Second treatment mean (at an angle of abduction of 55 degrees), 3: Third treatment mean (at an angle of abduction of 60 degrees).

Analysis in Table-2 shows that all contrasts were significant, because; (i) F-value$_{ov}$ = 63.46 and F-value$_{ov}$ = 253.69, were greater than $[F_{0.01}(1, 51)]_{cv}$ = 7.1595 (obtained from F-table). [*Where ov = observed value and cv = critical value*]. (ii) P-values for both F-value$_{ov}$ were found to be less than 0.0001 i.e. ($p<0.0001$), which was less than the set significance level i.e. $\alpha = 0.01$.

Furthermore, analysis showed that there was a significant difference between aggregates and the contrast [2 vs 3] was marginally significant however, the F-value 253.69 for the contrast [1 vs (2, 3)] was more significant, so the second contrast hypothesis was rejected. This indicated that a 45 degree angle of abduction level results in optimal operator performance (Figure 4).

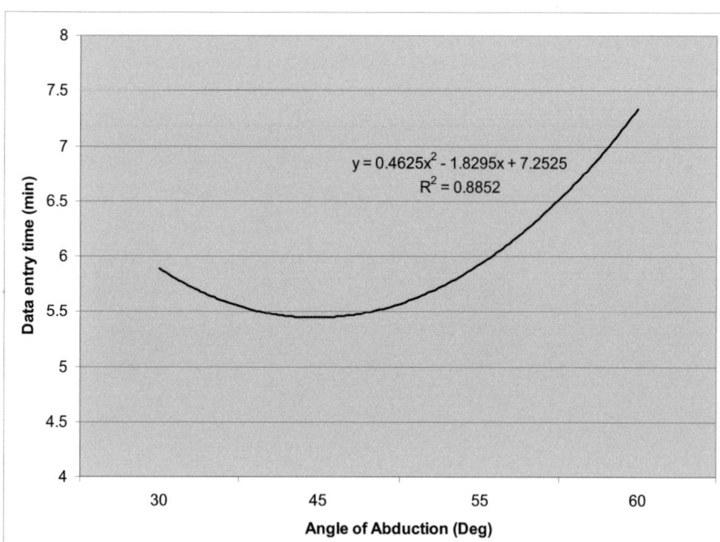

Fig. 4. Graph showing the performance in terms of data entry task time versus various levels of angle of abduction.

3.2 Study II

3.2.1 Subjects

Experimental investigation was carried out with three groups of 18 subjects each. Groups were divided according to the variation in height of the subjects; i.e. (Group1) - Subjects of height 5′ 9″, (Group2) - Subjects of height 5′ 6″ and (Group3) - Subjects of height 5′ 4″. All subjects were male, age varied from 21-26 years with mean age of 23.72 yrs (S.D = 1.592).

3.2.2 Experimentation

In order to conduct the investigation, an experiment was designed in a controlled CNC-EDM (Computer Numerically Controlled-Electro Discharge Machine) wire cutting environment, at "The National Small Industries Corporation Ltd." (NSIC) Aligarh, India.

Three levels of Viewing Angle, namely 15, 21 and 28 degrees above horizontal (Figure 5) were considered on the basis of findings discussed in the related works and comprehensive surveys conducted at various EDM centers. Before actual start of the experiment, each of the subjects was asked to go through the instruction sheet served by the experimenter. Specific time interval was allowed to perform the actual error searching task for one set of the experimental condition. To start and stop the task, instruction was given through prerecorded voice on a recorder. Errors were incorporated in the specially designed coded computer program (as used for study I on Electra, Maxi-cut-e Wire-cut EDM) for performing single pass cutting of alloy steel (HCHCr) work piece. Error searching time constituted the index of the human performance. The performance of each subject at a pre-specified time was recorded through error searching task (Figure 6).

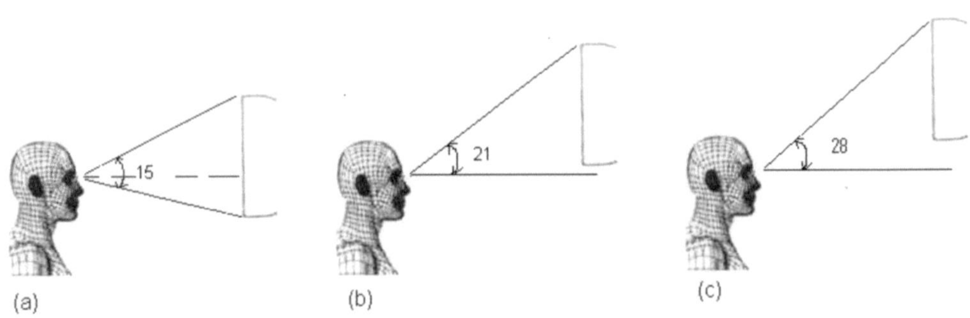

Fig. 5. Showing the EDM monitor and considered viewing angles for (a) 5′9″, (b) 5′6″ and c) 5′4″ height subjects, respectively.

Fig. 6. Picture showing subject performing the error searching task.

3.2.3 Statistical analysis

The experimental data collected, in terms of subject's performance in a CNC-EDM environment, was investigated using statistical analysis with repeated measures. A method of comparison of the mean was used to determine the optimum level of viewing angle.

3.2.4 Results II

The analysis of variance pertaining to the single factor repeated measure type of statistical design was performed over the data collected. The result is shown in the analysis of variance (ANOVA) Table 3;

S	Type III Sum of Squares	df	Mean Square	F-value	P-value
VA	17.297	2	8.648	80.932	<0.0001
E	5.450	51	0.107		
T	858.501	54			

Table 3. Summary of Analysis of Variance, S-Source, VA- Viewing Angle, E-Error, T-Total, df-degree of freedom.

F-ratio was used for testing the statistical hypothesis, and the level of significance for the test was set to 0.01. It was concluded that; (i) The null hypothesis, "Viewing Angle does not significantly affect the operator's performance in a CNC-EDM environment ", was rejected because of the aggregate's mean time difference (performance data in terms of error searching time). (ii) Null hypothesis rejected because the F-value$_{ov}$ = 80.932 (see Table 3) was greater than $[F_{0.01}(2, 51)]_{cv} = 5.0472$ obtained from the F-table using the values for degrees of freedom (2, 51). [*Where ov = observed value and cv = critical value*]. (iii) Null hypothesis rejected because the P-value for F-value = 80.932 was found to be less than 0.0001 i.e. ($p<0.0001$), which was less than the set significance level ($\alpha = 0.01$).

Since the viewing angle had statistically significant effect so far as the error searching task was concerned, an attempt was made to develop a mathematical model to search for the relationship between human performance and the viewing level. Then linear and non-linear regression analyses were performed. For the case of non-linear, exponential, hyperbolic and power function models were examined. The criterion fixed for selecting the best model was the value of the co-efficient of determination, R^2, i.e., the best one would have the highest value of R^2. Proceeding this way the exponential model was found to have the maximum value (0.774) of the R^2. The best fit model had the following form:

$$Y = 0.025 * X^2 - 1.0724 * X + 15.067$$

Where, Y = Human performance in a CNC-EDM environment and X = Viewing Angle level.

For the above mathematical model, data were generated and a graph was drawn showing relationship between the human performance and viewing angle level (see Figure 7).

3.2.5 Statistical conclusion

The null hypothesis stated above was rejected since F_{ov} = 80.932 was greater than F_{cv} = 5.0472 (obtained from F-table). Furthermore, the computed probability value (p-value) i.e. [$p<0.0001$] meant that the test was strongly significant at 1%; hence Ho (null hypothesis) must be unequivocally rejected at the critical value of 1% because 0.0001 is << 0.01. Thus, the above result indicated that the null hypothesis was rejected and it was found that the viewing angle had a significant effect on human performance in a CNC-EDM environment. Variation in performance under different levels of viewing angle was shown graphically in Figure 7. To establish which one out of the three considered viewing angles was optimal, the data was further analyzed by the method of mean comparison proposed by Winer (1971).

Contrast	Contrast sum of square	df	Mean square	F-value	P-value
2 vs 3	2.0736	1	2.0736	19.38	<0.0001
1 vs (2,3)	15.3228	1	15.3228	143.20	<0.0001

Table 4. Summary of the analysis.

Where; 1: First treatment mean (at a viewing angle of 15 degrees), 2: Second treatment mean (at a viewing angle of 21 degrees), 3: Third treatment mean (at a viewing angle of 28 degrees).

Analysis in Table 4 shows that all contrast were significant, because; (i) F-value$_{ov}$ = 19.38 and F-value$_{ov}$ = 143.20, were greater than $[F_{0.01}(1, 51)]_{cv}$ = 7.1595 (obtained from F-table). [*Where ov = observed value and cv = critical value*]. (ii) P-values for both F-value$_{ov}$ were found to be less than 0.0001 i.e. ($p<0.0001$), which was less than the set significance level i.e. $\alpha = 0.01$.

Furthermore, analysis showed that there was a significant difference between aggregates and the contrast [2 vs 3] was marginally significant however, the F-value 143.20 for the contrast [1 vs (2, 3)] was more significant, so the second contrast hypothesis was rejected. This indicated that a 21 degree viewing angle level results in optimal operator performance (Figure 7).

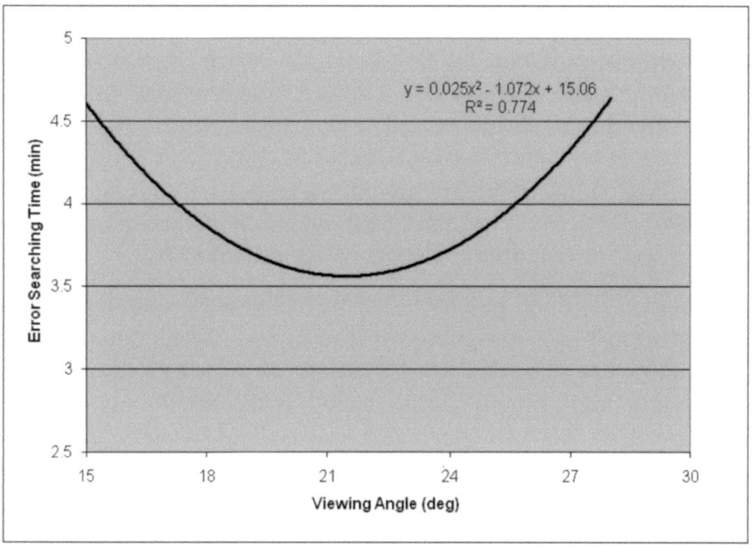

Fig. 7. Graph showing the performance in terms of error searching time versus various levels of viewing angle.

4. Discussion

World Health Organization (WHO) and Occupational Safety and Health Administration (OSHA) consider the cause of work related musculoskeletal diseases as multi-factorial. Management and workers in the recent scenario of automation are greatly concerned with working environment, ergonomics, quality of work and occupational safety and health. The development in information and communication technologies and specialized work requiring repetitive task add up to a need for human-machine interface design. Ergonomists are concerned with the complex physical relationships between peoples, machines, job demands and work methods. Nowadays major emphasis is on preventing musculoskeletal injuries in the work place. Prevention of these injuries is accomplished by understanding biomechanics and physiology of work, through the use of biomechanical models, laboratory simulations, field studies and job analysis.

Musculoskeletal disorders (MSDs) is a health disorder caused by repetitive motion, inadequate working posture, excessive exertion of strength, body contact with sharp surface, vibration, temperature, etc. MSDs can be minimized by prevention and management. Benefits from the prevention and management of MSDs show improvement of work environment, the relation between the labor and management, productivity and decrease in lost work days. From a long-term viewpoint, it can reduce financial losses and create the image of safe work place. MSDs are widespread and occur in all kind of jobs. However, work related musculoskeletal disorders are not only health problems; they also are a financial burden to society. The costs are related to medical costs, decreased productivity, sick leave and chronic disability (Danuta, 2010). Many studies proved that load sustained at very low levels can be a factor in MSDs development. Despite the fact that there is widespread awareness of the problem and measures to limit development of MSDs are being undertaken, according to an European survey up to 25% of workers report back pain and 23% muscular pain.

Some amounts of optical radiation are beneficial for humans but excessive exposure can cause many negative health effects to the skin and eyes and also can affect the immune system. Biological effects can be induced only by absorbed radiation. We could distinguish two types of reactions in biological tissues induced by optical radiation: photochemical and thermal. Exposure limit values represent conditions under which it is expected that nearly all individuals may be repeatedly exposed without acute adverse effects and based upon best available evidence, without noticeable risk of delayed effects.

In recent years, human-machine interface system has become one of the most promising areas for an ergonomist for designing, research and development. With the rapid technological advancement across the world, various new industries are emerging in large numbers day by day and the problems related with working environment are also increasing. The operator's posture, work place as well as machine and their interaction environment indicate significant effect on the performance. The optimum working environment can be designed if all the factors influencing the human performance are considered together. Factors such as angle of abduction and viewing angle are crucial from the ergonomic design point of view. Present work was taken to develop a better understanding of the effect of angle of abduction and viewing angle in a HMI environment. This work revealed that a 45 degree abduction angle and 21 degree viewing angle gives the optimal performance as far as human-CNC machine interaction environment is concerned.

The above mentioned findings in some way or the other are similar to those obtained by some earlier investigators also. Susan et al. (2006), for example, found significant reductions in the muscle activity by modifying the workstation arrangement of an ultrasound system's control panel. Similarly, Dennerlein et al. (2006) based upon their study revealed that designing for the optimal configuration of a computer controlled workstation was necessary to eliminate the postural discomfort. Also, Smith et al. (2002) found the optimum height of the table to position the handles of the laparoscopic instrument to minimize the discomfort. Another study by Lehman et al. (2001) explored that the modified workplace design of a retail supermarket industry minimizes the postural stress, fatigue and discomfort. Present study was also supported by Hongwei et al. (2002), which identified differences in various body measurements between occupational groups in the USA. The researcher concluded that the body size or the body segment measurements of some occupational groups differ significantly. The present finding was supported by Peter et al. (2006). The study revealed that the task completion in a computer controlled environment result the higher shoulder muscle activity, larger range of the motion and the larger velocities and acceleration of the upper arm. The finding was also supported by Fine et al. (2000). It was concluded in the referred study that the shoulder flexion or abduction is predictive of chronic or recurrent shoulder disorder. Therefore, based upon the research reviews, it can be significantly concluded that the anthropometric factors play a key role in the effective and efficient ergonomic design of the human-CNC machine interaction environment.

Furthermore, Kong-King et al., (2007), for example, found significant reductions in the eye muscle activity by modifying the workstation arrangement of an electronic paper displays. Dennerlein et al., (2006) based upon their study revealed that designing for the optimal configuration of a computer controlled workstation was necessary to eliminate the postural discomfort. In a VDU work environment, Svensson et al., (2001) found the optimum viewing angle which resulted lower load on the neck and shoulders. Also, Jan et al., (2003) explored that high viewing angle affects the activity of the neck extensor muscles. Results of the present study are supported by those of Batten et al., (1998), who determined the optimum viewing angle in a food service industry. The present findings also agree with the observations of Mon-Williams et al., (1998). This study revealed that as vertical gaze angle is raised or lowered, the effort required to binocular system also changes. Hence it can be concluded that the visual factor play a key role in the effective and efficient ergonomic design of the human-CNC machine interaction environment.

It is essential from the ergonomic point of view that the work place design of a CNC machine environment be compatible with the biological and psychological characteristics of the operators. The effectiveness of the human-CNC machine combination can be greatly enhanced by treating the operator and the CNC machine as a unified system. When the CNC operator is viewed as one component of a HMI system, the human characteristics pertinent to the ergonomic design are physical dimensions, capability for the data sensing, capability for the data processing, capability for the learning etc. Quantitative information about these human characteristics must be co-ordinate with the data on CNC machine characteristics, if maximum human-machine integration is to be achieved. The findings of the present work revealed that the levels of the angle of abduction and viewing angle have a statistically significant effect on the performance of the CNC-EDM operators. However, a 45 degree abduction angle and 21 degree viewing angle emerged to be the one which appears to offer a high level of compatibility in a human-CNC machine interface environment. Finally, it is observed that the application of ergonomics in the design of human-CNC machine interface would help to increase machine performance and productivity, but mostly help human operator to be comfortable and secure. Since nowadays, majority of the companies acquired CNC machines in order to be competitive, ergonomic and safety aspects must be considered.

5. Conclusion

In a human-machine interaction environment, machines are used to aid humans in the execution of various tasks. Therefore, human-machine interaction system should be designed to match the capabilities, limitations and characteristics of human beings. This work demonstrated that the angle of abduction and viewing angle have a marked effect on the operator's performance.

On the basis of the studies carried out, the following concluding remarks are drawn;

i. The level of angle of abduction has a significant effect on the performance of CNC-EDM operators.
ii. Findings of this work indicate that CNC-EDM systems should be re-designed so as to achieve a 45 degree angle of abduction for optimal performance.
iii. The level of viewing angle has a significant effect on the performance of CNC-EDM operators.
iv. Findings of this work indicate that CNC-EDM systems should be re-designed so as to achieve a 21 degree viewing angle for optimal performance.

The finding of this work can be directly applied to the practical field which will improve the design of a CNC-EDM system. This work suggests that those responsible for the function and operation of CNC-EDM workstations would have to redesign the system to reduce injuries, as far as visual, musculoskeletal and other related problems are concerned.

The present results are very important for the system designers of tomorrow. It is expected that more studies would be undertaken in this regard in near future and the new human-CNC machine interaction systems would be designed accordingly.

Bring to a close, the application of ergonomic principles in the design of human-CNC machine interface, would help to increase machine performance and productivity, but mostly help human operator to be comfortable and secure. Since at present time the vast majority of the companies acquired Automated Manufacturing Technology in order to be competitive, ergonomic and safety aspects must be considered.

6. Acknowledgment

The author would like to acknowledge the support provided by the national small industries corporation (NSIC), a government of India undertaking, Aligarh, India.

7. References

Alan R. H., Bente J. & Karen (2003). Intramuscular pressure and EMG relate during static concentrations but dissociate with movement and fatigue. Journal of Physiology,Vol-10, 1-31.

Antony N.T. & Keir P.J. (2010). Effects of posture, movement and hand load on shoulder muscle activity. Journal of Electromyography and Kinesiology, Vol- 20(2), 191- 198.

Ayako T., Hiroshi J., Maria B.. Villanueva G, Midori S. & Susumu S. (2002). Effects of the liquid crystal display tilt angle of a notebook computer on posture, muscle activities and somatic complaints. International journal of industrial ergonomics, Vol-29(4), 219-229.

Batten D.M., Schultz K.L. & Sluchak T.J. (1998). Optimal viewing angle for touch screen displays: Is there such a thing? International journal of industrial ergonomics, Vol-22(4-5), 343-350.

Bendix T., Krohn L., Jessen F. & Aaras A. (1985). Trunk posture and trapezius muscle load while working in standing, supported-standing, and sitting positions. Spine, Vol-10 (5), 433-439.

Burgess-Limerick, Robin, M. W., Mark C. & Vanessa L. (2000). Visual Display Height. The Journal of the Human Factors and Ergonomics Society, Vol- 42, 140-150.

Choudhury, M.D. Dewangan, K.N.. Prasanna K. G.V & Suja P.L. (2005). Anthropometric dimensions of farm youth of the north eastern region of India. International Journal of Industrial Ergonomics, Vol-35(11), 979-989.

Danuta Roman-Liu (2010). Tools of Occupational Biomechanics in Application to Reduction of MSDs. 3rd International conference on AHFE, ISBN 978-1-4398-3499-2, Miami, Florida, USA, july 2010, Book-6(37), 367-376.

David K.,.Ong C.N., Phoon W.O & Low A. (1988). Anthropometrics and display station preferences of VDU operators. Ergonomics, Vol-31(3), 337-347.

Dennerlein J.K. & Johnson P.W. (2006). Changes in upper extremity biomechanics across different mouse positions in a computer workstation. Ergonomics, Vol-49, 1456-1469.

Fine L.J., Punnett L., Keyserling W.M., Herrin G.D. & Chaffin D.B. (2000). Shoulder disorders and postural stress in automobile assembly work. Scandinavian Journal of Work, Environment and Health, Vol-26 (4), 283-291.

Fraser K., Burgess-Limerick R., Plooy A. & Ankrum D.R. (1999). The influence of computer monitor height on head and neck posture. International journal of industrial ergonomics, Vol -23(3), 171-179.

Gielo-Perczak K., Matz S. & An Kai-Nan (2006). Arm abduction strength and its relationship to shoulder geometry. Journal of Electromyography and Kinesiology, Vol-16(1), 66-78.

Gutierrez S., Levy J.C., Frankle M.A., Cuff D., Keller T.S., Pupello D.R. & Lee III W.E. (2008). Evaluation of abduction range of motion and avoidance of inferior scapular impingement in a reverse shoulder model. Journal of Shoulder and Elbow Surgery, Vol -17(4), 608-615.

Hongwei H., Daniel L. & Karl S. (2002). Anthropometric differences among occupational groups. Ergonomics, Vol-45 (2), 136-152.

Jan S., Arnaud J. & Arthur S. (2003). Posture, muscle activity and muscle fatigue in prolonged VDT work at different screen height settings. Ergonomics, Vol- 46, 714-730.

Jung-Yong K. Min-Keun C. & Ji-Soo P. (2003). Measurement of physical work capacity during arm and shoulder lifting at various shoulder flexion and ad/abduction angles. International Journal of Human Factors and Ergonomics in Manufacturing, Vol-13, 153-163.

Kong-King S. & Der-Song L. (2007). Preferred viewing distance and screen angle of electronic paper displays. Applied Ergonomics, Vol-38 (5), 601-608.

Koroemer K. H.E. & Hill S.G. (1986). Preferred line of sight angle. Ergonomics, Vol-29, 1129-1134.

Kuppuswamy A., Catley M., King N.K.K., Strutton P.H., Davey N.K. & Ellaway P.H. (2008). Cortical control of erector spinae muscles during arm abductions in humans. International Journal of Gait and Posture, Vol-27(3), 478-484.

Lehman, K.R.. Psihogios J.P & Meulenbroek R.G.J. (2001). Effects of sitting versus standing and scanner type on cashiers. Ergonomics, Vol-44, 719-738.

Levasseur A., Tetreault P., Guise J. de, Nuno N. & Hagemeister N. (2007). The effect of axis alignment on shoulder joint kinematics analysis during arm abduction. International Journal of Clinical Biomechanics, Vol-22(7), 758-766.

Mon-Williams M., Pooly A., Burgess-Limerick R. & Wann J. (1998). Gaze angle: a possible mechanism of visual stress in virtual. Ergonomics, Vol-41(3), 280-285.

Mukhopadhyay P., O'Sullivan L. & Gallwey T.J. (2007). Estimating upper limb discomfort level due to intermittent isometric pronation torque with various combinations of elbow angles, forearm rotation angles, force and frequency with upper arm at 90^0 abduction. International Journal of Industrial Ergonomics, Vol-37(4), 313-325.
Peter W. J. & Jack T. D. (2006). Different computer tasks affect the exposure of the upper extremity to biomechanical risk factors. Ergonomics, Vol-49, 45-61.
Shahnavaz H. (2009). Ergonomics intervention in industrially developing countries, Ergonomics in developing regions: Needs and applications, Taylor & Francis, 41-58.
Shahnavaz H., Naghib A. & Samadi S. (2010). Macro and Micro Ergonomic Application in a Medium Sized Company. 3rd International conference on AHFE, ISBN 978-1-4398-3499-2, Miami, Florida, USA, Book-6(35), 340-354.
Shallaly G.E. & Cuschieri A. (2006). Optimum viewing distance for laparoscopic surgery. International Journal of Surgical Endoscopy, Vol-20, 1879-1882.
Smith D.T., Ball K., Ellison A. & Schenk T. (2010). Deficits of reflexive attention induced by abduction of the eye. International Journal of Neuropsychologia, Vol-48(5), 1269-1276.
Smith, W.D. Berquer R.& Davis S. (2002). An ergonomic study of the optimum operating table height for laparoscopic surgery. Surgical Endoscopy, Vol-16, 416-421.
Susan. L. M. & Andy M. (2006). Surface EMG evaluation of sonographer scanning postures. Journal of diagnostic medical sonography, Vol-22, 298-305.
Svensson H.F. & Svensson O.K. (2001). The influence of the viewing angle on neck-load during work with video display units. Journal of Rehabilitation Medicine, Vol-33, 133 - 136.
Terrier A., Vogel A., Capezzali M. & Farron A. (2008). An algorithm to allow humerus translation in the indeterminate problem of shoulder abduction. International Journal of Medical Engineering and Physics, Vol-30(6), 710-716.
Westgaard, R. H. Aaras A. & Stranden E. (1988). Postural angles as an indicator of postural load and muscular injury in occupational work situations. Ergonomics, Vol-31 (6), 915-933.
Westlander G., Viitasara E., Johansson A. & Shahnavaz H. (1995). Evaluation of an ergonomics intervention programme in VDT workplaces. Applied ergonomics, Vol-26(2), 83-92.
Wickham J., Pizzari T., Stansfeld K., Burnside A. & Watson L. (2010). Quantifying normal shoulder muscle activity during abduction. International Journal of Electromyography and Kinesiology, Vol-20(2), 212-222.
Winer. B.J. (1971). Statistical principles in experimental design, 2nd edition, Tokyo: Mc Graw-Hill Kogakusha Ltd.
Yeow P. & Sen R. (2002).The promoters of ergonomics in industrially developing countries, their work and challenges. Proceedings: 3rd International cyberspace conference on Ergonomics, the CybErg 2002.
Yun G. L., Myung H. Y., Hong J. E. & Sang H. L. (2001). Results of a survey on the awareness and severity assessment of the upper-limb work-related musculoskeletal disorders among the female bank tellers in Korea. International Journal of Industrial Ergonomics, Vol-27, 347-357.
Yunis A.A. M. (2005). Anthropometric characteristics of the hand based on laterality and sex among Jordanian. International Journal of Industrial Ergonomics, Vol-35(8), 747-754.

Part 2

Human Robot Interaction

7

Risk Assessment and Functional Safety Analysis to Design Safety Function of a Human-Cooperative Robot

Suwoong Lee[1] and Yoji Yamada[2]
[1]*Yamagata University*
[2]*Nagoya University*
Japan

1. Introduction

Human-cooperative robots (HCRs) are expected to benefit various industries, and many studies related to physical human-robot interactions have been conducted (Moore et al., 2003; Kim et al., 2005; Tsuji et & Tanaka, 2005); some HCRs have been gradually introduced in manufacturing and welfare fields. For instance, power-assist systems in manufacturing assist workers in carrying heavy modular parts to the target site (Konosu & Yamada, 2003; Santos et al., 2010). In the welfare field, power-assisted meal-carrying carts enable caregivers to move numerous dishes at once (Fujiwara et al., 2002), and electro-hybrid wheelchairs make it easier for caregivers to move a person with weakened leg muscles (Seki et al., 2006).

Safety is regarded as a critical issue for HCRs. In particular, safety functions that can bring HCRs to a safe state in an emergency are essential because their hazardous movement may cause serious injuries to operators. The reliability of the safety functions must be sufficiently high in response to the estimated risk. Therefore, it is important to predetermine the required safety level for a HCR, to design a suitable safety function that ensures this safety level, and to analyze the validity of safety-function design.

Several attempts have been made to develop safety-design methodologies for HCRs in the related research fields. Ogorodnikova integrated several approaches related to risk estimation and safety design for a human-centered robotic work cell (Ogorodnikova, 2008). Kazanzides reported a tutorial overview of safety design for medical robots with a discussion of high-level safety requirements and methods for risk assessment (Kazanzides, 2009). Guiochet et al. studied a model-based, user-centered risk assessment that estimates the associated risks of an HCR (Guiochet et al., 2010). However, these studies mainly introduce methodologies for the overall safety design for HCRs, especially focusing on the inherent safety design, and do not present details on safety-function design involving validity analysis. On the other hand, Laible et al. studied safety-function design with a multichannel voting architecture that is based on the top-down risk assessment of an HCR (Laible et al., 2004). Okada et al. reported an example of the application of international safety-standard concepts to a robot cell-production system and showed that safety devices can be effectively used within a safety architecture (Okada et al., 2007). Nakabo et al. developed an integrated safety-function module for an HCR, which is designed to be compliant with international safety standards (Nakabo et al., 2009). However, these studies neither predetermine the safety level required by the system nor assess whether the designed safety functions match the requirement. An established safety-function design for HCRs has become a very important issue, but a methodology involving the validity analysis of safety-function design has not yet been examined.

IEC 61508, an international standard of safety-critical systems, has been gradually introduced in various industrial fields that adopt programmable controllers (IEC 61508 Technical Committee, 1998; 2002). This standard is concerned with functional safety, which is a part of the overall safety that depends on a system or equipment operating correctly in response to its inputs, and provides guidelines for not only determining the required safety-integrity level (SIL) but also analyzing the validity of safety-related system (SRS) design.

Therefore, we consider a methodology for safety-function design involving risk assesments and a functional safety analysis based on IEC 61508; this chapter introduces a case study that focuses on the system failures of an HCR in order to propose this methodology. The details of the methodology for Skill-Assist, an HCR we adopted as a platform system, are described in this chapter. Section 2 describes the outline of the Skill-Assist, and Section 3 explains the SIL determination for the Skill-Assist and risk assessments of the system failures. Section 4 describes an SRS designed on the basis of the risk-assessment results and the functional safety analysis of the SRS. The proposed methodology for safety-function design is discussed in Section 5, and the conclusion is presented in Section 6.

2. Skill-Assist

Figure 1 shows performing a task with Skill-Assist. Skill-Assist is a power assist system which is able to allow the operator to perform his/her task without disturbing the human skill by varying the virtual mechanical impedance (Konosu & Yamada, 2003). The Skill-Assist has been introduced in automobile assembly lines of a motor company, and is also expected to be applied to welfare field. Figures 2 presents the schematic overview of Skill-Assist. Skill-Assist has three degrees of freedom (DOF) and can move in transverse, traveling, and elevated directions using electric-powered actuators installed on lanes. The displacement and velocity of Skill-Assist are recorded using pulse linear encoders (Numerik JENA, RIA-22) attached to the lanes. An operator grips the lever of analog-type force sensor (Nitta, IFS-100M40A50-I63) and can maneuver the end effector of Skill-Assist to pick up and move the workload. The control computer (Advantech, IPC-610) of Skill-Assist processes sensor signals for impedance control, generates analog command signals with a D/A converter (Interface, PCI-3310), and drives the actuators using AC servo controllers (Mitsubishi, MR-J2S-40AS).

As fundamental safety measures, an enable switch is attached to the lever of the force sensor and an emergency stop switch is within close reach of the operator. Signal logic around the control system and power supply to actuators is managed by a programmable logic controller (PLC, Keyence, KV series). When the enable switch is not pushed or the emergency stop switch is pushed, the PLC disables the contactor (Mitsubishi, SD-Q19) to shut down the power supply and activates the regenerative brake (Mitsubishi, MR-RB12) simultaneously to bring Skill-Assist to a halt. Overcurrent, overheat, and openload protective functions are incorporated in the AC servo controllers.

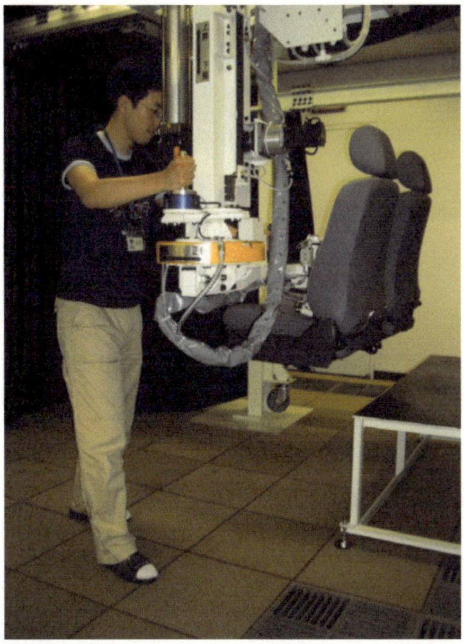

Fig. 1. Performing a task with Skill-Assist

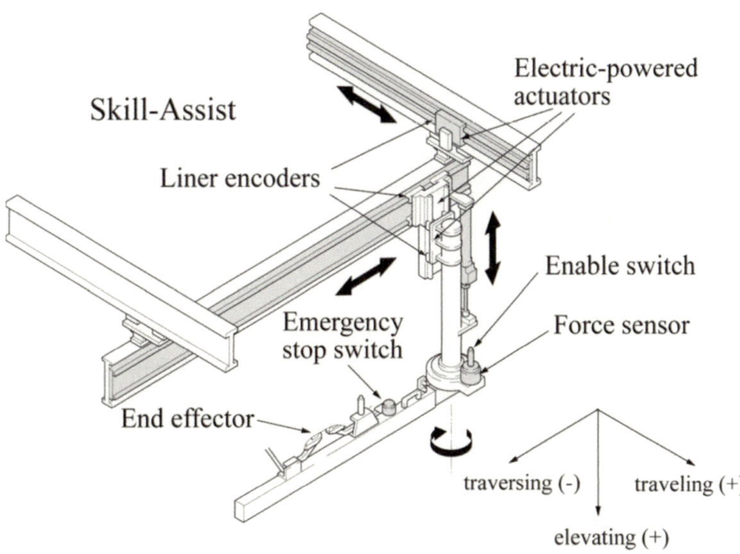

Fig. 2. Schematic overview of Skill-Assist

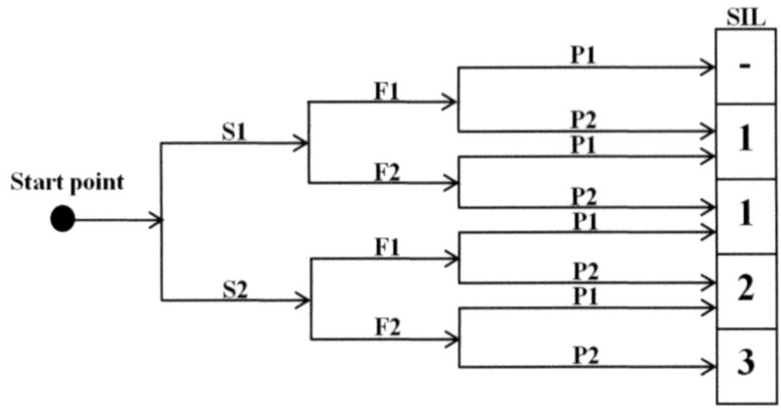

Fig. 3. Risk graph for determining required SIL

3. SIL determination and risk assessment

3.1 SIL determination for Skill-Assist

As the first step in the proposed safety-function design process, we determine the SIL for the Skill-Assist. SIL is defined in (IEC 61508 Technical Committee, 1998) as a relative level of risk reduction provided by a safety function, which is represented by SIL-1, SIL-2, SIL-3, and SIL-4. The most dependable level is SIL-4, which is required for an aircraft or a train, where catastrophic accidents can occur if the SRS fails. In general, the target SIL required for a system is determined by a qualitative or quantitative method; we use a risk graph, which is a qualitative method, for determining the target SIL from the information on risk factors (IEC 61508 Technical Committee, 1998). Fig. 3 shows the risk graph adopted in the proposed methodology and also used in the risk evaluation of a human-robot collaborative system (Behnisch, 2008; ISO Technical Committee 114, 2006). The risk graph is initiated at the start point on the left side and is implemented on the basis of risk parameters such as the severity of injury ($S1$, $S2$); the frequency of exposure to hazards ($F1$, $F2$); and the possibility of avoiding a hazard ($P1$, $P2$). The selection of the risk parameters leads to one of the five outputs on the right side, and the number at each output indicates the required SIL that must be achieved by the SRS.

3.1.1 Severity of injury ($S1$, $S2$)

$S1$ and $S2$ indicate "normally reversible injury" and "normally irreversible injury", respectively. Considering horizontal inertia (202 kg) and maximum velocity (1.43 m/s) of Skill-Assist, based on the results mentioned in (Haddadin et al., 2009), crushing or collision caused by its hazardous movement may result in a fracture-level or a serious permanent injury at worst. Hence, we select parameter $S2$ at the start point.

3.1.2 Frequency of exposure to hazards ($F1$, $F2$)

$F1$ and $F2$ indicate "seldom-to-less-often" and "frequent-to-continuous", respectively. A work-space that includes the Skill-Assist can be regarded as a hazardous zone because the operator usually makes contact with the Skill-Assist while conducting tasks. Therefore, it

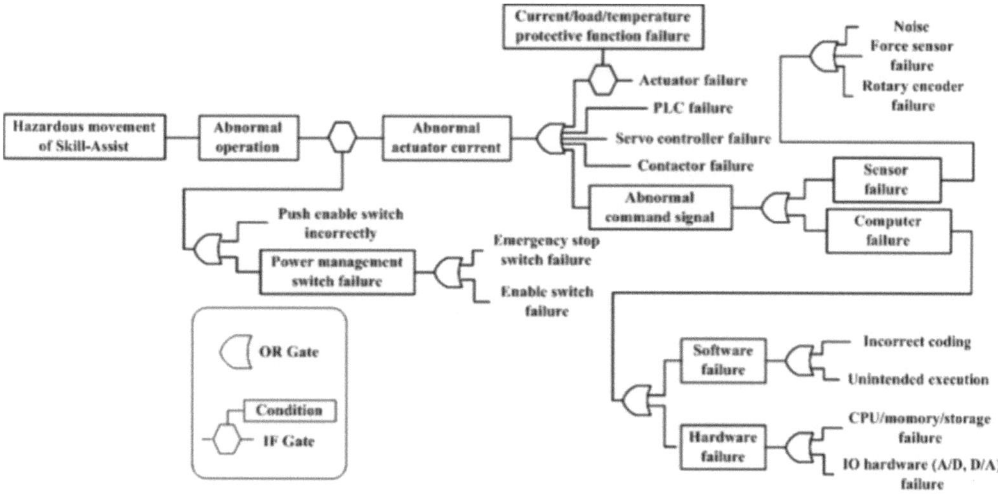

Fig. 4. Simplistic version of FTA that focuses on potential system failures

seems reasonable to assume that the operator is always exposed to the hazardous zone, and thus, we select parameter $F2$ at the second branch point.

3.1.3 Possibility of avoiding hazard ($P1$, $P2$)

$P1$ and $P2$ indicate "possible under specific conditions" and "scarcely possible", respectively. Considering the implementation of the enable and emergency stop switches, crushing or colliding caused by the hazardous movement of the Skill-Assist can be avoided by using the safety switches. Therefore, we select parameter $P1$ at the third branch point.

As a result of these risk parameters, the target SIL required for the Skill-Assist is SIL-2.

3.2 Fault Tree Analysis (FTA)

To examine the potential system failures and the appropriate safety measures against failures with unacceptable risk levels, we implement fault-tree analysis (FTA) (IEC 61025 Technical Committee, 2006).

Fig. 4 presents a simplistic version of the FTA, which focuses on the potential system failures that may cause the hazardous movement of the Skill-Assist. Note that we have omitted minor details, which are summarized in representative terms in Fig. 4, to focus on the sequence of safety-function design, because the actual FTA we conducted is more complex and too large to be represented in this chapter. The top event of the FTA is the hazardous movement of the Skill-Assist, which links to the lower-level events through IF and OR gates. The cumulative failure and simultaneous failure of multiple components are not considered in the FTA. An abnormal actuator current can be prevented if a human operator correctly pushes the power management switches or the switches normally work; otherwise, the abnormal current directly affects the movement of the Skill-Assist, resulting in crushing or colliding. The abnormal actuator current that occurs because of the failure of actuator, PLC, servo controller or contactor affects the hazardous movement of the Skill-Assist. We assume the actuator failure can be neglected if overcurrent, overheat, and openload protective functions incorporated in the AC servo controller normally work. The abnormal command signal can be

Parts	Failure mode	Effect	S	O	U	RPN	Safety measures
Force sensor	Continuous signal output	Runaway	3	2	1	6	Dual-channel voting, diverse programming
	Drift	Unstable operation	2	3	1	6	Drift compensation
	Noise (surge)	Unstable operation	2	3	1	6	Noise filter
Computer software	No output command	No operation	1	3	2	6	Dual-channel voting, diverse programming
	Continuous signal output	Runaway	3	3	2	18	Dual-channel voting, diverse programming
Computer hardware (D/A)	Continuous signal output	Runaway	3	2	1	6	Dual-channel voting, diverse programming
	Surge (short)	Unstable operation	2	3	1	6	Noise filter
PLC	Continuous signal output	Runaway	3	1	3	9	Safety PLC

Fig. 5. Simplistic version of FMEA that focuses on high RPN values

traced to sensor failures, such as noise or the malfunction of each sensor, or computer failures, such as software and hardware failures.

The FTA result enables us to easily trace the failures. Hence, we can develop safety measures for failures that may cause the hazardous movement of the Skill-Assist. For effectiveness, it is important to prioritize safety measures according to the effects and risks of the failures.

3.3 Failure Mode and Effects Analysis (FMEA)

To examine the potential failures and the appropriate safety measures against unacceptable risk levels estimated for the Skill-Assist, we next conduct a risk assessment based on a failure mode and effects analysis (FMEA) (IEC 60812 Technical Committee, 2006) on the basis of the FTA results.

In the FMEA, the consequences of a part failure are evaluated using three criteria: severity (S), likelihood of occurrence (O), and undetectability (U). The overall risk of each type of failure is called the risk priority number (RPN), which is the product of severity, occurrence, and undetectability ratings. S, O, and U have simplified ratings of low (1), medium (2), and high (3) in the proposed methodology. The ratings are each determined to suit the FMEA on the basis of the method mentioned in (IEC 60812 Technical Committee, 2006) and the experience of the control-system designers. The incidents of failure in the control system are graded on an RPN scale of 1–27, where a failure with a rating of 27 is regarded as the most hazardous.

Fig. 5 shows a simplistic version of the FMEA that especially focuses on failure modes with high risk-priority number (RPN) values. In Fig. 5, we have omitted the minor details and summarized in representative terms. The basic function of FMEA is to describe the parts of a system and to list the consequences of a part failure. The RPN threshold was determined to be four by several control-system designers. They consider it as the most suitable threshold value in the FMEA from a safety perspective, i.e., the failure modes with RPN more than the threshold are considered to be sufficiently serious to require safety measures. In Fig. 5, we categorize the severity of failure effects that may cause runaway, unstable operations, and no operation as high, medium, and low, respectively. The likelihood of the occurrence of noise and incorrect coding failure modes is rated as high. The undetectability of actuator failures are rated as low, while that of PLC is rated as high.

We then define a safety measure for each failure mode with a high RPN. For instance, a combination of dual-channel voting and diverse programming (Mitra et al., 1999; Littlewood, 2000; IEC 61508 Technical Committee, 1998) is adopted as an effective safety measure for sensor and computer failures, because it can address some common mode failures and is also recommended by a safety standard (BSR/T15.1 Technical Committee, 2002). A

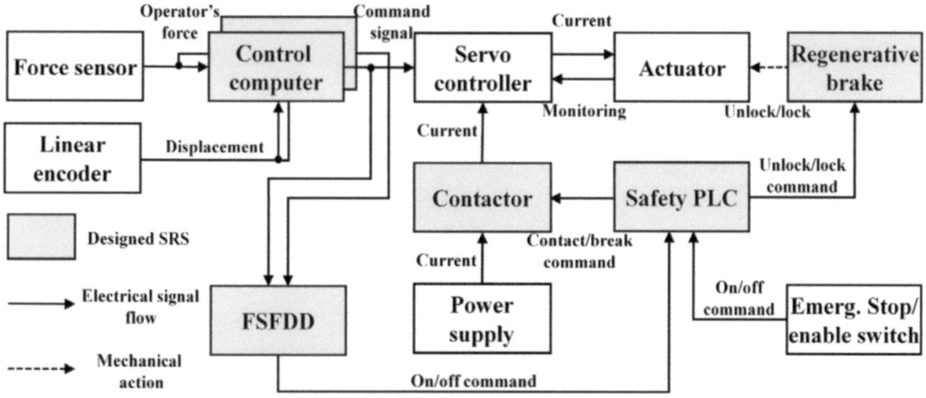

Fig. 6. Improved control system with the designed SRS

signal-monitoring function that utilizes dual-channel voting architecture is required for detecting abnormal command signal the control computer generates through the D/A converter. Safety PLC is adopted as an alternative of the PLC incorporated in the conventional control system of Skill-Assist.

4. Design of SRS and functional safety analysis based on IEC 61508

4.1 Control system for securing functional safety with the designed SRS

We design a SRS based on the risk assessment results and Fig. 6 shows an improved control system with the SRS. The designed SRS (shaded blocks in Fig. 6) consists of primary and secondary control computers, FSFDD (see also the Appendix), a safety PLC (JTEKT, TOYOPUC-PCS series), a contactor, and a regenerative brake.

The two control computers function as a dual-channel voter, diversely process sensor signals, and transfer two equivalent analog commands to the FSFDD. A force-sensor-based control algorithm is built into the primary computer and operates the Skill-Assist. Therefore, the command signal of the primary computer is also transferred to the servo controller. A diversely-programmed control algorithm is built into the secondary computer and calculates the redundant command signal to be compared with the command signal of the the primary computer. Unlike the command signal of the primary computer, that of the secondary computer is not transferred to the servo controller. Power is supplied to the DC servo motor through a contactor. The motor current is monitored by the servo controller by using the Hall-effect device.

When a fault is detected because of a difference in the command signals on the basis of the preset threshold, the FSFDD automatically shuts the power supply down and locks the drive wheels by using the contactor and regenerative brake through the safety PLC.

4.2 Configuration of the designed SRS

Fig. 7 depicts the architecture of the designed SRS. For the convenience of the functional safety analysis to be hereinafter described, the SRS is divided into the following sub-systems:

- Input sub-system: primary and secondary control computers

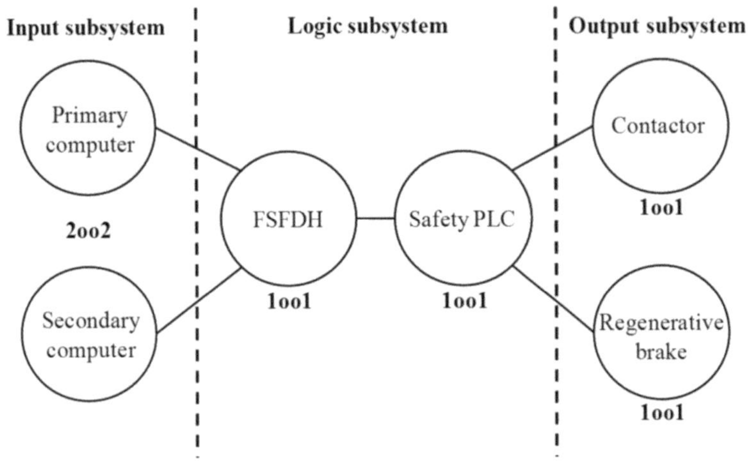

Fig. 7. Architecture of the proposed SRS

- Logic subsystem: FSFDD and safety PLC
- Output subsystem: contactor and regenerative brake

The input sub-system, which is expressed by 1 out of 2 (1oo2), enables the FSFDD to detect a fault in the command signals generated from the primary or secondary control computers. 1oo2 consists of dual channels connected in parallel, such that either channel can process the safety function. The logic sub-system comprises 1 out of 1 (1oo1) devices, where any dangerous failure leads to the failure of the safety function when a demand arises (IEC 61508 Technical Committee, 1998); therefore, in particular, the FSFDD and safety PLC involved in the logic sub-system should be highly reliable from the viewpoint of functional safety. The output sub-system comprises 1oo1 devices that can be actuated in a complementary manner in order to enhance the reliability of an emergency stop.

4.3 Process of functional safety analysis

To analyze the validity of the SRS design, we conduct functional safety analysis according to the approach mentioned in (IEC 61508 Technical Committee, 1998). We adopt the SIL, previously determined in subsection 3.1, as the quantitative criterion. Fig. 8 provides an overview of the functional safety-analysis process. First, the component failure rates, failure modes and failure mode distributions of the SRS are obtained. Second, failure modes, effects, and diagnostic analysis (FMEDA) [1] is implemented to examine the effects of the failure modes on the SRS (Goble et al., 1999). Next, the safety-failure fraction (SFF) and the probability of failures per hour (PFH) are calculated on the basis of the result of FMEDA in order to examine whether the target SIL has been achieved (IEC 61508 Technical Committee, 1998). Note that the evaluation process for the SRS software is not considered in Fig. 8, and we only consider the hardware of the designed SRS.

[1] FMEDA is a different process from FMEA.

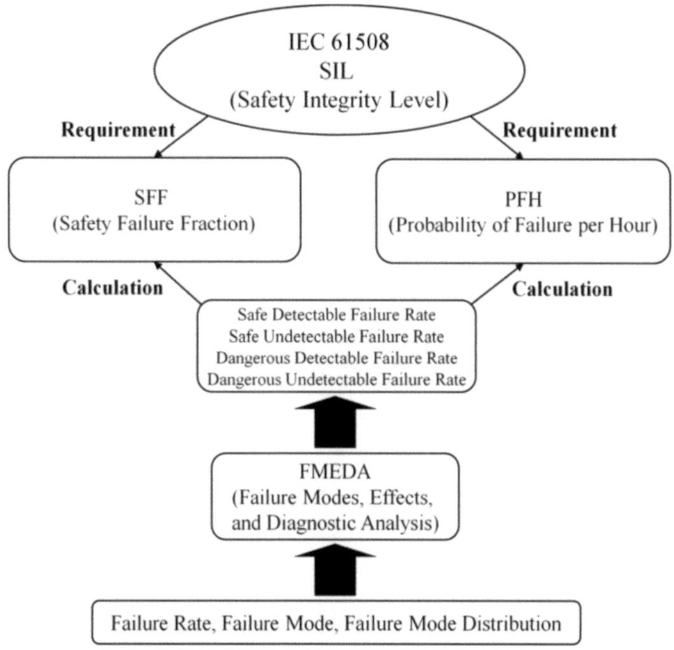

Fig. 8. Process of functional safety analysis

4.3.1 FMEDA

FMEDA is one of the steps required for analyzing the functional safety of a device. Fig. 9 shows a part of the FMEDA conducted for the FSFDD. Failure-in-time (FIT) denotes the unit of failure rate, and 1 FIT represents 10^{-9} failures per hour. In the FMEDA, we refer to (MIL-HDBK-217F Technical Committee, 1991) and (IEC 62380 Technical Committee, 2004) as references for the failure rate, failure mode, and failure mode distribution. The safe detectable, safe undetectable, dangerous detectable, and dangerous undetectable failure rates are denoted by λ_{sd}, λ_{su}, λ_{dd} and λ_{du} respectively and calculated as the result of the FMEDA. Furthermore, the safe failure rate λ_s, dangerous failure rate λ_d, and total failure rate λ of a component have the following relationships:

$$\lambda_s = \lambda_{sd} + \lambda_{su} \tag{1}$$

$$\lambda_d = \lambda_{dd} + \lambda_{du} \tag{2}$$

$$\lambda = \lambda_s + \lambda_d \tag{3}$$

A failure that gives an FSFDD output of 0 V and shuts down the power source of the actuator is considered to be a detectable failure, irrespective of whether it is safe or dangerous. A failure that does not change the output signal is considered to be a safe undetectable failure, whereas a failure that causes oscillations, drift, or surge in the output signal is considered to be a dangerous undetectable failure. A circuit simulator Micro-Cap 9.0 (Spectrum Software) is utilized for examining the effects of the failure modes.

FMEDA for the simply configured electrical components such as power switch and EM brake is conducted in a manner similar to that for the FSFDD. However, for complex components such as the control computer, where a detailed analysis of each failure

Parts	ID	Function	Failure mode	Effects of failure	FIT	Failure probability	Safe/dangerous failure mode	Detectable/undetectable failure mode	λ_{sd}	λ_{su}	λ_{dd}	λ_{du}	Remarks
Capacitor (Fixed ceramic dielectric capacitor)	C2	Stabilizing input signal to regulator 78M05F	Short	Continuous signal output	12.6	70%	Dangerous	Undetectable				8.82	
			Open	No output		10%	Safe	Detectable	1.26				
			Drift	No output		20%	Safe	Undetectable			2.52		
Variable resistor	VR1	Adjusting threshold of FS49B	Open	No output	138	80%	Safe	Detectable	110				
			Drift	No output		20%	Safe	Undetectable		27.6			
Transformer	T1	Rectifying output signal of FS57C	Short	Surge signal output	144	20%	Dangerous	Detectable			28.8		
			Open	No output		80%	Safe	Detectable	115				

Fig. 9. A part of FMEDA

SFF	Hardware fault tolerance		
	0	1	2
~60%	Not Acceptable	SIL1	SIL2
60%–90%	SIL1	SIL2	SIL3
90%–99%	SIL2	SIL3	SIL4
99%~	SIL3	SIL4	SIL4

Table 1. Architectural constraints determined by SFF and SIL

mode is impossible, a division of failures up to 50% λ_s and 50% λ_d is generally accepted (IEC 61508 Technical Committee, 1998). Furthermore, λ_{dd} and λ_{du} of the complex components are determined under the assumption that they have high diagnostic coverage (DC), which is expressed by following equation (IEC 61508 Technical Committee, 1998):

$$DC = \frac{\sum \lambda_{dd}}{\sum \lambda_d} \tag{4}$$

where $\sum$ denotes the summation of the failure rates of the components involved in each sub-system.

4.3.2 SFF

SFF is a parameter that specifies the architectural constraints required for an SRS (IEC 61508 Technical Committee, 1998). SFF can be calculated as follows:

$$SFF = \frac{\sum \lambda_s + \sum \lambda_{dd}}{\sum \lambda} \tag{5}$$

Table 1 shows the architectural constraints determined by SFF and SIL. A hardware fault tolerance of N indicates that N + 1 faults can cause a loss of the safety function. Because even a single fault cannot be allowed in the lool and loo2 architectures, in order to maintain the safety function, the architectures of all sub-systems in the designed SRS should meet an SFF in the range of 90%–99% to satisfy the target requirements of SIL-2.

SIL	PFH
4	$\geq 10^{-9}$ to $< 10^{-8}$
3	$\geq 10^{-8}$ to $< 10^{-7}$
2	$\geq 10^{-7}$ to $< 10^{-6}$
1	$\geq 10^{-6}$ to $< 10^{-5}$

Table 2. SILs according to PFH in high demand or continuous operation modes

4.3.3 PFH

The SIL of an SRS in high demand or continuous operational modes is measured by the PFH of the safety function, which must be low enough to achieve the required SIL (IEC 61508 Technical Committee, 1998). According to Table 2, which shows the relationship between the SIL and the PFH, the designed SRS must satisfy a PFH in the range of 10^{-7}–10^{-6} to achieve the target requirements of SIL-2.

The PFHs of the lool and loo2 architectures, PFH_{1oo1} and PFH_{1oo2}, respectively, are obtained by the following equations (IEC 61508 Technical Committee, 1998):

$$PFH_{1oo1} = \sum \lambda_{du} \tag{6}$$

$$PFH_{1oo2} = 2\left((1-\beta_d)\sum \lambda_{dd} + (1-\beta)\sum \lambda_{du}\right)^2 t_{ce} + \beta_d \sum \lambda_{dd} + \beta \sum \lambda_{du} \tag{7}$$

$$t_{ce} = \frac{\sum \lambda_{du}}{\sum \lambda_d}\left(\frac{T_1}{2} + MTTR\right) + \frac{\sum \lambda_{dd}}{\sum \lambda_d} MTTR \tag{8}$$

where β and β_d represent the fraction of common-cause failures that are undetected and detected by the diagnostic tests, respectively. The channel-equivalent mean down time, the interval of the periodic diagnostic test, and the total elapsed time from the initial failure to the reinitialization of the system status (mean time to repair) are represented by t_{ce}, T_1, and $MTTR$, respectively. Note that the unit of measurement for t_{ce}, T_1, and $MTTR$ is h.

4.4 Result of functional safety analysis

Table 3 summarizes the failure rates, SFF, and PFH that are acquired as a result of the functional safety analysis for the designed SRS. Each λ is provided by the manufacturers or determined by the failure-rate data obtained from (MIL-HDBK-217F Technical Committee, 1991; IEC 62380 Technical Committee, 2004). On the basis of the FMEDA results, we can determine λ_s, λ_{dd}, and λ_{du} for the SRS components. The SFFs of all the sub-systems are calculated using Eqs. (1), (3), and (5). The PFH of the input sub-system, which is configured with the loo2 architecture, is calculated using Eqs. (7) and (8), where $\beta = 20\%$ and $\beta_d = 10\%$ as the worst case, $T_1 = 8760$ h (one year), and $MTTR = 8$ h, on the basis of the parameter range in a typical example of the functional safety analysis (IEC 61508 Technical Committee, 1998). The PFHs of the logic and output sub-systems, which are configured with the lool architecture, are calculated using Eq. (6). The result of the functional safety analysis in Table 3 suggests that all sub-systems of the SRS are able to satisfy the target requirements of SIL-2, i.e., they have the SFFs in the range of 90%–99% and the PFHs in the range of 10^{-7}–10^{-6}.

Subsystem	Item	Failure rates ($\times 10^{-6}$)				SFF	PFH
		λ	λ_s	λ_{dd}	λ_{du}		
Input subsystem (1oo2)	Control computer	11.60	5.80	5.37	0.43	96%	3.3×10^{-7}
Logic subsystem	FSFDD	2.57	0.47	2.07	0.03	99%	4.0×10^{-8}
(1oo1)	Safety PLC	0.26	0.13	0.12	0.01		
Output subsystem	Regenerative brake	0.58	0.29	0.23	0.06	90%	1.6×10^{-7}
(1oo1×2)	Contactor	1.00	0.50	0.40	0.10		

Table 3. Result of functional safety analysis

5. Discussion

The sources of hazards in HCRs can be largely divided into human errors, the environment in which humans and robots interact, and the robot itself (Dhillon & Fashandi, 1997; Yamada et al., 1999; Alvarado, 2002). This research introduced a case study that focused on a robot, especially with regard to its system failures. The system failures of the robot could be identified by relatively simple risk assessments such as FTA, and the functional safety analysis was conducted by calculating the failure rates of different sub-systems the designed SRS comprises. Moreover, all equations in the functional safety analysis were deterministic and linear and all parameters in these equations took constant values; the parameters determined the SFF and PFH. However, if an operator and a robot are treated as a man-machine system, a human-robot cooperative system is stochastic and nonlinear, and in this case, human factors should be addressed by more sophisticated safety-analysis approaches. Therefore, the proposed methodology is limited to the design of the safety function for system failures and cannot be directly applied to other safety functions that can prevent hazardous events caused by human factors. To design the safety function for an HCR in consideration of human factors, human-behavior analysis must be considered, and the risk-analysis techniques proposed in related studies such as (Guiochet, 2003; Ogorodnikova, 2008; Ogure et al., 2009) may give us some hints for doing so.

From the viewpoint of safety-design issues of HCRs, conventional studies such as (Ogorodnikova, 2008; Kazanzides, 2009; Guiochet et al., 2010) mainly present methodologies that focus on the inherent safety design based on risk assessments. For instance, (Guiochet et al., 2010) proposes an approach based on a combination of well-known safety-analysis techniques and applies this approach to the safety design for an HCR. However, these studies do not present details of how to design the safety function for HCRs. On the other hand, (Laible et al., 2004), (Okada et al., 2007), and (Nakabo et al., 2009) propose design methodologies for the safety function for HCRs. However, they neither predetermine the safety level required by the system nor assess whether the designed safety functions match the requirement. The significance of our study compared to conventional studies is that the proposed methodology for safety-function design systematically evolves from a process of predetermining the safety level to that of analyzing it; the methodology enables the design of an adequate safety function for an HCR and provides an analysis process with the required safety level. We believe that the proposed methodology can be applied to safety-function design for system failures of HCRs such as power-assist systems or industrial robots with a hands-on control mode.

A dual-channel architecture can detect a fault that occurs in any one channel at a time. Therefore, if a component that is commonly connected to both channels causes a fault, a dual-channel voter such as FSFDD cannot detect the fault, because the same abnormal signals would be generated from the channels. Furthermore, the analog voting architecture proposed in this study limits the flexibility of the system configuration and has low performance in terms of noise tolerance. In the future, we will investigate the design of a dual-channel architecture that can address the simultaneous failure of both channels using digital processing.

A functional safety analysis of the software also needs to be implemented for an SRS involving programmable controllers. Unlike the case of hardware, which adopts a probabilistic approach as introduced in this paper, a software analysis is generally conducted by deterministic approaches and a specified software-development lifecycle (IEC 61508 Technical Committee, 1998). In particular, the method described in (IEC 61508 Technical Committee, 1998) concretely suggests software techniques, including safety specifications, architecture design, and programming languages, to be adopted in an SRS according to the required SIL. Such a functional safety analysis for software is also necessary for the proposed methodology, and the integration of safety-function design approaches for hardware and software should be discussed in the future.

System stability is an important issue related to the safety of HCRs. To stabilize a human-robot cooperative system constantly, it is primarily required to design a robust controller that can minimize the effects of uncertain factors in the system. As an additional safety measure, it is also required to establish a safety guideline for operators that prohibits aggressive maneuvering, which can cause the unstable movements of the system. The proposed methodology does not include the analysis for system stability because it focuses on the validity analysis of the safety-function design based on IEC 61508. To introduce the system-stability problem to the proposed methodology, it is necessary to analyze the maneuvering patterns of operators and the dynamics in the physical human-robot interaction, to quantify the analysis results to numerical parameters, and to apply these parameters to the process of safety-function design. Further discussion of how to implement system-stability analysis in the proposed methodology is an issue in the future.

6. Conclusion

In this chapter, we introduced a methodology for safety-function design involving functional safety analysis by using a case study on the system failures of the Skill-Assist. First, the target SIL required for the Skill-Assist was determined and the top-down and bottom-up risk assessments were then conducted. An SRS with two control computers, an FSFDD, and a safety PLC was designed on the basis of the risk-assessment results. We conducted a functional safety analysis for the designed SRS and found that it satisfied the target SIL.

7. Appendix – Fail-Safe Fault Detection Device (FSFDD): Signal-monitoring function for the analog voting architecture

Because an analog command signal is used in conventional control system of the Skill-Assist, we use an analog signal voting scheme to simplify the dual-channel architecture of the control computers. The analog voting scheme is also beneficial in simplifying the safety-related signal process once adequate measures are taken against noise. A fail-safe fault detection device (FSFDD) that we have developed can detect a fault by comparing the analog command

Fig. 10. Fail-safe fault detection device (FSFDD)

signals generated by the dual-channel control computer, and it reflects the result of the fault detection in the output signal (Lee & Yamada, 2007; 2009). By monitoring the command signals, the FSFDD is able to indirectly detect not only computer hardware/software failures, but also sensor failures that can cause hazardous movement of Skill-Assist. Fig. 10 shows the current version of the FSFDD. The fail-safe devices that dominate the FSFDD have the unique characteristic of generating an AC signal when the preset conditions for the input signals are met, and a constant DC signal otherwise (Kato, 1993; Sakai et al., 2000). The characteristics of fail-safe devices used in the FSFDD limit the effects of an internal failure on the output signal. Thus, the possibility of the FSFDD output signal reaching the inactive state of 0 V is high if if a fault is detected in the command signals or its components fail. A noise filter circuit is incorporated into the input terminal of the FSFDD to smoothen the high-frequency noise in the command signals. More details on the FSFDD have been completely documented in studies (Lee & Yamada, 2007; 2009; Kato, 1993; Sakai et al., 2000).

8. References

Moore, C., Peshkin, M., & Colgate, E. (2003). Cobot implementation of virtual paths and 3D virtual surfaces, *IEEE Transactions on Robotics and Automation*, 19 (2): 347–351, ISSN 1042-296X

Kim, Y., Lee, J., Lee, S., & Kim, M. (2005). A force reflected exoskeleton-type masterarm for human-robot interaction, *IEEE Transactions on Systems, Man and Cybernetics, Part A: Systems and Humans*, 35(2): 198–212, ISSN 1083-4427

Tsuji, T., & Tanaka, Y. (2005). Tracking control properties of human-robotic systems based on impedance control, *IEEE Transactions on Systems, Man and Cybernetics, Part A: Systems and Humans*, 35(4): 523–535, ISSN 1083-4427

Konosu, H., & Yamada, Y., (2003). Skill-Assist: assisting device helping human workers in automobile modular component assembly, *Proc. of IEEE/RSJ International Conference on Intelligent Robots and Systems*, pp.2514–2515, Las Vegas, USA.

Santos, P. G., Garcia, E., Sarria, J., Ponticelli, R., & Reviejo, J. (2010). A new manipulator structure for power-assist devices, *Industrial Robot: An International Journal*, 37(5): 452–458, ISSN 0143-991X

Fujiwara, S., Kitano, H., Yamashita, H., Maeda, H., & Fukunaga, H. (2002). Omni-directional cart with power assist system, *Journal of Robotics and Mechatronics*, 14(4): 931–937, ISSN 0143-991X

Seki, H., Iijima, T., Minakata, H., & Tadakuma, S. (2006). Novel step climbing control for power assisted wheelchair based on driving mode switching, *Proc. of IEEE Int. Conf. on Industrial Electronics*, pp. 3827–3832, Paris, France

Ogorodnikova, O. (2008). Methodology of safety for a human robot interaction designing stage", *Proc. of IEEE Int. Conf. on Human System Interactions*, pp. 452–457, Krakow, Poland

Kazanzides, P. (2009). Safety design for medical robots, *Proc. of Int. Conf. of the IEEE Engineering in Medicine and Biology Society*, pp. 7208–7211, Minneapolis, USA

Guiochet, J., Martin-Guillerez, D., & Powell, D. (2010). Experience with model-based user-centered risk assessment for service robots, *Proc. of 2010 IEEE 12th International Symposium on High-Assurance Systems Engineering*, pp. 104 -113, San Jose, USA

Laible, U., Bürger, T., & Pritschow, G. (2004). A fail-safe dual-channel robot control for surgery applications, *Safety Science*, 42(5): 423–436, ISSN 0925-7535

Okada, K., Maeda, I., Sugano, Y., Higuchi, & N., Fujita, T. (2007). Risk assessment of robot cell production system that achieved high productivity and safety in HMI environment, *Proc. of Int. Conf. on Safety of Industrial Automated Systems*, pp. 181–186, Tokyo, Japan

Nakabo, Y., Saito, H., Ogure, T., Jeong, S., & Yamada, Y. (2009). Development of a safety module for robots sharing workspace with humans, *Proc. of 2009 IEEE/RSJ Int. Conf. on Intelligent Robots and Systems*, pp. 5345–5349, St. Louis, USA

IEC 61508 Technical Committee (1998). *IEC 61508, Functional Safety of Electrical /Electronic/Programmable Electronic (E/E/PE) Safety Related Systems, Part 1: General Requirements*, IEC, Geneva, Swiss

IEC 61508 Technical Committee (2002). *Functional safety and IEC 61508 – A basic guide*, IEC, Geneva, Swiss

Homma, K., Yamada, Y., Matsumoto, O., Ono, E., Lee, S., Horimoto, M., Suzuki, T., Kanehira, N., Suzuki, T., & Shiozawa, S. (2009). A proposal of a method to reduce burden of excretion care using robot technology, *Proc. of IEEE 11th Int. Conf. on Rehabilitation Robotics*, pp.621–625, Kyoto, Japan

IEC 61508 Technical Committee (1998). *IEC 61508, Functional Safety of Electrical/ Electronic/Programmable Electronic (E/E/PE) Safety Related Systems, Part 5: Examples of Methods for the Determination of Safety Integrity Levels*, IEC, Geneva, Swiss

Behnisch, K. (2008). *White Paper Safe Collaboration with ABB Robots Electronic Position Switch and SafeMove*, ABB, Zurich, Switzerland.

ISO Technical Committee 114 (2006). *ISO13849-1, Safety of Machinery – Safety-Related Parts of Control Systems – Part 1: General Principles for Design*, ISO, Zurich, Switzerland.

Haddadin, S., Albu-Schäffer, A., & Hirzinger, G. (2009). Requirements for safe robots: measurements, analysis and new insights, *The International Journal of Robotics Research*, 28(11-12): 1507–1527, ISSN 1741-3176

IEC 61025 Technical Committee (2006). *IEC 61025, Fault Tree Analysis (FTA)*, IEC, Geneva, Swiss

IEC 60812 Technical Committee (2006). *IEC 60812, Analysis Techniques for System Reliability - Procedure for Failure Mode and Effects Analysis (FMEA)*, IEC, Geneva, Swiss

Mitra, S., Saxena, N. R., & McCluskey, E. J. (1999). A design diversity metric and reliability analysis for redundant systems, *Proc. of International Test Conf.*, pp. 662–671, Atlantic City, USA

Littlewood, B., Popov, P.T., Strigini, L., & Shryane, N. (2000). Modeling the effects of combining diverse software fault detection techniques, *IEEE Transactions on Software Engineering*, 26(12): 1157–1169, ISSN 0098-5589

IEC 61508 Technical Committee (1998). *IEC 61508, Functional Safety of Electrical/Electronic/Programmable Electronic Safety Related Systems, Part 6: Guidelines on the Application of IEC 61508-2 and IEC 61508-3*, IEC, Geneva Swiss

BSR/T15.1 Technical Committee (2002). *Draft Standard for Trial Use for Intelligent Assist Devices – Personnel Safety Requirements*, RIA, Ann Arbor, USA

Goble, W. M., & Brombacherb, A.C. (1999). Using a failure modes, effects and diagnostic analysis (FMEDA) to measure diagnostic coverage in programmable electronic systems, *Reliability Engineering and System Safety*, 66(2): 145–148, ISSN 0951-8320

MIL-HDBK-217F Technical Committee (1991). *Military Handbook 217F (MIL-HDBK-217F), Reliability Prediction of Electronic Equipment*, US Department of Defense, Arlington, USA

IEC 62380 Technical Committee (2004). *IEC TR 62380, Reliability Data Handbook - Universal Model for Reliability Prediction of Electronics Components, PCBs and Equipment*, IEC, Geneva Swiss

Dhillon, B., & Fashandi, A. (1997). Safety and reliability assessment techniques in robotics, *Robotica*, 15(6): 701-708, ISSN 0263-5747

Yamada, Y., Yamamoto, T., Morizono, T., & Umetani, Y. (1999). FTA-based issues on securing human safety in a human/robot coexistence system, *Proc. of IEEE Int. Conf. on Systems, Man and Cybernetics*, pp. II1058–1063,, Tokyo, Japan

Alvarado, M. (2002). *A Risk Assessment of Human-Robot Interface Operations to Control the Potential of Injuries/Losses at the XYZ Manufacturing Company (Master's thesis)*, University of Wisconsin-Stout, Menomonie, USA

Guiochet, J., Motet, G., Baron, C. & Boy, G. (2003). Integration of UML in human factors analysis for safety of a medical robot for tele-echography, *Proc of IEEE Int. Conf. on Intelligent Robots and Systems*, pp. 3212–3217, Las Vegas, USA

Ogorodnikova, O. (2008). Human weaknesses and strengths in collaboration with robots, *Periodica Polytechnica*, 25(33): 25–33,

Ogure, T., Nakabo, Y., Jeong, S., Yamada, Y. (2009). Hazard analysis of an industrial upper-body humanoid, *Industrial Robot -An International Journal*, 36(5): 469-476, ISSN 0143-991X

IEC 61508 Technical Committee, *IEC 61508, Functional Safety of Electrical/Electronic/Programmable Electronic (E/E/PE) Safety Related Systems, Part 3: Software Requirements*, IEC, Geneva, Swiss

Lee, S., & Yamada, Y. (2007). A highly-reliable force control system with a fail-safe fault detecting hardware for functional safety of Skill-Assist, *Proc. of Int. Conf. - Safety of Industrial Automated Systems*, pp. 403–408, Tokyo, Japan

Lee, S., & Yamada, Y. (2009). Skill-Assist safety and intelligence technology, *International Journal of Automation Technology*, 3(6): 643–652, ISSN 1881-7629

Kato, M. (1993). LSI implementation and safety verification of window comparator used in fail-safe multiple valued logic operations, *IEICE Transactions on Electronics*, E76-C(3): 356–366, ISSN : 1745–1353

Sakai, M., Shirai, T., Mukaidono, M. (2000). A construction method of fail-safe interlocking module based on separation between safety-related parts and non-safety-related parts, *Proc. of 4th Int. Conf. on Engineering Design and Automation*, pp. 966-971, Orlando, USA

8

Improving Safety of Human-Robot Interaction Through Energy Regulation Control and Passive Compliant Design

Matteo Laffranchi, Nikos G. Tsagarakis and Darwin G. Caldwell
Department of Advanced Robotics, Istituto Italiano di Tecnologia
Italy

1. Introduction

Modern production processes continuously require enhancement in production time and the quality of the products. The use of robots in this field of application has formed an increasingly important aspect of the drive for efficiency. These robots typically work in restricted areas to prevent any harmful interaction with humans and are designed for repeatability, speed and precision. However, new opportunities are arising in homes and offices that mean that robots will not be confined to these relatively restricted factory environments and this sets new demands in terms of safety and ability to interact with the environment. These new requirements make industrial heavy and stiff manipulators controlled with high gain PID controllers not suited to cooperate and work closely with humans. In order to cope with this, impedance control (Hogan, 1985; Ikeura and Inooka, 1995; Zollo, Siciliano et al., 2002; Zollo, Siciliano et al., 2003) for decreasing the replicated output impedance of the system to safe values and safety-oriented control strategies (Heinzmann and Zelinsky, 1999; Bicchi and Tonietti, 2004; Kulic and Croft, 2004) to react safely when a Human-Robot Interaction is detected have been introduced. The mentioned control algorithms work well for slow interaction transients and within specific frequency bands, however when the frequencies are above the closed loop bandwidth of the robot, these strategies are ineffective in reacting safely making the resulting system to be dangerous. When a sudden and fast impact occurs, the output impedance of the robot is dominated by the link and the rotor reflected inertia. This latter term is usually high due to the high reduction ratio of the gear making the overall robot output impedance large and dangerous meaning that the system's safety is once again compromised. An alternative to this "active" approach is the incorporation of intrinsically safe structures particularly focusing on the actuation systems design. Several actuator prototypes have been developed embedding either passive compliant elements in the structure (Pratt and Williamson, 1995; Sugar, 2002; Yoon, Kang et al., 2003; Hurst, Chestnutt et al., 2004; Zinn, Khatib et al., 2004; Hollander, Sugar et al., 2005; Tonietti, Schiavi et al., 2005; Schiavi, Grioli et al., 2008; Tsagarakis, Laffranchi et al., 2009; Catalano, Grioli et al., 2010; Jafari, Tsagarakis et al., 2010; Tsagarakis, Laffranchi et al., 2010) or, more recently, clutches/damping devices (Lauzier and Gosselin, 2011; Shafer and Kermani, 2011) to decouple the link (i.e. the part usually interacting with the human) from the rotor during interaction with either the environment or people. Considering the first class of actuation devices, compliance is not only beneficial from the safety perspective but it also can be used to gain higher energy efficiency levels (Jafari, Tsagarakis et al., 2011), as protection from shock loads, (Kajikawa and Abe, 2010) or to achieve mechanical power peaks which could not be obtained with a stiff structure (Laffranchi, Tsagarakis et al., 2009). Series Elastic Actuators (SEAs) are a particular class of actuators with passive compliance (Pratt and Williamson, 1995; Sugar, 2002; Zinn, Khatib et al., 2004; Hollander, Sugar et al., 2005; Tsagarakis, Laffranchi et al., 2009). They employ a fixed stiffness passive elastic element located between the actuator-gear group and the output link. The introduced decoupling action makes the high frequency output impedance to be dominated by the link inertia only, removing the effect of the actuator's reflected inertia which dominates in rigid robots. In addition, its main disadvantage of the preset passive mechanical compliance can be at some degree minimized by combining the unit with an active stiffness control. From what has been mentioned previously it can be concluded that the implementation of a safety-oriented control algorithm on an inherently compliant system (e.g. SEA) can guarantee the safety of the Human-Robot Interaction over the frequency spectrum.

Although no standard is defined for such "human friendly" robots[1], the safety of a robotic structure is usually characterized by means of safety indexes which were developed in fields that are different from robotics. A well known safety criterion is the Head Injury Criterion, or HIC (Versace, 1971) which was born in the automotive industry and has been used in robotics in (Haddadin, Albu-Schaffer et al., 2008; Bicchi and Tonietti, 2004; Zinn, Khatib et al., 2004). These indexes are based on tests made on human and animal cadavers consisting in the replication of collisions where the orders of magnitude of the physical variables (e.g. velocity) are significantly different from those of a generic robotic system. In addition, the computation of this index uses only the acceleration of the head during the impact, without taking into account the sequence of events and the boundary conditions. For instance, it does not distinguish between the case of a collision with a free head or a collision with a clamped head, despite the fact that the risks are very different for the two cases (Haddadin, Albu-Schaffer et al., 2008). It is clear from the above that these criteria are not suited to characterize the safety of a robotic system. In addition, as far as the HIC is concerned, the complexity and the computation requirements of this index make difficult the real time implementation of this criterion within the control system of a robotic device in order to ensure safety.

Motivated by these demands this Chapter presents an approach which enhances Human-Robot Interaction safety by combining a passive compliant actuator with a control technique, based on the regulation of the energy stored in the robotic system, with the aim of limiting this energy to specified safe energy thresholds. These maximum safe values are obtained by analysing collisions against a constrained and a free head and experimental data of energy absorption to failure of cranium bones and cervical spines. The proposed Energy Regulation Control (ERC) has been applied on a series elastic actuator (SEA) to evaluate the presented concept. ERC is a position-based controller that modifies the trajectory reference as a function of the maximum energy value imposed by the user. The

[1] The International Organization for Standardization (ISO) defines guidelines and requirements for inherent safe design, information for use and protective measures for use of industrial robots, (ISO-10218-1, 2006; ISO-10218-2, 2011). Their aim is to provide guidelines to reduce risks associated with industrial robots, however they do not apply to non-industrial robots as those considered in this work.

proposed control method is designed, simulated and tested on a prototype series elastic robotic joint. The experimental results show the capability of the combined unit in limiting the system stored energy to the maximum set threshold. The presented strategy is designed, simulated and evaluated on a prototype series elastic robotic joint. The paper is structured as follows: the critical human-robot interaction scenarios considered in this work are analysed in Section 2 which also reports on the calculation of the safety thresholds and on the energy exchange during collisions. Section 3 introduces the dynamic model of the series elastic actuator prototype used in this work and the energy regulation control scheme. Section 4 presents a simulation analysis with section 5 validating the effectiveness of the control strategy by means of experimental results. Section 6 covers the conclusions and future work.

2. Critical scenarios in human-robot Interaction and related safe energy thresholds

2.1 Critical human-robot collision scenarios

In this study, the collision between the robot and the human head is considered as a reference case since the head is one of the most delicate parts of the human body. Two collision cases are analyzed. In the first case, Figure 1a, the robot is colliding against a clamped head, while in the second case the robot is colliding against a free head which can therefore accelerate after the collision with the robot link.

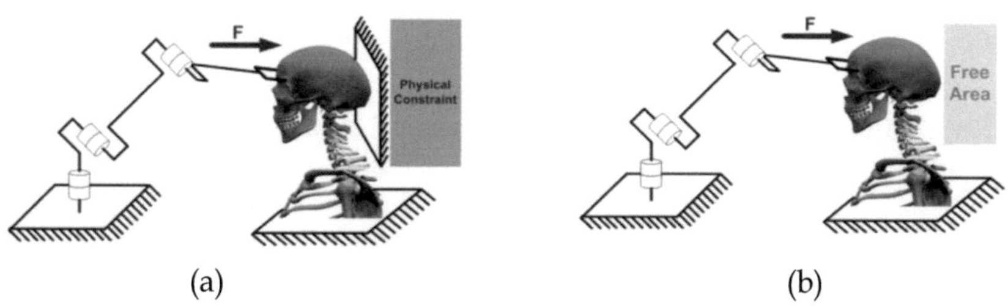

Fig. 1. (a) Constrained and (b) free head impact scenarios.

In the first case the impact forces are only exerted on the skull bones, while in the second case, after the first stage of the impact, the head can be subject of high acceleration/velocity motion exerting stress on the neck that can be equally or more significant than the stress exerted on the skull bones. In the first case the energy absorbed by the human cranial bone is examined, while for the second case it is useful to take also into consideration the energy absorbed by the human upper cervical bone.

2.2 Safe energy thresholds for the cranial bone in the constrained head collision scenario

Data on the amount of energy required to cause the failure of the cranial bones can be found in (Wood, 1971; Margulies and Thibault, 2000). In (Wood, 1971) skulls of adult humans were exposed to dynamic tests with stress rates ranging from 0.005 s^{-1} to 150 s^{-1}. The results show that the energy absorbed to failure is constant over the frequency spectrum (Wood, 1971) meaning that this parameter is independent of the collision velocity. The above suggests that bounding the energy level of the robotic device can be a suitable strategy which can guarantee low accidental risks during collisions between the robot and the human. From (Wood, 1971) the linear regression of the values of energy absorbed to failure measured in 120 specimens over the spectrum returns an energy/volume ratio of $\varepsilon_{failure\_adult} \approx 0.29$ mJ $\cdot$mm^{-3}.

The volume of the cranium can be computed using the following formula from (Manjuath, 2002):

$$V_{adult\_head} \cong 0.5238 \cdot L \cdot B \cdot H \tag{1}$$

Where L is the maximum antero-posterior length of the skull, B is the breadth and H is the height. For the typical adult skull L = 196 mm, B = 155 mm, H = 112 mm (Tilley and Associates, 1993). By multiplying (1) with the energy/volume ratio, the energy level that can cause the failure of a typical adult skull can be derived to be equal to:

$$\varepsilon_{ABS\_failure\_adult} = \varepsilon_{failure\_adult} \cdot V_{adult\_head} \cong 517\,J \tag{2}$$

The above energy level is just an indicative value of the energy required to break a typical adult human skull. In this work a more conservative level is considered in order to prevent not only the failure of the skull bone but also to minimize the risk of a serious injury. Such a conservative level can be the energy required to produce the same effects on an infant human head instead of an adult human head. In contrast to the stiff adult cranium, the infant skull is a compliant structure capable of substantial deformation under external loading and is thus much more delicate. In (Margulies and Thibault, 2000) experiments were carried out to check the rupture of the three-point bending at two velocity rates: in a first case a quasi-static excitation is forced on the cranium with the velocity of the loading nose equal to 2.5mm/min ($42.3 \cdot 10^{-6}$ m/s), while in the second case the loading nose is moving at a velocity that is 2540mm/min ($42.3 \cdot 10^{-3}$ m/s).

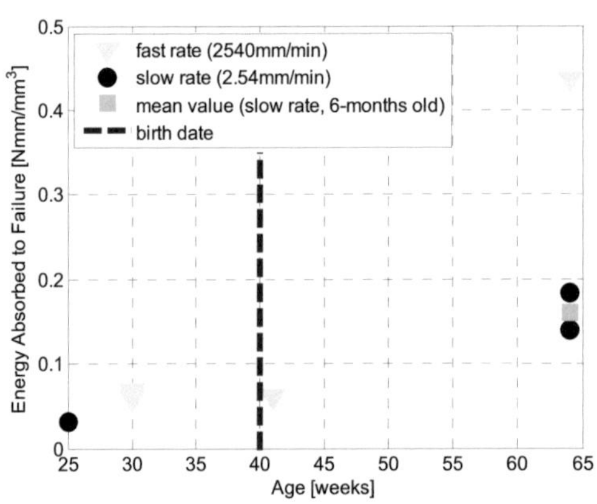

Fig. 2. Energy absorbed to failure versus age – human cranial bone in three point bending, (Margulies and Thibault, 2000)

In the case of the "slow" loading nose the amount of energy absorbed is smaller if compared with the other case. In contradiction to the human adult cranium case, the absorption of energy to failure is a function of the strain rate and, of course, of the age of the infant (Fig. 2).

As expected, the energy absorbed to failure in this case is smaller than that of the adult human head and equal to $\varepsilon_{failure\_child} \approx 0.16$ mJ·mm^{-3}. This is the mean value of the results obtained from specimens of 6 months old infants (Margulies and Thibault, 2000), see Fig. 2.

The typical volume of infant skulls can be found in (Sgouros, Goldin et al., 1999). For a 6-months old infant this is equal to:

$$V_{child\_head} \cong 750 \cdot 10^3 mm^3 \tag{3}$$

Therefore, the level of energy that can cause the failure of a typical 6 months old child skull is equal to:

$$\varepsilon_{ABS\_failure\_child} = \varepsilon_{failure\_child} \cdot V_{child\_head} \cong 120 J \tag{4}$$

It is reasonably lower compared with the one shown in (2) and therefore far from the dangerous energy levels required to seriously injure the cranium of an adult human being.

2.3 Safe energy thresholds for the cranial bone in the free head collision scenario

Injuries to the cervical spinal cord are of special concern, because damage in this region may result in deficits ranging from slight motor and sensory losses in the lower limbs to complete quadriplegia and lifelong ventilator dependency.

Case	**Analyzed structure**	**Energy [J]**
Clamped case	Adult cranium	517
	6-months old infant cranium	120
Unclamped case	Adult neck	30

Table 1. Safe energy thresholds.

In (Bilston and Thibault, 1995)it has been shown that, during normal human head motion, quite large axial strains occur in the cervical spinal cord, although these probably occur at low and not dangerous strain rates. However, during accidental sudden impacts strains in the spinal cord occur very rapidly, resulting in temporary or permanent loss of neural function that is closed to the injured region. Measures of the level of the absorbed energy that may cause the failure of the cervical spinal cord can be found in (Yoganandan, Pintar et al., 1996). An average value for this parameter experimentally estimated using 7 intact adult specimens is

$$\varepsilon_{mean\_neck} \cong 30 J \tag{5}$$

The value in (5) represents a mean energy value which takes into account different kinds of pathologies, from the disruption of ligaments to the fracture of certain bones of the cervical spinal cord. It can be noticed that this value is much smaller than those in (2) and (4). This implies that from the energy absorption and failure point of view, the neck is a much more delicate structure compared to the cranial bone.

Table 1 summarizes the minimum absorbed energy levels, which may cause critical injuries in a human head or neck, during accidental collision of the clamped or free human head with a robot.

3. Energy regulation control

The basic concept of this control strategy is to limit the energy stored into the structure of the robot[2] (joint and link) in safe levels below those introduced in section II. During the accidental collision the worst case condition is assumed, that is, all the energy stored in the link is transferred to the collided body. The proposed energy regulation control was implemented and evaluated on a single SEA joint. The employed actuator consists of three main components: a typical brushless DC motor, a harmonic reduction drive and the rotary passive compliant module.

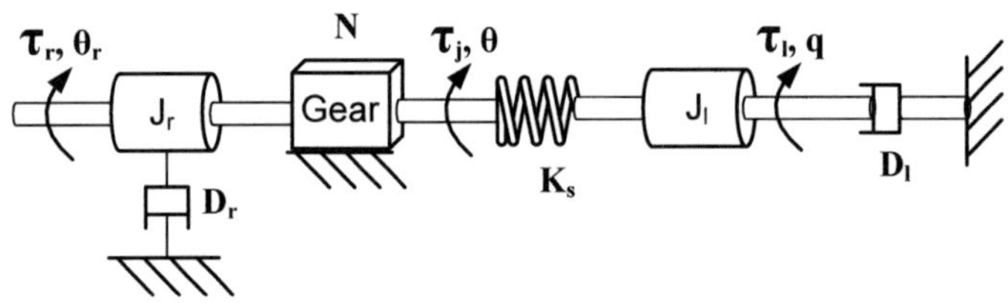

Fig. 3. The CompAct SEA mechanical conceptual schematic.

These three components can be represented by the mechanical model shown in Fig. 3. The model is composed of the rotary inertia and viscous damping of the rotor J_r, D_r, the gear drive with reduction ratio N, the elastic module with an equivalent spring constant of K_s, the output link inertia and axial damping coefficient J_l, D_l. In addition, θ_r, θ are the motor mechanical angles before and after the reduction drive, q is the angle of the output. Finally, τ_r is the torque provided by the actuator while τ_j is the input torque of the elastic element and τ_l is the torque imposed to the system by the load and/or the environment.

The above system can be described by the following set of dynamic equations.

$$\left(J_r N^2 s^2 + D_r N^2 s + K_s\right)\theta - K_s q = \tau_j \tag{6}$$

$$\left(J_l s^2 + D_l s + K_s\right) q - K_s \theta = \tau_l \tag{7}$$

3.1 Trajectory shaping based on energy regulation control

Considering the scenario of a single DOF robotic system, based on the actuation unit of Fig. 3, (Tsagarakis, Laffranchi et al., 2009), interacting with the body of the human operator as shown in Fig. 4, the amount of energy stored by the generic robot link body shown in Fig. 4 is:

---

[2] A similar concept was introduced in (Hannaford and Jee-Hwan, 2002), however in this work the saturation of stored energy (specifically the balance of energy flow from-to the controlled system) was used to ensure the passivity of the system and therefore its stability rather than from the perspective of safety in human-robot interaction.

$$\varepsilon_{tot} = \varepsilon_k + \varepsilon_e + \varepsilon_g \quad (8)$$

where ε_k is the translational and rotational kinetic energy, ε_e is the elastic potential energy and ε_g is the gravitational potential energy. The energy stored into the prototype link as function of the parameters of the joint model introduced in Fig. 3 is:

$$\varepsilon_{tot} = \frac{1}{2}J_l\dot{q}^2 + \frac{1}{2}J_r\left(N\,\dot{\theta}\right)^2 + \frac{1}{2}m_L\left(l_{COG}\,\dot{q}\right)^2 + \frac{1}{2}K_S\theta_S{}^2 + m_L\,g\sin(q)l_{COG} \quad (9)$$

where the additional introduced parameters are the mass of the link m_L, the acceleration of gravity g and the distance between the axis of rotation and the center of gravity of the link l_{COG}. Furthermore, the angle θ_S corresponds to the compression angle of the compliant element such that:

$$\theta_L = \theta_0 + \theta_S \quad (10)$$

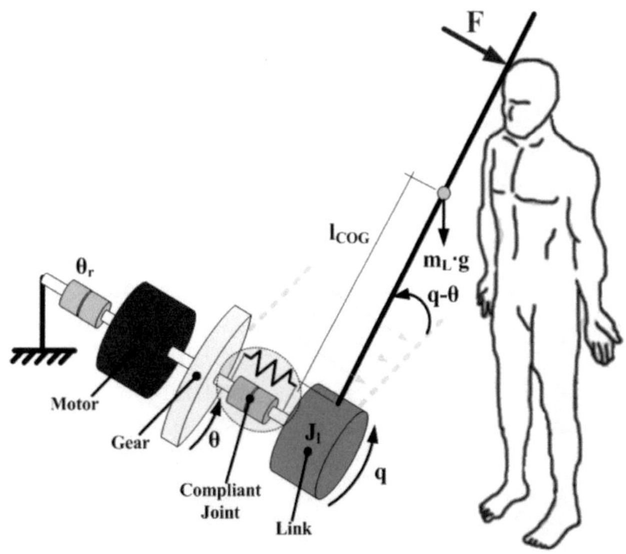

Fig. 4. Conceptual mechanical schematic of a series elastic actuator interacting with a human.

Imposing an upper bound ε_{max} to the total stored energy results in:

$$\varepsilon_{tot} < \varepsilon_{\max} \quad (11)$$

From the above energy limit ε_{max} the limit of the spring deflection angle θ_S can be derived from (9) given the instantaneous kinetic and gravitational energy stored in the link:

$$\theta_{SMAX} = \sqrt{2\left(\varepsilon_{\max} - \varepsilon_k - \varepsilon_g\right)K_S{}^{-1}} \quad (12)$$

However, (12) gives a solution only if the term under the square root is greater than zero, i.e. when the total energy stored is dominated by the elastic potential energy, which is the case when an unexpected collision occurs. The term under the square root is negative when the sum of the kinetic and the gravitational potential energy is greater than the maximum energy allowed. Assuming that the robot manipulator is designed for safety, the maximum gravitational potential energy stored would be much smaller than the maximum energy threshold, and thus the condition in which the term becomes negative would be when the total energy stored is dominated by the kinetic energy, which is the case of a free motion at a velocity that makes the kinetic energy to reach the energy threshold ε_{max}.

$$\Delta\theta = \sqrt{-2\left(\varepsilon_{\max} - \varepsilon_k - \varepsilon_g\right)K_S^{-1}} \tag{13}$$

In this case and given the current angle θ, the term described by (12) is used to generate a new reference angle according to (13). In particular, (13) uses a proportional control law to regulate the reference trajectory. During the interaction the trajectory regulation law uses the difference between the instantaneous spring deflection angle θ_S and the maximum deflection angle θ_{SMAX} given by (11). For the free motion case the correction term of (12) is used to compute the modified reference trajectory of the joint θ_{D_MOD} from the measured angle θ. The combined trajectory regulation law for both cases can be expressed as:

$$\theta_{D\_MOD} = \begin{Bmatrix} \theta_D & \varepsilon_{tot} < \varepsilon_{\max} \\ \theta + \left(\theta_S - \theta_{S\_MAX}\right) & \varepsilon_e > \varepsilon_{\max} - \varepsilon_k - \varepsilon_g > 0 \\ \theta + \Delta\theta\ K_{p\_FM} & \varepsilon_{\max} - \varepsilon_k - \varepsilon_g < 0 \end{Bmatrix} \tag{14}$$

where the term K_{p_INT} is the proportional gain used for the interaction case and K_{p_FM} is the proportional gain used for the free motion case. When the total energy stored exceeds the maximum allowed, the control system switches the value of the reference angle θ_D to the modified one in function of the detected condition, according to (13). When the total energy stored is lower or equal than the maximum allowed, the system switches back to the reference value of the desired trajectory angle θ_D.

POSSIBLE INTERACTION	$\theta_S > 0 \Rightarrow \theta_{SMAX} > 0$
	$\theta_S < 0 \Rightarrow \theta_{SMAX} < 0$
POSSIBLE FREE MOTION	$\dot{\theta} > 0 \Rightarrow \Delta\theta < 0$
	$\dot{\theta} < 0 \Rightarrow \Delta\theta > 0$

Table 2. Working conditions.

Table 2 reports how the sign of the terms introduced in (12) and (13) is determined. When the condition $\varepsilon_e > \varepsilon_{max} - \varepsilon_k - \varepsilon_g > 0$ is verified the case of "possible interaction" is detected, whereas $\varepsilon_{max} - \varepsilon_k - \varepsilon_g < 0$ identifies the condition of "possible free motion".

To prevent the high frequency components, introduced by the switching between reference trajectory and the safety imposed value, from entering the servo loop, a weighted mean between the desired trajectory angle θ_D and the modified reference trajectory of the joint θ_{D_MOD} was implemented.

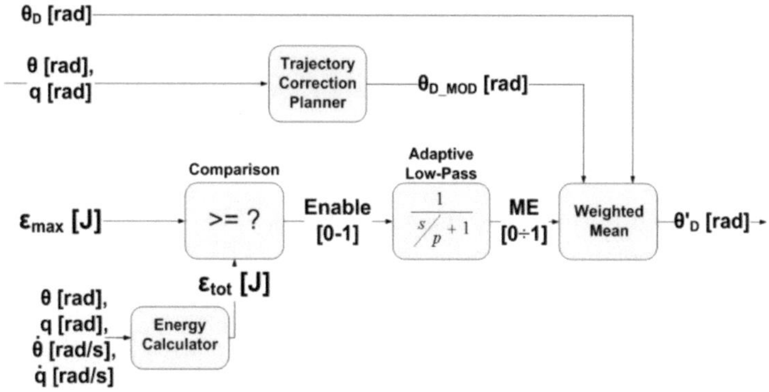

Fig. 5. Block scheme of the ERC trajectory modification module.

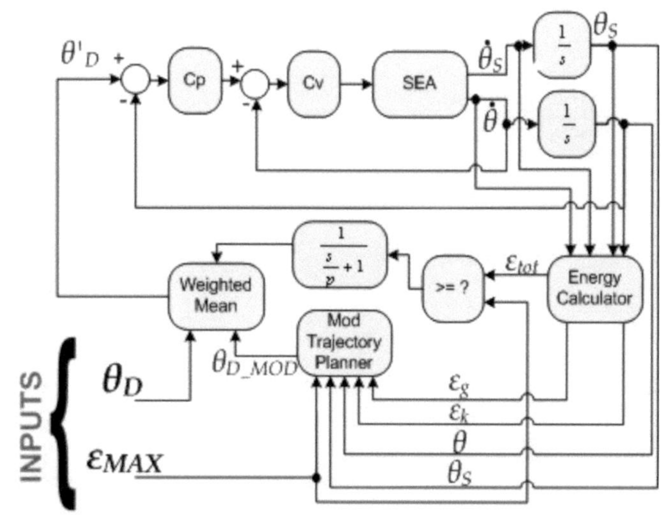

Fig. 6. ERC block scheme.

The signal "Enable" is the switching signal generated from the results of the comparison between the total energy stored, ε_{tot} and the maximum energy threshold ε_{max}. This signal, is low-pass filtered to give *ME* (Mean Enable), which is used as a weight for the "Weighted mean" block. The filter in Fig.5 is an adaptive first order filter with bandwidth set in function of the difference between θ_D and θ_{D_MOD}. In detail, the pole of this filter is set to

$$p = \dot{\theta}_{MAX}\left|\left(\theta_D - \theta_{D\_MOD}\right)^{-1}\right| \tag{15}$$

In this way, the maximum value of the derivative of the position reference (velocity) is limited to a maximum value $\dot{\theta}_{MAX}$ obtained from a safety-based criterion (in this case, $\dot{\theta}_{MAX}$ is the velocity that makes the kinetic energy to reach the maximum allowed ε_{MAX}). This makes the controller to not to inject large magnitude commands that can result unsafe during transitions from θ_D to θ_{D_MOD} and vice versa. The signal θ'_{0D} is the output of the block "Weighted Mean" and is given by

$$\theta'_D = ME\ \theta_D + (1 - ME)\theta_{D\_MOD} \tag{16}$$

The overall energy regulation control scheme is shown in Fig. 6.

4. Simulation results

Simulations are carried out to validate the effectiveness of the introduced ERC scheme. The model used for the simulations is linear and does not take into account torque, velocity, current saturations to make the system free from these effects to better evaluate the efficacy of ERC. The simulation consists in setting a sinusoidal reference trajectory θ_D with frequency of 2 rad/s and amplitude of 5 rad to the ERC-controlled system at the same time applying an intermittent output torque disturbance (amplitude: 20Nm, frequency 1.57 rad/s) to simulate accidental collision/interactions.

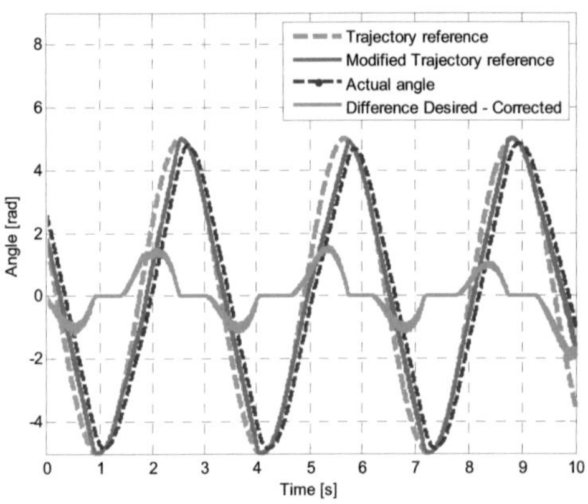

(a)

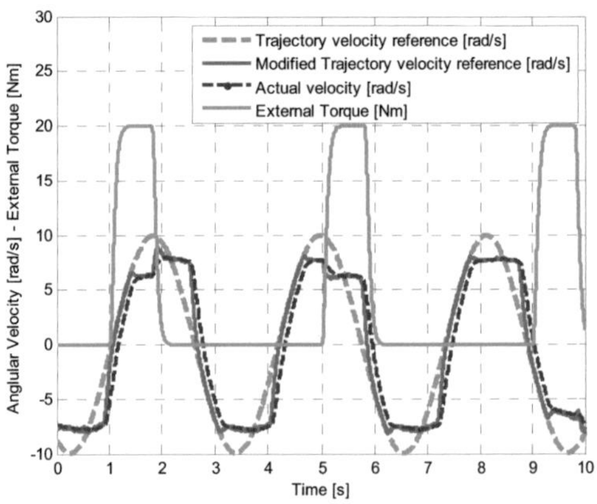

(b)

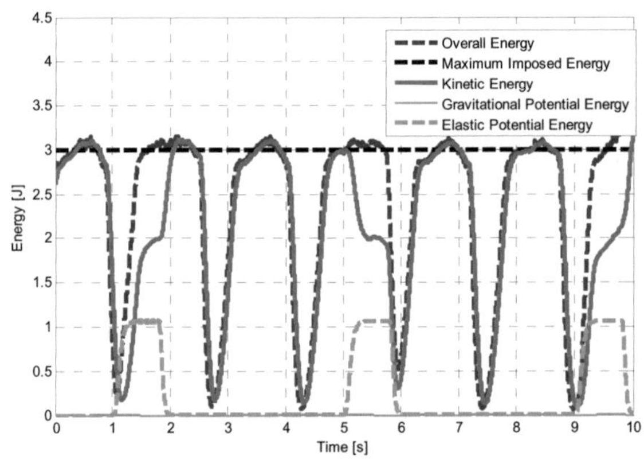

(c)

Fig. 7. (a) Position and (b) velocity trajectory modifications due to ERC. (c) Trend of the different components of the stored energy.

The energy threshold ε_{MAX} was set to 3J which is much lower than the safe values reported in Tab. 1 to trigger the ERC with link/motor velocity or spring deflection angle values well within the available ranges of the real system. The reason for this is that given the intrinsically safe properties of the actuator used for this study (i.e. soft and lightweight), these safe energy thresholds are reached only for extremely large deflection angles (potential energy storage) and/or velocities (kinetic energy storage).

Figs. 7a, 7b show the modification of the trajectory reference due to the action of ERC. The modified trajectory reference is different from the desired trajectory reference. The maximum differences between these two values occur when the velocity of the link is maximum (high kinetic energy storage, Fig. 7c) and/or with the external torque disturbance, which determines a high elastic energy storage due to the deflection of the compliant element. The sinusoidal position reference has been planned such that the corresponding velocity level could grow over the energy limit and trigger the ERC.

Fig. 7c presents each component of the energy stored in the link. When no external torque is applied ERC acts mostly on the kinetic energy (the deflection angle is very small in this case due to the high stiffness/inertia ratio, $K_S = 190$ Nm·rad^{-1} $J_l = 4.98 \cdot 10^{-3}$ kg·m^2), however, when the disturbance collision torque is applied, the regulation is made on the overall energy. At the same time, the gravitational potential energy is almost equal to zero due to the lightweight link.

5. Experimental results

Experiments were conducted in order to verify the performance of the energy regulation control scheme introduced in the previous sections. The experiments were performed using the prototype actuation unit (Tsagarakis, Laffranchi et al., 2009) shown in Fig. 8.

Two potentially risky scenarios were analyzed: the case of free motion at a high velocity and that of an accidental interaction. For both cases the highest contribution on the total energy stored into the actuator is given either by the kinetic (free motion) or the elastic potential energy (unexpected interaction). The gravitational potential energy is not giving a relevant contribution to the overall energy, this is because this system has a lightweight link (m_L = 0.41 kg) contributing with a maximum value of $\varepsilon_{g_max} \approx 0.45$J when the link centre of gravity is at its highest position.

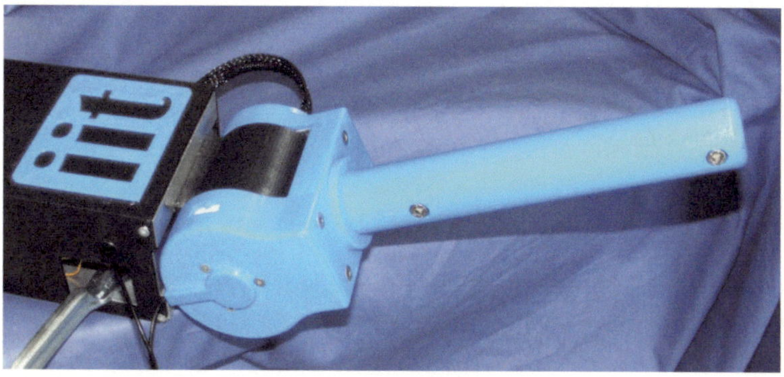

Fig. 8. The actuator used for the experiment – Free motion experiment.

5.1 Free motion experiment

In the first experiment the joint performed a free motion driven by a sinusoidal trajectory with the parameters shown in Table 3. The parameters of the reference trajectory were selected to make the system exceed the maximum energy in order to demonstrate the control action of ERC.

In this case, apart from the gravitational potential energy that is very small due to the light weight link, the elastic potential energy is also close to zero since the deflection of the spring is minimum during the free motion due to the high stiffness - link inertia ratio (K_S = 190 Nm rad^{-1}; J_l = 4.98·10^{-3} kg m^2). Therefore the overall energy is determined by the kinetic energy. Fig.9a shows the energy components of the joint.

Parameter	Value
Amplitude of the trajectory reference A	0.92 rad
Frequency of the trajectory reference ω	0.32Hz
Maximum energy value imposed ε_{max}	0.8 J

Table 3. Parameters of the free motion experiment.

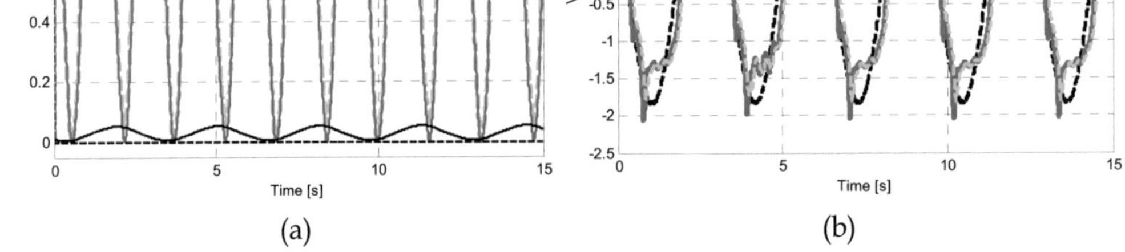

Fig. 9. Free motion case: a) Energy components b) Trajectory modification.

As expected the overall energy is very close to the kinetic energy. In Fig. 9b it can be seen how the link velocity trajectory is limited in order to constrain the total energy of the system within the maximum set value. As the trajectory velocity exceeds 1.5 rad/s the control adjusts the reference in order to limit the total energy. As the trajectory velocity becomes smaller than the 1.5 rad/s threshold the reference velocity trajectory is tracked again.

5.2 Unexpected interaction experiment

In this experiment the motor was commanded to follow a sinusoidal trajectory while interactions were generated within the range of motion of the link using a soft obstacle made of polyethylene, Fig. 10.

The trajectory parameters and the energy limit applied are illustrated in Table 4. The maximum imposed energy was set equal to 0.8J, which is much smaller than the values shown in Table 1. This was done in purpose in order to test the behaviour of the control system avoiding big force-torque exchanges that can damage the test equipment.

It can be observed that during interaction the kinetic energy drops to zero as a consequence of the decrease of the velocity of the link. The potential energy grows accordingly with the spring deflection due to the impact, making the overall energy to exceed the maximum allowable value. In this case the control works to limit the elastic potential energy, because the kinetic energy and the gravitational potential energy are constant due to the fact that the link is not in motion. Fig. 11b shows how the trajectory angle is modified in order to achieve the goal.

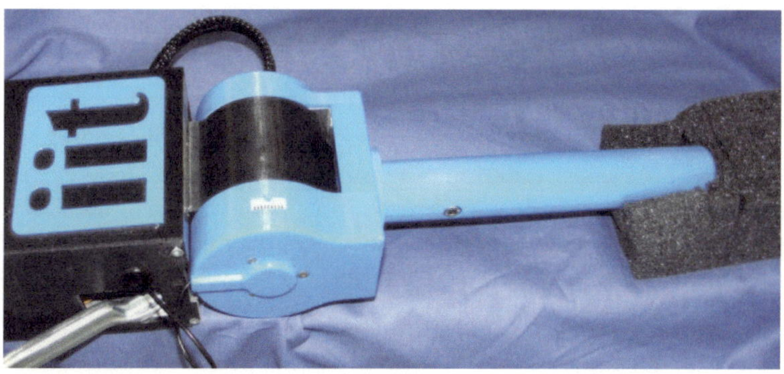

Fig. 10. Unexpected interaction test setup.

Parameter	Value
Amplitude of the trajectory reference *A*	0.7 rad
Frequency of the trajectory reference ω	0.25 Hz
Maximum energy value imposed ε_{max}	0.8 J

Table 4. Parameters of the unexpected interaction experiment.

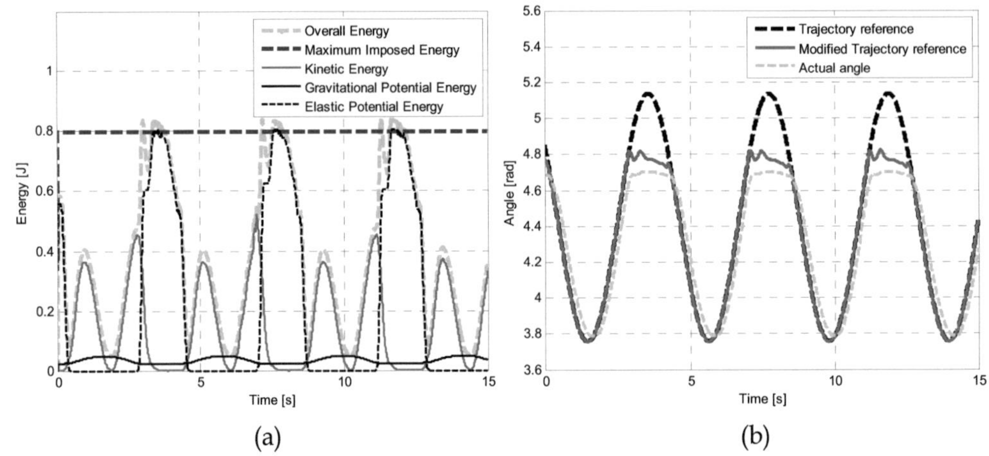

Fig. 11. Unexpected interaction case: a) Energy components b) Trajectory modification.

6. Conclusions and future work

In this paper a safe-oriented strategy to control a SEA system was presented. By combing series elastic mechanical design and energy regulation control an approach to cope with the problem of safety during the first instants of the impact, (i.e. the problem occurring in rigid torque-controlled robots) is proposed. The specific case presented here can be extended to a generic compliant actuation design.

The presented technique constrains the energy stored into the robotic link to a maximum value that is derived by a safety criterion. The proposed control scheme is a position based controller that adjusts the trajectory reference position as a function of the desired maximum energy threshold using the states of the system. The overall system was experimentally evaluated using a prototype SEA unit.

Future developments will include the formulation of ERC for multi degree of freedom systems and the implementation of the resulting scheme in a robotic arm. The manipulator on which this method will be tested has to be designed following safe-oriented criteria (e.g. soft and lightweight): this will allow lower amounts of energy storage which would be well below the energy safe thresholds. In such a case, performance (speed, dynamics) will not be limited during the execution of normal operations. The described ERC-controlled robot will be then used to carry further experiments to characterize the energy losses occurring during unexpected interactions to validate the safety level of the presented control strategy. A last research to be investigated in the future is the use of Energy Regulation Control in compliant actuators with variable physical damping such as VPDA systems, (Laffranchi, Tsagarakis et al., 2010; Laffranchi, Tsagarakis et al., 2011). ERC can be revised to exploit the passive properties of physical damping to safely dissipate excess of stored energy.

7. References

Bicchi, A. and Tonietti, G. 2004. "Fast and soft arm tactics." *Ieee Robotics & Automation Magazine*, Vol. 11, (3).

Bilston, L. and Thibault, L. 1995. "The mechanical properties of the human cervical spinal cordIn Vitro." *Annals of Biomedical Engineering*, Vol. 24: 67-74.

Catalano, M. G., Grioli, G., Bonomo, F., Schiavi, R. and Bicchi, A., 2010. VSA-HD: From the enumeration analysis to the prototypical implementation. *Intelligent Robots and Systems (IROS), 2010 IEEE/RSJ International Conference on*, pp. 3676-3681.

Haddadin, S., Albu-Schaffer, A. and Hirzinger, G., 2008. The role of the robot mass and velocity in physical human-robot interaction - Part I: Non-constrained blunt impacts. *Robotics and Automation, 2008. ICRA 2008. IEEE International Conference on*, pp. 1331-1338.

Hannaford, B. and Jee-Hwan, R. 2002. "Time-domain passivity control of haptic interfaces." *Robotics and Automation, IEEE Transactions on*, Vol. 18, (1): 1-10.

Heinzmann, J. and Zelinsky, A. 1999. "A safe control paradigm for Human-Robot Interaction." *Journal of Intelligent and Robotic Systems, Springer*, Vol. 25.

Hogan, N. 1985. "Impedance Control: an approach to manipulation: parts I-III." *Journal of Dynamic Systems, Measurement, and Control*, Vol. 107.

Hollander, K., Sugar, T. and Herring, D. (2005). A Robotic 'Jack Spring' for Ankle Gait Assistance. *International Design Engineering Technical Conference*. Long Beach, CA, USA, ASME.

Hurst, J. W., Chestnutt, J. E. and Rizzi, A. A., 2004. An actuator with physically variable stiffness for highly dynamic legged locomotion. *Robotics and Automation, 2004. Proceedings. ICRA '04. 2004 IEEE International Conference on*, pp. 4662-4667 Vol.4665.

Ikeura, R. and Inooka, H. (1995). Variable impedance control of a robot for cooperation with a human. International Conference on Robotics and Automation. IEEE. Nagoya, Japan.

ISO-10218-1 (2006). Robots for industrial environments -- Safety requirements -- Part 1: Robot.

ISO-10218-2 (2011). Robots and robotic devices -- Safety requirements for industrial robots -- Part 2: Robot systems and integration.

Jafari, A., Tsagarakis, N. G. and Caldwell, D. G. (2011). Exploiting Natural Dynamics for Energy Minimization using an Actuator with Adjustable Stiffness (AwAS). International Conference on Robotics and Automation. IEEE. Shanghai, China.

Jafari, A., Tsagarakis, N. G., Vanderborght, B. and Caldwell, D. G. (2010). A Novel Actuator with Adjustable Stiffness (AwAS). International Conference on Intelligent Robots and Systems, IROS. IEEE. Taipei, TW.

Kajikawa, S. and Abe, K. 2010. "Robot Finger Module With Multidirectional Adjustable Joint Stiffness." *Mechatronics, IEEE/ASME Transactions on*, Vol. PP, (99): 1-8.

Kulic, D. and Croft, E., 2004. Safe planning for human-robot interaction. *Robotics and Automation, 2004. Proceedings. ICRA '04. 2004 IEEE International Conference on*, pp. 1882-1887 Vol.1882.

Laffranchi, M., Tsagarakis, N. G. and Caldwell, D. G. (2009). Antagonistic and Series Elastic Actuators: a Comparative Analysis on the Energy Consumption. International Conference on Intelligent Robots and Systems. St. Louis.

Laffranchi, M., Tsagarakis, N. G. and Caldwell, D. G. (2010). A Variable Physical Damping Actuator (VPDA) for Compliant Robotic Joints. *International Conference on Robotics and Automation*. Anchorage, Alaska.

Laffranchi, M., Tsagarakis, N. G. and Caldwell, D. G. (2011). A Compact Compliant Actuator (CompAct™) with Variable Physical Damping. *International Conference on Robotics and Automation (ICRA)*. IEEE. Shanghai, China: 4644-4650.

Lauzier, N. and Gosselin, C. (2011). Series Clutch Actuators for Safe Physical Human-Robot Interaction. Robotics and Automation, International Conference on. IEEE. Shanghai, China: 5401-5406.

Manjuath, K. 2002. "Estimation of Cranial Volume - an Overview of Methodologies." *J. Anat. Soc.*

Margulies, S. and Thibault, K. 2000. "Infant Skull and Suture Properties: Measurements and Implications for Mechanisms of Pediatric Brain Injury." *Journal of Biomechanics*, Vol. 122.

Pratt, G. A. and Williamson, M. M. (1995). Series elastic actuators. *Intelligent Robots and Systems 95. 'Human Robot Interaction and Cooperative Robots', Proceedings. 1995 IEEE/RSJ International Conference on.* 1: 399-406 vol.391.

Schiavi, R., Grioli, G., Sen, S. and Bicchi, A. (2008). VSA-II: a Novel Prototype of Variable Stiffness Actuator for Safe and Performing Robots Interacting with Humans. *International Conference on Robotics and Automation*. IEEE. Pasadena, CA, USA.

Sgouros, S., Goldin, J. H., Hockley, A. D., Wake, M. J. C. and Natarajan, K. 1999. "Intracranial volume change in childhood." *Journal of Neurosurgery*, Vol. 91, (4): 610-616.

Shafer, A. S. and Kermani, M. R. (2011). Design and Validation of a Magneto-Rheological Clutch for Practical Control Applications in Human-Friendly Manipulation. Robotics and Automation, International Conference on. IEEE. Shanghai, China: 4266-4271.

Sugar, T. G. 2002. "A novel selective compliant actuator." *Mechatronics*, Vol. 12, (9-10): 1157-1171.

Tilley, A. R. and Associates, H. D., 1993. *The Measure of Man and Woman: Human Factors in Design*, Whitney Library of Design.

Tonietti, G., Schiavi, R. and Bicchi, A. (2005). Design and Control of a Variable Stiffness Actuator for Safe and Fast Physical Human/Robot Interaction. *International conference on robotics and automation*. Barcelona, Spain.

Tsagarakis, N. G., Laffranchi, M., Vanderborght, B. and Caldwell, D. G., 2009. A compact soft actuator unit for small scale human friendly robots. *Robotics and Automation, 2009. ICRA '09. IEEE International Conference on*, pp. 4356-4362.

Tsagarakis, N. G., Laffranchi, M., Vanderborght, B. and Caldwell, D. G., 2010. Compliant Actuation: Enhancing the Interaction Ability of Cognitive Robotics Systems. *Advances in Cognitive systems*. London, Institution of Engineering and Technology.

Versace, J. (1971). A Review of the severity index. *15th Stapp Car Crash Conference*. New York: 771-796.

Wood, J. L. 1971. "Dynamic response of human cranial bone." *Journal of Biomechanics*, Vol. 4.

Yoganandan, N., Pintar, F. A., Maiman, D. J., Cusick, J. F., Sances, A. and Walsh, P. R. 1996. "Human head-neck biomechanics under axial tension." *Medical Engineering & Physics*, Vol. 18, (4): 289-294.

Yoon, S., Kang, S., Kim, S. J., Kim, Y. H., Kim, M. and Lee, C. W. (2003). Safe arm with MR-based passive compliant joints and visco-elastic covering for service robot applications. International Conference on Robots and Systems. Las Vegas, USA.

Zinn, M., Khatib, O. and Roth, B. (2004). A new actuation approach for human friendly robot design. *Robotics and Automation, 2004. Proceedings. ICRA '04. 2004 IEEE International Conference on.* 1: 249-254 Vol.241.

Zollo, L., Siciliano, B., De Luca, A., Guglielmelli, E. and Dario, P. (2003). Compliance control for a Robot with Elastic Joints. International Conference on Robotics and Automation. IEEE. Coimbra, Portugal.

Zollo, L., Siciliano, B., Laschi, C., Teti, G., Dario, P. and Guglielmelli, E., 2002. An impedance-compliance control for a cable-actuated robot. *Intelligent Robots and Systems, 2002. IEEE/RSJ International Conference on*, pp. 2268-2273 vol.2263.

9

Monitoring Activities with Lower-Limb Exoskeletons

Juan C. Moreno and José L. Pons
Grupo de Bioingeniería, Consejo Superior de Investigaciones Científicas
Spain

1. Introduction

Advances in sensor technologies and data storage have led to the development of portable systems that can measure aspects of human behaviour in everyday life. Measuring the progressive change in physical activity in people with different types of diseases in real conditions means that rehabilitation, training and physical education programmes can accordingly adapt. Monitoring activities has been acknowledged as an integral part of optimum healthcare. [2]. There are multiple disciplines in which activity is monitored, such as medicine, physiotherapy, behavioural sciences, psychophysiology and ergonomy.

Parallel development in techniques for measuring movement and mass storage means that is possible to measure physical activity in real conditions. Daily physical activity is defined as the total voluntary movement produced by the musculoskeletal system during daily functioning, [3]: measuring movement with sensors is related to measuring body movement or specific parts of the body depending on the location of the sensor.

Different configurations of monitors of physical activity have been primarily applied on rehabilitation programmes of different types of pathologies. To configure pulmonary rehabilitation in people with chronic pulmonary diseases the application of activity monitors that help with daily activity and physical activity have been researched. The development and application of such systems involves measuring movement, and methodological, practical and analytical aspects. A review presented by Steele, [91], describes different monitoring systems of daily activity and exercise with movement sensors in people with pulmonary diseases, by analysing the different sensor technologies used in commercial devices. Among the clinical uses, observation processes are included which are of interest to obtain variables like improved exercise and increased daily activity. Functional capacity, self-sufficiency for movement, quantification of gait and measuring physical capacity by calculating energy consumption over time are the principal variables of interest that have been calculated with systems that use movement sensors, [8], located on the waist, ankle and wrist of subjects.

As well as the energy consumption associated with any type of physical activity (both static and dynamic), the estimate of variables related to gait and lower-limb movements, such as the number of steps or distance covered, are measurements that have also been shown to be valid and have been obtained with high reliability in versions of pedometers available commercially, like the Digiwalker pedometer, which measures wrist vertical accelerations, or the Caltrac system, [3], which uses uniaxial accelerometers located on the hip and estimates energy consumption depending on the age, height and gender of the user. It has been observed that estimates with these devices may vary according to:

- the velocity and frequency of the movement or activity;
- the location and degree of freedom of the sensors;
- the calibration equations applied.

The quantification of activity is a method to measure physical activity that may help as a motivation tool. Advanced monitors of physical activity aim to establish the type of activity according to the data captured using portable systems to measure movement. In the literature we find portable systems that classify movement into different applications. It is important to mention the recent exploration of applying accelerometers on body segments to study activities. The concept of an activity monitor based on ambulatory measurement of posture and movement, albeit not new, is mentioned in relatively few cases in the literature.

Recognising activities from signals of accelerometers mounted on the torso has been researched in, [7], whereby a model of multiple classes was proposed by combining Markov chains and Gaussian models from characteristics extracted from the analysis with the fast Fourier transform (FFT). In a study analysing different accelerometer orientations on the sternum, to recognise activities and postures, [7], the viability of discriminating dynamic and static activities with methods for processing signals to extract characteristics was confirmed.

In the literature we found, [49], the combination of accelerometers with gyroscopes integrated into a portable device on the waist of subjects and a proposal to analyse the morphology of the signals from/ of the two types of transducers and the application of thresholds to discriminate specific activities. The classification method proposed identifies the level of velocity of movements in categories according to fuzzy rules. Another system for monitoring activities, presented by Groeneveld, [9], proposes training a neuronal network to classify movement data.

Among the classification methods applied to identify activities we find Bayes classifiers, hidden Markov chains, decision trees, Gaussian models and frequency component analysis. Generally, a problem found in obtaining a model to classify multiple activities (classes) is the high probability of overadjusting the data to the group of training data with the resulting loss of expected generality. It is important to note that the quantitative comparison of the validity of systems for monitoring activities is a complex task and not always attainable given the differences between the classification, adjustment and application criteria of the different methods proposed. However, it is possible to do qualitative comparisons, knowing the methodology applied to obtain the results of a system and the behaviour of different methods to discriminate specific activities.

The most relevant studies found to date in the literature pose discriminating activities with portable sensors of movement mounted directly on the torso or waist. Only pedometers, as monitoring methods offering specific information, have been applied to the lower limb and configured as commercial systems to count steps or estimate energy output. Instruments available in the market to monitor activities from wrist motion (Motionlogger, Ambulatory Monitoring, Inc.) enable long-term data logging and objective detection of sleep, hyperactivity or daytime activity levels. Other devices attached to the lower limb are capable of measuring important motion variables and foot pressures for analysis of walking features, e.g. WalkinSense, Tomorrow Options. To date, we have not found any study on monitoring physical activities in users with ambulatory gait aids in the literature. We present the concept and experimental study of monitoring activities with lower-limb exoskeletons below.

2. Exoskeleton activity monitor (EAM)

Traditional techniques to analyse gait (video- and force-platform-based systems) restrict mobility and do not represent very natural conditions due to spatial limitations. In a preliminary study, [1], where a multidisciplinary group of experts involved in the manufacture, prescription and evaluation of lower-limb orthoses was considered, the necessary guidelines were defined to include devices to monitor users with lower-limb functional compensation systems both in the laboratory and in real-world conditions, so that new objective information might be obtained that could be used by physiotherapists, orthopaedic specialists and physiologists.

The exoskeleton activity monitor (EAM) approach presented is based on these requirements and fits into a context of clinical application as a tool to analyse the daily activity of subjects in a clinic or rehabilitation centre and the functioning of the gait aid system in an orthopaedic workshop. The portable gait compensation system is equipped with the activity monitor that captures lower-limb movement. In the application scenario, the subject develops one or several activities freely with the system that captures biomechanical data. Later in the clinic or rehabilitation centre the session data related to the subject information (data bases with anthropometrical, historical, statistical data, etc), are downloaded into a base platform where they are processed and presented to assess the daily activity and keep a track record of system use. Figure 4.1 shows a diagram of this concept of monitoring subjects with lower-limb exoskeletons or orthoses.

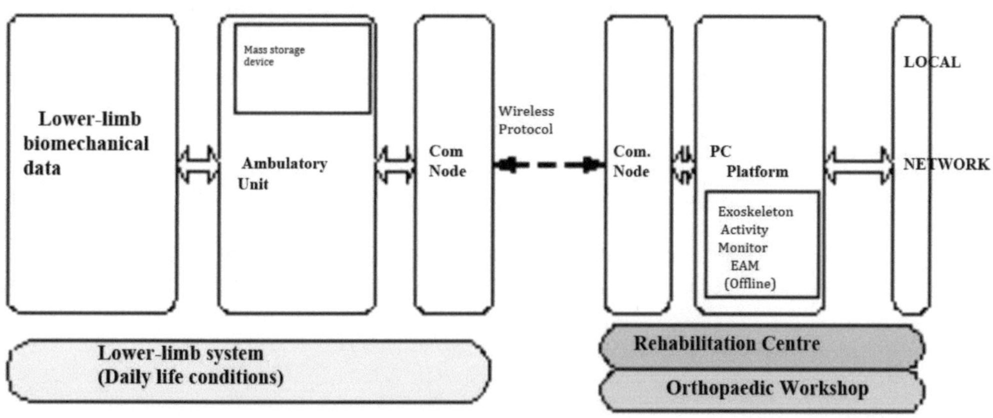

Fig. 4.1. Diagram of the context of monitoring physical activities with a lower-limb exoskeleton activity monitor (EAM).

2.1 Objectives

The monitor aims to offer information on the exoskeleton by monitoring a set of activities or categories. Accordingly, we also consider the following subset of activities:

- Sitting
- Standing
- Walking on level ground
- Walking (going up/down) ramps of approximately 5 degrees
- Going up or down stairs
- Other or not known

2.2 Ambulatory platform

The entire system includes hardware, methods for recognising activities and the positioning of sensors on the lower limb. The ambulatory unit that controls the exoskeleton contains two 8-bit AVR microcontrollers, which manage acquisition (up to 16 analogue channels), wireless communication and data storage on SD (Secure Digital) card removable flash memory. The autonomy of the activity monitor must be such that measurements can be taken for one whole day. The prototype that we have developed is fed by a 900-mAh lithium-ion battery that offers 4 hours of autonomy in continuous use. The storage capacity of this prototype is conditioned by the storage capacity of the SD flash card and the capacity of the battery used. The Atmega32L microcontroller manages the data writing and reading, updates an initialisation file containing the session record, the times (given by a real-time clock) and the sensor gains according to prior calibration. The sensors used in the monitor are a uniaxial accelerometer on the foot, gyroscopes on the foot and leg (to measure rotations on the sagittal plane) and an angular position sensor on the knee.

The monitoring system in offline mode continually measures and stores the sensor configuration signals at a frequency of 33 Hz, with an 8-bit resolution. The attachment of the inertial sensor boxes to the exoskeleton structure reduces to a great extent the appearance of artefacts because of relative vibrations or movements between the sensor and the segment in question. The ambulatory measurement unit is attached to the subject's waist. The vector of input variables of/from the activity monitor describes movement in relation to the state of the lower limb is defined in accordance with the following expression:

$$u(t) = \{ay\ foot\ (t),\ \omega\ foot\ (t),\ \omega\ leg\ (t),\ \theta\ \ knee\ (t)\} \tag{4.1}$$

From the conclusions of the analysis of movement in 3D, we assume that in the subset of activities of interest, the components resulting from movements outside the sagittal plane and changes in direction of movement are low and their effect is negligible on the results of the identification methods that we propose below

3. Methodology

The processing method concept is based on processing a posteriori the lower-limb movement signals to extract the discriminating characteristics that make it possible to group them into a number of known categories, where univocal transitions between the different activities are not assumed. The data processing consists of several stages: (1) filtering; (2) extracting characteristics to detect static activities, cyclical activities and to analyse the energy of the time series for which two methods are proposed; and (3) discriminating a subset of categories.

- Signals
- Standardisation
- Filtering

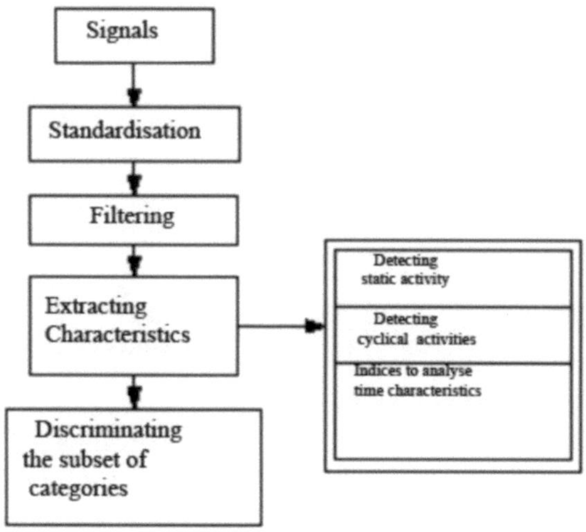

Fig. 4.2. Activity monitor schema.

3.1 Signal acquisition and filtering

The inertial sensors are located on the foot and leg. The accelerometer gives an output equal to zero when its measurement axis is perpendicular to the gravity acceleration axis. The gyroscopes give a signal equal to zero in static conditions and a voltage proportional to their rate velocity. The angle of the knee estimated from the position sensor measurement on the exoskeleton joint may vary between approximately 0 to 100 degrees during the set of activities. Signal acquisition is done with an 8-bit resolution AD converter, at a sampling frequency of 33Hz, values that were established by a compromise between resolution, autonomy and computation time (a sampling frequency sufficient for gait at natural velocity and corresponding to the maximum rate of writing in SD format for our data package structure). The signals are filtered initially using a first-order, low-pass filter with a cutoff frequency of 30 Hz.

3.2 Detecting static activity

In static conditions, constant acceleration on the sensor depending on the inclination φfoot of the segment, in relation to the axis of the force of gravity g, can be calculated via the cosine, according to the expression

$$Ai = -g\cos(\varphi foot) + n \tag{4.2}$$

where n is white noise.

On the other hand, during static activities the gyroscope signals will be equal to zero. These conditions can be used to determine whether the activity is dynamic or static. In the literature we find the application of this principle proposed by Veltink, [9 7], establishing the attachment of accelerometers on the trunk (middle sternum) as the methodology for discrimination. The method that we propose for the EAM to detect the nature of the activity from measuring lower-limb segment movement consists of: i) low-pass filtering of the accelerometer signal on the foot segment with a cutoff frequency of 0.2Hz, ii) demodulation of the signal (absolute value) and application of a second-order, low-pass, Butterworth filter with a cutoff frequency of 0.1 Hz to obtain the signal envelope and weight it (by multiplication) with the velocity magnitude (filtered with a low-pass filter of 0.2 Hz) of the foot rotation, iii) application of a threshold to the resulting signal. Once the detection of the static activity has been generated it is possible to discriminate directly between the sitting and standing categories, by applying a threshold to the knee flexion angle.

3.3 Detecting periods of cyclical activity

Earlier studies have indicated the viability of separating the activities of body segments into cycles using accelerometers mounted on the human torso [5]. We propose a method using accelerometers and gyroscopes on the lower limb. By estimating the intervals corresponding to dynamic activities (gait on level ground, going up and down ramps, going up and down stairs) we pose the possibility of detecting cyclical activities with a combined technique of: a) identifying high-sensitivity heel or foot contact, considering different support types (such as flat support on stairs, initial support after point drag, etc.) and detecting minimums of the time series of foot angular velocity and b) signal oversampling in fixed width time windows, between periods of dynamic activity greater or equal to a window width that defines the detector time resolution. Below this threshold the dynamic activities will be considered in the indeterminate category and could correspond to activities not considered in the subset of categories or to transitions between these activities.

3.4 Extracting characteristics

From the input signals at each instant of time measured, methods are applied to discriminate rotation intervals (RIs) from the segments and intervals of cyclical dynamic activity. Likewise, methods are proposed to extract signals representing dynamic movement characteristics, for which two discriminating indices (EAF and PFT) and the frequency contents (FC signal) are proposed. We describe the procedures to obtain each of the characterisation signals used in the activity monitor below.

3.4.1 Frequency response

The inertial sensor signals are passed through a finite impulse response (FIR) digital filter designed to pass frequencies in the 0.3-2 Hz band, (limits in the 0.1-3 Hz band) generating FC signals, with the frequency content in the oscillatory bandwidth of interest, whose instantaneous amplitude is related to the signal frequency content of linear acceleration and rotation velocities.

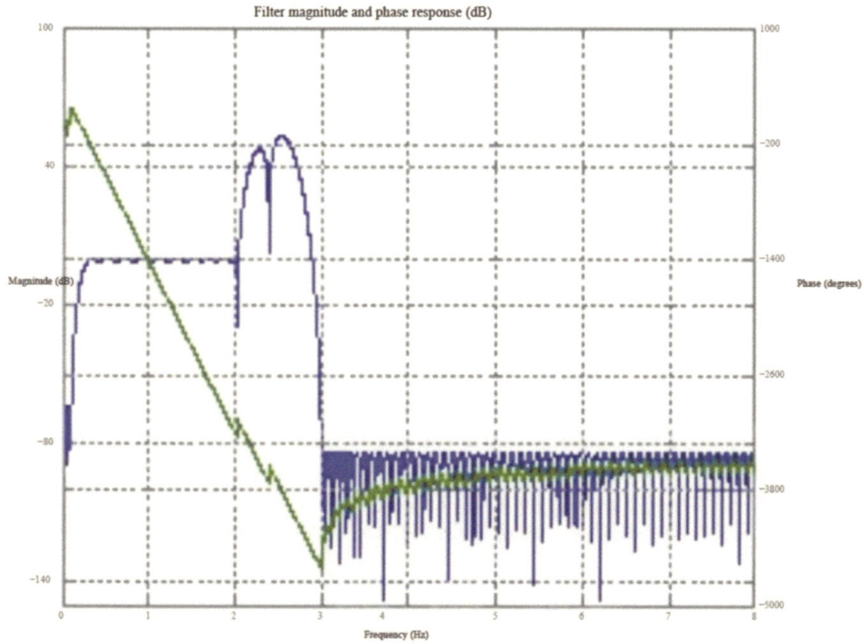

Fig. 4.3. Band pass filter magnitude and phase response to extract signal frequency characteristic from segment movement.

3.4.2 Segment rotation interval

Signal frequency characterisation corresponding to leg rotation velocity, ωleg, is rectified. Two consecutive zero-pass instants, which correspond to the changes in gyration direction of the segment, define the intervals. Throughout these intervals a numerical integration is applied obtaining,

$$IR(n) = \sum_{i}^{i+1} \theta_k, \tag{4.3}$$

which are defined as the rotation intervals of the dataset. Two methods (indices) to characterise the signals for clustering into activities are proposed below.

3.4.3 RLM index

We define the rotational and longitudinal movement (RLM) index as the characteristic for classifying the cyclical activity between the subset of categories. The RLM index is calculated from the signal resulting from the composition of acceleration filtered signals at Y on the foot, a y foot , and angular velocities of the foot, ωfoot , and leg, ωleg. For each sample k of the period n of cyclical activity of duration s, the RLM index is calculated using the signal composition integral.

$$RLM(k, n) = \{a\ y\ foot[k] * \omega foot\ [k] * \omega leg\ [k]\}\ k{=}s\ _{k=0} \quad (4.4)$$

Accordingly, an RLM value is defined for each dynamic activity interval. This index is directly related to the mean amplitude of the acceleration and angular velocity signals and is an indication of the quantity of combined movement (rotational and longitudinal) of the two segments, required for the activity. We propose calculating the integral over the composed signal because rotational and longitudinal movements are thereby considered at each instant of time. The possibility of grouping data from the RLM mean value calculated at each period of cyclical activity is considered by obtaining specific thresholds for separating categories.

$$PFT(n) = \int_{k=0}^{k=s} \log(\sigma_M)$$

3.4.4 Frequency vs. time: PFT index

Analysis of the signal power spectrum over time is a characteristic which, similarly to the RLM index, can be used to define a metric for classifying activities. The calculation on the pre-defined signal composition is done with the FFT of a specific number of samples, with an H-size Hamming window and number of overlapping samples ns. As a criterion for analyser design, we select the ns value from which we calculate the size of the window using the expression

$$H = ((ns * (K - 1))/ K) + 1 \quad (4.5)$$

where K is the total number of samples of the composed signal. We thus obtain the frequency component matrix in M frequency [f, t] of 1024 × (K – ns) elements. The mean and standard deviation of the frequency components obtained at each instant are measured from the total signal power for each sample. An abrupt change in the content of M [f] between consecutive samples, can be detected by tracking the deviation from a reference value at each instant. We define the PFT index as the area under the curve from the result the standard deviation σM, for each period n of cyclical activity. The logarithmic function was used to change the base to adapt the range of the output of the matrix M elements and define tresholds.

4. Experimental methods

4.1 Subjects

A group of experiments were conducted with 3 subjects with no mobility problems (numbered 1, 2 and 3), with ages ranging between 25 and 35 years, stature between 1.70 and 1.88 m and weighing between 60 and 70 kg. The passive version of the exoskeleton was attached to the subjects. The exoskeleton was equipped with the monitoring system to evaluate the activity monitor: detecting static periods, cyclical activities and discriminating the total set of activities.

4.2 Protocol

The group of experiments were developed following a specific protocol that determined a sequence of activities that included repetitions of the categories selected in a circuit: cyclical and non-cyclical dynamic activity (ramps, stairs, gait on level ground), and static activity (standing, sitting). The circuit defined the trajectory of the subject, adopting his preferred velocity of movement and for the static activities fixed intervals of time were defined. In order to divide the movements into activities a posteriori, either assisted direct observation with a chronometer or observation of a video afterwards was used. The sensors were calibrated statically prior to each trial and signal unbalances were corrected to guarantee that the measurement conditions were identical. All the signals corresponding to each trial were stored in files in the mass storage device of the exoskeleton ambulatory measuring system. The data processing methods that the activity monitor applied were programmed in the base platform of the system.

4.3 Detecting static activity

To detect static activities, a threshold equal to 0.05 was applied to the filtered and rectified signal. The threshold applied to the knee angle to detect sitting activity was 30 degrees.

4.4 Detecting periods of cyclical activity

Signal frequency oversampling was 100 Hz. The detector time resolution was defined by applying a window width to discriminate cyclical activities equal to 1.5 seconds. The sensitivity of the method for detecting minimums (section 5.3.1.3) was adjusted to obtain errors less or equal to 1%.

4.5 Discriminating dynamic and static activities

From the inertial sensor signals with the impulse response filter (IRF) (with limits in the 0.1-3 Hz band) the FC signals were generated for each subject assay. From the leg angular velocity rectified signal the RIs were found in the datasets.

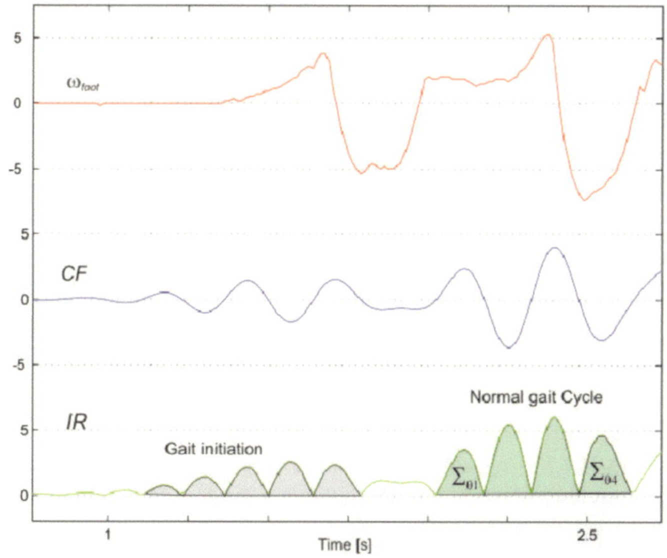

Fig. 4.4. Example of extracting dynamic characteristic signals during foot transitions (static condition) to gait on level ground. The signal measured ωleg is used to calculate FC and RI.

The grouping thresholds of the satisfactory RLMs in the classification in our studies are: i) gait on level ground: RLM > 25; ii) going up/down stairs: RLM < 8; iii) going up/down ramps: 10 < RLM < 20. Calculation of the power spectrum was developed over time with an FFT of 2048 samples, on the composed signals, with an overlapping ns equal to 81, applying the equation 4.5 for each assay with its specific number of samples K. For the grouping of the PTFs (equation 4.6) we define the following thresholds in our studies: i) gait on level ground: PTF > 6; ii) going up/down stairs: PTF < 3.3; iii) going up/down ramps: 3.5 < PTF < 5.

5. Results

Figure 4.5 shows an example of the results of the activity monitor in the experiment with one of the subjects. These results show the discrimination of static and dynamic activity, the identification of Intervals of cyclical activity and the RLM and PFT indices. Based on video observation, situations were established where the monitor detected dynamic activities, either cyclical or indeterminate activities. This example represents the dynamic characteristic signals obtained and calculated from the methods proposed and the identification response of dynamic activities with the two grouping methods presented for a circuit with all the activities.

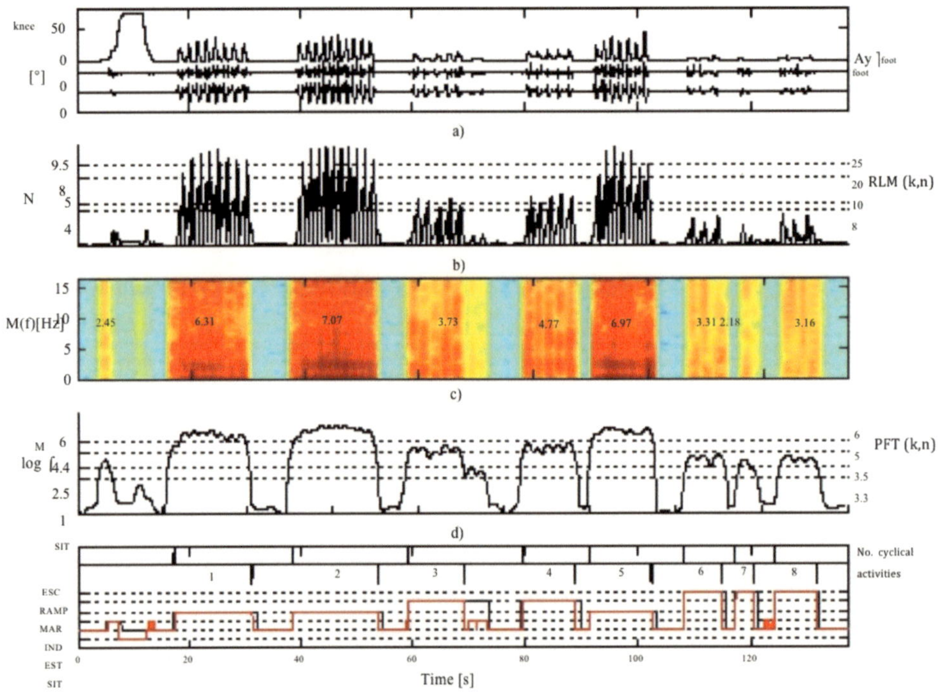

e)

Fig. 4.5. Example of the EAM method results for subject 1 corresponding to a circuit of activities with the exoskeleton. Input signals to the monitor (a), signal N to extract the RLM index based on thresholding (b), instantaneuos frequency components over time and average during periods of activity (c) to calculate the PFT index (d) and EAM outputs (e) calculated based on RLM (red) and PFT (black). The detector presents the classification in categories (ESC: stairs; RAMP: slopes; MAR: walking; IND: undetermined; EST: standing; SIT: sitting).

5.1 Detecting static activity

The results of detecting static activity based on the time invariant state of the foot accelerometer and gyroscope signals show the viability of detecting the static condition irrespective of type – sitting or standing– in the set of categories. Figure 4.6 shows an example of detecting static activity with the resulting filtered and rectified signal, obtained from the two sensor signals, in the transition between the two static activities. The configuration of the detector depends primarily on the threshold value applied to the resulting signal. The cutoff frequency value of the filter and its order are also configuration variables that define the attenuation level of the resulting signal. In our studies we conclude a second-order, Butterworth filter with a cutoff frequency of 0.1Hz and a resulting signal threshold equal to 0.2 as adequate values for the design of the static activity detector with the exoskeleton.

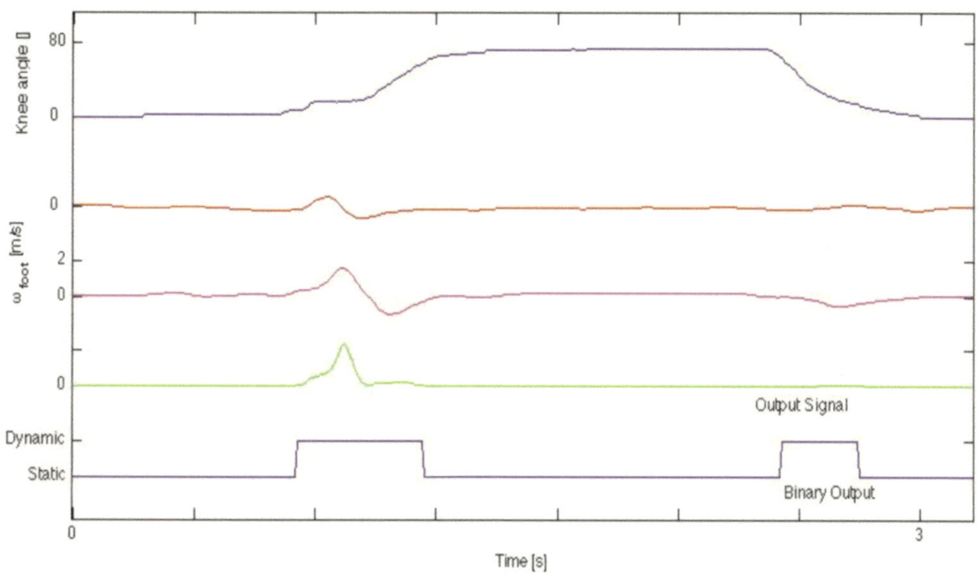

Fig. 4.6. Example of the static activity detector functioning when sitting down and standing up. The degree of knee flexion, foot gyration acceleration and velocity filtered signals ayfoot and ωfoot, the signal from demodulation, calculation of envelope and weighting.

It is concluded that by combining the two inertial sensor signals, the static activities of the other activities can be clearly grouped. This fact is verified in the analysis on the plane of the mean values of the (FC) signals generated from the two sensor signals in the foot segment (see figure 4.10). The activity not identified as static in the dataset is labelled in this stage of the monitor as dynamic activity.

5.2 Detecting periods of cyclical activity

The method proposed and applied to the experimental dataset can identify the cyclical dynamic activities establishing the starting and finishing times of dynamic activity and determining roughly periodical contacts of the lower limb with the ground during this interval.

5.3 Discriminating dynamic activities

To detect minimums of the foot angular velocity signals, we consider a minimum point if it corresponds to the greatest value in a window with a width equal to a tenth of the sampling period and if this corresponds to an increase in velocity greater than 50 degrees/s, compared with the previous sample. The configuration of the width of the detector window must correspond to a criterion defined according to the application context. The instantaneous amplitude of the FC signals is used as a characteristic to apply the grouping indices of dynamic activity proposed.

Figure 4.7 shows the mean values and standard deviations of the FC signals calculated from the foot accelerometer and the leg and foot uniaxial gyroscope tangential signals in the entire periods of dynamic activity. A significant separation can be concluded between subjects for mean values of gait activity on level ground from the foot angular velocity sensor, as information for discrimination. For the FC of ωfoot with the Wilcoxon non-parametric signed rank test, [12], a mean probability of equality p in the data medians compared with the other activities equal to 0.1 was concluded. For FC of ωleg, p was found equal to 0.2. The separation between the gait on sloping ground and stairs for the three subjects with foot gyration velocity showed a statistical distinction for the amplitude of the FC signals, with a p equal to 0.2 obtained using the Wilcoxon signed rank test.

No significant differences were found in the mean FCs of going up and down stairs and ramps, compared with gait on level ground. The activities labelled as indeterminate (transitions between cyclical static and dynamic activities) showed a significant statistical separation with the FCs of the three signals, greater for the FC calculated from the foot rotation velocity. The differences between subjects for cylical gait signals, fundamentally due to the velocity assumed by each subject, make it possible to apply just one threshold to distinguish gait from the other activities. However, the standard deviations of the FC mean values of foot gyration velocity are statistically significant, so it is better to calculate the RLM discriminating index. Figure 4.8 shows the mean values and the standard deviations of the FC signals calculated from the foot accelerometer and the leg and foot uniaxial gyroscope tangential signals, averaged from individual periods (rotation intervals (RIs) in periods of cyclical activity. Using the mean value of the FCs of all the cycles of a cyclical activity, the distinction of gait activity on stairs with regard to gait on sloping ground using the gyroscope on the foot is significant, with p equal to 0.12, for all subjects. The mean standard deviation for each subject of the FCs of foot tangential acceleration in independent cycles of cyclical activity is greater for all subjects when the values for the entire periods of cyclical activity are considered, as can be observed in figure 4.10 with the grouping of activities. The conclusion is that it is best to use the mean values of the cyclical periods for calculating the RLM index.

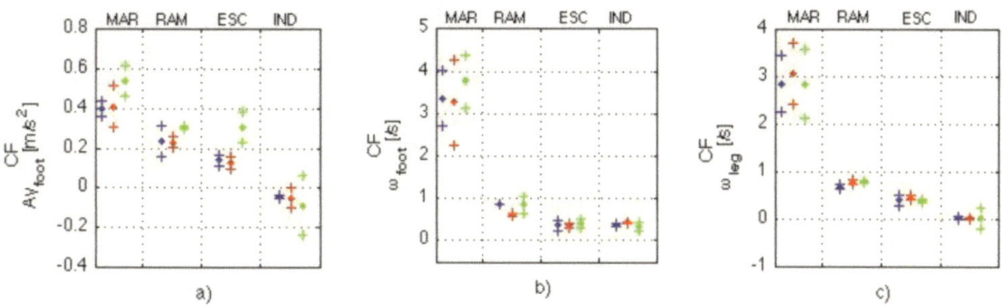

Fig. 4.7. Mean values (± standard deviation) of the FC signals calculated from the foot accelerometer and foot and leg uniaxial gyroscope tangential signals of the periods of indete-rminate, cyclical activity /cyclical and indterminate activity (MAR: gait, RAM: gait on sloping ground, ESC: stairs IND: indeterminate), for the three subjects (S1 blue, S2 red and S3 green).

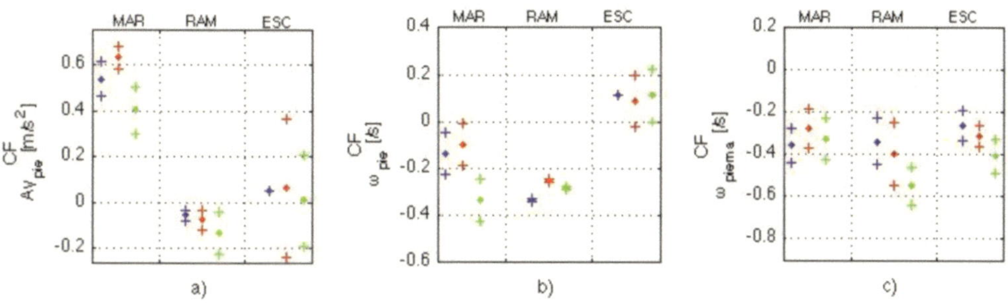

Fig. 4.8. Mean values (± standard deviation) of the FC signals calculated from the foot accelerometer and the foot and leg uniaxial gyroscope tangential signals of the total of individual cycles (rotation intervals, RIs) for each cyclical activity (MAR: gait, RAM: gait on sloping ground, ESC: stairs), for the three subjects (S1 blue, S2 red and S3 green).

5.4 RLM index vs. PFT index

The detection of dynamic activities was calculated with the RLM cyclical activity index (equation 4.4) and the PFT index based on the FFT with the thresholds found experimentally (shown in section 4.4.5). The dependency of the activity monitor response on the configuration of these thresholds must be researched according to the type of application and the subset of categories to be discriminated. Figure 4.9 compares the mean values of the RLM and PFT indices calculated for the three subjects. The detection errors were calculated by correlating the output signals using the two methods with the reference signal obtained from observation. The PFT indices vary to a greater extent than the RLMs for the standard deviations.

The variation in the RLM index for the subjects and repeated activities of going up/down stairs is significant and the detection mean error of this activity with this method is 8%. The detection mean error for the three subjects walking on sloping ground (RAM) with the RLM index was 10%, whereas for the detection with the PFT index the mean error was 18%. The detection of cyclical gait with the two methods did not reflect any significant differences statistically, with an overall mean error of 1.5%, a fact that was verified by separating the gait mean values from the other activities.

It is observed that the detections classified as indeterminate occur during the transitions between dynamic and static activity in 90% of the cases, as a result of overlapping between values of the indices discriminating activity on sloping ground and static activity. The overall viability for detecting activity in this study with the EAM is 4.2 %.

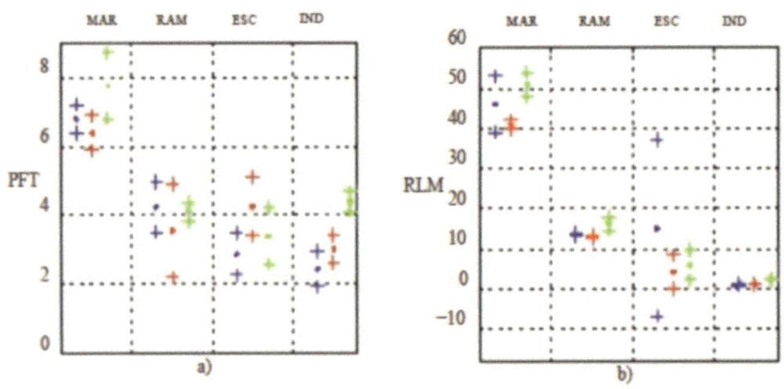

Fig. 4.9. Mean values (± Standard deviation) of the resulting PFT and RLM indices for discriminating dynamic activities (EST: static, MAR: gait, RAM: gait on sloping ground, ESC: stairs, IND: indeterminate), calculated for all the set of tests with the three subjects (S1 blue, S2 red and S3 green).

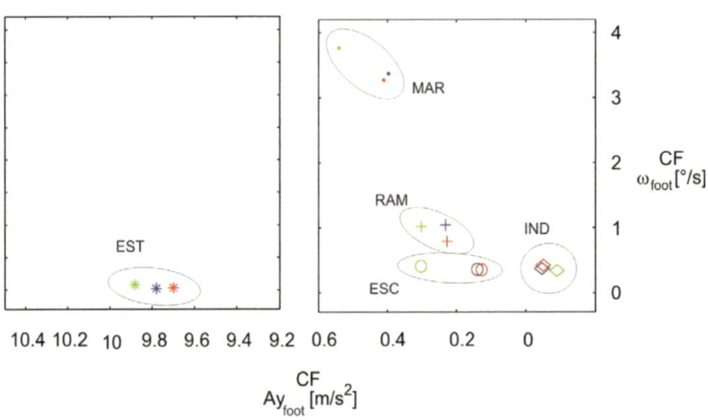

Fig. 4.10. Mean values on the plane of FC signals calculated from the foot accelerometer tangential signal vs. the foot gyroscope tangential signal, for periods of dynamic and static activity detected in the set of tests (EST : static, M AR : gait, RA M : gait on sloping ground, ESC: stairs, IND : indeterminate), for the three subjects (S1 blue, S2 red and S3 green).

Subject	Activity	PFT (log σM)	RLM
1	MAR	6.78 (± 0.41)	46 (± 7)
	RAM	4.25 (± 0.73)	13.59 (± 0.26)
	ESC	2.83 (± 0.63)	15.04 (± 21.84)
	IND	2.45 (± 0.51)	1.10 (±0.32)
2	MAR	6.37 (± 0.49)	41 (± 4)
	RAM	3.55 (± 1.35)	12.87 (± 0.45)
	ESC	4.2 (± 0.85)	2.11 (± 4.19)
	IND	3.02 (± 0.4)	1.15 (±0.23)
3	MAR	7.74 (± 0.94)	51 (± 3)
		4.1 (± 0.28)	16.25 (± 1.59)
	RAM ESC	3.4 (± 0.81)	5.93 (± 3.96)
	IND	4.4 (± 0.27)	2.3 (±0.3)

Table 4.1. Mean values and standard deviations of the RLM and PFT indices from all the set of repetitions, grouped into dynamic activities.

6. Discussion and conclusions

The discrimination of dynamic activities in the EAM groups characteristics with signal thresholds that describe morphological characteristics of the signals and the frequency content of lower-limb movements. It has been proven that sensitivity to differences between subjects is acceptable with this method, which does not require an initial reference measurement of each subject to configure the monitor. Nevertheless, a large scale study including a larger number of subjects will be required in order to test the robustness of the proposed method. In this study we have considered a set of five categories with a low classification mean error in a small group of healthy subjects. The capacity of the monitor to detect gait on sloping ground was lower, probably due to different strategies adopted by the subjects with the exoskeleton. The width of the detector window of the cyclical activity obtained in this study is satisfactory for the experimentation proposed to evaluate the activity monitor. Analysis of the standard deviation of the mean values of the two indices proposed showed a better functioning of the monitor with the proposed RLM discriminating index in the overall results, although it was more sensitive to subject differences. Moreover, the computational efficiency of applying this method, compared with the PFT, resulting from applying the FFT, is improved, with a ratio of 1 to 20, in processing time.

The capacity of the configuration of inertial measurement units in the exoskeleton segments and the knee angle precision sensor to distinguish movements and postures was confirmed. The transition between sitting down and standing up with the method proposed showed excellent functioning. The potential of this method in different applications for other types of portable technical aids (standing frames, walking frames, wheelchairs) is high.

It is important to highlight that the applicability of these methods to pathological cases considers that the gait compensation system approximates pathological patterns to normal patterns and, therefore, it is considered that the applicability is for general use. Adapting classification methods to particular cases, such as for patients who require a permanent joint block will necessitate adjusting the activity monitor subsystems. We take the study of pathological cases as a field of future work which will depend on the viability of the application during prolonged use of the compensation system (adaptations in the medium and long term).

With the system it is possible to quantify the number of knee flexions attained with the compensation system, depending on the time used and in relation to the dynamic activity. Thus, detector functioning and sensitivity to cyclical dynamic activities can be studied considering cyclical activities in different conditions where abrupt changes in trajectory or activity may occur. We highlight the need to analyse multiple aspects relative to the validity of the methods in different conditions and in the application of exoskeletons and orthoses in the daily life of subjects with muscular weakness.

7. References

[1] J. Fahrenberg and M. Myrtek. Ambulatory assessment: Computer-assisted psychological and psychophysiological methods in monitoring and field studies. Seattle: Hogrefe and Huber, 1996.

[2] C.J . Casperson, K .E. Powell, and G .M. Christianson. Physical activity, exercise, and physical fitness: definitions and distinctions for health related research. Public Health Rep, 100(3):26- 31, 1985.

[3] B.G. Steele, B. Belza, and K. Cain. Bodies in motion: Monitoring daily activity and exercise with motion sensors in people with chronic pulmonary disease. Journal of Rehabilitation Research and Development, 40(5):45–58, 2003.

[4] G.C. Le Masurier, S.M . Lee, and C . Tudor-L ocke. Motion sensor accuracy under controlled and free-living conditions. M ed Sci Sports E xerc, 36(5):905–10, 2004.

[5] D.R Bassett, B.E. Ainsworth, A.M. Swartz, S.J . Strath, W .L. O'Brien, and G .A. King. Validity of four motion sensors in measuring moderate intensity physical activity. Medicine and Science in Sports and Exercise, 32(9):905–10, 2000.

[6] A. Pentland. Healthwear: medical technology becomes wearable. Computer, 37(5):55–65, 2004.

[7] P.H. Veltink, H. Bussmann, W W. de Vries, W. Martens, and R.C. Van Lummel. Detection of static and dynamic activities using uniaxial accelerometers. IEEE Trans. on Neural Systems and Rehabilitation, 4(4):375–385, 1996.

[8] S. Lee and K . Mase. Activity and location recognition using wearable sensors. IE E E P ervasive C om puting, 1(3):24–32, 2002.

[9] W.H. Groeneveld, K.J. Waterlander, A. De Moel, H. Konijnendijk, and C.K. Snijders. Instrumentation for ambulatory monitoring of patient movement. In Proceedings of the 12th International Symposium on Biotelemetry, 1992.

[10] GAIT Project. Development of user req uirements specificaction. Technical report, Roessingh Research and Development (RRD), 2003.

[11] W.L.J. Martens. Exploring the information content and some applications of body mounted piezoresistive accelerometers. Dynamic Analysis Using Body Fixed Sensors, pages 8-11, 1994.

[12] F. Wilcoxon. Individual comparisons by ranking methods. Biometrics, 1:80–83, 1945.

10

Sensori-Motor Appropriation of an Artefact: A Neuroscientific Approach

Yves Rybarczyk[1], Philippe Hoppenot[2],
Etienne Colle[2] and Daniel R. Mestre[3]
[1]*New University of Lisbon*
[2]*University of Evry*
[3]*University of Mediterranean / CNRS*
[1]*Portugal*
[2,3]*France*

1. Introduction

The required objective for the design of a machine to be used by a human operator is its adaptation to the user's capabilities. According to this logic, the ideal system should fit perfectly into the human sensori-motor loop. The system would disappear from the field of consciousness and the operator would use it as a "natural" extension to her/his own body. In order to complete this goal we first have to know what the human capacities of appropriation of an artefact are. This chapter proposes to answer this question from a review of a series of studies in the field of psychology, neuropsychology, neurophysiology and information technologies.

We will understand that the appropriation, or ownership, is achieved not only thanks to the natural adaptation properties of the human being, but also through artificial processes designed by the HMI engineer. The human adaptation is described as involving two complementary processes, taking place in opposite directions, called *assimilation* and *accommodation* (Piaget, 1952). This adaptation occurs because the nervous system's plasticity makes it possible to integrate an artefact in the body schema (Maravita & Iriki, 2004, for a review). The fundamental aim in the HMI field is to further natural processes of adaptation via an implementation of artificial ones. Like natural processes, artificial ones can be carried out according to two directions. On one hand, the way in which the machine works can be brought closer to the human skills (Rybarczyk et al., 2001). This approach is called anthropocentric. On the other hand, the individual her/himself can be modified in order to plug electro-computational devices into the nervous system and to become a cybernetic organism or *cyborg*. This last research area is not science fiction anymore, but has already demonstrated its advantages in the field of assistive technologies (Hochberg et al., 2006) or in enhancing the human capabilities (Warwick, 2009). Figure 1 represents the sensori-motor appropriation of artefacts such as introduced here. The following sections of this chapter will describe in detail each module through an explanation supported by neuroscientific evidences.

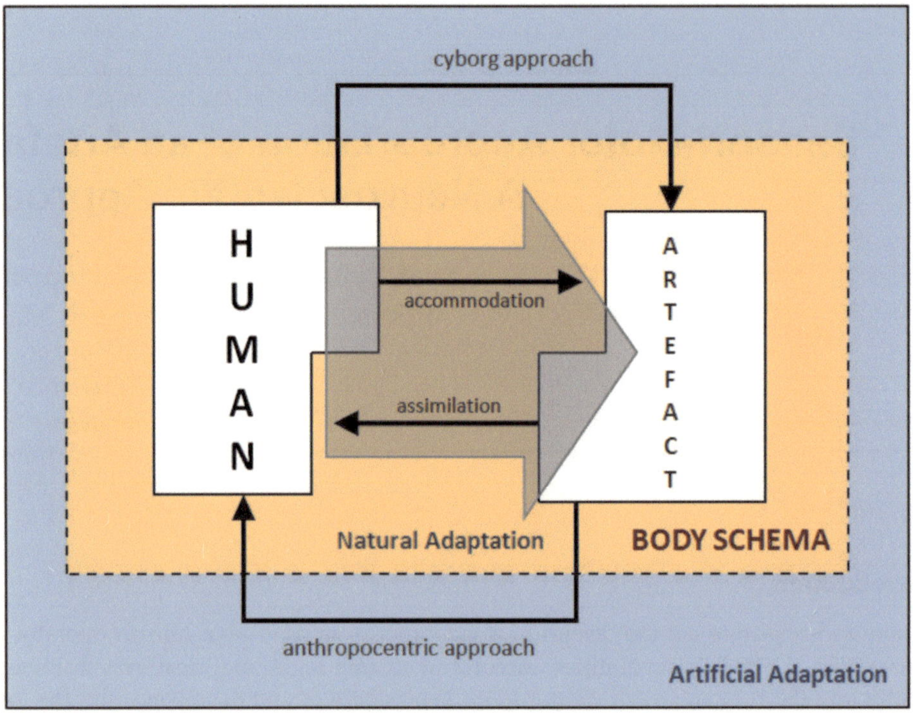

Fig. 1. Principle of the appropriation process that involves an integration of the artefact into the human body schema. To notice that the natural adaptation (accommodation + assimilation) can be boosted by artificial implementations from the artefact to the human being (anthropocentrism) or/and from the human being to the artefact (cyborg).

2. Natural processes

When a living being interacts with the environment, natural processes of adaptation are triggered to enable the individual to fit with her/her surrounding world. Since a long time ago, numerous psychological schools have tried to understand the underlying mechanisms of the human-artefact interaction. Today, some of these theories can be supported by the recent finding in the field of the neuropsychology and neurophysiology. This knowledge has a direct implication to comprehend the user's appropriation of electronic devices. The first part of this chapter will describe the natural human-artefact adaptation process from the point of view of the different scientific areas until its last involvement in the field of information technologies.

2.1 Psychological evidences

2.1.1 Instrumental approach

To understand clearly the concept of a machine appropriation, or more generally an instrument appropriation by a human being, it is necessary to put it back into the original psychological context. The first researcher who attempted to mix psychology and technology was Vygotsky. His approach tried to put activities with instruments as the central problem of the construction and functioning of cerebral processes of the human being (Vygotsky, 1930). He noted that the integration of an instrument into a behavioural process induces actions linked to its use and to its control. The existence of this mediator between the organism and the surrounding environment transforms the execution of the psychological processes involved in the *instrumental action*. This expression is defined by Vygotsky as a collection of functions that are specifically associated and coordinated following the characteristics of the instrument itself.

Studies by Rabardel, in the context of robotics, extend this approach to the re-composition of the action, following an instrumental approach to human-machine relationships (Rabardel, 1995). An instrument is a hybrid entity that is not reducible to an artefact, which is just the physical component of an instrument. Actually, an instrument emerges from two entities. On one hand, it is composed by the artefact, usually a manufactured product. On the other hand, it is also composed from one or more of its schemes[1] of use, which are the result of the individual construction itself. So overall, the instrument is not only a part of the external world - an artefact - but also a product of the operator's action - the schemes.

However, although artefacts and schemes are associated to define an instrument, they can be relatively independent. Indeed, one scheme can be applied to different artefacts of the same class (e.g., same driving schemes can be used to steering different vehicles) or neighbouring classes (sometimes with possible dramatic consequences, like using heating properties of microwave ovens to dry a pet). On the contrary, one artefact can be associated to different schemes for different functions (e.g., a screwdriver can be used to make a hole).

Consequently, a constant instrument, with qualities of preservation and reuse, consists of a stable association of two variables which, jointly, represent processing and action as a solution to deal with a determinate situation. However, the question is how the construction of this constant instrument begins and happens. Whatever the scheme's side or the artefact's side, this construction does not typically occur ex nihilo. Generally, artefacts are pre-existing, even though they have to be processed by the individual to become instruments. Schemes usually come from the individual repertoire and they are generalized or accommodated to a new artefact. Sometimes, when the artefact design is completely unknown, entirely new schemes have to be constructed. To explain the way in which the construction process of the instrumental entity is carried out, it is necessary to understand the *piagetian* theory of the individual adaptation to her/his surrounding environment.

2.1.2 Adaptation theory

According to Piaget, intelligence is, in the first place, adaptation (Piaget, 1936). The complexity of the living being's organisation is understandable through the balanced relationship that occurs between the individual and the environment. This balance is possible because of the transformations occurring inside the organism, following the characteristics of the environment in which the individual evolves. The aim of these

[1] The scheme of an action is a structured collection of generalized features of the action, which enables to repeat a same action or to apply this action to new contexts. Thus, a scheme consists of a general template that can reoccur in different circumstances and complete various achievements. For instance, in the case of a prehension task, although we extend more or less an arm or we open more or less a hand according to the object's distance, it is always the same scheme of catching.

modifications is to promote the environment-individual interactions, favourable to the conservation of the living being. Piaget - who analyses the emergence of intelligence according to its sensori-motor aspect - divides adaptation into two complementary processes.

The first one is the assimilation process. According to Piaget, all the external realities, regarding the individual organisation cycle, that respond to an organism's need can be potentially assimilated. This process is defined as a behavioural trend to be preserved. This is possible thanks to the behaviour repetition that becomes schematized, which means that it is supported by one or more schemes. These schemes, composed by a structured collection of generalized features of the action, enable to reproduce a same action and to apply it in new contexts (Piaget & Beth, 1961).

Besides, the schemes represent an active organization of the lived experience, integrating the past. They have a structure with a history and they are transformed following the new experienced situations. So, the story of a scheme is that of its generalization but also its differentiation from the contents it is applied to. The generalization is conceptualized by the assimilation process. In concrete terms, because of an apparent proximity, the use of new objects can be assimilated by pre-existing schemes. On the other hand, the differentiation property is linked to the second process implicated in adaptation: the accommodation process.

When the external realities do not allow a direct assimilation, mechanisms of accommodation are triggered at the scheme level. The example of a stick manipulation learning by the child (Piaget, 1936) helps to understand the complementary nature of the assimilation and accommodation processes. In this experiment, a child is in front of a sofa on which a bottle is placed. The child has a stick with which s/he had learned to hit objects. First, the child tries to catch the bottle directly, which is not possible, and then begins to hit it with the stick. The bottle falls by chance. The child goes on hitting the bottle when it is on the floor. S/he observes the movement of the bottle and begins to push it with the stick to bring it towards her/him. Later, without a stick, s/he uses a book to bring again the bottle towards her/him.

The experiment shows that the child has first used a pre-existing scheme (hit with a stick), but such assimilation does not allow to catch the bottle. The scheme is progressively accommodated, in order to obtain the movement of the object and a new scheme: push with a stick. Then, this last one is generalized to other objects, here a book. Rybarczyk et al. (2002) argue that human-machine interaction follows the same logic. When the machine presents operating modes that are close to those of the operator, they can be directly assimilated. On the contrary, if the device is completely "different", the operator must accommodate her/his schemes to the new device (figure 2). This is this *piagetian* principle of adaptation applied to human-machine relationship which is described here as the mechanism of appropriation[2].

Consequently, in order to achieve a successful ergonomic design, it is essential to take into account the gap existing between the schemes and representations of the operator and the

---

[2] This term, which is often employed in the field of educational research to refer to the child's capability of learning to use a pedagogical tool, is not directly used in this sense. Actually, we apply the word following the meaning given by Bullinger (1987), who stresses the appropriation process to the level of sensori-motor integration.

schemes and representations that are necessary to control the machine. Two directions are possible. The first one consists in reducing the gap between the pre-existing schemes of the operator and the schemes that are relevant to control the machine, with the objective of extending the sensori-motor repertoire of the operator. In this case, the operator will try to attribute her/his characteristics to the machine. The second direction is to take into account the existing gap - then ergonomic conception will try to point it out, in order to help the operator to conceptualize it.

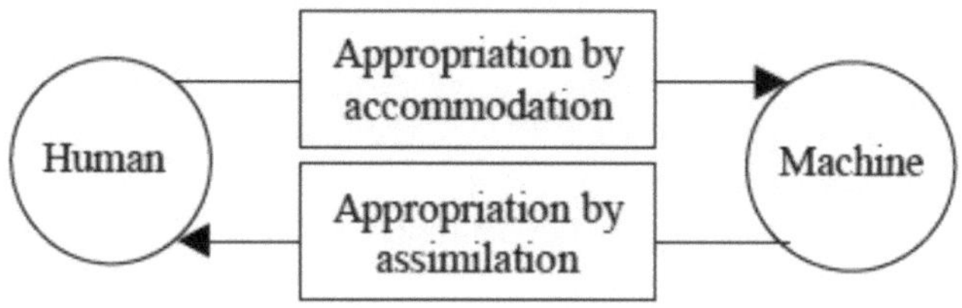

Fig. 2. Application of the adaptation *piagetian* model to human-machine interaction.

2.2 Artefact integration into the body schema

2.2.1 What is body schema?

The precedent section clearly explained that human sensori-motor and cognitive development is achieved primarily through interaction with the surrounding environment. This statement means that each of our interactions with the environment will trigger a sensorial cue, carried out to the central nervous system, to inform this latter about our physical capacities. This mental representation of our functional body, created and updated by the central nervous system, is known as the body schema (Paillard, 1991). More precisely, the body schema is defined as a mental construction or internal model we have about our body and parts of it, with relation to the environment, in movement or in rest. It is built through experience, thanks to the combination of multi-modal sensations. If, indeed, the individual has a more or less conscious representation of his/her body action capabilities, this implies that s/he must have a more or less precise idea of the limits of this body. In others words, if I have the consciousness that my arm has a length of about 70cm, I have the implicit knowledge that my range of action, by simple arm extension, is approximatively an arc of 70cm radius. As motor processes contribute in the first place to the organism construction (O'Regan & Nöe, 2001; Borghi & Cimatti, 2010; Gallese & Sinigaglia, 2010), it suggests a different sensori-motor processing, depending on whether the space considered is reachable vs. unreachable by the hand.

The strongest evidence for distinct representations of near and far space in the human's brain comes from studies of subjects with a well-known neuropsychological disorder called neglect. In a majority of subjects, the lesion involves the right inferior parietal cortex, especially the supramarginal gyrus (Heilman et al., 1983; Husain & Kennard, 1996). In the most common form of neglect, the subject ignores an entire side, or hemifield, of egocentric space, usually the left side (Jeannerod, 1987; Halligan & Marshall, 1994). For example, subjects will incorrectly bisect horizontal lines to the right of the midpoint, thus neglecting the left side of the line. However, recent studies have found that neglect is not a single monolithic disorder but can be fractionated into a variety of more specific disorders, each of which reflects the involvement of certain components of the brain highly multifaceted architecture for spatial representation (Bisiach, 1997; Vallar, 1998). For the purpose of this paper, the most important type of neglect is sometimes referred to as proximal/distal neglect.

Using exactly the same methods, two different studies described brain-damaged subjects who exhibited opposite types of neglect. The first study, conducted by Halligan and Marshall (1991), concerned a single subject with a large right temporal-parietal lesion. The main experiment consisted in two additional line bisection tasks in the following conditions. First, the subject used an ink pen to bisect horizontal lines at a distance of 45cm, well within arm reach. In a second condition, he used a laser pointer to perform a similar line bisection task at a distance of 244cm, well beyond arm reach. Results show a pointing deviation on the right side in the first condition and a correct pointing in the second condition. This pattern suggests that the subject has a selective impairment of the representation of the near left sector of space. The second study was conducted by Cowey et al. (1994) and employed the same experimental procedures to test other patients with neglect. Contrary to the precedent case, subjects pointed correctly only in the proximal space, which means they had a specific neglect to the far sector.

The fact that these two studies demonstrate opposite performance profiles strongly suggests that the brain contains separate neural systems for representing stimuli in near (or peripersonal) space on the one hand, and in far (or extrapersonal) space on the other side. Neurophysiological studies done with macaque monkeys confirm, from the anatomo-functional point of view, the presence of distinctive neural pathways to process information in each spatial sector. More data are available regarding near space, as compared to far space. Neuro-anatomical substrates dedicated to analyze peripersonal space stretch from the parietal lobe (medial, ventral and anterior intraparietal aeras) to the frontal lobe (premotor areas). These circuits are implicated for reaching, for grasping and for monitoring limb movements in relation to the face. The majority of these neurons has bimodal tactile and visual response properties for a stimulus delivered at a distance inferior to about 100 cm in relation to the skin surface (Graziano & Gross, 1995; Fogassi et al., 1996). This bimodal property delimits the well-know pericorporal (or peripersonal) sector, where the integration of kinaesthetic and visual information will be facilitated, in order to improve the coordination of limb movements with respect to a corporal frame of reference (Rizzolatti et al., 1997; Previc, 1998).

In spite of these evident proofs of differential cerebral treatment, depending on whether action space is proximal or distal, we do not have the consciousness of living in a segmented environment. What could explain the phenomenal continuity of space? A partial answer has been provided by Cowey et al. (1999), investigating whether the boundary between near and far regions of space is abrupt or progressive. To address this question, they asked neglect patients to perform a series of line bisection tasks, at six increasing distances, from 25 to 400cm. Results show an increase in the pointing error at progressively farther distances, suggesting a continuous change from peripersonal to extrapersonal space. In the same way, neurophysiological recordings among animals confirm this overlapping between the two regions of space. So far, it has been shown that neurons in area F4 (pathway of the peripersonal system) have a gradient firing response that is strongest to stimuli within the proximal region and steadily declines as stimuli are placed farther away (Graziano et al., 1997). The receptive field depth of these neurons also progressively expands as the speed of stimuli towards the body part increases (Fogassi et al., 1996).

2.2.2 Neuroscientific evidences of integration

Such a fuzzy border between spatial sectors suggests, therefore, that spatial layouts are relatively extensible from one to the other. It is, in part, because of this dynamic property that the representation of space around us seems homogenous and coherent, whatever the situation. However, this representational flexibility has certain limitations. Some works trying to delimit more precisely the dynamic properties of the body schema have focused, principally, on the evaluation of the peripersonal space around the hand. To address this question, they have employed, in the majority of case, the experimental paradigm of tool manipulation (Cardinali et al., 2009; Maravita & Iriki, 2004, for a review).

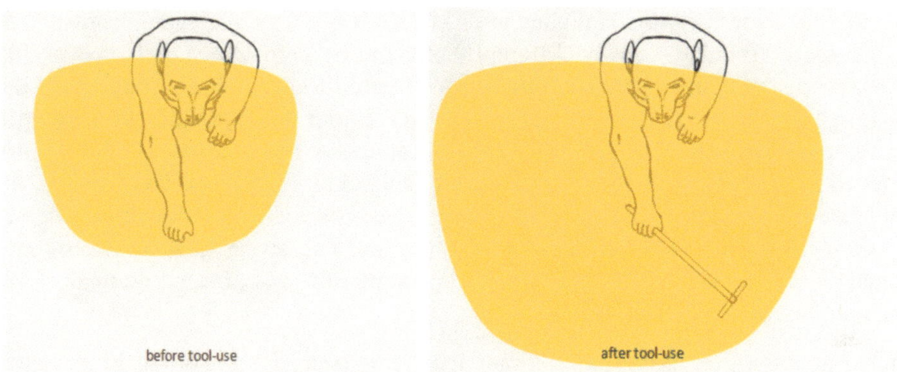

(a) (b)

Fig. 3. Visual receptive fields (vRF) of bimodal neurons for the monkey right arm (yellow area), before (a) and after tool-use (b). Immediately after tool-use the dimension of vRF is enlarged in order to include the length of the rake (adapted from Iriki et al., 1996).

Iriki et al. (1996) have shown, in monkeys, that the activation of far and near space maps can be influenced by the use of tools when the action modifies the spatial relationships between the body and environmental objects (figure 3). They found bimodal neurons in the monkey parietal lobe that coded for the schema of the hand, similar to those studied by Graziano and Gross (1995), and by Fogassi et al. (1996). As already discussed, these neurons fire when a tactile stimulus is delivered to the monkey's hand and when visual objects are presented near the hand tactile receptive field. The most striking feature described by Iriki et al. (1996) was that visual receptive fields of the bimodal neurons could be modified by a purposeful action. Indeed, when the monkeys reached for far objects with a rake, the visual receptive field was enlarged to include the entire length of the rake and to cover the expanded accessible space. The authors explained their results by postulating that, during the reaching movement, the tool was assimilated to the animal's hand, becoming part of the hand representation (Aglioti et al., 1996; Paillard, 1993). The space now reachable by the prolongation of the hand was enlarged, including part of what had previously been far space, and the spatial relationship between the body and objects was modified by the action of reaching with a tool. As a consequence, far space was remapped as near space and the neurons that fired for near space also fired when what had previously been coded as far space was reached by the rake. Moreover, this extension was reversible, because the elongation of bimodal neurons receptive fields contracted towards the hand after a certain delay after tool use. This constitutes further demonstration of the remapping plasticity of the primate spatial representation.

This modulation of space coding can also be observed in human beings. Berti and Frassinetti (2000) showed in a right brain-damaged patient that, when the cerebral representation of pericorporal space was extended to include a tool used for a purposeful action, the space previously mapped as far was then treated as near, like in monkeys. Patient "PP" had a clear neglect in near space in many different tasks including reading and line bisection. Line bisection in near space was affected by neglect both when the patient had to perform a pointing task with the index finger of the right hand and, when she had to point with a projection light-pen. When the lines were positioned far from the body, neglect was much less severe or even absent when tested using the projection light-pen. This result is very similar to that described by Halligan and Marshall (1991) and, again, shows that the functional space around us can be differently affected by brain damage. However, in Berti and Frassinetti's experiment, the patient was also asked to bisect lines in far space using a stick through which the patient could reach the line. Under this condition, neglect appeared also in far space and was as severe as neglect in near space. This result might be explained in reference to neurophysiological data reported by Iriki et al. (1996). Like in monkeys, the use of a tool extended the body schema, thus enlarging the peripersonal space to include all the space between the patient's body and the stimulus. Far space was, as a consequence, remapped as near. And, because near space representation was affected by neglect, neglect became manifest also in far space.

A similar remapping of distal as proximal space has been demonstrated in patients with cross-modal visuo-tactile extinction (Farnè & Làdavas, 2000). This term refers to a clinic symptom, whereby some patients with right-hemisphere damage fail to report a tactile stimulus delivered to their contralesional left hand when a concurrent visual stimulus is presented to their ipsilesional right hand (Di Pellegrino et al., 1997). This phenomenon can be easily explained by neurophysiological recordings in monkeys, which stress the bimodal characteristic of neurons coding the peripersonal space surrounding each part of the body and especially the hand (Fogassi et al., 1996; Grazziano & Gross, 1995). Indeed, if a similar cell population exists in humans, a visual stimulus near one hand might thereby enhances the representation of that hand (Driver & Spence, 1998), to compete (Driver et al., 1997) with the activity produced by touch on the other hand, thus producing cross-modal extinction when the other hand has been "disadvantaged" by a unilateral lesion (Làdavas et al., 1998).

In Farnè and Làdavas' experiment (2000), cross-modal visuo-tactile extinction was assessed by presenting visual stimuli far from the patient's ipsilesional hand, in correspondence of the distal edge of a rake statically held in their hand. The results show that cross-modal extinction was more severe after the patients used the rake to retrieve distant objects with respect to a condition in which the rake was not used. Again, the evidence of an expansion of peri-hand space lasted for only a few minutes after tool use. Finally, pointing movements towards distant objects also produced cross-modal extinction entirely comparable with that obtained in the pre-tool-use condition, showing that the expansion of hand peripersonal space is strictly dependent upon the use of the tool, aimed at physically reaching objects located outside the hand reaching space, and it does not merely result from directional motor activity.

2.3 Appropriation of electronic devices

The tool appropriation into the body schema presented above refers to experiments that have been limited to direct interaction with simple tools. In these conditions, perceptivo-motor relationships are relatively straightforward and natural for the human being. So, the question remains whether the user can incorporate an artefact into her/his body schema when the correlation between motor actions and their perceptual consequences is more complex, like in remote control situations.

2.3.1 Virtual reality

The concept of *presence,* defined in the field of virtual reality, resembles the concept of appropriation in certain aspects. The sensation of "being there", in place of the avatar that represents the operator in the virtual world is one example. In Minsky (1980) the term "tele-presence" is used to describe the operator's sensation to be physically present in the space where s/he acts via the machine. Sheridan (1992) proposed to distinguish between virtual presence for virtual reality and "tele-presence" for remote control situations. This separation is not useful in neuroscience (Ijsselsteijn et al., 2000). In fact, the central question is the mental representation of one's human body. Subjects in virtual reality situations say they were mentally more "situated" in the virtual world than in the physical world (Slater & Usoh, 1993). Loomis (1992) distinguishes between the phenomenal body and the physical body to explain the *distal attribution* of an avatar to her/himself in the virtual world. According to this author, in this singular situation, there are three entities. The first one is the objective entity, which is the physical body of the individual. The second is the virtual body, represented by the user body inside the virtual environment (the avatar). The last entity is the body schema or mental representation the user has of her/his own body. When the individual interacts with a mediated world, her/his body schema can be deteriorated by swapping between virtual body and physical body (Meyer & Biocca, 1992). Evidences of *presence* the can be showed following multi-level of analysis, from the phenomenology to the neural activity underlying the embodiment feeling (Ijsselsteijn, 2002).

From the phenomenological point of view, one of the most famous demonstrations of the distal attribution is the rubber hand illusion (Botvinik & Cohen, 1998). In this experiment, a left rubber hand is placed on a table, visible from the participant. On the contrary, the left real hand of the participant is hidden from her/his field of view. When the experimenter synchronously stimulates the subject's hand and the fake hand, by means of two brushes, subject came to feel that the life-size rubber hand was their own. This experiment was reproduced in virtual reality to know whether this phenomenon is replicable in mediated environments (Yuan & Steed, 2010). The participant is placed in a situation of virtual immersion thanks to a head-mounted display. S/he is sat in front a physical table and has to perform various tasks in the virtual environment with her/his right arm. One task is to point at coloured stimuli in a specific order (adaptation of the Simon game) and another one is to drop a ball to a hole. Also, in one condition, an emotional stimulation is induced to the subject, seeing a lamp falling over the virtual hand. The avatar that the participant sees is displayed from a first person point of view. The presence feeling is gauged through a questionnaire and the galvanic skin response (GSR). The questionnaire results show the participants have the real feeling that the virtual arm is her/his own arm. Furthermore, the increase of the GSR immediately after the falling lamp event is a physiological recording that confirms the self-identification with the avatar. As the magnitude of the response ownership is similar to those demonstrated for the rubber hand illusion, we can deduce that the process of appropriation of a simple artefact would be similar to one occurring with an electronic device.

Fig. 4. Brain parietal lobe processing of primates acting in virtual reality environment. (a) Visual receptive fields (vRF) of each hand are activated around the video recording of the monkey's hand displayed on the screen. (b) Active tool-use extends, along the rake, the vRF of the hand image on the monitor (adapted from Iriki et al., 2001).

For a further exploration of this distal attribution, Iriki et al. (2001) have analysed neurophysiological data of brain monkeys, when the animal is set in remote control situation. Authors carried out an experiment in which monkeys were trained to recognize their own hand on a video monitor. Simultaneously, investigators recorded the activity of bimodal neurons receptive fields localized around the hand (figure 4). First, results showed that visual receptive fields (vRF) were formed around the image of the monkey's hand in the monitor. After tool-use, the vRF around the image of the hand on the monitor extended along the image of the handheld rake, like the vRF extension when viewing the hand directly. In other conditions in the experiment, the size and position of the vRFs of these bimodal neurons were modified accordingly with the expansion, compression or displacement of the hand's image in the video monitor, even though the posture and position (and of course the size) of the real hand remained constant. Furthermore, vRFs for the same neurons were formed around a restricted spot left around the tip of the tool (akin to a computer cursor) when all other images on the monitor were filtered out. These results suggest that the visual image of the hand (and even its "virtual" equivalent, such as a spot of light) in the monitor was treated by the monkeys as an extension of their own body.

2.3.2 Teleoperation

In the neuroscientific studies presented before, tools are relatively simples and the perceptual-motor relationships are quite straightforward for the user. So the question remains about what the appropriation process is when the human-artefact interaction is highly complex, like in teleoperation of a robotic device. Indeed, in the case of the remote control of an electromechanical machine, in addition to an indirect contact with the artefact, the interface is significantly more refined. The appropriation of a telerobot according to a process of device embodiment into the operator's body schema was studied by Rybarczyk and Mestre (2011). To do that, the authors compared the performance of human beings in a natural condition vs. other in a teleoperated condition, in a discrimination task of the reachable area of an effector (participant's arm vs. telerobotic arm). The study is presented in this section.

Method

The originality of this experiment is thus to reveal the body schema's alteration, not through the study of neuropsychological cases, but using behavioural assessment in normal subjects placed in a teleoperation situation. This assessment is based on the concept of affordance, describing the interaction relationships between an actor (or an effector) and the surrounding environment. The affordance of an object or situation is related to the activities that it offers or "affords" for an organism possessing given action capabilities (Gibson, 1979; Turvey & Shaw, 1979). Such functional possibilities for action are determined by the fit between properties of the environment and properties of the organism. For example, an object "affords" grasping if its size, shape and surface texture are compatible with the functional morphology of the organism's prehensile limb (Newell & Scully, 1987). In a similar way, an object at distance affords a simple extension movement (to touch it) if its length is smaller than the human's arm dimension.

Warren and Whang (1987) have proposed a measurement method to describe the attunement of environmental variables to organism's action variables. They defined the "Pi" dimensionless numbers, being a ratio between an environmental dimension and a body dimension. As the ratio is varied, optimal points in the ecosystem may emerge for preferred states at which a given action is most comfortable or efficient, and critical points will emerge, at which the limits on an action are reached and a phase transition to a qualitatively different action occurs. Warren (1984) studied the case of stair climbing, showing that there is a particular ratio between the stairs height and leg length for which ascending a stair is optimally comfortable and efficient (in energetical terms). In the following experimental conditions, the object to catch is at a variable distance (D) in relation to the robotics' arm length (R). Thus, as distance increases, appears a critical distance for which the grasping by simple extension becomes impossible, and requires the transition to a prehensile action that would be coupled, for example, with a locomotion movement of the mobile arm's mounted platform. The value of this critical distance is given by the Pi ratio ($\Pi = D/R$) becoming superior to 1.

If we ask an operator to estimate the maximum reachable distance, the value of the Pi ratio will inform us about the operator's representation of space, caused by his interaction with the machine. Indeed, to estimate the distance in which an extension of the arm is not enough to catch an object, the operator needs to carry out a translation from absolute coordinates of the environment into robotics' system coordinates (Fitch & Turvey, 1978). The Pi ratio thus delivers a numerical estimation of the operator's body schema, on which statistical analysis can be conducted. Pi ratio is thus defined as the subject's estimation of the maximal distance of grasping divided by the arm's length. Thus, the more the ratio is close to 1, the more the individual has a good representation of his range of action in space and therefore the more his/her body schema conforms to actual action capabilities. Afterwards, in robotic conditions, the Pi ratio obtained when the subject is using the manipulator is compared with that obtained in natural conditions (with the subject's own arm). If the Pi ratio calculated for the peribrachial space is not statistically different between the two conditions, this result might be interpreted in terms of an extension of the operator's pericorporal space to the remote manipulator arm length.

Procedure

During the experiment, the robot or the human being, depending on the condition, was placed in front of a table (figure 5a). The rotation axis of the subject's or robotic shoulder was aligned along the median axis of the table. From the centre of this axis radiated five rays, visible only for the experimenter. These straight lines were 20 degrees apart. They stretched out with respect to the median line, which was the 0° ray, on an angular sector, from -40 to 40 degrees (figure 5b). In the teleoperated condition, the camera position was located up, on the left and slightly behind (to compensate for the limitation of camera optical field of view) in relation to the rotation axis (or shoulder) of the robot. In the "natural" condition, individuals were put exactly in the same location, relatively to the experimental device, than the robot. This means that their right shoulder was centered on a position identical to that of the robot arm's rotation axis.

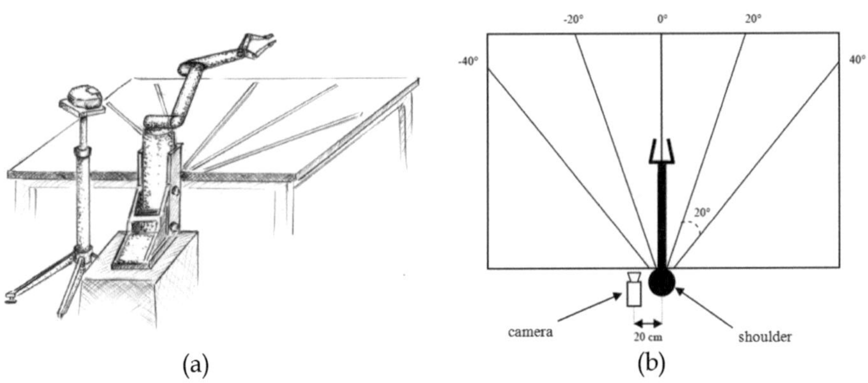

(a) (b)

Fig. 5. (a) Schematic representation of the experimental device (robotic condition only), in ¾ right back view. (b) Details of the experimental configuration characteristics, in top view.

The experimental procedure followed three successive steps. In a first step, each subject had to grasp a cylindrical object, 2.5cm in diameter and 8cm high, by extending their right arm or with the robotics' arm, depending on the condition. This grasping was carried out for each ray, for four random positions close (inferior and superior) to the maximal length of arm's extension. So, subjects were always confronted with reachable and unreachable objects in all rays. Whatever the case, subjects were ordered to try to catch the cylinder the more rapidly and precisely possible by a simple arm's extension, that is to say without coupling it with a chest's movement. Indeed, during all the experiment, the subject's back was kept in close contact with the back of the chair. Finally, the starting point of each movement was always the same, the pair of pliers or hand's main axis aligned with the ray where the grasping occurred.

After this motor stage came a calibration stage. Here, subject must put the object, held between the thumb and the index finger or the pair of pliers end, the farthest possible along each ray, by a movement of simple arm's extension. Thus, the distance obtained for each ray gives us the reference value (R) of the range of action or peripersonal space of human's arm and robotics' arm. This value is used as denominator to calculate the Pi ratio.

The last stage was designed to estimate the threshold distance for which one subject estimated a transition between his grasping space and his locomotion space. To do that, eight object positions have been chosen according to the reference length value (R) obtained in the calibration stage. Precisely, these eight positions were symmetrically distributed on both sides of the reference length so as to have four supraliminal and four infraliminal values. Thus, these positions had a value of ±1cm, ±4cm, ±8cm and ±13cm in relation to the reference (R). Subject's task was to answer by "yes" or "no" to the question: "Do you think you could catch the object presented with a simple arm's extension?". To obtain a precise threshold value, each eight positions were presented ten times for each five rays. The presentation order of object positions and rays tested has been randomised in each condition. Then, the 80 answers have been counted to obtain the threshold (S), which is the distance value in respect of a same percentage of answers "yes" and "no", equal to 50% (Bonnet, 1986).

Results

As shown on the figure 6, Pi in the robotic condition is not statistically different from Pi in the natural condition ($F[1, 6] = 2.48$; NS). This result suggests that, in a remote control situation, the capacity of the human being to delimit his grasping space is the same whatever the effector's organ is his own arm or a teleoperated robotics' arm. Furthermore, this similarity happens rapidly, since no effect of interaction between conditions and experimental sessions is recorded ($F[3, 36] = 0.48$; NS). These data mean that a human operator, acting on the environment through a robotics' telemanipulator tool, can circumscribe her/his range of action almost as precisely as when s/he performs the action with her/his own arm. Also, because of this remapping occurs after limited training, humans appear to rapidly perceive the affordance of the remote control arm. So overall, the study suggests that a teleoperated device can rapidly be appropriated and incorporated into the operator's body schema, in the same way that was demonstrated for more simple tools (Maravita et al., 2001; Carlson et al., 2010).

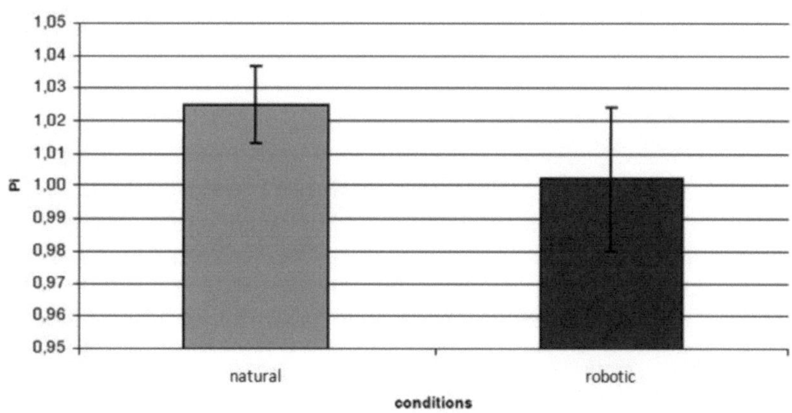

Fig. 6. Pi index values of grasping distance evaluation for each experimental condition.

3. Artificial processes

Beyond the obvious natural processes of appropriation described earlier, the "matching" between the human operator and the electromechanical machine can also be achieved through artificial processes. As the natural adaptation occurs in both directions, the artificial adaptation can also be implemented according to two approaches. The first approach, called anthropocentric, is applied from the machine to the human. The objective is to bring closer the way in which the machine works to the human skills and, consequently, promote an adaptation mainly through an assimilation process. The other approach is carried out in the opposite direction. In this case, the human-machine interaction is improved via an implementation of electro-computational components in the biological organism. Because the living being gets some machine-like capacities, this new generation of individuals is called cyborg - the contraction between cybernetic and organism. This section explains these two complementary approaches through examples coming from neurorobotics studies.

3.1 Anthropocentric approach

Human operators tend to attribute properties of themselves to a used tool, at least in an initial stage (Laborde & Mejias, 1985; Mendelsohn, 1986). So, artefact movements are translated by the user in terms of her/his own motricity. Moreover, Mendelsohn (1986) noticed that the construction of an anthropocentric representation of the machine is enhanced by the similarity between the machine's characteristics and the operator's schemes. This similarity ensures that the individual makes an easier first contact with the system. When this projection is relevant, it involves an assimilation process in the cognition and action schemes of the user. For instance, the control interface of the telemanipulator presented by Gaillard (1993) facilitates such assimilation. In this device, the Cartesian coordinate system of the robot is isomorphic to the corporal coordinate system of the operator. Therefore, the device can be qualified as egocentric. The operator can make a projection of her/his body schema into the working space of the robot. The readjustments are few and the learning process is improved because the system's design preserves the natural movement direction. In such configuration, the human operator is rapidly able to apply an efficient internal control and planning of the movement, thanks to the spatio-temporal isomorphism between the human and the machine. In order to demonstrate the advantages of the anthropocentric approach, two experiments of implementation of human-like properties in the machine are presented below, being one from a morphological point of view and the other from a functional point of view.

3.1.1 Morphological aspect

In the section 2.3.2, signs of appropriation appear when the topological relationship between the camera and the robotic arms is designed according to an anthropomorphic architecture (camera located up and on the left in relation to the robot shoulder, in order to mimic a right arm). So, another point studied by Rybarczyk and Mestre (2011) was to test the effects of the anthropomorphism reduction on the appropriation process. This experiment is described next.

Experimental design

The same experimental configuration, procedure and evaluation factor ("Pi") as described in section 2.3.2 are used in this study. The only differences in relation to the previous description are the kind and number of conditions and data analysed. Here, three teleoperation conditions were tested. In the three conditions the robotic arm's position never changed, it was only the camera locations in relation to it which changed (figure 7). The camera locations were at equidistance with respect to the centre of table. So, they were arranged along a virtual circle of radius equal to the half length of the table. Consequently, it was only the angular position on the circle which distinguished one teleoperation condition from the other.

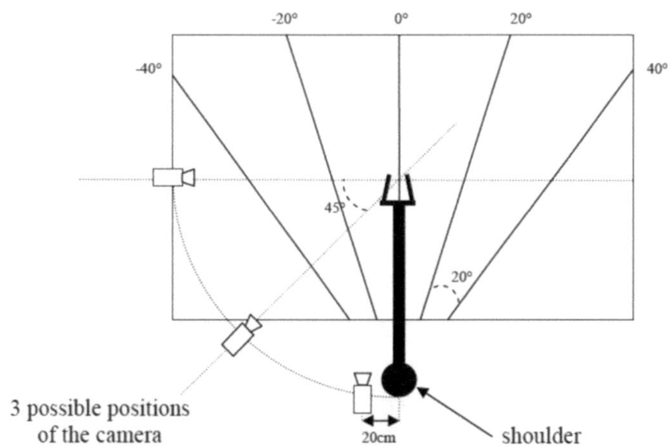

Fig. 7. Three camera position conditions tested in the experiment.

The first camera position was positioned up and on the left in relation to the robot shoulder. Such configuration was defined as "anthropomorphic", because it respects the topological relationship between the cephalic organ and the right superior limb of the human being. So, this design will be called more specifically "right anthropomorphic". In the second condition, known as "bias" condition, the camera was placed at a bigger eccentricity angle, compared to the first one. This angle was equal to 45° in relation to the 0° ray. Finally, the last camera was positioned perpendicularly in comparison with the antero-posterior arm's axis, which broke all morphological identity with the human model. This last configuration was called "side" condition.

In terms of data, three other factors (in addition to "Pi") were analysed. First, the execution time was recorded in each experimental condition. Second, another index of the movement quality has been calculated from this motor task. It was called "spatial error". It was defined as the ratio of the movement length of the robotics' pliers, carried out by the operator, on the shorter distance between the starting point and the arrival point of the movement. Finally, this movement length has been used to calculate a second "Pi" value, called "Pi2", which is the ratio of the estimated distance of catching (D) on the movement length executed by the subject, and not the robotics' arm length (R), as in the Pi index.

Results

Figure 8a shows a general tendency for a greater velocity in the execution time of the movement in an anthropomorphic condition, even if this superiority is only significant with regard to the side condition (F [1, 6] = 6.1; p < 0.05). On the figure 8b, we can observe the same tendency of the anthropomorphic condition to produce less spatial error than the others conditions. Precisely, the anthropomorphic condition ensures a more direct movement from the starting to the arrival point than in the side condition (F [1, 6] = 6.05; p < 0.05), but this difference is not significant in comparison with the bias configuration (F [1, 6] = 3.14; NS). It means that the sensori-motor effort to carry out the catching task has linearly increased as the camera eccentricy was increased.

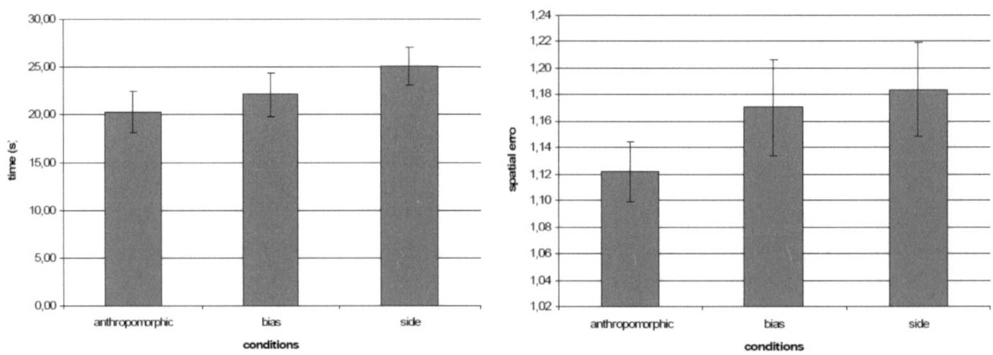

(a) (b)

Fig. 8. (a) Average times of the execution of the movement following the three relative positions of the camera with respect to the arm. (b) Spatial error according to the three teleoperated conditions.

From the point of view of the perception task, as shown in figure 9a, "Pi" values of grasping distance evaluation by arm's extension are not the same depending on the teleoperated condition (F [2, 9] = 9.05; p < 0.007). We notice an elevation of the "Pi" from the 1 reference value (and the "Pi" obtained in "natural" condition) the more the teleoperated condition moves away from the anthropomorphic configuration, with a significant difference between natural and side condition (F [1, 6] = 16.8; p < 0.006). "Pi2" analysis may explains such increment in "Pi". Indeed, when the estimated distance of catching is divided by the distance carried out by the operator in the motor stage, the Pi value of the side condition is close to 1 (figure 9b). Moreover, this second Pi index decreases linearly toward the anthropomorphic configuration. This observation suggests a strong influence of sensorimotor efforts on the catching distance estimation, the more the teleoperated condition moves away from an anthropomorphic configuration.

The fundamental result of this experiment is to stress that the body schema extension has certain limitations, in particular when the visual organ/effector organ topological relationship is too much distorted to lead to a perception of "distal attribution" (Loomis, 1992). Such is the case in the side condition, in which results show that the operator cannot have a correct representation of the robotics' arm capacities. The more the operator's vision is shifted forward and to the side (with respect to the effector's axis), the more s/he overestimates the maximal grasping distance. The overestimation can be explained by a motor account, since the motor effort seems to increase too. Besides, it has been demonstrated that perceived distances increase with an augmentation of motor activity and difficulty (Proffit et al., 2003; Witt et al., 2004). These fundamental differences between the anthropomorphic levels of each condition suggest that the appropriation process occurs, at least in teleoperated situation, only under restricted conditions. The study shows that static morphological features can interact on the dynamic mental construction of the body schema. These results are supported by works demonstrating that the rubber hand illusion can be elicited even if the effector has no visual resemblance to a human hand (Armel & Ramachandran, 2003) - which is the case of the robotic manipulator - but does not happen if the shift between the visual referential of the individual and the effector organ exceeds the peripersonal area (Lloyd, 2007).

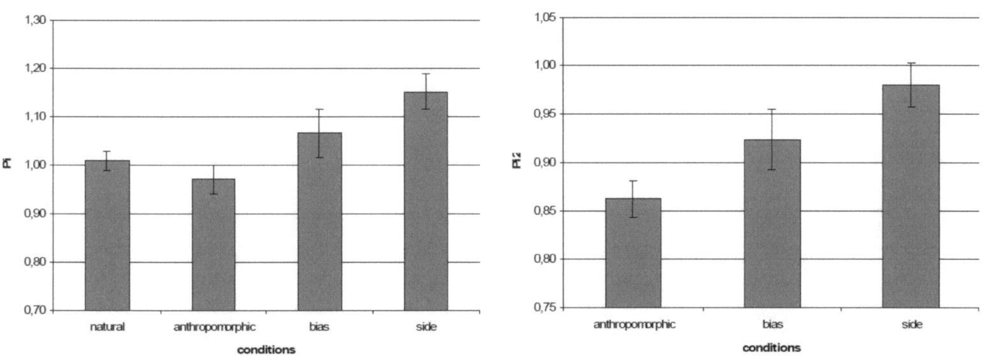

(a) (b)

Fig. 9. (a) Pi index values of grasping distance evaluation following each experimental condition (the natural value is added from the previous study). (b) Pi2 index values of grasping distance evaluation for each condition. On the contrary of the previous Pi, in this case the estimated distance is divided by the distance carried out by the arm in the first motor task of the experiment.

3.1.2 Functional aspect

The anthropocentric approach can be applied not only on the morphological design, but also on the functional architecture of the system. To complete this approach in the field of teleoperation, Rybarczyk et al. (2004) researched whether the implementation of a human-like behaviour in the way in which the telerobot works could improve the HMI. In this experiment - summarised below - visuo-motor mechanicals of anticipation inspired from the living beings were implemented in a mobile platform, in order to improve the steering control.

Modelling of the human behaviour

Teleoperation is a situation characterized by the deterioration or absence of many sensorimotor contingencies, in comparison with natural conditions. However, one sensorial modality that is still present, and thus overexploited, is vision (Terré, 1990). One consequence is that any degradation of visual information and feedback will have serious consequences for the quality of robot control. Conversely, the control of the machine displacement can be strongly improved by the "quality" of visual information. In teleoperation, the visual limitations are mainly related to the important reduction of the visual field size and to the transmission delay of images (Massimo & Sheridan, 1989). In fact, these constraints are associated with spatio-temporal characteristics of human visual perception. One strategy that has developed during evolution to cope with limited bandwidth problems is visuo-motor anticipation. This strategy consists in directing the gaze to a place in space, which is a goal or sub-goal of displacement, before actually moving the body in that direction. For example, during the control of locomotion around corners, the subject does not preserve his/her gaze axis rigorously aligned with the rest of the body, but directs this one towards the inside of the trajectory (Grasso et al., 1996). Thus, gaze orientation would anticipate displacement orientation, by systematically anticipating the changes in the direction of locomotion by a temporal interval of about one second. A control strategy following an organization of the type "I go where I look" seems to underlie the guidance of locomotion (Land, 1998). The same thing occurs for the bypassing of a reference mark. The gaze and body movements' recordings show that the gaze is directed to the reference mark before the individual reaches its level, the realignment of the head in the direction of walk being carried out only after its crossing (Grasso et al., 1998). This suggests that gaze orientation is controlled step by step according to a predictive mechanism of the new direction to follow.

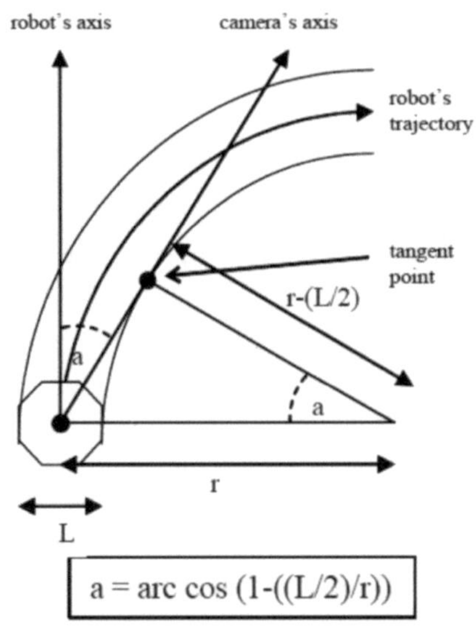

Fig. 10. Implementation of visuo-motor anticipation according to a non-human-like model. The camera's rotation angle is computed by the curve radius (r) of the robot's trajectory, using trigonometric laws. Here, cos a=(r(L/2))/r, where the semi-width of the robot equals L/2. The radius (r) is obtained by dividing the translation velocity by the rotation velocity of the robot.

Such observations were also collected in the case of automobile control. Under these conditions, the driver's gaze axis is directed to the tangent point of the curve one to two seconds before reaching the convexity of the curve (Land & Lee, 1994). By this strategy the driver seeks to use the particular optical properties of the tangent to the turn, in order to guide the trajectory. The tangent point corresponds to a singularity in the optic flow field, being motionless when the driver's trajectory is aligned with the road's curvature.

Psychophysical studies show that this gazing strategy corresponds to an optimization of information pick-up for the control of the trajectory (Mestre, 2001). As a consequence, it seems that this visual anticipation behaviour is useful for trajectory control. Rybarczyk et al. (2004) implemented this type of behaviour on a teleoperated mobile robot, in order to test whether this could help human-machine cooperation. To do that, an analogy was made between the human gaze during locomotion control and the mobile camera on the mobile robot. The figure 10 describes the camera-robot coupling that simulates the human-like visuo-motor anticipation. The expected result was a facilitation of the navigation control of the robot, following the example of human locomotion supported by predictive properties of the brain.

Experimental design

The telerobotic system was composed of two principal elements: a mobile platform and a control station. The robotic platform was equipped with a mobile camera. The robot was moved by two independent driving wheels, a free wheel in front of the vehicle allowing its stability. The engines were of the same type as those which equip electric wheelchairs. The optical camera field of view was 50° in the horizontal and 38° in the vertical dimension. This sensor "sent" to the operator an image of the environment in which the robot evolved, on a terminal display having a height of 23 cm and a width of 31 cm. The whole system, engines and sensors, was controlled by a PC embarked on the robot. This PC was connected to the computer of the control station through a TCP/IP HF connection. Client/server software architecture structured the informatics part. The control interface was using the PC keyboard, by which the operator controlled the direction and displacement velocity of the platform.

The first situation was a "non-human" condition, in which there was no anticipation, since the camera was motionless, aligned with the orientation of the robot. In the second condition, called "human-like", the camera orientation anticipated the platform displacement. In the two cases, the subjects were placed in a teleoperated situation, i.e. they only had an indirect vision of the experimental environment. The task of the subjects consisted in making the robot a slalom course between four boundary marks. The instruction given to them was to carry out the course as soon as fast as possible without colliding with the boundary marks. The analysis of the results was carried out on three parameters: the path execution time and the collision number and the trajectories smoothness.

This last parameter brings deep behavioural information, since it is not only based on a pure performance (as the first two parameters) but on the motor skills the task is completed. To calculate the smoothness of trajectories, an index was computed on the basis of the frequency distribution of the instantaneous curve radius of each trajectory (Péruch & Mestre, 1999). The following formula was used:

$$r(m) = \frac{v(m/sec)}{w(radians/sec)},$$

where r corresponds to the curve radius, v is the instantaneous speed, and w is the absolute instantaneous rotation speed. Then, the curve radius is converted in decimal logarithm. If the vehicle nearly stops and makes a single rotation, the curve radius is very small (< 1), and the logarithmic value of r is negative. If the vehicle makes a combination of translation and rotation, the curve radius is ≥ 1 and its logarithm is ≥ 0. If before each curve the participant stops and makes a single rotation, the distribution of curve radii will be bimodal, with one spike centered on negative values of the logarithm and the other spike centered on positive values. If the participant makes a smooth (or curvilinear) trajectory, the distribution will rather be unimodal and centered on a value ≥ 0 of the logarithm of the curve radius. For each trajectory, the distribution of the logarithm of the curve radii was computed and distributed in categories from -4 to +3. The distributions were normalized, the occurrences of curve radii in each category being expressed as a percentage of the total number of occurrences for each trajectory.

Results

The figure 11a shows that the average time for the execution time of the travel is significantly lower when the camera anticipates (human-like) over the platform displacement in comparison with the motionless camera (non-human) ($F [1, 12] = 7.58$; $p < 0.02$). Also, data displayed on the figure 11b show that the same significant effect in favour of the mobile camera is obtained for the number of collisions ($F [1, 12] = 5.52$; $p < 0.04$).

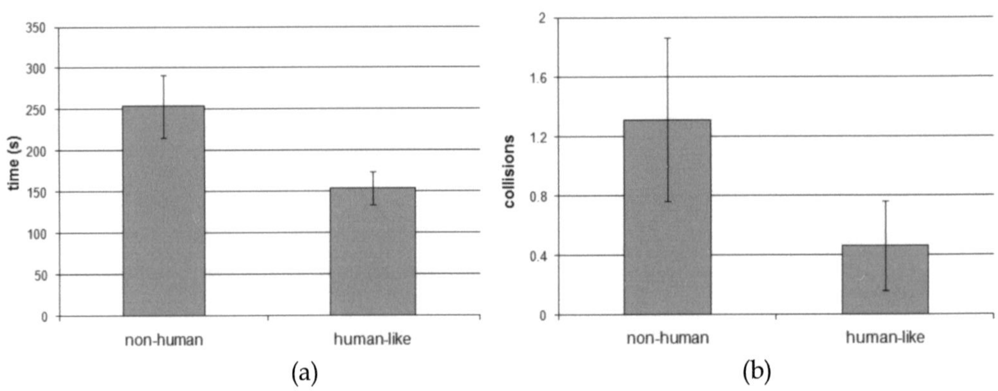

Fig. 11. (a) Mean time of execution. (b) Mean number of collisions.

Also, the trajectory smoothness is different following the conditions. When the camera anticipates over the robot's displacement, the path is more curvilinear than when this human-like behaviour is not implemented on the mobile platform (figure 12). ANOVA test confirms a statistically higher percentage of occurrences of curvilinear trajectories (higher peak) for the anticipating camera in comparison with the motionless camera condition ($F [1, 12] = 69.31$; $p < 0.00001$). In addition, curves negotiated with stops (smaller peak) are significantly fewer in human-like condition than non-human condition ($F [1, 12] = 19.90$; $p < 0.0008$). These data tend to show that the steering control is more natural when the visuo-motor anticipation is implemented in the remote mobile device. So overall, these results demonstrate a better HMI when the machine exhibits human-like behaviours in the way in which the system works. Beyond the pure performance improvement, the anthropocentric approach seems to make easier and intuitive the human control over the machine, by promoting a human-machine cooperation through an appropriation process by assimilation dominance.

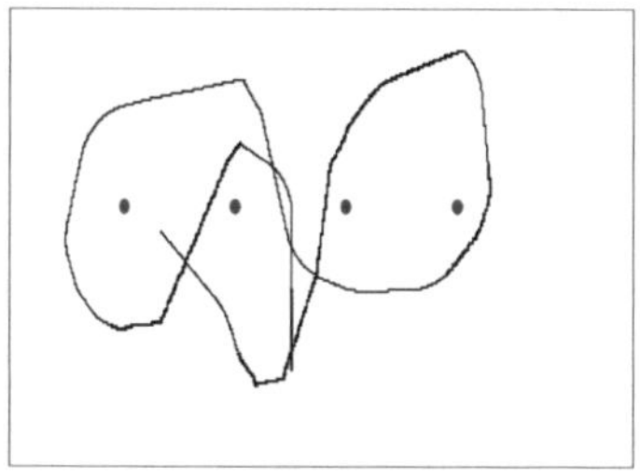

(a)

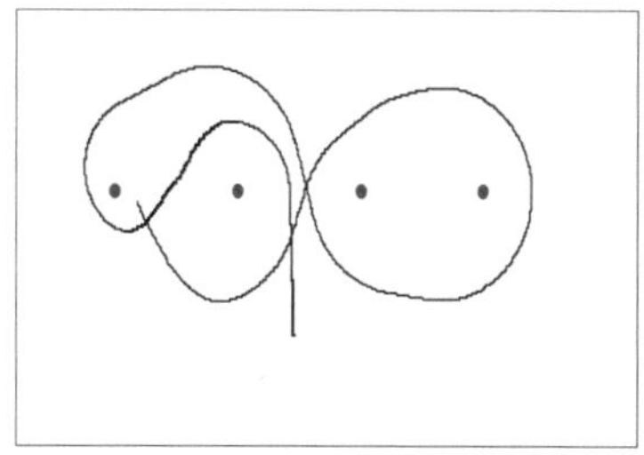

(b)

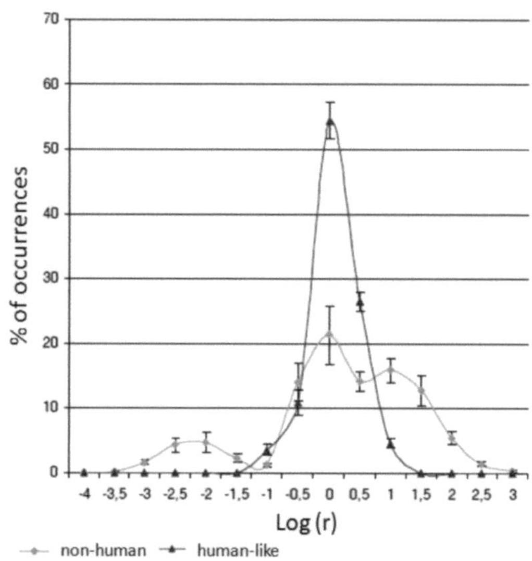

(c)

Fig. 12. Trajectories in fixed camera mode – non-human – (a) and anticipating camera mode – human-like – (b). Average distribution of (logarithms of) curve radius, expressed as a percentage of the total number of occurrences, following the two experimental conditions of vision (c).

3.2 Cyborg approach

Another way to reduce the gap between the human and the machine is to implement an approach in the direction opposite to the previous one, which means from the human to the machine. In other words, the idea of the cyber approach is to bring some human functions closer to the way in which the machine works. This paradigm of the HMI has first been applied in assistive technologies (Hochberg et al., 2006). Most motor handicapped people are really dependent on electromechanical artefacts in order to carry on a "normal" life. However, many of them have lost capabilities in using lower or upper members. Consequently, traditional Human-Machine Interfaces are useless for them. With the cyborg paradigm and the numerous possible implementations, such as Brain-Computer Interface (BCI), severely disabled people may compensate a capability loss with a tight linkage between the machine and their nervous system. Indeed, the idea of a cyborg implementation is to directly connect the human nervous system to the control system of an electronic device. Therefore, a simple nervous impulse would be enough to interact with the machine.

Besides bringing back functionalities to a brainstem stroke victim, a cyborg has many other advantages over a usual interface. Since the motor command is directly measured from the nerve, it avoids a noisy signal and enables a better discrimination of the human intention. Moreover, the close human-machine relationship may be achieved not only for the motor control but also for the sensorial feed-back. If electrodes are implanted on sensorial fibres, a signal collected from electromechanical sensors of the machine can provide the user the sensations similar to those of a stimulation of her/his own biological sensor. An application for sensate prosthesis has already been investigated (Warwick, 2009). An adaptation to superficial electrodes could be imagined for sensate robotic arms, which would allow the operator to employ lower level reflexes that exist within the central nervous system, making control of the robot more subconscious.

The simplification of the control interface and, subsequently, the mental workload diminution, are a key idea brought by the cyborgs. It is common that a mediated action, carried out through a robot, for instance, implies a complex combination of motor movement which can be completely different in comparison to the same action performed in natural conditions, because of the interface. However, if the input and output are correctly connected between the human and the machine, the emitted brain signal to control the device will be the same as to control the human body itself, with the obvious advantages in terms of HMI. At last, the introduction of an electronic device inside the biological organism may enhance the human properties too, as it was demonstrated by an experiment carried out by Warwick et al. (2005) in which an extra sensory input (signals from ultrasonic sensors) is directly transmitted to the nervous system, allowing this information to be recognised and used by the individual. The acquisition of these extra abilities implies the human to make a high effort of adaptation to a device that brings a completely new source of information. In this case, the appropriation process will be essentially supported by an accommodation of pre-existing schemes and a possible creation of new ones.

4. Conclusion

The tool appropriation occurs when the artefact is completely integrated into the human sensori-motor loop (or schemes) in order to become transparent, which means it disappears from the field of consciousness. From a psychological point of view, the appropriation involves two complementary processes - accommodation and assimilation - in which the gap between the operator and the way in which the machine works is reduced. During this adaptation, the tool is progressively integrated into the operator's body schema, which is not only a phenomenological but also a neurological transformation of the individual. A better knowledge of this phenomenon is crucial to improve the HMI. Indeed, anthropocentric implementations can boost the human-machine cooperation through an appropriation process mainly based on assimilation mechanisms. On the other hand, a cyborg approach may enhance the human abilities by stimulating schemes' accommodation.

5. References

Aglioti, S., Smania, N., Manfredi, M., & Berlucchi, G. (1996). Disownership of left hand andof objects related to it in a patient with right brain damage. *Neuroreport,* Vol. 8, pp. 293-296.

Armel, K.C., & Ramachandran, V.S. (2003). Projecting sensations to external objects: Evidences from skin conductance response. *Proceedings of the Royal Society of London B,* Vol. 270, pp. 1499-1506.

Berti, A., & Frassinetti, F. (2000). When far becomes near: remapping of space by tool use. *Journal of Cognitive Neuroscience,* Vol. 12, pp. 415-420.

Bisiach, E. (1997). The spatial features of unilateral neglect. In: *Parietal Lobe Contribution to Orientation in 3D Space,* P. Thier and H.O. Karnath (Eds.), Springer: Berlin.

Bonnet, C. (1986). *Manuel Pratique de Psychophysique,* A. Colin: Paris.

Borghi, A.M., & Cimatti, F. (2010). Embodied cognition and beyond: acting and sensing the body. *Neuropsychologia,* Vol. 48, No. 3, pp. 763-773.

Botvinick, M., & Cohen, J. (1998). Rubber hands "feel" touch that eyes see. *Nature,* Vol. 391, p. 756.

Bullinger, A. (1987). Space, organism and objects, a Piagetian approach. In: *Cognitive processes and spatial orientation in animal and man,* P. Ellen and C. Thinus-Blanc (Eds.), Martinus Nijhoff Publishers: Dordrecht.

Cardinali, L., Frassinetti, F., Brozzoli, C., Urquizar, C., Roy, A.C., & Farnè, A. (2009). Tool use induces morphological updating of the body schema. *Current Biology,* Vol. 19, No. 12, pp. 478-479.

Carlson, T., Alvarez, A., Wu, D., & Verstraten, F. (2010). Rapid assimilation of external objects into the body schema. *Psychological Science,* Vol. 21, No. 7, pp. 1000-1005.

Cowey, A., Small, M., & Ellis, S. (1994). Left visuo-spatial neglect can be worse in far than in near space. *Neuropsychologia,* Vol. 32, pp. 1059-1066.

Cowey, A., Small, M., & Ellis, S. (1999). No abrupt change in visual hemineglect from near to far space. *Neuropsychologia,* Vol. 37, pp. 1-6.

Di Pellegrino, G., Làdavas, E., & Farnè, A. (1997). Seeing where your hands are. *Nature,* Vol. 338, p. 730.

Driver, J., Mattingley, J.B., Rorden, C., & Davis, G. (1997). Extinction as a paradigm measure of attentional bias and restricted capacity following brain injury. In: *Parietal Lobe Contribution to Orientation in 3D Space,* P. Thier and H.O. Karnath (Eds.), Springer: Heidelberg.

Driver, J., & Spence, C. (1998). Attention and the crossmodal construction of space. *Trends in Cognitive Science,* Vol. 2, pp. 254-262.

Farnè, A., & Làdavas, E. (2000). Dynamic size-change of hand peripersonal space following tool use. *Neuroreport,* Vol. 11, pp. 1645-1649.

Fitch, H., & Turvey, M.T. (1978). On the control of activity: some remarks from an ecological point of view. In: *Psychology of motor behavior and sport,* D. Landers & R. Christina (Eds.), Human Kinetics Pub: Urbana.

Fogassi, L., Gallese, V., Fadiga, L., Luppino, G., Matelli, M., & Rizzolatti, G. (1996). Coding of peripersonal space in inferior premotor cortex (area F4). *Journal of Neurophysiology,* Vol. 76, pp. 141-157.

Gaillard, J.P. (1993). Analyse fonctionnelle de la boucle de commande en télémanipulation. In: *Représentations pour l'Action,* A. Weill-Fassina, P. Rabardel and D. Dubois (Eds.), Octares: Toulouse.

Gallese, V., & Sinigaglia, C. (2010). The bodily self as power for action. *Neuropsychologia,* Vol. 48, No. 3, pp. 746-755.

Gibson, J.J. (1979). *The ecological approach to visual perception,* Houghton Mifflin: Boston.

Grasso, R., Glasauer, S., Takei, Y., & Berthoz, A. (1996). The predictive brain: Anticipatory control of head direction for the steering of locomotion. *NeuroReport,* Vol. 7, pp. 1170-1174.

Grasso, R., Prévost, P., Ivanenko, Y.P., & Berthoz, A. (1998). Eye-head coordination for the steering of locomotion in humans: An anticipatory synergy. *Neuroscience Letters,* Vol. 253, pp. 115-118.

Graziano, M.S.A., & Gross, C.G. (1995). The representation of extrapersonal space: a possible role for bimodal, visual-tactile neurons. In: *The Cognitive Neurosciences,* M.S. Gazzaniga (Ed.), MIT Press: Cambridge.

Graziano, M.S.A., Hu, X.T., & Gross, C.G. (1997). Visuospatial properties of the ventral premotor cortex. *Journal of Neurophysiology,* Vol. 77, pp. 2268-2292.

Halligan, P.W., & Marshall, J.C. (1991). Left neglect for near but not for far space in man. *Nature,* Vol. 350, pp. 498-500.

Halligan, P.W., & Marshall, J.C. (1994). Spatial neglect: position papers on theory and practice. *Neuropsychological Rehabilitation,* Vol. 4, special issue.

Heilman, K.M., Watson, R.T., Valenstein, E., & Damasio, A.R. (1983). Localization of lesion in neglect. In: *Localization in Neuropsychology,* A. Kertesz (Ed.), Academic Press: New-York.

Hochberg, L.R., Serruya, M.D, Friehs,G.M., Mukand, J.A., Saleh, M., Caplan, A.H., Branner, A., Chen, D., Penn, R.D., & Donoghue, J.P. (2006). Neuronal ensemble control of prosthetic devices by a human with tetraplegia. *Nature,* Vol. 442, pp. 164-171.

Husain, M., & Kennard, C. (1996). Visual neglect associated with frontal lobe infarction. *Journal of Neurology,* Vol. 243, pp. 652-657.

Ijsselsteijn, W., De Ridder, H., Freeman, J., & Avons, S.E. (2000). Presence: Concept, determinants and measurement. *Proceedings of the SPIE, Human Vision and Electronic Imaging,* San Jose, CA, USA.

Ijsselsteijn, W. (2002). Elements of a multi-level theory of presence: phenomenology, mental processing and neural correlates. *Proceedings of Presence,* Porto, Portugal.

Iriki, A., Tanaka, M., & Iwamura, Y. (1996). Coding of modified body schema during tool use by macaque postcentral neurons. *Neuroreport,* Vol. 7, pp. 2325-2330.

Iriki, A., Tanaka, M., Obayashi, S., & Iwamura, Y. (2001). Self-images in the video monitor coded by monkeys intraparietal neurons. *Neuroscience Research,* Vol. 40, pp. 163-173.

Jeannerod, M. (1987). *Neurophysiological and Neuropsychological Aspect of Spatial Neglect.* North Holland: Amsterdam.

Laborde, C., & Mejias, B. (1985). The construction process of an interaction by middle-school pupils: an experimental approach. *Proceedings of the Ninth International Conference PME,* Utrecht, Netherlands.

Làdavas, E., Di Pellegrino, G., Farnè, A., & Zeloni, G. (1998). Neuropsychological evidence of an integrated visuotactile representation of peripersonal space in humans. *Journal of Cognitive Neuroscience,* Vol. 10, pp. 581-589.

Land, M.F., & Lee, D.N. (1994). Where we look when we steer? *Nature,* Vol. 369, pp. 742-744.

Land, M.F. (1998). The visual control of steering. In: *Vision and Action,* pp. 163-180, L.R. Harris and K. Jenkin (Eds.), University Press: Cambridge.

Lloyd, D.M. (2007). Spatial limits on referred touch to an alien limb may reflect boundaries of visuo-tactile peripersonal space surrounding the hand. *Brain and Cognition,* Vol. 64, pp. 104-109.

Loomis, J.M. (1992). Distal attribution and presence. *Presence: Teleoperators and Virtual Environments,* Vol. 1, pp. 113-118.
Maravita, A., Husain, M., Clarke, K., & Driver, J. (2001). Reaching with a tool extends visual-tactile interactions into far space: evidence from cross-modal extinction. *Neuropsychologia,* Vol. 39, pp. 580-585.
Maravita, A., & Iriki, A. (2004). Tools for the body (schema). *Trends in Cognitive Sciences,* Vol. 8, pp. 79-86.
Massimo, M., & Sheridan, T. (1989). Variable force and visual feedback effects and teleoperator man/machine performance. *Proceedings of the Nasa Conference on Space Telerobotics,* Pasadena, CA, USA.
Mendelsohn, P. (1986). La transposition de schèmes familiers dans un langage de programmation chez l'enfant. In: *Psychologie, Intelligence Artificielle et Automatique,* C. Bonnet, J.M. Hoc and G. Tiberghein (Eds.), Mardaga: Bruxelles.
Mestre, D. (2001). Dynamic evaluation of the functional visual field in driving. *Proceedings of Driving Assessment 2001,* Aspen, CO, USA.
Meyer, P., & Biocca, F. (1992). The elastic body image: an experiment on the effect of advertising and programming on body image distortions in young women. *Journal of Communication,* Vol. 42, pp. 108-133.
Minsky, M. (1980). Telepresence. *Omni,* Vol. 2, pp. 44-52.
Montangerons, J., & Maurice-Naville, D. (1994). *Piaget ou l'Intelligence en Marche,* Mardaga: Liège.
Newell, K.M., & Scully, D.M. (1987). *The Development of Prehension: Constraints on Grip Patterns.* Unpublished manuscript, University of Illinois at Urbana- Champaign.
O'Regan, K. & Nöe, A. (2001). A sensorimotor account of vision and visual consciousness. *Behavioral and Brain Sciences,* Vol. 24, pp. 939-973.
Paillard, J. (1991). *Brain and Space,* Oxford University Press: Oxford.
Paillard, J. (1993). The hand and the tool: the functional architecture of human technical skills. In: *The Use of Tools by Human and Non-Human Primates,* A. Berthelet and J. Chavaillon (Eds.), Oxford University Press: New-York.
Péruch, P., & Mestre, D. (1999). Between desktop and head immersion: Functional visual field during vehicle control and navigation in virtual environments. *Presence,* Vol. 8, pp. 54-64.
Piaget, J. (1936). *La Naissance de l'Intelligence chez l'Enfant,* Delachaux et Niestlé: Paris, Lausanne.
Piaget, J. (1952). *The Origins of Intelligence in Children,* The Norton Library, WW Norton & Co, Inc.: New York.
Piaget, J., & Beth, E.W. (1961). Epistémologie mathématique et psychologie: Essai sur les relations entre la logique formelle et la pensée réelle. In: *Etudes d'Epistémologie Génétique,* PUF: Paris.
Previc, F.H. (1998). The neuropsychology of 3-D space. *Psychological Bulletin,* Vol. 124, pp. 123-164.
Proffitt, D.R., Stefanucci, J., Banton, T., & Epstein, W. (2003). The role of effort in distance perception. *Psychological Science,* Vol. 14, pp. 106-112.
Rabardel, P. (1995). *Les Hommes et les Technologies. Approche Cognitive des Instruments Contemporains,* A. Colin: Paris.

Rizzolatti, G., Fadiga, L., Fogassi, L., & Gallese, V. (1997). The space around us. *Science,* Vol. 277, pp. 190-191.

Rybarczyk, Y., Galerne, S., Hoppenot, P., Colle, E., & Mestre, D.R. (2001). The development of robot human-like behaviour for an efficient human-machine co-operation. *Proceedings of AAATE 2001,* Ljubljana, Slovenia.

Rybarczyk, Y., Ait Aider, O., Hoppenot, P. & Colle, E. (2002). Remote control of a biometrics robot assistance system for disabled persons. *AMSE Modelling, Measurement and Control,* Vol. 63, No. 4, pp. 47-56.

Rybarczyk, Y., Mestre, D., Hoppenot, P. & Colle, E. (2004). Implémentation de mécanismes d'anticipation visuo-motrice en téléopération. *Le Travail Humain,* Vol. 67, No. 3, pp. 209-233.

Rybarczyk, Y., & Mestre, D.R. (2011). Body schema deformation in teleoperation: effects of sensori-motor contingences. Psychology Research (to appear).

Sheridan, T.B. (1992). Musings on telepresence and virtual presence. *Presence: Teleoperators and Virtual Environments,* Vol. 1, pp. 120-125.

Slater, M., & Usoh, M. (1993). Representations systems, perceptual position, and presence in immersive virtual environments. *Presence: Teleoperators and Virtual Environments,* Vol. 2, pp. 221-233.

Terré, C. (1990). *Conduite à Distance d'un Robot Mobile pour la Sécurité Civile: Approche Ergonomique.* Thèse, Université René-Descartes, Paris, France.

Turvey, M.T., & Shaw, R.E. (1979). The primacy of perceiving: an ecological reformulation of perception for understanding memory. In: *Perspectives on Memory Research,* L.G. Nilsson (Ed.), Erlbaum: Hillsdale.

Vallar, G. (1998). Spatial hemineglect in humans. *Trends in Cognitive Sciences,* Vol. 2, pp. 87-96.

Vygotsky, L.S. (1930). La méthode instrumentale en psychologie. In: *Vygotsky Aujourd'hui,* B. Schneuwly and J.P. Bronckart (Eds.), Delachaux et Niestlé: Paris, Lausanne.

Warren, W.H. (1984). Perceiving affordances: visual guidance of stair climbing. *Journal of Experimental Psychology: Human Perception and Performance,* Vol. 10, pp. 683-703.

Warren, W.H., & Whang, S. (1987). Visual guidance of walking through apertures: body-scaled information for affordances. *Journal of Experimental Psychology: Human Perception and Performance,* Vol. 13, pp. 371-383.

Warwick, K., Gasson, M., Hutt, B., & Goodhew, I. (2005). An attempt to extend human sensory capabilities by means of implants technology. *Proceedings of the IEEE Int. Conference on Systems, Man and Cybernetics 2005,* Hawaii, USA.

Warwick, K. (2009). Hybrid brains - Biology, technology merger. In: *Biomedical Engineering Systems and Technologies, Communications in Computer and Information Science.* A. Fred, J. Filipe and H. Gamboa (Eds.), pp. 19-34, Springer-Verlag: Berlin.

Witt, J.K., Proffitt, D.R., & Epstein, W. (2004). Perceiving distance: a role of effort and intent. *Perception,* Vol. 33, pp. 577-590.

Yuan, Y, & Steed, A. (2010). Is the rubber hand illusion induced by immersive virtual reality? *Proceedings of the IEEE Virtual Reality Conference 2010,* Waltham, MA, USA.

11

Cognitive Robotics in Industrial Environments

Stephan Puls, Jürgen Graf and Heinz Wörn
Karlsruhe Institute of Technology
Germany

1. Introduction

Industrial robotics is a challenging domain for cognitive systems, especially, when human intelligence meets solid machinery with many degrees of freedom like most of today's industrial robots. Hence, for guaranteeing safety for human workers, safety fences are installed to separate humans and robots. As consequence no time and space sharing interaction or cooperation can be found in industrial robotics.

Some progress has gained in the past to the extent that some modern working cells are equipped with laser scanners performing foreground detection. But with these systems one is not able to know what is going on in the scene and, therefore, could not contribute something meaningful for challenging tasks like safe human-robot cooperation. We are conducting research on reconstruction of human kinematics based on 3D imaging sensors. The resulting kinematical model is tracked and fused with knowledge about robot kinematics and surrounding objects into an environmental model. This allows for efficient risk estimation and subsequent risk minimization through adaption of robot motion. Based on these processing steps, recognition of and reasoning about actions and situations in a human centred production environment is performed. All components and modules are merged into a single framework for human-robot cooperation (MAROCO), in order to pave the way for interactive and cooperative scenarios.

In the following, the framework MAROCO and its components are described and it is shown how the presented approaches contribute to achieve the vision of close productive human-robot collaboration.

In Sec. 2, the state-of-the-art for the major research topics concerning this work is presented. This includes works about human-robot cooperation, human pose reconstruction and research about situation and activity recognition. Afterwards, a system overview is given, which highlights the system architecture of the developed framework. In Sec. 4, theoretical considerations and algorithmic approaches are detailed. The section about experimental evaluation follows, in which all implementations and developments are put on trial and demonstrate their effectiveness. Conclusions are drawn and hints for future work are given in Sec. 6.

2. State-of-the-art

The vision of humans achieving a common goal with robot co-workers offers manifold possibilities for robots application. In the past few years several research groups around the globe contributed to this specific field of robotics research. At first, an introduction of the state-of-the-art for safe human-robot cooperation and interaction is given. Afterwards follows an overview about human pose reconstruction which builds an important basis for the here presented approaches. The elaboration takes into account the work of manufacturers, research institutes, and universities.

2.1 Human-robot cooperation

There are just a few camera based vision systems dealing with safe human-robot cooperation. One such system was introduced by the company Pilz in 2007. The system is based on three cameras which are mounted under the ceiling of a robot cell. Stereo vision tools are then applied to the image sequences. The main idea is dividing the robot cell in up to 50 static parts. The recognition capability of the system seems to be foreground detection. Dynamic scenes couldn't be processed efficiently. A meaningful real-time interpretation of the robot cell is not feasible, due to missing means to distinguish between humans and background objects.

The working group Robot Systems of the Fraunhofer Institute IPA from Stuttgart, Germany, incorporated a time-of-flight camera system into the robot cell (Winkler, 2008). This system deals with dynamic safety zones, which are established in a virtual environment model of the working cell. The system defines three types of regions:

- Regions which must provide measurements of the camera system to detect occlusions generated by the robot.
- Critical regions in which no person or objects may appear.
- Areas in which collision detection may not occur.

To reduce the risk for the human co-worker the maximal velocity of the robot can be limited.

A system dealing with direct human-robot cooperation is presented in (Thiemermann, 2005). The research foci are optimizing safety and ergonomics. The robot cell is build up with a SCARA-robot and a CCD-camera based vision system. This scientific work concentrates on hand tracking realised by colour segmentation techniques. Then the shortest distance between the estimated hand positions and the tool centre point of the robot is calculated. The risk recognition part is realized applying a classic fuzzy logic system. The parameters of the fuzzy logic system are trained by an artificial neural network. This work takes also velocities and accelerations into account to finally control the maximal speed of the robot.

Application of CCD-cameras for realisation of such a system seems to be plausible. But there are several open questions regarding stability analysis, robustness against changing illumination conditions, etc. Mere concentration on the co-workers hands can also be restricting.

Another approach for safe human-robot cooperation was published in (Kulic, 2005). The setup of the robot cell is a PUMA robot (type 560). The sensor system is, compared to other approaches, more complex, since several hardware kits like stereo colour vision system, an electrocardiograph or an electromyography are applied. From a scientific point of view, this approach is interesting, but there is little hope that system integrators would spend the necessary effort in integrating such an amount of sensors. Thus, unfortunately, this approach seems to be too complex and cost intensive.

Another way establishing safe human-robot cooperation was published in the works of (Henrich & Gecks, 2008b). The proposed approach for scene reconstruction is based on an image analysis module originally based on the work of (Henrich et al., 2008a). The vision system tries to identify pixels that belong to the real robot. The system provides some foreground detection with a pixel classification method, which identifies single pixels belonging to the robot, to foreground objects or to the static background. This research group also implemented a dynamic path planning module. But without knowing significant parameter of the human kinematics, path planning is restricted to avoidance of obstacles. Human-robot cooperation is otherwise not feasible.

At a first glimpse, the work of (Knoop et al., 2006) has a similar goal of introducing the human pose which is motivated by service robotics taking into account a humanoid robot and a human co-worker. Significant differences are that the author reported by applying his method for markerless reconstruction of the human body is dependent on hand skin colour detection. The proposed system, called VooDoo, runs in less than 15 frames per second as was reported by the authors (Knoop et al., 2006). Thus, this foregoing is not capable to deal in a safety critical industrial robotic cell. Furthermore, no occlusion detection was reported, which are of great interest especially when it comes to cooperation, due to safety considerations and reasoning about human actions in a blind spot.

An extended version of the VooDoo system was later published in (Lösch et al., 2009). This work concentrates on the time consuming initialisation which is based on a silhouette-based approach. The method proposed argues the negative influences of colour image dependant methods and thus uses the silhouette-approach for the initialisation. But the same author applies the VooDoo system after initialisation of the human kinematical model which is strongly dependant on the skin colour detection.

It is interesting, that all of the authors deal with safe human-robot interaction or cooperation, but only few of the authors are really trying to estimate and calculate significant parameters of the human kinematics. Also, there are approaches that are taking into account hand skin colour detection and simultaneously call these methods markerless.

2.2 Human pose reconstruction

In the subsequent section an overview for pure markerless human body tracking approaches will be given. The overview cannot raise a claim to be complete. The papers are presented in chronological order.

The paper of (Fua et al., 2002) presents an implicit surface approach for a generic and robust method handling articulated structures of the human body. The main contribution of this work is the description of a mathematical formalism with simplified and robust implementation of articulated soft objects. The soft object approach is advantageous because of using stereo and silhouette data, providing accurate shape description by a small number of parameters and explicit modelling of 3-D geometry.

The work of (Kehl et al., 2005) proposes a markerless full body pose tracking method which is based on the integration of multiple cues such as edges, colour information and volumetric data. The human model is reconstructed by applying the stochastic meta descent (SMD) method to super-ellipsoids. The colour information is used to resolve self-occlusions, while edge information provides better accuracy and more robustness.

The work of (Caillette & Howard, 2004a) presents a robust method for real-time visual human body tracking by applying a hierarchical 3-D reconstruction from multiple camera views. Individual body parts are tracked by using 3-D blobs. The blob tracking is based on volume and colour information. The dynamics of the blob model is the highlight of the paper. Self-occlusions and noisy data are also investigated by experiments.

Real-time full human-body tracking based on markerless multi-view image sequences is presented in (Caillette & Howard, 2004b). The full approach is realized taking into account three steps: acquisition, reconstruction and tracking. The main idea of the method is based on reconstructing a 3-D voxel based representation of a person using multiple web cams providing colour images. Self-occlusions are also discussed as well as ambiguous poses. The novelty of the approach is a statistical reconstruction method taking colour features and blobs into account.

The authors of (Jenkins et al., 2006, 2007) present a method for kinematic pose estimation based on monocular image sequences as well as action recognition based on the results of the kinematic reconstruction. The motion primitives are modelled as nonlinear dynamic systems which are applied to predict expected motions. Goal of this paper is the inversion of the estimation process which means estimating motion primitives from measurements of the nonlinear dynamical human body. For these reasons, a particle filter is applied to fulfil this task.

The authors in (Azad et al., 2008) argue that the most challenging problem in human motion capture is the high-dimensional search space. A novel approach presented by the authors is build up on a particle filter framework which combines edge cues and 3-D hand tracking as well as a distance cue for upper body tracking as was proposed by the authors in an earlier paper. To overcome the problem of finding the inverse kinematics for the arm model the authors suggest a solution based on the so-called annealed particle filter approach. Another advantage is that this method does not depend on an initialization method. Proper model alignment is achieved by using fusion method and an adaptive shoulder approach.

The paper (Wan et al., 2008) proposes a method for markerless kinematic reconstruction which is based on voxel information generated from a multi camera set-up and the shape from silhouette method. The volume data is then considered as a Markov random field. A predefined human body model is then matched with the volume data. The matching task is formulated as an energy minimizing function. Thus, the problem is transformed into a 3-D graph construction. The minimizing of the graph problem is achieved by application of max-flow theory. The final reconstruction of the model is calculated using Powell's algorithm.

Based on video streams from a time-of-flight camera, the work of (Zhu et al., 2008) presents a model-based, Cartesian control theoretic approach for human pose estimation. The human body model consists of 17 degrees of freedom and models the upper body. The overall runtime cycle achieves about 10 frames per second. The presented approach is also feature based. Special features are the implemented joint limit avoidance and self-penetration avoidance.

The paper of (Jensen & Paulsen, 2009) is focused on gait analysis using a time-of-flight camera. Thus, an articulated model is fitted in each frame to the data by using a Markov random field. Self-occlusions are treated by smoothing missing data. The created model is cut into cycles, which are then fitted via Fourier method to achieve a cyclic model. The final features that are calculated are speed, cadence, step length and range of motion.

Based on the combination of several particle filters with physical simulation of a flexible body model, the work of (Hecht et al., 2009) describes a new approach for markerless human motion tracking. No inverse kinematics is needed for the physical simulation. Experimental results show that this approach runs with 10 FPS on regular PCs.

The dissertation thesis of (Zhu 2009) presents a computational framework for human-pose estimation from depth image sequences. The approach is feature based and takes kinematic constraints including joint limits and self-collision avoidance into account (see Zhu et al., 2008). Another approach is based on dense correspondence between consecutive frames of articulated human models. Both approaches are coupled via temporal prediction using Bayesian information integration.

The paper of (Mussi et al., 2010) presents a GPU-based implementation of a markerless full-body articulated human motion tracking system. The body reconstruction is based on image sequences from multiple cameras. The tracking task is formulated as a multi-dimensional nonlinear optimisation problem and solved by the particle swarm optimisation (PSO) method. The optimisation searches the best matched between a virtual pose silhouette and the actually pose extracted from the image sequences.

The problem of human pose reconstruction is of great interest and presents a challenging research topic, as exemplified by all presented publications. In the realm of human-robot cooperation and interaction, its purpose follows the higher goal of recognising human actions and situations.

2.3 Situation and activity recognition

Recognition of human activities and situation awareness is a premise for advanced safe human-robot cooperation. The most prominent methods used for action recognition systems are based on probabilistic methods, e.g., hidden Markov Models (HMMs) (Krüger et al., 2007; Raamana et al., 2007; Wu et al., 2008). These methods are widely used for application in speech recognition and other domains and, thus, their capabilities have been demonstrated. Moreover their theoretic foundations are well understood and investigated.

Though, according to (Shi et al., 2004), HMM are not suitable for recognition of parallel activities. Thus, propagation networks have been introduced. In these networks each node is associated with an action primitive and embeds a probabilistic duration model. Temporal and logical constraints are enforced by conditional joint probabilities. Similar to HMMs, a multitude of propagation networks are evaluated for approximating the observation probability.

(Minnen et al., 2003) states, that purely probabilistic methods are not suitable for recognition of prolonged activities. Their presented approach implements parameterised stochastic grammars.

The application of knowledge based methods for action recognition tasks is scarce, but work on scene interpretation using logical formalisms has been conducted. In the realm of semantic web, Description Logics are used for defining ontologies and knowledge management. Efficient algorithms have been developed for reasoning with Description Logics. Thus, its application in logics based situation and activity recognition became accepted.

In (Hummel et al., 2007), Description Logics are used for reasoning about traffic situations and understanding of intersections. Deductive inference services are used to reduce the intersection hypotheses space and to retrieve useful information for the driver.

In (Tenorth & Beetz, 2009), a system is presented, which uses Prolog in order to process knowledge in the context of robotic control. It is especially designed for use with personal robots. Knowledge representation is based on Description Logics and processed via an Ontology Web Language (OWL) Prolog plug-in. In contrast to our approach, the Prolog based reasoning system is not used to recognize activities or reason about situations. Instead, it is used to query on its environmental model. Actions and events are observed by the processing framework and used as knowledge facts. The knowledge base can be extended by using embedded classifiers in order to search for groups of instances that have common properties.

Scene interpretation by analysing table covers using Description Logics was conducted by (Neumann & Möller, 2008). Reasoning was based on temporal and spatial relations of visually aggregate concepts. Besides probabilistic information for generation of preferred interpretations, visual evidence and contextual information is used. In (Möller & Neumann, 2008), this work was broadened to cope with general multimedia data.

A comprehensive approach for situation-awareness is introduced in (Springer et al., 2010). This approach includes context capturing, abstraction and decision making. The combined framework manages sensing devices and reasoning components which allow using different reasoning facilities. Thus, logical reasoning can be used for high level decision making.

These last examples including our contributions show that the usage of Description Logics bears great potential. Hence, its adoption in the situation and action recognition task incorporated into the MAROCO framework.

3. System overview

The MAROCO framework implements an architecture achieving human centred computing realising safe human-robot interaction and cooperation due to advanced sensor technologies and fancy algorithms. An introduction of an intermediate state of the MAROCO system is given in (Graf & Wörn, 2009a). In the following, the advanced and augmented architecture is presented (Fig. 1). In this section, modules and functions are introduced and linked to Fig. 1 by referencing the given numbers in brackets.

Closing the kinematic chain in an environment with human agents and robots is especially meaningful and a premise in case of contact based cooperation scenarios. Thus a sensor calibration step is part of the framework {1}. The kinematic chain consists of the robot coordinate systems, the coordinate systems of human agents, the environmental model and finally the coordinate system of the 3D camera system.

The sensor system consists of a single depth sensing camera based on the time-of-flight principle which is developed and distributed by the company PMD Technologies. The resolution of the camera system is at the moment limited to 200x200 pixels. The advantage about the used 3D sensor technology is that it provides depth images as well as amplitude images. Amplitude values are a means to evaluate remissions of the active illumination of the camera system. The remission is influenced by objects in the scene and allows for adaption of algorithms towards increased robustness and effectiveness.

Due to this fact, the usage of cheaper sensors like the Microsoft Kinect camera is not feasible. Furthermore, because our sensor is mounted at the ceiling, the included human tracking of the Kinect system would render useless. The installation of the sensor system at the ceiling is meaningful in order to avoid the reach of humans or machinery, thus, allowing for a consistent sensor setup and enforce safety requirements.

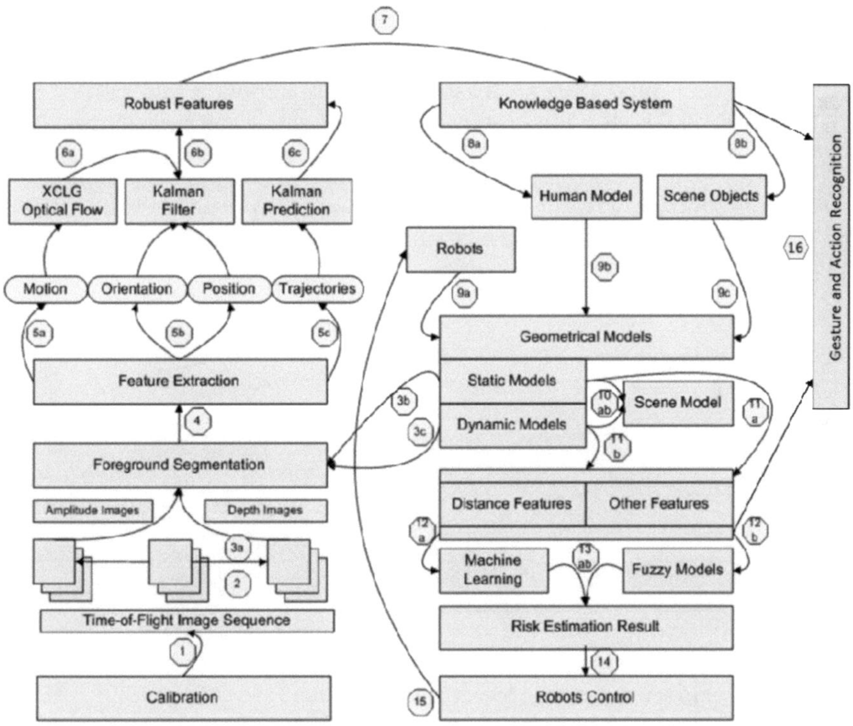

Fig. 1. System architecture of the MARCOCO framework.

In order to isolate relevant information from background clutter {4}, background subtraction techniques are used. Our approach is based on Gaussian Mixture Models and advances on works of (Stauffer & Grimson, 2000; Lee, 2005) with adaptions due to requirements of human-robot interaction and the used sensor model. Background modelling incorporates a priori knowledge and can be learned by applying a variety of techniques.

Detection of human presence is done by a decision process depending on selective discriminating features based on foreground information {4}. Therefore, algorithms based on eigenvalue analysis, depth measurements of pixel distributions, the distribution of connected components and finally motion features generated from optical flow computations {5a} are applied to decide whether the pixel cluster is generated by a human being or not.

MAROCO, the framework realising the system-architecture, provides also a flexible and complex kinematical model for human bodies {8a}. Due to the usage of a single 3D sensing camera mounted at the ceiling, a limited subset of degrees of freedom of the human kinematics is modelled. The kinematic features to be estimated are

- the shoulder and elbow angles of the left and right arm,
- the head position,
- the height of the person, and
- the upper body position {5b}.

These features are processed and generated by means of sequence analysis. Temporal information is incorporated by methods like Kalman filtering, Kalman prediction (Bar-Shalom et al., 2001) and optical flow estimation (Graf et al., 2010b). Thus, robust features are generated out of noisy data. Then all these features are supplied to a pattern recognition module which decides whether the provided features belong to a human model or a scene obstacle {7}. Obstacles are not recognized but represented by their bounding cylinders.

All gathered information and features are then used to construct geometrical models {9a, 9b, 9c}. Static and dynamic objects and agents are merged into an environmental scene model {10a, 10b} (Fig. 2).

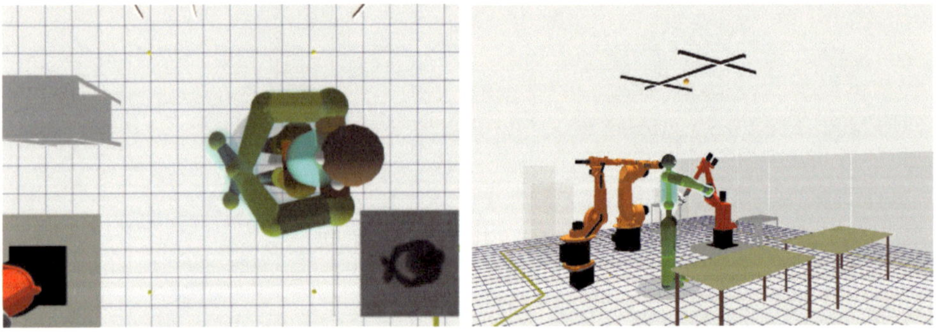

Fig. 2. Reconstructed human kinematics and environment model. Left image also shows depth coded grey scale sensor data in lower right corner.

Working with geometric information rather than pixel-based models results in great benefits concerning runtime behaviour. Using the 3D sensor and applying algorithms purely based on pixel processing (e.g. Graf & Wörn, 2008) is expensive in the meaning of computational time.

The generated robust features are used, besides other distance measurements, to estimate the risk. Feature estimates and distance calculations are then passed to machine learning methods {12a} and to functional evaluation {12b} (Graf et al., 2010a). Risk quantification can be used for influencing robotic behaviour {14} by either reducing motion velocity or adapting the motion path (Graf et al., 2009). This in turn changes representation of robot models {15}.

All information about human and robot kinematics can be used to reason about situations and human activities (Graf et al., 2010c) {16}. This allows recognising actions and drawing conclusions about expectations towards robotic behaviour.

4. Theoretical considerations and algorithms

In this section, more detailed insights into our approaches and implementations are given. First, estimation and computation of robust features is detailed. Afterwards, methods for risk estimation and minimisation are presented. This section concludes with a description of the recognition module of MAROCO which allows reasoning about situations and activities.

4.1 Robust features

In order to model human kinematics many features have to be robustly estimated. One kind of these features is based on motion analysis of the 3D sensor data. A means of motion analysis presents the estimation of the Optical Flow field. This technique is used in image sequence analysis and robotics for a long time (Horn & Schunk, 1981; Lucas & Kanade, 1981). It can be understood as the apparent motion of intensity structures in an image sequence. Our approach of computing Optical Flow fields advances on the combined local and global method (CLG) first introduced by (Bruhn et al., 2005a). The CLG method uses an isotropic Gaussian in order to reformulate the original data term formulated by (Horn & Schunk, 1981).

Our approach extends on this procedure by adapting Gaussians to the underlying distribution of pixels. Thus, it is called XCLG method (Graf et al., 2010b). The Optical Flow is influenced by its neighbourhood and, therefore, pixels at positions of edges or curves need special consideration. Through analysis of image edges, Gaussians are oriented and stretched along the principal axis which is congruent to the edge. The isotropic Gaussian of the CLG method is then substituted by the adapted Gaussian (Fig. 3).

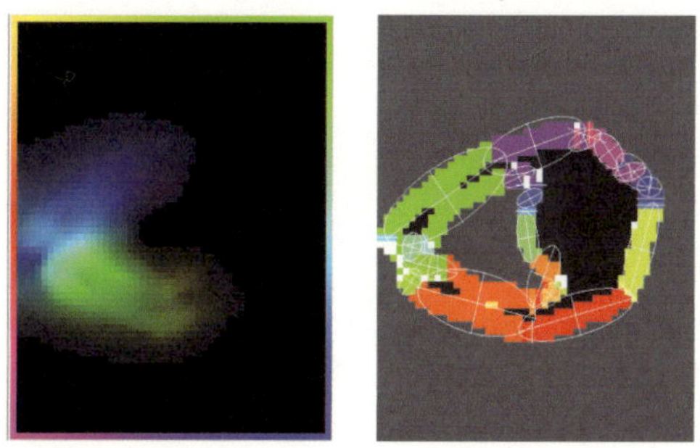

Fig. 3. Optical Flow field and anisotropic Gaussians adapted to underlying edges. The arms are moved towards each other.

Due to the fact that Optical Flow computations are an iterative process, usually, thousands of point wise iterations have to be applied to achieve significant results. For achieving real-time capabilities, application of standard numerical techniques, like Jacobi, Gauss-Seidel or successive over relaxation (SOR), is not feasible. The probably most efficient technique known today solving this kind of equation systems are so called multigrid solvers. They are often applied to sparse equation systems. In (Bruhn et al., 2005b) real time computations of

Optical Flow fields are reported using multigrid solvers. Thus, our approach uses multigrid solvers, which are implemented for general purpose GPU processing. This allows for real-time computations and effective use of motion analysis for robust features.

Other features include estimates about head and body orientation. These are computed through eigenvalue/eigenvector extraction of spatial pixel distributions. For this purpose, the depth images are segmented using additional estimations about body height and body part size relations. The orientations are determined by following assumptions:

- The head orientation is assumed to be the eigenvector corresponding to the larger of the two eigenvalues of the covariance matrix of the head pixel distribution.
- The upper part of the body orientation is assumed to be the eigenvector corresponding to the smaller of the two eigenvalues of the covariance matrix of the shoulder pixel distribution.

Through application of a windowed Kalman filter to past angles calculated from eigenvector analysis, estimations of orientations achieve greater robustness. An adapted Kalman filter is also used to fuse different information sources, such as motion analysis through Optical Flow computations, orientation estimates and arm poses. More details concerning the Kalman filter can be found in (Graf & Wörn, 2009a; Graf et al., 2010b).

The arm poses are also important features. These are estimated through the identification of three key points: shoulder, elbow and hand. Arm segments between these points can be linearly interpolated. In order to estimate the positions of the key points, skeletonisation succeeds a segmentation step. Afterwards the skeleton is mapped onto a graph and the arm poses are determined through path analysis in the graph. This approach takes also occlusions into account. Occlusions can be caused by either arms covering each other or by a robot pose covering human arm segments (Graf, 1010).

4.2 Risk quantification

Todays' application of robotics in industrial environments is characterized by isolation of robots and humans due to safety concerns. Realising close human-robot collaboration requires evaluation of situations regarding a measure of danger for the human. Risk quantification depending on human and robot kinematics can result in adaption of robot motion and, thus, guarantee safety for human co-workers.

Assignment of a risk value to a situation has to take into account many different parameters of the human and robot kinematics. The main idea is that there is greater danger for a human co-worker, if he is not aware of robot movement. Also the distance between robots and the human agent are of importance.

A method for providing great flexibility in building a knowledge base is the application of two-threaded fuzzy logics (Kiendl, 1997). Two-threaded fuzzy logics allow encoding positive and negative rules in a knowledge base. That reduces the number of necessary rules compared to standard fuzzy logic systems. A detailed description of the implemented fuzzy system and the corresponding rules can be found in (Graf et al., 2010a).

In order to connect the results from the positive and negative rules accumulations, so called hyperinference operators are necessary. In (Kiendl, 1997) a few operators, like a strong and a weak veto, are introduced. The strong veto operator is defined by (1), where $\mu(u)$ defines the association function of fuzzy sets, μ^+ and μ^- define the results of the accumulation of positive rules and negative rules respectively.

$$\mu(u) = \begin{cases} \mu^+(u), \text{ if } \mu^-(\text{u}) = 0 \\ 0, \text{ otherwise.} \end{cases} \tag{1}$$

Thus, this operator does not respond to the area under the activated positive rule and the negative rule is overly weighted. The great flexibility of two-threaded fuzzy logic systems is bypassed through application of the strong veto operator.

The weak veto operator is defined by:

$$\mu(u) = \begin{cases} \mu^+(u), \text{ if } \mu^+(\text{u}) \geq \mu^-(\text{u}) \\ 0, \text{ otherwise.} \end{cases} \tag{2}$$

Therefore, if the area under the negative rule is greater than the one under the positive rule the veto is applied. This action is desirable. On the opposite, if the area corresponding to the negative rule is smaller than the area under the positive rule the veto is not applied. Thus, the area under the negative rule has no influence on the outcome in all those cases. This behaviour is not desirable.

As consequence, a novel operator was implemented which is a trade-off in comparison to the strong and weak veto operators. It is defined as:

$$\mu(u) = \begin{cases} \mu^+(u) - \beta^-(u), \text{ if } \mu^+(\text{u}) > \mu^-(\text{u}) \\ 0, \text{ otherwise.} \end{cases} \tag{3}$$

In Fig. 4, the response characteristics of the proposed operator are presented. The construction of the novel veto operator begins by subdivision of the area under μ^- into three parts. At first, the α -cut of the curve is determined according to the output of the activated negative rule. Then, an orthogonal line is generated as shown in Fig. 4 (bottom row). This defines three parts of the area under the operator. The outer area elements are identical due to the symmetric characteristic of the operator and described by β^-. The adequate output of the veto operator is then generated by μ^+ - β^-.

This proposed method for risk estimation can be implemented to evaluate a situation in real-time. Furthermore, its effectiveness is demonstrated in the section about experimental evaluation (Sec. 5).

4.3 Risk minimisation

As stated in the last section, the risk evaluation is used to influence robotic behaviour in order to guarantee safety for the human agent. In the context of industrial robotics, the efficiency of task performance of robots is very important. Thus, simple adaption of motion velocities does not suffice. A more advanced method is to actually re-plan the robots' path with dynamic safety constraints imposed by the moving human agent.

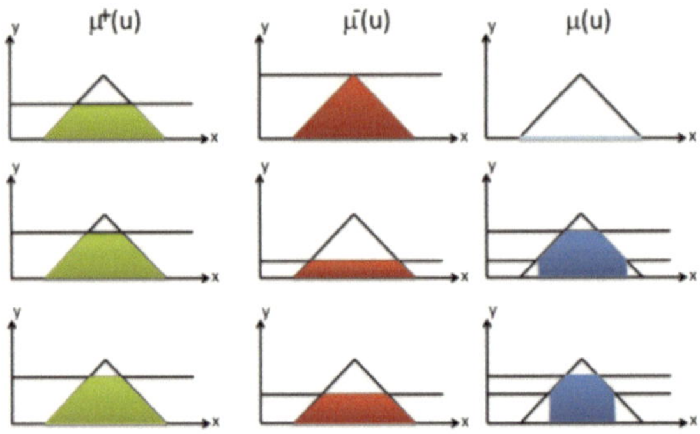

Fig. 4. Response characteristic of the novel veto operator.

The path planning takes place in the robots' configuration space. This space is interspersed with nodes which are connected to a graph structure. Association of risk estimates and configuration space is achieved by evaluation of each node in the graph. The path planning takes these evaluations of configurations into account and returns a safe and shortest path from and to given configurations. It uses a modified A* search in configuration space to do so. A look-a-head functionality is used to re-evaluate a future path segment and detect impending collisions before they actually occur. In such a case a re-planning is invoked.

The implemented technique allows for fast and responsive re-planning without violating real-time constraints. Details about its implementation can be found in (Graf et al., 2009).

4.4 Situation and activity recognition

All the methods and functionality presented above enable safe human-robot interaction and cooperation. But in order to actually achieve cooperation, situations and human activities need to be recognised and according conclusions about robotic behaviour need to be drawn. As pointed out in Section 2.3. Description Logics are suited for reasoning about context and, therefore, about situations and actions.

In (Graf et al., 2010c), a first approach towards the application of Description Logics for situation awareness is presented. An external reasoning system is used as inference facility. A MAROCO module must, therefore, fulfil at least the tasks of establishing a communication interface with the Description Logics reasoner, managing the knowledge base and managing the reasoner results. An overview of the subcomponents is given in Fig. 5. The communication is achieved through the so called DIG-interface which was defined by the Description Logic Implementation Group. It uses a TCP connection to transmit XML messages. Many reasoners support this interface definition, which allows the separation of application and reasoner by the means of programming language and execution place.

General knowledge and knowledge about individuals in the domain can be distinctly separated and defined in a Description Logic knowledge base. Common knowledge defines the terminology of the domain and, thus, is declared in the terminology box, hence TBox. Declarations about individuals and their properties are centralised in the assertion box, hence ABox. This allows for modular and reusable knowledge bases and, thus, for more efficient coding of knowledge (Hummel et al., 2007).

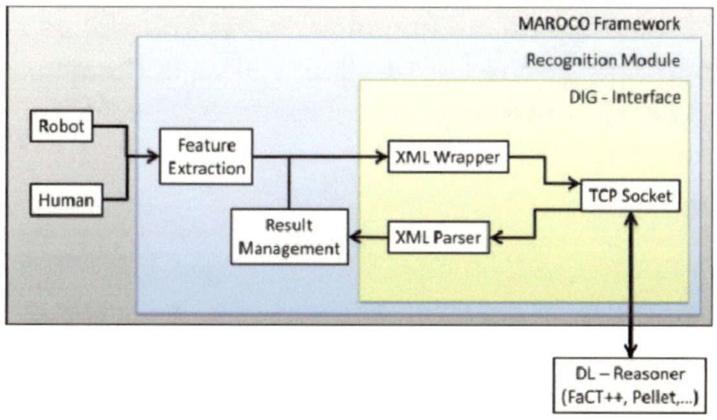

Fig. 5. Components of the recognition module embedded in the MAROCO framework.

The DIG-interface implements a so called *Tell&Ask* (Baader et al., 2010) functionality. The definition of the knowledge base is achieved through *tell* operations. Reasoner results and information can be retrieved through *ask* operations. Modifications successive of *ask* operations are not defined by the DIG-interface. Consequently, the knowledge base needs to be re-established in each runtime cycle in order to incorporate changed sensor data into the recognition process. The differentiation of domain knowledge and assertional knowledge of Description Logics is disregarded by the DIG-interface.

The recognition module handles assertions depending on the current kinematical human model and robot specific parameters and domain specific knowledge. Thus, the distinction of TBoxes and ABoxes is represented internally.

As the assertional knowledge depends on kinematical parameters, a feature extraction component is applied in order to fill the attribute values of the assertions (Fig. 5).

Due to the fact that there is currently no object recognition implemented in the MAROCO framework, objects are included into the situation recognition through means of simulation. Thus, a human agent can hold working tools or measurement devices in his hands. Also, the simulation enables the robot gripper to be holding objects like work pieces. In future works, these purely simulated features will be incorporated into the demonstrator as well. For now, these virtual features enable evaluation of effectiveness and capabilities of the recognition system. Moreover, by incorporating virtual features, the recognition module can reason about probable interactions and generate expectation towards robotic behaviour, e.g., prepare a work piece or hand tools on to a human co-worker. These expectations can be used directly or in context of the recognized actions as input for a possible task planner for realizing concrete close human-robot collaboration. Implementation of a task planning module is a logical consequence and will be done in near future.

Taking temporal information into account during reasoning is accomplished by defining an *after*-role between different actions. This role can be regarded as precondition for actions, because certain actions can only be recognised if certain other actions occurred prior. In order to facilitate temporal dependencies between actions, previously recognised actions are stored and retrieved during knowledge base recreation. This functionality is taken over by the reasoner result management component (Fig. 5).

Furthermore, the knowledge base implements concepts of complex actions which consist of other actions. The temporal relationship includes these complex concepts. Thus, parallel and subsequent occurring actions can be processed and recognized.

Detailed description of the implemented ontologies and knowledge base are given in (Graf et al., 2010c). Evaluation and discussion of effectiveness and capabilities of the presented recognition module conclude the section about experimental evaluation (Sec. 5).

5. Experimental evaluation

Due to the application of diverse methods in the framework MAROCO, there is a need for diverse testing and evaluation. In the following sections, especially experimental evaluation of accuracy, efficiency and effectiveness are presented. Also, the capabilities of the proposed methods and their fusion in the framework are discussed.

5.1 Robust features and human kinematics

Determination of motion features through computation of Optical Flow fields allows interpretation about direction and apparent motion. These can be identified by representing the Optical Flow field as vector field. In the context of human-robot interaction, rates of changes are of great importance, as they indicate motion intensity. Thus, the vector length plays an important role in the estimation and filtering of robust features. For evaluation purposes, the XCLG method was compared with the CLG method by computing the Optical Flow field of an image sequence and by evaluation of magnitude differences of both vector fields. As shown in (Graf et al., 2010b), the CLG method underestimates vector lengths by 26%-47%. These results demonstrate the greater accuracy of the XCLG method considering vector lengths.

Due to the implementation of the Optical Flow computation using general purpose graphics unit processing, the presented method achieves real-time capability. The computation times are also compared to the CLG method. Each method was implemented with SOR solver and multigrid solver. Different camera systems with differing resolutions were used. Moreover, the publicly available "Yosemite" image sequence was used to verify the results with internationally respected data. The results of these runtime tests are presented in Table 1.

In [ms]	**IFM O3D (50x64)**			
	CLG		**XCLG**	
	SOR	**MG**	**SOR**	**MG**
CPU	*164*	2	*172*	11
GPU	20	**5**	23	**8**
In ms	**PMDTec CamCube 2.0 (204x204)**			
	CLG		**XCLG**	
	SOR	**MG**	**SOR**	**MG**
CPU	*2150*	25	*2225*	85
GPU	89	**20**	102	**33**
In ms	**Yosemite**			
	CLG		**XCLG**	
	SOR	**MG**	**SOR**	**MG**
CPU	*4020*	48	*4260*	295
GPU	164	**32**	220	**85**

Table 1. Overall time for computation of Optical Flow using CLG and XCLG.

Due to lack of ground truth data, evaluation of tracking results in real world applications is challenging. Thus, testing implemented algorithms was done indirectly through examination of overlap of sensor data and tracked kinematics. In order to compare sensor data and tracking results, the human kinematics is projected back onto the image plane. Thus, the cycle from sensor data to tracking data and back again is closed (Fig. 6). Congruency of foreground pixels and back-projection can be interpreted as accuracy of the kinematics reconstruction step and, thus, is a measure of the reliability of the algorithm.

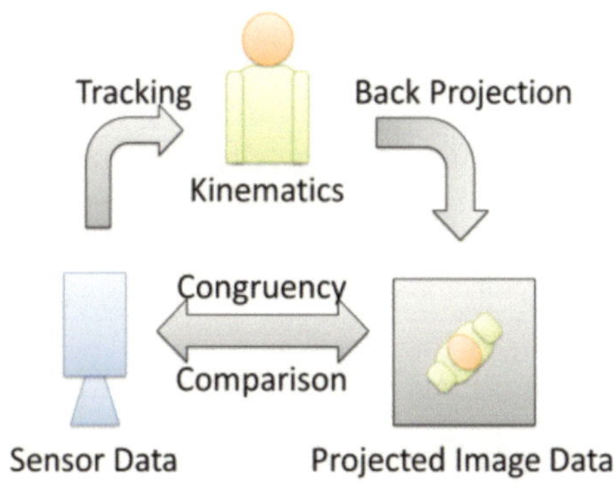

Fig. 6. Data processing cycle for evaluation of tracking data.

In order to analyse the congruency, different human motion sequences were used. Each sequence consists of approximately 600 frames. In Table 2, the results are summarised. The motion sequences include simple motions like forward and backward (1), only arm movements (2), turning around (3), standing still (4), and arbitrary motion (5).

Sequence	Mean	Variance
1	96.60	19.82
2	89.46	14.71
3	90.07	9.67
4	93.13	2.33
5	91.60	14.53

Table 2. Quantification of the congruency rate.

These results show that the reconstruction of the human kinematics is congruent with the observed sensor data to a large degree. Due to the fact that risk estimation is based on the kinematics reconstruction, this degree of congruence has great importance. After all, it influences directly the safety capabilities of the system, because risk estimation is done purely based on reconstructed kinematics.

5.2 Risk management

For the evaluation of selected risk estimation methods, different experiments with varying methods have been conducted. These methods include e.g., simple measures like shortest distance between human and robot, methods of differing complexity implemented as Gaussian mixture models and Support Vector Regression.

Compared to simple distance measures and Gaussian mixture models, the two-threaded fuzzy system allows for precise modelling of situations and according risk assignments. For examination purposes the same sensor input sequence was evaluated by the above mentioned methods and risk assignments were compared. The results confirm our assumption about flexibility and effectiveness of the here presented fuzzy method (Fig. 7). Further details can be found in (Graf et al., 2010a).

The conducted experiments also demonstrate that training a Support Vector Regression resulted in unreliable and noisy risk estimation compared to the implemented two-threaded fuzzy system. Thus, the fuzzy system outperforms the Support Vector Regression and is used as preferred risk estimation method. Grounded on the results of the here described fuzzy logic implementation, safety and efficiency for human-robot cooperation is achievable in real-time.

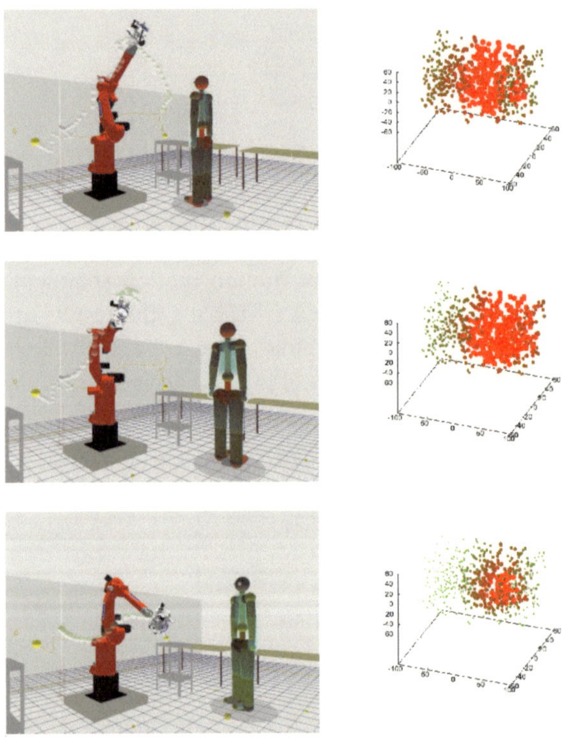

Fig. 7. Selected situations of human posture and corresponding configuration subspace for first three robot axes. Size and colour of each node of the subspace is determined by risk assignment.

For the experimental analysis of the path re-planning technique different scenarios were tested in simulation. Especially, the size of the configuration space graph was subject of evaluation in order to capture scalability of the algorithm. For testing, a sequence of human motion was recorded and played back during simulation (Fig. 7). Thus, arbitrary movements were recorded and thereby the simulation was related to real-world setups. The tested scenarios do not consider human-robot interaction or cooperation, but instead, the robot has a given repetitive task and has to avoid human co-worker in its working area. The overall hold-up time of the robot reaches about 27% during evaluation. The results are presented in Table 3. Further details are explained in (Graf et al., 2009).

# Vertices of Graph	100	1000	2000
Avg. Path Length	4.62	5.98	7.34
Hold-up Time [%]	63.96%	27.34%	38.96%

Table 3. Results of path planner run-time analysis.

The presented results concerning risk quantification and minimisation demonstrate the effectiveness of guaranteeing safety for human agents in the realm of close human-robot collaboration.

5.3 Situation awareness

In order to evaluate the situation and activity recognition module of the MARCOCO framework, different courses of action were executed. On the one hand, efficient analysis of different scenarios requires automated means of feature value setting. Thus, value pre-sets were incorporated into the framework which allows for usage of pre-defined feature vectors. Such pre-sets enable investigation of interesting use cases without capturing sensor data. Also, recognition results can be directly related to defined feature changes through pre-sets. Nevertheless, recognition based on actual sensor data is compulsory in order to evaluate recognition results over time and prolonged actions (Fig. 8).

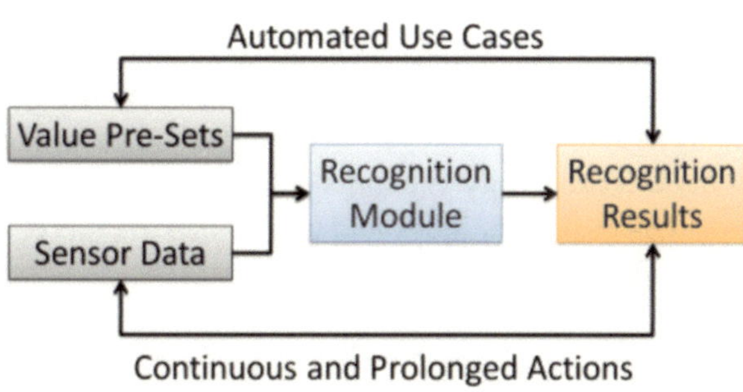

Fig. 8. Usage of feature value pre-sets and actual sensor data.

Based on these pre-sets and on actual sensor data all experiments were conducted. Natural movements and transitions between actions have been tested and special use cases have been investigated.

Table 4 summarises the results of 2140 recognition cycles. The average processing time amounts to approximately 550 ms. The lower bound is less than half of this. There are also casual outliers which take up to 10 seconds. Further investigations based on feature value pre-setting have shown that long duration times might not be directly linkable to the recognition module itself (Graf et al., 2010c). Though, further research needs to be conducted on optimising runtime behaviour of the recognition module.

# Recognition cycles	2140		Max [ms]	9705
Ø Response time [ms]	551.78		# > 1000 ms	17 (0.79%)
Min [ms]	216		# > 5000 ms	4 (0.18%)

Table 4. Results from evaluation of the recognition module.

In Fig. 9, results of the recognition module depending on the human pose are depicted. It demonstrates the capabilities of analysing solely kinematical features of the human agent and its relations to a robot.

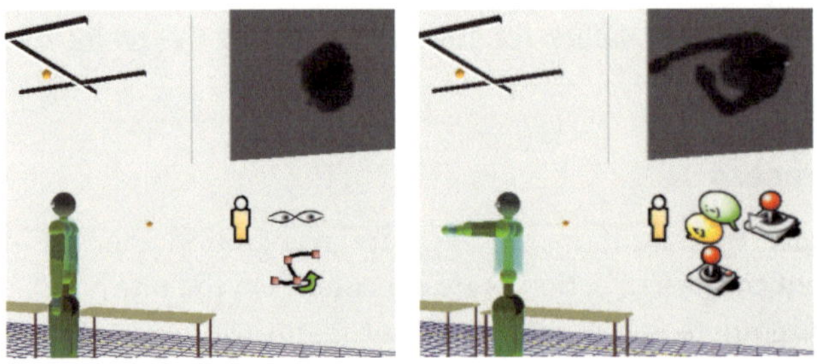

Fig. 9. Left: Human agent is watching the robot. Recognized situation: Monitoring. The robot is expected to carry on with its task of following a planned path. Right: Human agent is communicating. The complex action to signal a left turning movement is recognized. The robot is expected to comply with user instructions.

By adapting the virtual features according to the generated expectations the interaction between reasoner results and robotic behaviour can be demonstrated. Thus, the capabilities of the presented approach reach beyond sole activity and situation recognition. By generating expectations towards robot behaviour, an understanding of the situation can be achieved. This induction of relations between concepts can hardly be realized by purely probabilistic methods. The achieved processing cycle time of approximately 550 ms does not allow for safe cooperation based only on the recognition module. Thus, the MAROCO framework uses its implemented techniques and algorithms to enforce safety and real-time capabilities during robot motion.

6. Conclusion

The presented framework MAROCO and the incorporated approaches are based on the identification of different modules that have to be taken into account when designing a system for close human-robot collaboration based on a depth imaging sensor. Experimental results give confidence in continuing to strive for true contact based cooperation between robot and human. Thus, our work is a stepping stone for future development.

Thus far, a system was implemented which analysis depth images taken from a 3D camera system mounted beneath the ceiling. Robust features like motion, head and body orientation, position and arm poses are robustly end efficiently estimated. Evaluation has shown that high accuracy is achieved.

All these features are used to reconstruct the human kinematics which is the foundation for risk quantification. A two-threaded fuzzy system with a novel hyperinference operator is implemented for risk evaluation of situations according to human pose features and relation between human and robots. The system is flexible and effective. In comparison to Support Vector Classification and other means of risk estimation the two-threaded fuzzy system is the most reliable and accurate one.

Results of risk estimation are used for adapting robotic behaviour. Adaption is realised by path re-planning if a look-a-head functionality determines impending collisions of human and robot before they occur. That allows for safe and efficient path traversal and, thus, reduced time of robot hold-up times.

In order to achieve true human-robot cooperation situation awareness and action recognition is necessary. A module for realising this task was implemented using Description Logics for defining appropriate ontologies and for reasoning. The presented system is capable of recognising subsequent, parallel and dependent actions and can generate expectation towards robotic behaviour. Thus, the system reaches beyond sole situation recognition and enables understanding human activities.

Future work will carry on development towards a system that achieves close human-robot collaboration. There are still many open challenges that need to be tackled before this goal is reached. The usage of more than one camera can either widen the supervised work area or enable multi-view capturing of the scene.

Currently, only one human agent can be detected and its kinematics can be reconstructed. Extension of the presented algorithms is needed for multi-human pose estimation. Moreover, the algorithms need to be adapted in order to cope with more arbitrary movements of human co-workers. Some movements are not covered by the current human pose reconstruction process, e.g., stooping down.

Object recognition and semantic mapping of the work area are also important means for modelling interactions of human agents and robots with the surrounding environment. Particularly object recognition will enable more diverse and differentiated analysis of situations. Semantic mapping of objects and places in the robots' work area will allow for recognition of human action plans and, thus, a better understanding of intentions behind human actions.

As pointed out above, implemented virtual features need to be realized for the demonstrator. Moreover, runtime optimisations of the current situation and activity recognition module need to be investigated and implemented. This will allow for evaluation of real-world scenarios of interaction and cooperation. Also, realisation of industrial applications with the MAROCO system will enable evaluation of capabilities and user acceptance. This experimental evaluation can be realised stepwise beginning with simple risk minimisation and collision avoidance, advancing on to telepresence-like systems and concluding in fully autonomous human-robot cooperation.

The MAROCO system emphasises on real-time computation and safety for human co-workers. Nevertheless, the implemented system is a research base and does not permit safety certification. Hopefully, achievements of the human-robot cooperation research community will migrate into applicable industrial systems. Safety regulations and engineers have to adapt to this young field of research.

7. Acknowledgment

We acknowledge support by Deutsche Forschungsgemeinschaft (DFG) and Open Access Publishing Fund of Karlsruhe Institute of Technology (KIT).

8. References

Azad, P., Asfour, T., & Dillmann, R. 2008. Robust Real-time Stereo-based Markerless Human Motion Capture. *Proceedings of the IEEE/RAS International Conference on Humanoid Robots*, Daeheon, Korea, pp. 700-707

Baader, F., Calvanese, D., McGuinness, D., Nardi, D., & Patel-Schneider, P. 2010. "The Description Logic Handbook", 2nd Edition, Cambridge University Press

Bar-Shalom, Y., Li, X. R., & Kirubarajan, T. 2001. *Estimation with Applications to Tracking and Navigation: Theory, Algorithms, and Software*, Wiley, New York

Bruhn, A., Weickert, J., & Schnörr, C. 2005a. Lucas/Kanade Meets Horn/Schunck: Combining Local and Global Optic Flow Methods. In: *International Journal of Computer Vision* 61(3), pp. 211-231

Bruhn, A., Weickert, J., Feddern, C., Kohlberger, T., & C. Schnörr, C. 2005b. Variational Optical Flow Computation in Real Time. In: *IEEE Transactions on Image Processing 14:5*, pp. 608-615

Caillette, F., & Howard, T. 2004a. Real-Time Markerless Human Body Tracking Using Colored Voxels and 3-D Blobs, *Proceedings of the 3rd IEEE/ACM International Symposium on Mixed and Augmented Reality*

Caillette, F., & Howard, T. 2004b. Real-Time Markerless Human Body Tracking with Multi-View 3-D Voxel Reconstruction, *Proceedings of the British Machine Vision Conference* (BMVC), pp. 597-606

Fua, P., Gruen, A., D'Apuzzo, N., & Plankers, R. 2002. Markerless Full Body Shape and Motion Capture from Video Sequences, *Symposium on Close Range Imaging*, International Society for Photogrammetry and Remote Sensing, Corfu, Greece

Graf, J. 2010. Sichere Mensch-Roboter-Kooperation durch Auswertung von Bildfolgen, *Dissertation*, Fakultät für Informatik, Karlsruhe Institut of Technology, Germany

Graf, J., & Wörn, H. 2008. An Image-Sequence Analysis System with Focus on Human-Robot-Cooperation using PMD-Camera. *Proceedings of Robotik 2008*, München, pp. 223-226

Graf, J., & Wörn, H. 2009a. Safe Human-Robot Interaction Using 3D Sensor, In: *VDI Berichte 2067 Automation 2009*, VDI/VDE Gesellschaft Meß- und Automatisierungstechnik, Baden-Baden, Germany, pp. 1-12

Graf, J., Czapiewski, P., Wörn, H. 2010a. Evaluating Risk Estimation Methods and Path Planning for Safe Human- Robot Cooperation, *Proceedings of ISR/Robotik 2010*, München, Germany

Graf, J., Dittrich, F., & Wörn, H. 2010b. High Performance Optical Flow Serves Bayesian Filtering for Safe Human-Robot Cooperation. *Proceedings of Int. Symposium of Robotics (ISR) and VDI/VDE Robotik 2010*, München, Germany, 8 pages

Graf, J., Puls, S., & Wörn, H. 2009. Incorporating Novel Path Planning Method into Cognitive Vision System for Safe Human-Robot Interaction. *Proceedings of IARIA Computation World: Cognitive 2009*, Athen, Greece, pp. 443-447

Graf, J., Puls, S., & Wörn, H. 2010c. Recognition and Understanding Situations and Avtivities with Description Logics for Safe Human-Robot Cooperation, *Proceedings of the 2nd International Conference on Advanced Cognitive Technologies and Applications: Cognitive 2010*, Lisbon, Portugal, pp. 90-96

Hecht, F., Azad, P., & Dillmann, R. 2009. Markerless Human Motion Tracking with a Flexible Model and Appearance Learning, *Proceedings of the IEEE International Conference on Robotics and Automation* (ICRA), Kobe, Japan, pp. 3173-3179

Henrich, D., Fischer, M., & Gecks, T. 2008a. Sichere Mensch/Roboter-Koexistenz und Kooperation. In: *Robotik 2008*, München, Germany

Henrich, D., & Gecks, T. 2008b. Multi-Camera Collision Detection Between Known and Unknown Objects. *Proceedings of 2nd ACM/IEEE International Conference on Distributed Smart Cameras* (ICDSC), Stanford, USA

Horn, B., & Schunck, B. 1981. Determining optical flow. In: *Artificial Intelligence*, pp. 185–204

Hummel, B., Thiemann, W., & Lulcheva, I. 2007. Description Logic for Vision-based Intersection Understanding, *Proceedings of Cognitive Systems with Interactive Sensors* (COGIS), Stanford University, USA

Jenkins, O., Gonzalez, G., & Loper, M. 2006. Monocular Virtual Trajectory Estimation with Dynamical Primitives. *Proceedings of the American Association for Artificial Intelligence Workshop on Cognitive Robotics* (AAAI), Boston, Massachusetts, USA

Jenkins, O., Gonzalez, G., & Loper, M. 2007. Recognizing human pose and actions for interactive robots. In: *Human-Robot Interaction*, chapter 6, pp. 119-138

Jensen, R.R., & Paulsen, R.R. 2009. Analysis of Gait Using a Treadmill and a Time-of-Flight Camera, *Proceedings of the DAGM Workshop on Dynamic 3D Imaging*, Jena, Germany, pp. 154-166

Kiendl, H. 1997. *Fuzzy Logik methodenorientiert* , R. Oldenbourg Verlag, München, Wien

Lee, D. S. 2005. Effective Gaussian Mixture Learning for Video Background Subtraction, *Proceedings of IEEE Trans. Pattern Analysis and Machine Intelligence (27)*, pp. 827-832

Lucas, B. D., & Kanade, T. 1981. An Iterative Image Registration Technique with an Application to Stereo Vision. In: *Proceedings of Imaging*, pp 121-130

Lösch, M., Gärtner, S., Knoop, S., Schmidt-Rohr, S.R., & Dillmann, R. 2009. A human body model initialization approach made real-time capable through heuristic constraints, *Proceedings of the 14th International Conference on Advanced Robotics* (ICAR), Munich, Germany

Minnen, D., Essa, I., & Starner, T. 2003. Expectation Grammars: Leveraging High-Level Expectations for Activity Recognition, *Proceedings of Computer Vision and Pattern Recognition*, Vol. 2, pp. 626-632

Mussi, L., Ivekovic, S., & Cagnoni, S. 2010. Markerless Articulated Human Body Tracking from Multi-View Video with GPU-PSO, *Proceedings of the 9th International Conference on Evolvable Systems*, York, UK

Möller, R., & Neumann, B. 2008. Ontology-Based Reasoning Techniques for Multimedia Interpretation and Retrieval, In: *Semantic Multimedia and Ontologies*, Part 2, pp. 55-98, Springer London

Neumann, B., & Möller, R. 2008. On Scene Interpretation with Description Logics, In: *Image and Vision Computing*, Vol. 26, pp. 81-101

Kehl, R., Bray, M., & Van Gool, L. 2005. PHI'05 Workshop in Conjunction with ICCV 2005, Beijing, China

Knoop, S., Vacek, S., & Dillmann, R. 2006. Sensor Fusion for 3D Human body Tracking with an Articulated 3D Body Model. *Proceedings of the 2006 IEEE International Conference on Robotics and Automation* (ICRA), Orlando, Florida, USA

Krüger, V., Kragic, D., Ude, A., & Geib, C. 2007. The Meaning of Action: A Review on Action Recognition and Mapping, *Proceedings of Advanced Robotics*, Vol. 21, pp. 1473-1501

Kulic, D. 2005. Safety for Human-Robot Interaction. Dissertation, Faculty of Graduate Studies, Mechanical Engineering, University of British Columbia, December 2005

Raamana, P., Grest, D., & Krüger, V. 2007. Human Action Recognition in Table-Top Scenarios: An HMM-Based Analysis to Optimize the Performance, In: *Lecture Notes in Computer Science*, Vol 4673, pp. 101-108

Shi, Y., Huang, Y., Minnen, D., Bobick, A., & Essa, I. 2004. Propagation Networks for Recognition of Partially Ordered Sequential Action, *Proceedings of Computer Vision and Pattern Recognition*, Vol. 2, pp. 862-869

Springer, T., Wustmann, P., Braun, I., Dargie, W., & Berger, M. 2010. A Comprehensive Approach for Situation-Awareness Based on Sensing and Reasoning about Context, In: *Lecture Notes in Computer Science*, Vol. 5061, pp. 143-157, Springer Berlin

Stauffer, C., & Grimson, W. E. L. 2000. Learning Patterns of Activity Using Real-Time Tracking, *Proceedings of IEEE Trans. On Pattern Analysis and Machine Intelligence*, Vol. 22, No. 8, pp. 747-757

Tenorth, M., & Beetz, M. 2009. KNOWROB - Knowledge processing for Autonomous Personal Robots, *Proceedings of the IEEE International Conference on Intelligent Robots and Systems* (IROS)

Thiemermann, S. 2005. Direkte Mensch-Roboter-Kooperation in der Kleinteilmontage mit einem SCARA-Roboter. *Dissertation*, Fakultät für Maschinenbau der Universität Stuttgart

Wan, C., Yuan, B., & Miao, Z. 2008. Markerless Human Body Motion Capture using Markov Random Field and Dynamic Graph Cuts, In: *The Visual Computer* 24(5), pp. 272-380

Winkler, B. 2008. Konzept zur Sicheren Mensch-Roboter-Kooperation auf Basis von Schnellen 3-D Time-of-Flight Sensoren. A. Verl und M. Hägele (Eds.), VDI/VDE Gesellschaft für Meß- und Automatisierungstechnik (GMA), Düsseldorf, Deutsche Gesellschaft für Robotik: *Robotik 2008*, pp. 147-151. Tagung München

Wu, Y., Chen, H., Tsai, W., Lee, S., & Yu, J. 2008. Human action recognition based on layered-HMM, *Proceedings of the IEEE International Conference on Multimedia and Expo*, pp. 1453-1456

Zhu, Y., Dariush, B., & Fujimura, K. 2008. Controlled human pose estimation from from depth image streams. *Proceedings of the IEEE Computer Society Conference on Computer Vision and Pattern Recognition*, pp. 1-8

Zhu, Y. 2009. Model-Based Human Pose Estimation with Spatio-Temporal Inferencing, *Dissertation*, The Ohio State University

12

Intelligent Object Exploration

Robert Gaschler[1], Dov Katz[2], Martin Grund[1],
Peter A. Frensch[1] and Oliver Brock[2]
[1]*Humboldt-Universität zu Berlin,*
[2]*Technische Universität Berlin*
Germany

1. Introduction

Tool use is considered to be the hallmark of higher cognitive abilities (compare e.g. Blaisdell, 2008). It is therefore the target of an extensive body of work in psychology. The mechanisms that enable the discovery of affordances in humans and animals are still not fully understood. Tool use has been observed predominantly in primates but also in other animals such as crows. Weir and Kacelnik (2007), for instance, report on a New Caledonian Crow modifying aluminum strips in order to retrieve food. The crow correctly chooses between bending and unbending aluminum strips, depending on the specific type of jar it is presented with. Studies on tool use suggest that the potential application of objects to achieve manipulation objectives can be discovered through exploration. When an affordance of an object is discovered, it becomes a tool.

Recently, tool use has begun to gain the attention of a different research field: robotics. The goal of research in robotics is to produce artificial agents capable of accomplishing manipulation tasks. Many of these manipulation tasks require the usage of tools. Thus, significant progress in robotics will be achieved by developing the necessary mechanisms for tool use.

We believe that much can be gained by integrating the methods of psychology and robotics. The mutual interest in tool use creates an opportunity for fruitful collaboration. On the one hand, roboticists can leverage insights gained by decades of research on tool use in humans and animals. On the other hand, psychologists can benefit from quantifiable and easy-to-reproduce experiments conducted on artificial agents. A theory about tool use, for example, could be tested on a robotic system, allowing for precisely controlled experimental conditions, without the complexity involved in testing human subjects.

In this chapter, we present a new collaborative effort between researchers from the areas of psychology and robotics. We focus on exploration of kinematic structures as a first step towards advancing our understanding of human and robotic tool use. Through the study of kinematic structures, we hope to gain insights into the principles that govern tool use at a more general level. The work presented here is still in its early stages. Nevertheless, our preliminary results are encouraging.

To assess whether a new object can be a useful tool for a certain task, an agent must be able to explore the object's properties, such as its shape or the possible relative motions its constituent parts are able to perform. An understanding of object exploration is therefore a prerequisite for explaining tool use in humans and in robots. As in many environments exploration is costly, learning of efficient exploration strategies and transfer to novel objects is a major concern of the current chapter. To understand the principles underlying object exploration and the acquisition of exploration strategies, we turn our attention to a specific class of objects: rigid articulated objects. Articulated objects are objects composed of rigid parts that are connected to each other via degrees of freedom (joints). Exploration provides an agent with an understanding of how an object's degrees of freedom can be used and thus with knowledge about the potential use or the function of the object. Consequently, the ability to explore the kinematic structure of an object is a prerequisite for using it as a tool.

We describe a novel simulation environment, which will allow for robots and humans to interact with the same objects, in order to determine their kinematic structure. This simulated environment enables us to study object exploration in humans and robots. We hope that by studying exploration of articulated objects we can advance the current level of understanding of human object exploration and tool use, and that this improved understanding will play an important role in advancing robotic tool use. We also hope that this collaborative research will encourage a greater exchange of ideas and techniques between robotics and psychology.

In the following paragraphs we will discuss what psychology and robotics can contribute to intelligent object exploration in terms of representational formats, the dilemma of exploration vs. exploitation, and the interplay of passive knowledge accumulation and active testing. In each case we will briefly sketch how the robotics approach to object exploration can benefit from incorporating approaches from psychology and how psychological studies and applications concerning object exploration can be fostered by borrowing from and providing interfaces with robot object exploration. After this, we will describe in more detail our current approach and results concerning robot object exploration. Finally, we report findings on human exploration that render as highly promising future attempts to provide robots with human exploration strategies and to construct interfaces that allow for humans and robots to manipulate the same objects.

1.1 Symbolic and relational representations

The form of representation of object structure is highly relevant for intelligent object exploration. In order to benefit from past exploration episodes, experience needs to be stored in a way that allows application to novel cases and abstraction from irrelevant features. Both of the latter criteria pose a serious challenge to instance-based models that have been proposed in psychology and robotics for improving performance by storing processing episodes. We argue that symbolic and relational representations will be crucial to capture human and robot object exploration.

In cognitive psychology, instance-based approaches have been developed that successfully model human skill acquisition with narrow sets of stimuli (e.g., Logan, 1988). In these models, processing episodes (e.g. an arithmetic problem and its solution) are stored in memory. When the situation reoccurs, the solution can be retrieved from memory which is often faster and more efficient than the original way of computing the solution. While successful in explaining some aspects of human skill acquisition, these models are less helpful for capturing exploration. However, research on information reduction (e.g., Haider & Frensch, 2002; Gaschler & Frensch, 2007, 2009) suggests that humans spontaneously explore object structure and parse objects into relevant and irrelevant parts - even in repetitive tasks with a narrow set of material that would be solvable by an instance-based approach. They generate knowledge about abstract structural properties of the task material which allows them to process novel and unfamiliar objects just as efficiently as highly practiced ones.

Roboticists have also been using instance-based approaches to link specific states of the environment to actions. While machines are good at storing tables of states and actions, the problem of applying the knowledge to novel situations remains. Instance-based representations usually contain too much information due to the storage of irrelevant features. Unless repeated exposure to various exemplars of objects allows for pruning of the irrelevant features, they will hinder application of the knowledge to novel situations (e.g., Sun, Merrill, & Peterson, 2001 for an interesting approach). This is because novel situations that might in principle be suitable for application of the instance knowledge might have low similarity on irrelevant features. Other research in artificial intelligence and robotics has tried to tackle the problem of matching knowledge to states of the environment by considering more abstract representation formats. Katz and Brock (2008) proposed to capture information about robot object exploration episodes by symbolic relational representations. This work focuses on the domain of articulated objects. It leverages a representation of link properties that only includes properties that are relevant for manipulation. Application of the knowledge of the structural properties of the object therefore does not depend on irrelevant features such as the configuration of an object in every exploration episode. This type of approach avoids problems of combinatorial explosion when planning and learning from specific physical interactions that instantiate exploration episodes. Also, a robot system that has a clear-cut representation of an exploration event allows for an interface with a human. More specifically, a robot may learn from human exploratory behavior through observation.

In psychology and robotics representation can be regarded as an important component of intelligent object exploration and tool use. Representation format is crucial to solve the problem of the application to novel cases and abstraction from irrelevant features as well as the problem to provide an interface between human and robot exploration behavior. A high-dimensional world can be represented such that human and robot object exploration can rely on helpful restrictions of what has to be considered to solve a task. Through experiments, psychologists can reveal insights about the representations used by humans for solving exploration and tool use tasks. Roboticists can then test such representations in real-world or simulated experiments and try to design mechanisms that can choose or generate the most appropriate representation format for a new tool use task. Psychologists can gain from strict validation of their experimental results on a robotic platform. Human theories of exploration and tool use can be cast in the representation used for robot exploration and then tested in a simulation environment that allows for a large array of systematic variations of object structure.

1.2 Exploration vs. exploitation

Object exploration can lay the ground for tool use by delivering the knowledge about structural properties that is necessary to infer functional properties. If exploration is a means rather than an end, efficiency considerations are relevant. Humans or robots can either invest more time and energy in acquiring more knowledge about the structure of an object or rather capitalize on the (potentially incomplete) knowledge acquired so far and exploit it to boost performance.

Based on human and animal research, learning and decision theories have proposed models that balance exploration and exploitation by proposing that the probability to choose an option different from the one that is currently associated with the highest reward is inversely related to the strength of the evidence for the option deemed best (e.g., Luce, 1959). Through updating of the estimates choice preferences will change from trial to trial. Crucial for adaptation to dynamic reward structures, reinforcement learning will provide estimates that grant opportunities for further learning as eventually the option deemed less profitable is chosen occasionally. Indeed, humans often show probability matching. If human participants are instructed to choose between options (e.g. card decks) in reward discrimination experiments, probability matching has been frequently observed (e.g., Gaissmaier & Schooler, 2008). Their participants did not constantly choose the deck with the highest reward probability (i.e., optimizing) but rather chose all decks - with frequencies paralleling reward probabilities. Probability matching ensures quick adaptation to changes in the reward schedule as information on all options is constantly gathered. If, for instance, the previously less rewarding option would surpass the previously most rewarding option, a participant relying on optimization would miss the chance to profit from the new highest reward, while one engaging in probability matching would not. Notably, the authors furthermore showed that probability matching was not the result of probabilistic action selection in all cases. Rather, some of the participants constantly tested hypotheses about potential deterministic regular structures in the reward schedule of the task (even when the task was still probabilistic). Exploring various hypotheses subsequently led to choice patterns that were consistent with probability matching. Once a regular rather than a probabilistic structure was present in the material, many of the participants discovered it and switched to exploitation of the discovered regularity. Thus, human behavior can, at least on the aggregate level, be captured well by probabilistic approaches linking the strength of evidence to the balance between exploration and exploitation. This however does not preclude the development and usage of rule knowledge.

In a similar way, reinforcement learning approaches used in robotics inherently balance exploration and exploitation and are flexible enough to adapt to probabilistic as well as deterministic regularities in object structure. For instance, Katz and Brock (2008) have proposed a reinforcement learning approach to make robot object exploration more efficient. Robot actions that lead to the discovery of properties of the structure of an object are assigned a reward. The higher the evidence that a specific action will lead to a substantial increase in the amount of knowledge about the structure of an articulated object, the more likely it is to be executed. By this mechanism regular object structures will lead to strong manipulation knowledge which is exploited in order to boost exploration performance.

While reinforcement learning had originally been developed in psychology, the extension to temporal difference learning that is nowadays of high impact in model-based neuroscience and behavioral research has been sparked by work conducted from a machine learning perspective (e.g., Sutton & Barto, 1998). Investigating how humans balance exploration and exploitation will enable us to develop robots that are capable of exploring their environment in an efficient way. For instance, the conditions under which humans discard (seemingly) irrelevant object features from processing or, alternatively, start to rely on a feature first deemed irrelevant that then turned out to be highly correlated with outcomes and easy to assess might be of special interest for efficient object exploration and tool use in robots. Hypotheses about potentially efficient exploration strategies can be tested on simulated or physical artificial agents. Furthermore, heuristics for efficient exploration discovered or validated in robotic systems can be provided to humans. For instance, the visual saliency of object parts in a virtual environment can be dynamically adapted in order to guide attention of a human novel to a task based on comparing online eye tracking data and exploration knowledge of the robot.

1.3 Watching vs. doing

To explore a new object, we typically begin by poking it, rotating it, etc. This indicates that for humans action and perception are closely linked. Nevertheless, action and perception have often been studied separately. Similarly, robots are usually modeled as input-computing-output devices. Indeed, the most dominant paradigm in robotics is called sense-plan-act. This paradigm has led to a separation in the study or robot perception and robot motion.

In psychology, integrative approaches have been flourishing on different levels. On the one hand, this relates to the issue of action-enabled perception. On the other hand, this relates to the issue of how learning can lay the ground for developing agency and specifically for the ability to choose actions according to goals. Concerning the issue of action-enabled perception, animal research has early on pointed out that active movements are necessary in order to develop a functioning visual cortex (e.g., Held & Hein, 1963). While kitten actively moving in a controlled visual environment developed normal vision, yoked-control kittens being exposed to the very same movements passively did not. Recent findings by Craighero, Leo, Umiltà, and Simion (2011) suggest that based on a bias in perception, action and perception are linked in humans even before own action starts. They reported that two-day-old human newborns preferentially attend movements directed toward an object. The authors systematically manipulated (a) presence of an object, (b) direction of the arm movement, and (c) hand shaping, and found that the newborns oriented more frequently and looked longer at a hand shapes that were consistent with a movement goal. Apart from this, research and everyday experience suggests that moved or moving objects are detected faster as compared to items stationary to the background.

One of the first examples of robots interacting with the environment to simplify perception was proposed by Katz and Brock (2008; see also Katz, Pyuro, & Brock, 2008, and Katz, Orthey, & Brock, 2010). This work proposes that by pushing and pulling on an object, a robot can distinguish the object from the background and track which parts of the object are connected to each other by degrees of freedom. Consequently, when faced with a novel object, the robot can discover its kinematic structure by interacting with it.

The link between perception and action leads to an interesting perspective when considering how learning enables action. Perception and learning of co-variations between states in the environment and own movements can enable robots and humans to later exploit their knowledge about useful interactions to explore new objects. One line of research on human action control, often referred to as ideo-motor theory, proposes that we develop the capability to intentionally influence our environment by inverting observations of accidental moves and effects in the environment. For instance, Elsner and Hommel (2001) suggested that humans become intentional agents in a two-step procedure. Due to a lack of knowledge relating own movements to changes in the environment, a baby might at first have little basis for intentional action in the form of selecting motor programs that lead to desired goals. At first, a baby may in fact randomly execute motor programs and observe changes in objects. The co-occurrence of movements (i.e., shaking the leg) and changes in object (i.e., the mobile starts to move) are stored. Once established, associations between motor programs and changes in objects can be applied in reverse direction in the next step. For instance, a representation of the moving mobile might evoke the motor program that made it move accidentally in the first place. The baby becomes an active agent as it can select the motor programs leading to desired goals, because pleasurable states are linked to motor programs that anteceded them. By this it can test and establish causal knowledge linking motor programs to changes in objects. While later in life, we surely possess action-effect knowledge with respect to many objects and domains, we might use similar ways to obtain structured knowledge about novel objects. We develop the capability to intentionally use novel objects as tools by storing co-occurrences of movements and effects and by active exploration. To this end we can employ principled testing, but also learn from effects that were not brought about by active testing.

A central motivation of our work on combining the study of object exploration in humans and in robots is our belief that much can be gained by better integrating learning from watching and learning from doing. Humans and robots can explore objects successfully by capitalizing on our embodiment, as well as by taking advantage of opportunities for passive learning. While active exploration and systematic experimentation is the key strategy to test hypotheses about causal relations between own movements and changes in the object, the hypotheses to be tested might in part be derived from a rather passive subsystem that observes movements in the actor and the object. Research on implicit learning in humans (e.g., Frensch & Rünger, 2003) suggests that co-occurrence statistics about a multitude of features in the actor and the object might accumulate and the strongest of the co-variations may fuel active testing that can lead to causal knowledge and a symbolic level of representation. We thus propose that it may be beneficial to follow the human example, and develop robotic systems that combine active exploration with passive learning. Likely humans can, if novel to an object exploration or tool use task, profit from a robot model as a starting point for generating and testing hypotheses. Furthermore, human object exploration might benefit from robot systems that dynamically adjust training schedules in order to foster efficient hypothesis testing. For instance, the robot might track the hypothesis space explored by the human and enforce overlooked tests by blocking access to object parts, visual highlighting of object parts or online composition of transfer objects that pinpoint hypotheses about object structure.

1.4 From puzzle boxes to virtual environments

Since Thorndike's research on cats learning to escape from puzzle boxes and gaining access to food (Thorndike, 1911), various researchers have employed similar devices in order to study exploration. Approaches have to balance between (a) the goal of providing a rich environment to explore and (b) the consideration that data logging and quantification of behavior are necessary for most research purposes. If participants are provided with a rich environment and can explore it in a multitude of different ways, researchers will be faced with the task of categorizing and summarizing many instances of rather unique behavior. For instance, they will have to determine which motor patterns are functionally equivalent.

We are currently developing a virtual environment in which humans can explore and use kinematic structures through a haptic interface. This system allows to log the forces applied to the object and object movements. As discussed in the previous sections, it is often far from obvious whether or not a behavior allows to conclude that a system is behaving in a goal directed manner and through exploration is building up a knowledge base capturing relevant parts of the structure of the object - unless one has designed the system and has access to the process parameters. Braitenberg (1984) provided a vivid demonstration of how a few simple mechanical building blocks can, when combined, produce complex behavior in purely reactive creatures that nevertheless readily leads to attribution of agency by humans. Braitenberg suggested combining the analysis of biological systems with a synthetic approach in order to (a) guard against the pitfalls of attributing agency where there is none and to (b) generate fruitful research hypotheses from one approach to the other and vice versa. This is exactly the research agenda we are currently following to understand exploration of kinematic structures of objects. Robots and humans are faced with very similar tasks. In a virtual environment, humans can interact with kinematic objects over haptic devices transmitting force back and forth between hand and object. Simulated robots can explore the same objects in the same environment. Apart from offering the possibility to test robots and humans on the same task, the virtual environment has several other advantages. Data logging is precise and easy to automate. Different variants of fully specified and exactly reproducible objects can be created. Experimental manipulations of perceptual capabilities, regularities in the structure of the object, and manipulation capabilities are possible. Most importantly, depending on research goals, objects and manipulation capabilities can be designed in such a way that prior knowledge is either of key relevance or has little impact.

Our current approach to study how humans and robots explore the kinematic structure of objects and how exploration strategies change with experience is twofold. We are using high and low constrained environments in order to combine the strengths of both approaches. In each case we are using kinematic chains as objects that can be explored. The chains are equipped with different types of joints. The agent has to determine what type of joint is located at which part of the object in order to capture the structure and functionality of the chain. In the environment with few constraints the agent can apply continuous amounts of force to different parts of the object. By pushing or pulling, the agent creates the opportunity to track movements of the different parts of the chain. Based on observing how the parts of the chain move in relation to one another, the agent can (a) distinguish object from background, (b) infer which parts of the moving object(s) are linked rather than independent objects, and (c) infer which type of joint is located at which position.

2. Robot learning to explore objects by manipulating them through grounded relational reinforcement learning

Undirected object exploration can be time consuming. In many environments, an agent may thus be required to explore new objects efficiently. The ability to plan an exploration sequence by considering past experience with similar objects is therefore essential.

To decide how to explore an articulated object, a robot must determine a sequence of interactions with it. These interactions would result in relative motion between the parts of the object, enabling the robot to acquire knowledge of the object's shape and kinematic structure. In this section, we describe a simulation environment within which an agent can interact with novel objects. We will demonstrate that it is possible to gather and generalize manipulation expertise that will enable the robot to efficiently direct its future interactions within the environment. Our robot interacts with an object by pushing or pulling it, while observing the object's motion. As these interactions create a change in the configuration of the object, the robot incrementally discovers the object's intrinsic and extrinsic degrees of freedom (intrinsic = between the parts of a single object, extrinsic = between different objects). The robot learns to select interactions that are most likely to reveal the maximum information about the kinematic structure. The acquired manipulation knowledge substantially reduces the number of interactions required to obtain an accurate kinematic model. Furthermore, manipulation knowledge acquired by modeling one object transfers to other objects even if they have different kinematic structures.

In the approach introduced by Katz and Brock (2008), manipulation expertise is learned based on a relational state representation. This representation is essential, as it renders learning tractable by collapsing large regions of the state space onto a single, task-relevant, relational state. The symbolic representation is carefully grounded in the perceptual and interaction skills of the robot. This grounding ensures that relationally learned knowledge remains applicable in the physical world. We begin our discussion by introducing the relational representations of kinematic structures that forms the basis of our learning-based approach to manipulation. Next, we describe how this representation can be grounded using the perception and manipulation capabilities of the robot. We proceed to discuss the relational learning framework and how it can be grounded with respect to the relational representation. Finally, we demonstrate the effectiveness of our approach in manipulation experiments with articulated objects.

2.1 Relational representation of kinematic structure

To describe the state space associated with manipulating rigid articulated objects using a propositional representation, we would have to include a proposition for every object encountered by the agent. We would also have to include a proposition for every action applicable to this object. Gathering and generalizing manipulation expertise becomes impossible with this representation due to the combinatorial explosion of actions and states. A relational representation allows us to describe an infinite number of states and actions using a finite set of relations. It is thus critical to the success of our learning-based approach to manipulation. Our relational representation leverages the following insight: an agent may encounter, for example, many types of scissors. These scissors may vary in color, shape, and size. All scissors, however, have the same kinematic structure. This kinematic structure can be captured by a single relational formula.

What object properties should our relational representation include? To represent the kinematic structure of an object, we must consider joint types (revolute, prismatic, or disconnected), link properties (e.g. color and size), and the kinematic relationships between links. Therefore, our relational representation uses the following predicates:

1. Revolute Joint: R(·,·,...)
2. Prismatic Joint: P(·,·,...)
3. Disconnected: D(·,·,...)

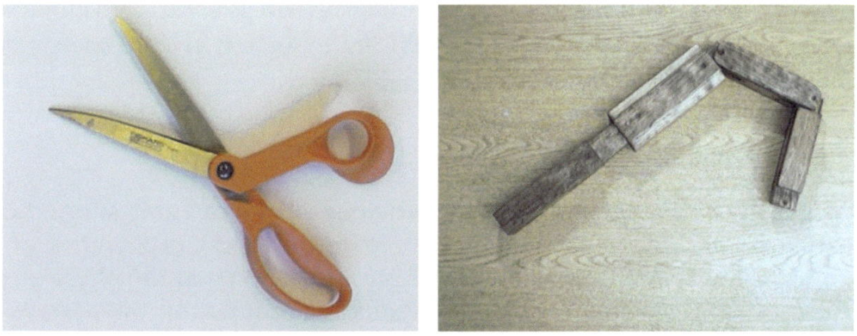

Fig. 1. Two examples of kinematic structures: scissors with a single revolute joint and a wooden toy with a prismatic joint and two revolute joints.

Fig. 1 shows two examples of kinematic structures. The scissors have a single revolute degree of freedom and the wooden toy is a serial kinematic chain with a prismatic joint (on the left of the figure) and two revolute joints. Our relational representation enables us to describe the kinematic structure of the scissors as: $D(L_B,R(L_1,L_2))$, where L_1 and L_2 represent the two links of the scissors and L_B is a disconnected background link. Similarly, the kinematic structure of the wooden toy can be represented as $D(L_B,R(L_4,R(L_3,P(L_1,L_2))))$. The notation is constructed based on a table that indicates the kinematic relationship between every pair of rigid bodies.

This representation is not unique. The wooden toy could also be represented as: $D(P(L_4,R(R(L_1,L_2),L_3)),L_B)$. The specific representation used by the agent depends on the order of discovery of the joints. The most deeply nested relation is the one discovered first. The representation of links can also be extended to an m-ary relation: L(·,·,...) where m>0 (m can be any positive integer implying that any finite number of properties can be captured by the representation). This representation supports a variety of link properties such as size, color, and composition. In the work we describe here, we limit ourselves to a single link property: size. The extension to a larger number of link properties, however, is straightforward. Using the extended link representation, the wooden toy can be described by: $D(L_B,R(L(S,F_4),R(L(S,F_3),P(L(S,F_1),L(S,F_2)))))$ where S stands for the property size=small and F_i spatially identifies link i in the physical world. To complete our relational representation, we must also provide a representation for the actions performed by the agent. The actions that we allow are limited to pushing or pulling a link. Each action can be applied either along the major axes of the link or at a forty-five degree angle to the major axes. An action is represented as A(L(·,·,...),α), where L(·,·,...) represents a link and α is an atom describing one of the six possible actions. The relational representation of links, joints, and actions allows us to reason and learn about objects based on their kinematic structure. The experience that an agent may acquire by manipulating scissors can be applied to all other scissors. The properties of an object that affect its manipulation behavior may not be limited to its kinematic structure. The relational representation of a link can be extended to include other relevant properties. With additional link properties, our agent will be able to distinguish between identical kinematic structures. The advantage of this approach is that it ignores information about the physical manifestation of objects (i.e. position, orientation, and configuration), as well as other properties irrelevant for generic description and control of manipulation. As a result, we achieve a significant reduction in the dimensionality of the state space, rendering the learning problem tractable.

2.2 Grounding the relational representation

The relational representation described in the previous section can only support the learning of manipulation knowledge if it is grounded in the physical capabilities of the robot. Grounding bridges between the symbols of our representation and the physical, continuous world (Harnad, 1990). It ensures that we can symbolically interpret the observations made by the robot with regards to its interactions with the world. At the same time, grounding ensures that the resulting symbolic manipulation knowledge maintains its relevance and predictive power for the robot's real-world interactions.

To ground our relational representation, we bind the relations $R(\cdot,\cdot,\ldots)$, $P(\cdot,\cdot,\ldots)$, and $D(\cdot,\cdot,\ldots)$ as well as the links' properties to real-world perceptual capabilities of the robot. These perceptual capabilities enable a robot to model rigid articulated objects (Katz & Brock, 2008). The robot's perceptual capabilities provide adequate grounding for our relational representation of links and their kinematic relationship.

2.3 Acquiring manipulation expertise

With the grounded relational representation of states (links and joints) and actions, we can now cast the problem of incremental acquisition of manipulation knowledge as a relational reinforcement learning problem (Džeroski, de Raedt, & Driessens, 2001; Tadepalli, Givan, & Driessens, 2004; van Otterlo, 2005). In reinforcement learning, an agent learns an optimal policy for solving a task. This policy tells the agent which action to perform in a particular state (e.g., where to affect the object and whether to push or to pull). The process of acquiring the policy is incremental; the agent learns the policy through a sequence of interactions with the environment. With every action, the robot may or may not discover new information. To formulate this process as a reinforcement learning problem, in our experiments, we simply assign a reward for every degree of freedom and every link property discovered by the robot. We expect the robot to incorporate new experiences into its policy, improving it over time. If learning succeeds, our robot will have acquired an effective policy for modeling the kinematic structure of novel rigid articulated objects. For more information about the implementation, we refer the reader to Katz, Pyuro, and Brock (2008).

Given unlimited time for exploration, an agent can gather enough manipulation experiences to learn an optimal policy. To comply with the time constraints imposed by manipulation in unstructured environments, our agent must be able to discover an optimal (or nearly optimal) policy quickly. To that end, it must balance between exploration and exploitation. Exploration refers to the execution of an action to improve the robot's estimate of the associated reward. In other words, when an agent explores, it either chooses an action it has never tried before, or the action the outcome of which the agent is most uncertain about. Exploitation, in contrast, refers to action selection based on maximizing reward. The balance between exploration and exploitation is important. If the agent explores too much, it will miss to employ knowledge. If it exploits too early, it will perform poorly because it has not gathered enough experience.

To decide if a new action should be executed, we compute the fraction of actions for which the robot already has gathered experience. It then selects one of the actions associated with its current knowledge about the object unless the random number generator indicates that exploration should be executed instead. If the robot is to retrieve an action based on its experience, we use Interval Estimation (IE) (Kaelbling, 1993), which picks the action that has the highest potential to perform well. Thus, IE also balances between exploration and exploitation.

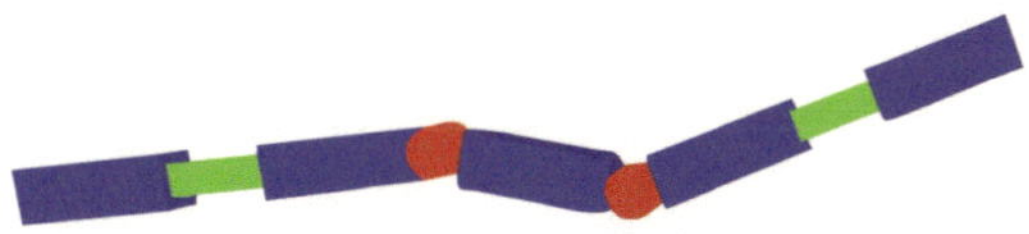

Fig. 2. Example of an articulated object. Links (rigid bodies) are shown in blue. Revolute joints are represented by red cylinders, and prismatic joints are illustrated as green boxes. Joint types are only marked for illustrative purposes but not in the experiments.

2.4 Experiments with planar objects

To evaluate the effectiveness of our learning-based approach to manipulation of articulated objects, we perform two types of experiments, previously published in Katz and Brock (2008). First, we show that manipulation knowledge can be gathered from experience. And second, we show that the acquired experience transfers to previously unseen objects. We perform experiments in a simulated environment. This environment is based on the Open Dynamics Engine (ODE), a popular dynamics simulator. ODE is an open source, high-performance library for simulating the dynamics of rigid bodies. It features various joint types and integrated collision detection. It simulates gravity, various sources of friction, and allows for some non-determinacy. In our experiments, a robot interacts with an articulated planar (two-dimensional) object to extract its kinematic structure. An example object is shown in Fig. 2. Links (rigid bodies) are shown in blue. Revolute joints are represented by red cylinders, and prismatic joints are illustrated as green boxes.

An experiment consists of a sequence of trials. A trial is composed of a number of steps. In each step, the robot applies a pushing or pulling action to the articulated object. The trial ends when an external observer (independent thread of the simulation) signals that the robot has obtained the correct kinematic structure of the object. In each step of every trial the robot accumulates manipulation experiences that improve its future performance. The number of steps per trial measures the number of interactions necessary to discover the correct kinematic structure of the articulated object. It therefore measures the efficiency with which the robot accomplishes the task. Each step of a trial can be divided into three phases:

1. The robot selects an action and a link for interaction. The action is instantiated using the current state and the experience stored in the agent's memory.
2. The selected action is applied to the link, and the resulting object motion is simulated. The observed motion is reported to the agent. If the agent pushes or pulls the object at a suitable location, the resulting object motion might deliver information concerning multiple links at the same time.

3. The agent analyzes the observed motion and determines the kinematic properties of the rigid bodies observed so far. These properties are then incorporated into the robot's current state representation.

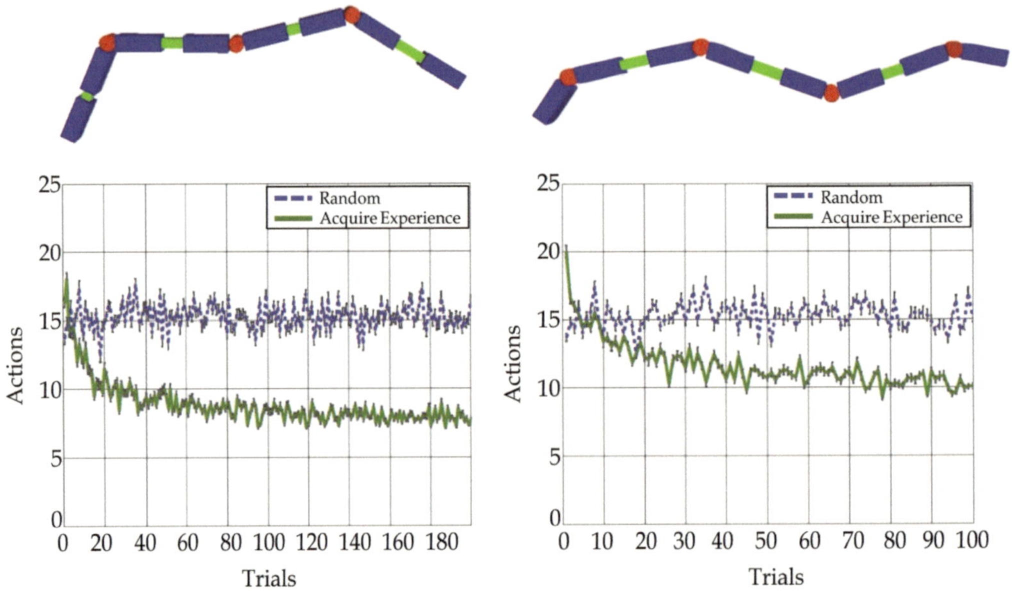

Fig. 3. left panel. Experiments with a planar kinematic structure (PRPRPRP). The object possesses seven degrees of freedom (R = revolute, P = prismatic). The right panel shows the experiment with the structure (RPRPRPR; seven degrees of freedom). Error bars in all figures reflect the standard error of the mean.

2.5 Gathering manipulation knowledge

Our first type of experiments shows that manipulation knowledge can be gathered from experience. To demonstrate the effectiveness of learning, we observe the practice-related decrease in the number of actions required to discover a kinematic structure. We compare the performance of the proposed grounded relational reinforcement learning approach to a random action selection strategy. Fig. 3 and 4 show the objects presented to the robot, as well as the results (learning curves) of four experiments. For each trial, we report the average number of interactions used to discover the correct kinematic structure. This average is computed over 10 independent replications.

In the first experiment, we presented the robot with an object with seven degrees of freedom and eight links. The resulting learning curve is shown in Fig. 3 (left panel). Action selection based on the proposed relational reinforcement learning approach results in a substantial reduction of the number of actions required to correctly identify the kinematic structure. As to be expected there is a stable and high number of actions required in the baseline, random action selection. This improvement already becomes apparent after about 10 trials. Using the learning-based strategy, an average of eight pushing actions is required to extract the correct kinematic model of the object. Compared to the approximately 16 pushing actions required with random action selection, learning achieves an improvement of about 50%. In the second experiment, we presented the robot with another object with seven degrees of freedom and eight links. The resulting learning curve is shown in the right panel of Fig. 3. The improvement achieved by our learning approach becomes apparent after about 20 trials. Using the learning-based strategy, an average of 10 pushing actions is required to extract the correct kinematic model of the object. Compared to the approximately 15 pushing actions required with random action selection, learning achieves an improvement of about 30%.

In the third experiment, we presented the robot with an object with eight degrees of freedom and nine links. The resulting learning curve is shown in Fig. 4 (left panel). The learning-based strategy requires an average of eight pushes at asymptote, whereas the random strategy uses approximately 20 pushing actions. Learning achieves an improvement of about 60%. In the fourth experiment, we present the robot with an object with nine degrees of freedom and ten links. The resulting learning curve is shown in the right panel of Fig. 4. The learning-based strategy requires an average of 10 pushes, whereas the random strategy uses approximately 22 pushing actions. Learning achieves an improvement of about 60%. These four experiments demonstrate that our approach to manipulation enables robots to gather manipulation knowledge and to apply this knowledge to improve manipulation performance.

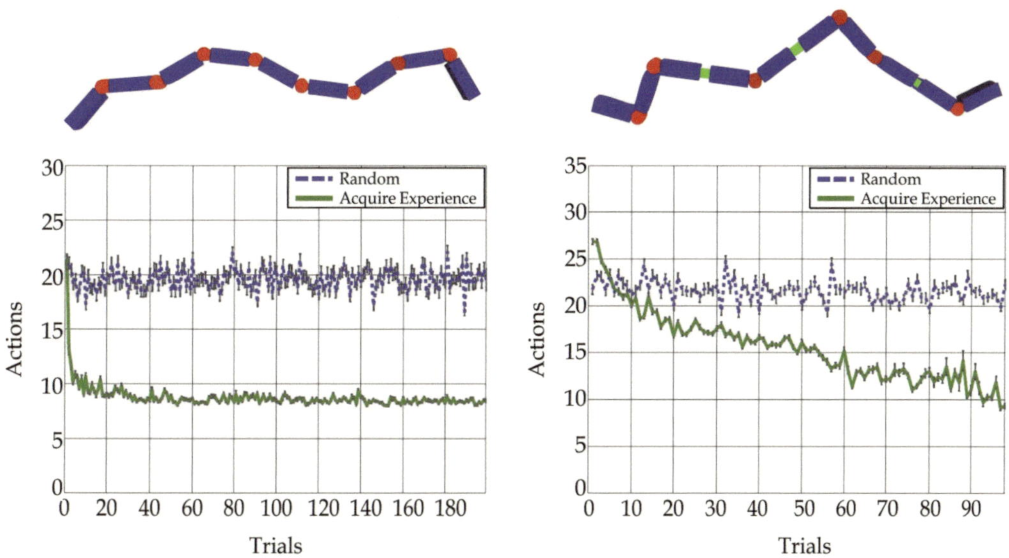

Fig. 4. Structure RRRRRRRR (eight degrees of freedom) plus learning curve and baseline on the left panel as well as structure RRPRPRRPR (nine degrees of freedom) on the right panel.

2.6 Transferring manipulation knowledge

Our second type of experiment shows that manipulation experience acquired with one object transfers to other objects. To demonstrate the effectiveness of knowledge transfer, we again observe the number of actions required to discover a kinematic structure. We compare the performance of the proposed grounded relational reinforcement learning approach with and without prior experience. Fig. 5 and 6 show the objects presented to the robot, as well as the results (learning curves) of four experiments.

In the first transfer experiment, the robot gathers experience with an articulated object with seven degrees of freedom (see Fig. 5, left panel). After 50 trials, the robot is given a simpler object with only five degrees of freedom. The simpler structure is a substructure of the more complex one. We compare the robot's performance with that of a robot without prior experience. The robot with prior experience consistently outperforms the robot without experience. In the first trial, which is the most important for real-world manipulation, the experienced robot requires only 40% as many pushes. Over the following five trials, the performance improvement is approximately 20%. In trials 5 to 20, the performance improvement is much smaller.

In the second transfer experiment, the robot learns to manipulate a complex articulated object with five revolute joints (see Fig. 5, right panel). After 50 trials, the robot is given a slightly simpler structure that only possesses four revolute joints. Again, the simpler structure is a substructure of the more complex one. We compared the robot's performance after these initial 50 trials to the performance of a robot without prior experience. The experienced robot achieves convergence almost immediately. This corresponds to a performance improvement of about 50% in the first trial, relative to the robot without experience. After about 15 trials, both robots converge to approximately the same performance. This is to be expected for simple structures, exclusively consisting of revolute joints. The third transfer experiment complements the second experiment. Here, the robot learns to manipulate an articulated object with four revolute degrees of freedom (see Fig. 6, left panel). After 50 trials, the robot is given a structure with an additional revolute joint (five altogether). We compare the robot's performance after these initial 50 trials to another robot's performance without prior experience. Again, experience results in an improved performance in the first few trials (about 30%). After about eight trials, both robots converge towards the same number of interactions.

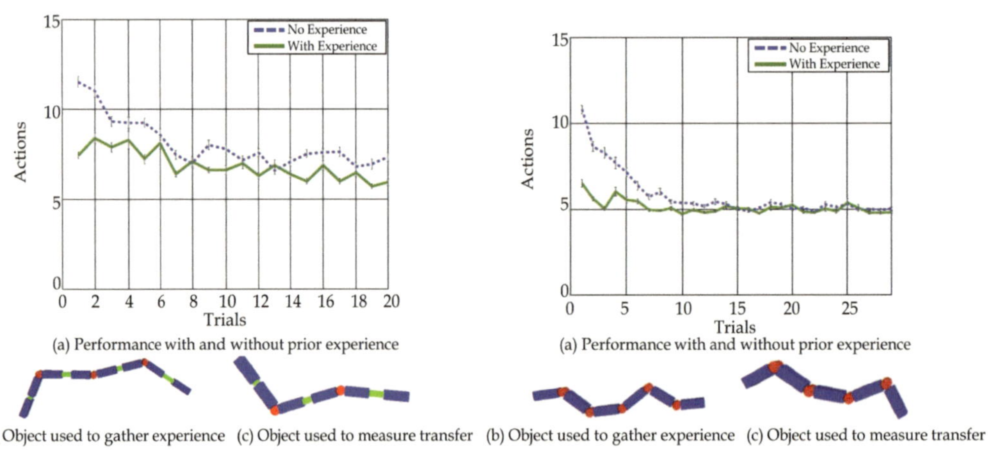

Fig. 5. left panel. Experiment on transfer of knowledge acquired with PRPRPRP to PRPRP. The right panel shows the experiment on transfer from RRRRR to RRRR.

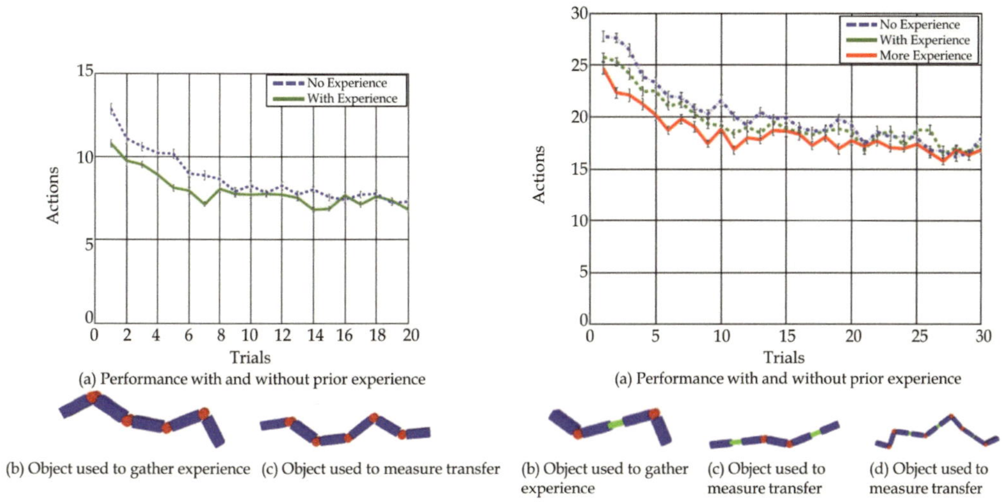

Fig. 6. Left panel. Experiment on transfer of knowledge acquired with RRRR to RRRRR. The right panel shows the transfer (RPR to PRRP and RRPRPRRPR).

The fourth experiment (see Fig. 6, right panel) takes a step towards long term learning of manipulation expertise. Here, we compare the performance of three robots: The first has no prior knowledge, the second's prior knowledge is based on interactions with one object, and the third's prior knowledge relies on interactions with two objects. The results show the advantage that the more experienced robots have in the first few trials. More importantly, this experiment suggests that the more experience a robot gathers, the more it can transfer to new situations.

To summarize, our experimental results provide strong evidence that learning from past experience can significantly boost the robot's manipulation performance. Learning enables a robot to autonomously acquire manipulation expertise by interacting with the environment. Our results show that this expertise transfers across different instances of the manipulation task and substantially improves manipulation performance. Learning and generalization of manipulation knowledge become possible due to our relational representation of states and actions. This representation collapses the otherwise intractable state space and renders reinforcement learning feasible. We believe that the effectiveness of our approach is due to the proper, task-specific grounding of our relational representation in the robot's perceptual and interactive capabilities.

2.7 Experiments with 3-D objects

We are currently working on the development of a new simulation environment for three-dimensional objects. This work is still in its early stages. Our primary objective is to replicate the success of learning for planar objects in the more general case of 3-D articulated objects. An example of the type of three-dimensional objects we plan to explore in the new simulation environment is shown in Fig. 7 (left panel). In this simulation environment, we also intend to explore the relevance of a variety of object properties, such as size, color, texture, the existence of parallel lines, or sharp changes in contrast.

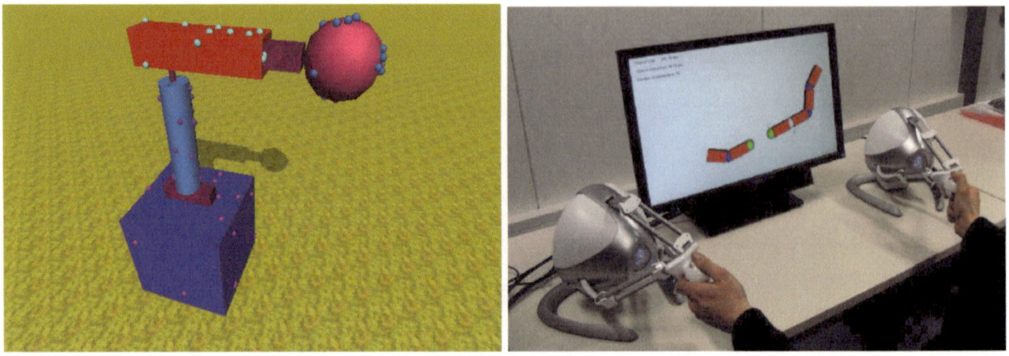

Fig. 7. Left panel. Simulated three-dimensional rigid articulated object. On the right side: two haptic devices operated by a human subject to interact with an object.

The new simulator is designed to facilitate research in the intersection between human and robotic object exploration. The simulator features a haptic interface (see Fig. 7, right panel), enabling human subjects and the simulated robots to interact with the same kinematic structures. Encouraged by the success of our learning approach for the domain of planar objects, we intend to use the new simulation environment to further develop our robot's skills in exploring new objects. We hope that by studying how human subjects approach object exploration, balance exploration and exploitation we will be able to extract knowledge that will advance the state of the art in autonomous manipulation.

3. Exploration of simple structures in humans

If, in the long run, robot exploration is to take advantage of adaptive strategies from human exploration behavior, one has to demonstrate in the first place that there is in fact an adaptive processing in humans while performing an exploration task that is suitable for robots. This is the goal of this section. Ideally, one could substantiate the notion that participants make use of clever exploration strategies, show systematic exploration and generate rules about the characteristics of the material. This could motivate research that employs these behavioral patterns for robot object exploration. To this end, we study here human exploration of simple structures with a simplified interface. We aim first to demonstrate principled exploration in a narrow environment before expanding to more complicated object structures and elaborate interfaces in the future. For instance, in the virtual 3-D environment described above, humans will use haptic interfaces to manipulate objects. Robots can (a) observe and try to learn from human moves and (b) manipulate the same objects. Notably, on the human side, psychomotor abilities and cognitive aspects of exploration will jointly determine performance. Failure can either be attributed to lack of knowledge about where and how to physically affect the object in order to learn the most about its structure, or can be attributed to difficulties in skillfully executing and completing manipulation plans. Likewise, for a researcher or a robot trying to extract valuable patterns of exploration behavior from human manipulation there is the problem of parsing behavior into discrete attempts to affect the object by applying force to a specific part of the object.

In order to provide a firm basis for our future attempts to tackle these problems, we first tried a divide and conquer strategy, setting apart the more cognitive aspects of exploration from the more psychomotor aspects. As detailed below, we started our work on human exploration of articulated objects with a highly simplified exploration environment excluding the need for skillful application of force and limiting the space of possible tests and strategies. With this, we wanted to provide evidence for systematic and adaptive exploration strategies in a variant in which the parsing of the exploration by a machine would be trivial. This should lay the ground for tackling more complicated object structures and less constrained continuous exploration behavior while making use of a haptic interface. As described in detail in the next section, in the high constrained environment participants were confronted with a short chain with space for three joints on each trial. Participants were asked to conduct discrete tests for each of the different potential types of joints in each of the locations of the chain in order to discover the structure of the chain.

3.1 Setup of the task

We designed an experiment to test whether and how systematic exploration of highly constrained structures occurs in humans. On each trial, participants were provided with a chain on the screen and were asked to test the different joints (compare Fig. 8).

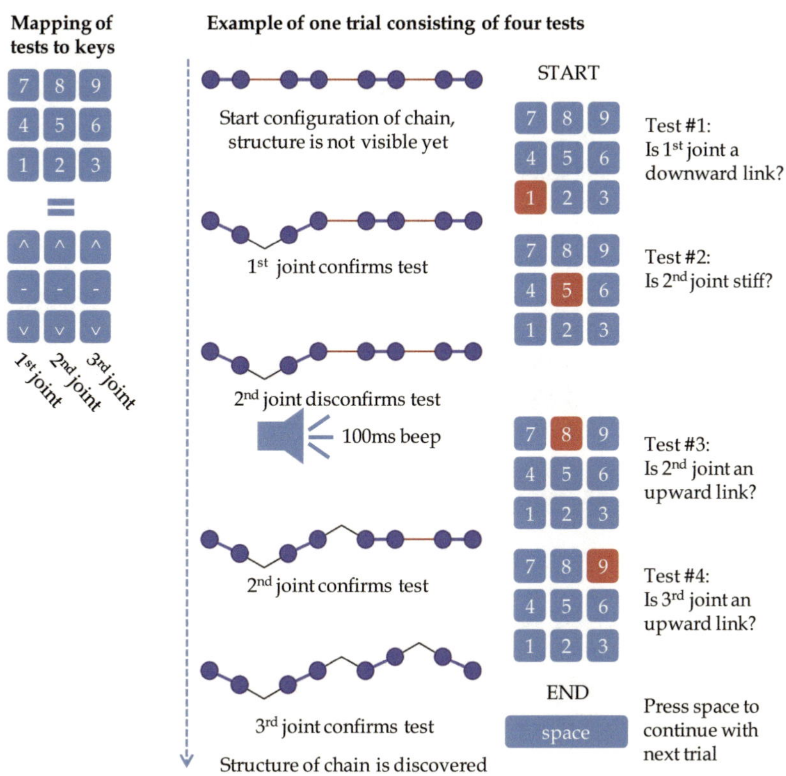

Fig. 8. Setup and example trial of the highly constraint exploration task for humans.

Each chain had three joints. There were three different kinds of joints: bending upward, bending downward, and stiff connections. We used the number pad of a regular keyboard. The leftmost column of the 3 by 3 matrix of the number pad was assigned to testing whether the leftmost joint was bending upward (upper key), was stiff (middle key) or bending downward (lower key). The same arrangement was in place in the second and third column of the number pad with respect to the second and third joint (counted from the left). Tests were executed in a discrete manner. If the participant wanted to test whether the leftmost joint was able to bend upward, the participant pressed the upper left key on the 3 by 3 matrix of the number pad. Then, the display on the screen indicated if the joint indeed bended upward (if this was the characteristic of this joint) or if it was instead either a stiff joint or one able to be bent downwards. Then a tone sounded as feedback on the discrete test while the visual display remained constant.

3.2 Selection of training material

In order to test for systematic and adaptive exploration in humans we used material that normatively favored some strategies over others. We judged the systematism of human exploration behavior based on whether participants adapted to the structure of the material. On a finer level, we inquired whether humans either developed rule-like knowledge about the structure of the chains occurring in the training material or rather learned which exemplars of chains existed in the practice set. While we first describe the different regularities we built into the material for different groups of participants, we then discuss how it is possible to distinguish between an adaptation to these regularities that is based on rule knowledge vs. one based on exemplar knowledge.

We distinguished four conditions with different training materials. As we constructed chains with three joints each selected from three different types of joints, there were 27 different chains in principle. The training material was selected from the pool of 27 possible chains according to one of three different rules. Each of the rules led to the selection of twelve chains and allowed for clear predictions on how learning should change exploration. The first rule was tested on two different groups of participants. They explored chains in which *joints 2 and 3 were never stiff* (they were either bending upward or bending downward). If participants learned about the structure of the chains, they should stop testing whether the joints 2 and 3 are stiff. As detailed below, we varied the frequency of specific chains during training in 13 participants so that four of the twelve chains were repeated four times per learning block and others just once. For nine participants the same chains were presented with balanced frequencies - each twice per block of 24 trials. The third group of participants (N=9) was provided with chains in which *no neighboring joints were identical*. If participants adapted to the structure of the material, they should often switch to a different type of test when switching to test another joint. The fourth group of participants (N=9) explored the structure of chains in which *two neighboring joints were identical*, either the joints 1 and 2 or 2 and 3. We hypothesized that participants would adapt to the material by often executing identical tests on neighboring joints, especially once one joint had been correctly classified.

3.3 Frequency variation to test for rule knowledge

In the following we consider the condition in which *joints 2 and 3 were never stiff* in some more detail for two reasons. First, this training material allows for a strategy change towards faster exploration by discarding irrelevant aspects of the exploration task (refraining from stiffness tests on joints 2 and 3). Research on information reduction (i.e., Gaschler & Frensch, 2007, 2009) has argued that the discarding of irrelevant aspects of tasks from processing is a major basis of skill acquisition and of expertise acquisition. One can argue that by learning which aspects are relevant and which can be ignored, experts learn to use their time and cognitive resources very efficiently (in their domain of expertise). Similarly, learning to avoid less useful tests on kinematic objects helps to focus on hypotheses concerning their structure, to save time and energy, and to reduce risks that might be involved in executing tests in adverse environments. Second, in the research on information reduction we have proposed means to test whether simplification of task processing is based on rule-like knowledge and voluntary strategy change. We therefore wanted to apply such a test first on the data of the group with the setup most similar to the one used in research on information reduction so far. A test of rule-based performance is very useful for our goal to demonstrate systematic, principled exploration behavior in humans.

In research on information reduction we have been arguing that observations of people simplifying task processing, for instance by ignoring irrelevant aspects of stimuli, are widespread in various domains of applied psychology. However, special manipulations are necessary in order to test exactly how the simplification of task processing takes place and what kind of knowledge about regularities in the task material is acquired. For instance, the widespread observation *that* after some practice, participants ignore aspects of stimuli that are less relevant does not suffice to judge whether rule-like knowledge has developed or whether participants have instead adapted to the specific training exemplars. We successfully applied manipulations of exemplar frequency to specify the type of knowledge being acquired during practice and the mode of exploitation that this knowledge leads to. In particular, we varied the frequency with which specific training exemplars were processed during practice. If knowledge about the structure of the material would be bound to the specific instances encountered during training, then one would expect that learning should occur early in training for the frequently encountered exemplars, but much later for the examples presented only infrequently. Already early in training, participants could accumulate substantial experience with frequently presented exemplars and, for instance, start to ignore irrelevant parts in these exemplars, while still fully processing the infrequent exemplars until a similar amount of experience with these has been gathered. If, however, participants generate rule-like knowledge, then practice should modify the processing of the frequently and less frequently encountered instances at the same time and to the same extent. The latter is what we observed in the studies on information reduction. Participants learned to ignore the irrelevant parts of infrequently presented exemplars at the same point in time during practice and managed to ignore these to the same extent as the frequently encountered exemplars. It was not the case that participants dared to ignore the irrelevant parts of well-known items while still fully processing infrequently presented and novel exemplars. Rather, there was an all-or-none strategy change.

Here we employed a similar approach in order to judge whether or not participants developed rule knowledge when confronted with material in which the joints 2 and 3 were never stiff. Counterbalanced across participants, either the four chains with the first joint bending upward or the four chains with the first joint bending downward were repeated four times rather than once per block. The frequency manipulation allowed to distinguish between gains in exploration efficiency based on rules knowledge vs. on representations of specific exemplars of chains. If, on the one hand, participants rely on knowledge about specific exemplars, then the rate of testing whether joint 2 and 3 are stiff should decrease much more quickly per block of practice for the four frequent in comparison with the infrequently presented chains. People would e.g. learn that for the four frequently presented chains starting with an upward bending joint 1 there is no need to test whether joints 2 and 3 are stiff, but learn little about the other eight chains confirming to the rule that were presented less frequently. If, on the other hand, participants acquire knowledge that can be described as a rule, then the frequency of training exemplars should be irrelevant. The rate of testing whether joints 2 and 3 are stiff should decrease at the same rate per block and to the same level for both frequently and infrequently presented chains.

3.4 Procedure

Participants were instructed that their task was to explore chains by determining in each trial the types of the joints. Participants were provided with the mapping of keys and tests for the three different types of joints. They then performed four blocks of 24 trials on the training material selected as detailed above. In block 5, participants from all conditions were exposed to all 27 possible chains. We randomly sorted the chains in each of the five blocks for each participant . From the perspective of the participants, there was no signal for the beginning or end of a block.

3.5 Results

3.5.1 Overall learning

As an initial learning check, we analyzed whether practice led to a decrease in the number of tests required to determine the structure of a chain. This analysis confirmed that participants learned to explore chains more efficiently from block to block (compare Fig. 9, left panel). A mixed analysis of variance with training block as factor varied within participants and composition of training material varied between participants confirmed the general training effect as there was a significant main effect of training block, $F(2.24, 80.52) = 20.1$, $MSE = 253$, $p < .001$, $\eta_p^2 = .358$. We applied Greenhouse-Geisser correction here and whenever warranted in the analyses of variance (ANOVAs). The average amount of tests per trial was similar in each of the four groups and decreased at the same rate over blocks. The ANOVA neither showed a main effect of the composition of training material ($F = 1.07$) nor an interaction of training material and training block ($F < 1$).

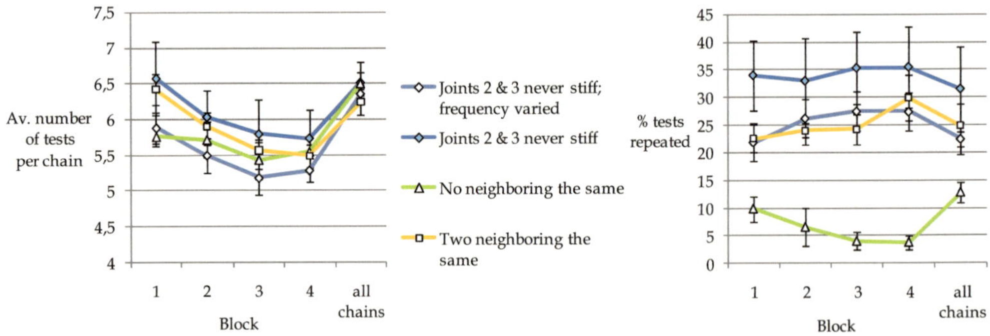

Fig. 9. Practice-related changes in human exploration performance. The left panel shows the decrease of the average number of tests executed per trial to determine the structure of the chain. The right panel depicts the average % of test repetitions that were observed when participants changed from testing one joint to testing a different one.

The decrease in the number of tests per chain in blocks 1 to 4 could either be the result of learning about the structure of the chains or of other practice effects (e.g., learning to operate the keyboard to execute the tests or learning to avoid test repetitions). Therefore, transfer to a situation in which the pool of chains changed while the exploration task stayed constant was essential. Comparison of the last block of training with the subset of the material and the final block with all possible 27 chains suggests that participants indeed learned of the structure of the chains presented in blocks 1 to 4. There was a sharp increase in the average number of tests executed per chain between block 4 and the final block, bringing performance back to the starting level. This rules out that the decrease in the number of tests executed per chain was due to general training effects unrelated to the chains presented. An ANOVA of the last two blocks confirmed the visual impression. There was a main effect of block, $F(1, 36) = 89.46$, $MSE = .125$, $p < .001$, $\eta_p^2 = .713$. Again the specific rule applied to select the training set neither influenced the average amount of tests per chain in main effect nor in interaction with block (*F*s < 1).

3.5.2 Practice related changes in tests on neighboring joints

While the above analyses suggest that participants learned about the chains they encountered during training, it does not specify what exactly was learned. In the next two sections we therefore analyzed the groups of participants separately according to whether and how they adapted to the specific regularity present in their training material.

First we analyzed the average rate of trials in which one type of test was repeated on subsequent tests on different joints of the same chain. Participants confronted with chains selected from the pool of 27 possible chains under the constraint that no neighboring joints were identical should refrain from repeatedly executing the same test. After having tested, for instance, whether joint 1 bends upward, they should not execute the same test on joint 2 but rather check for the ability of joint 2 to bend downwards. The right panel of Fig. 9 suggests that this was indeed the case. Participants adapted to the regularity during the first few trials. The proportion of subsequent identical tests on different joints was already very low in this condition as compared to the other conditions in the first block and decreased further over the three training blocks. The reverse should hold true for participants trained on chains selected so that 2 neighboring joints were identical. They should execute the same tests on neighboring joints. Unexpectedly however, no marked boost of the rate of executing identical tests subsequently on different joints was evident. Differences in overall rate of repeating tests subsequently on different joints amongst the conditions as well as differences in the dynamics were confirmed by an ANOVA on the data of training blocks 1 to 4. There was a main effect of the composition of the training material, $F(3, 36) = 18.98$, $MSE = 774.15$, $p < .001$, $\eta_p^2 = .613$, as well as an interaction of composition condition and training block, $F(7.49, 89.86) = 2.75$, $MSE = 103.17$, $p = .011$, $\eta_p^2 = .187$.

3.5.3 Practice related changes in tests as joints 2 and 3 were never stiff

Testing for systematic exploration in humans, we next analyzed the data of the participants trained on chains in which joints 2 and 3 were never stiff. We focused on how the average number of tests for whether joints 2 or 3 were stiff decreased with practice. As detailed above, in and of itself a practice-related decrease in the average number of tests is compatible with many views on what exactly is being learned. For testing whether exploration leads to rule-like knowledge and systematic exploration, the variation of the frequency with which specific chains were presented per block has to be taken into account.

Consistent with the view that exploration is systematic and related to rule knowledge, we found that participants learned as quickly to perform efficient exploration on *infrequently presented* chains as they did on frequently presented chains. General knowledge about the characteristics of the chains rather than knowledge about specific chains that were frequently presented was driving performance. Fig. 10 shows average frequencies of testing joints 2 and 3 in the group with the frequency variation (lines named high frequency vs. low frequency) and in the group of participants in which all chains were presented twice per block of practice (equal frequency line). In order to investigate the impact of presentation frequency on the number of tests for stiff joints 2 and 3, we charted the same data in two different ways. On the left panel we averaged the data per block (which we consider first), while on the right panel we averaged the data based on counting the occurrence of the specific exemplar of a chain during training. In the blockwise analysis we can, for instance, determine whether the rate of tests for stiff joints 2 and 3 had decreased to the same level by training block 4 in the infrequent (fourth presentation) and the frequent chains (14th-16th presentation). Indeed, there was no difference in the rate of tests for stiff joints 2 and 3 for the latter chains. More generally, the performance on high and low frequency chains was highly similar in all blocks of training. The uniform increase in exploration efficiency is in line with an account proposing that participants are acquiring rule knowledge that is applied to frequently encountered and infrequently encountered chains alike.

Interestingly, in tendency more of the stiffness tests on joints 2 and 3 were observed in the first training block of the group of participants exploring each chain with equal frequency as compared to the number of tests in the group of participants with frequency variation. This might suggest that learning of the regularity in the structure of the material was faster or was exploited faster for efficient exploration in participants with frequency variation. It is conceivable that knowledge of regularities in the material is generated relatively quickly based on the chains presented four times per block and then immediately transferred to the chains presented less frequently (compare Gaschler & Frensch, 2007). However further experimentation would be necessary to determine in detail whether knowledge develops in the frequent chains and transfers to the infrequent ones or vice versa. This would, first of all, include a replication of the data pattern as the ANOVA was not fully decisive with regard to the question of whether the equal frequency group deviated from the course of practice observed in the group of participants with frequency variation. There was a main effect of block, $F(2.19, 43.7) = 23.98$, $MSE = .016$, $p < .001$, $\eta_p^2 = .545$. The interaction of block and training group was marginal, $F(2.19, 43.7) = 2.59$, $MSE = .016$, $p = .082$, $\eta_p^2 = .115$. There was no main effect of group of participants ($F < 1$).

The blockwise analysis suggests equal increases in exploration efficiency for the high and the low frequency chains. While this null effect is consistent with the interpretation that participants were acquiring and employing rule knowledge to increase exploration efficiency, one could wonder whether the setup is actually suitable to demonstrate any influence of the rate of presentation of specific chains on performance. We therefore also charted the same data based on counting the occurrence of the specific example of a chain during training. As the high frequency chains were presented four times in each of four blocks, we have 16 data points. The four presentations of the low frequency chains over the course of practice lead to four data points, and sorting the presentation of the specific instances in the equal frequency group led to eight data points. The graph suggests that the reduction in the rate of tests for stiffness in joints 2 and 3 was much faster for low frequency compared to high frequency chains when plotted based on the instance counter. On average, the very first encounter with an infrequent chain led to a much lower rate of testing joints 2 or 3 for stiffness as compared to the first encounter with a high frequency chain. Notably, the first encounter with a specific low frequency chain usually occurred at a point in time during training in block one, when several frequently presented chains had already been processed. Apparently, the knowledge acquired during the processing of the latter was immediately transferred to the former. As practice on high frequency chains affected performance on low frequency chains from their first presentation onwards, the knowledge acquired cannot be specific to the high frequency chains. Rather, it seems to be rule-like. The observation that learning changed the performance on low frequency chains faster than on high frequency chains (if charted per presentation of the specific chain) was substantiated with a within-subjects ANOVA on the data of the group of participants with the frequency variation. This analysis was restricted to the first four encounters with each specific high frequency chain and included all four encounters with low frequency chains. As the rate of stiffness tests on joints 2 and 3 was overall lower in the low frequency chains, the ANOVA showed a main effect of frequency, $F(1, 12) = 6.24$, $MSE = .063$, $p = .028$, $\eta_p^2 = .342$. The overall decrease in the rate of testing stiffness in the joints 2 and 3 was reflected in a main effect of instance counter, $F(2.18, 26.19) = 15.4$, $MSE = .03$, $p < .001$, $\eta_p^2 = .562$. The steeper slope of learning on the high frequency as compared to the low frequency chains over the first four encounters led to an interaction of frequency and instance counter, $F(1.98, 23.75) = 3.72$, $MSE = .04$, $p = .04$, $\eta_p^2 = .237$.

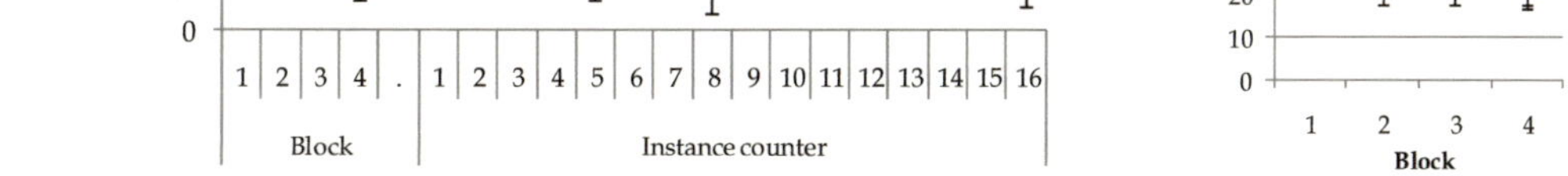

Fig. 10. For participants exposed to a selection of chains in which the joints 2 and 3 were never stiff, the average number of tests for stiffness per joint (2 and 3 averaged) is displayed over the course of practice, either by aggregating per block of practice or by aggregating per encounter with the specific chain. On the right side, we display the practice related decrease in the percentage of participants still testing stiffness in joints 2 or 3.

In summary, we can conclude that participants adapted to the regularity in the material. When confronted with material in which joints 2 and 3 were never stiff (but rather bending upward or downward) participants showed a marked reduction in the average number of tests for stiffness per chain on these joints. As exploration efficiency increased at the same time in practice and to the same extent for high and low frequency chains, we suggest that participants employed systematic exploration and developed rule knowledge on the structure of the chains. The data are consistent with the view that humans develop relational representations that capture high-level features and regularities of the objects. For the future, this encourages us to provide robots with human behavior in this and similar exploration situations in order to grant them with a set of adaptive exploration sequences they can expand upon. Comparison with robot object exploration will in turn allow us to judge what aspects of human exploration behavior come close to optimal exploration sequences and which aspects might be improved. This also counts for approaches to the exploration-exploitation dilemma. For instance, our analyses suggest that most of the participants eventually ceased exploration and started exploitation of the acquired knowledge. As shown in the right panel of Fig. 10 from block 3 onwards, the majority of participants did not check stiffness in joint 2 or 3 at all. They switched from exploration to exploitation mode. For instance, they would not have noted whether multiple characteristics had been ascribed to single joints. While all participants tested stiffness in the high frequency chains in block 1, results of these tests were apparently transferred to low frequency chains, by some participants already within the first block.

4. Summary

In this chapter we have described first steps for studying tool use in humans and robots in a common framework by focusing on how humans and robots explore the kinematic structure of objects. We have gathered initial evidence that representational formats, which make the problem of discovering and representing kinematic structure tractable for robots, may have similar counterparts in humans. Exploration experience could be used to render exploration more efficient both by robots and by humans. As we observed that humans adapt their exploration strategies to the constraints present in the pool of objects, future work can target the possibility that robots use the observation of human exploration behavior as a starting point for acquiring efficient strategies. So far we have used tasks in which exploration was applied to completely unravel the kinematic structure of an object. Expanding upon our results on humans exploiting redundancies in the structure of the objects, future research can address how exploration can be terminated once sufficient structural properties are discovered for tool use according to the current goal.

5. References

Blaisdell, A. P. (2008). Cognitive Dimension of Operant Learning, In: *Learning and Memory: A Comprehensive Reference*, Vol.1, R. Menzel, & J. Byrne, (Eds.), pp. 173-195, Elsevier, ISBN 0-12-370504-5, Oxford, Great Britain

Braitenberg, V. (1984). *Vehicles: Experiments in Synthetic Psychology*, MIT Press, ISBN 0-262-02208-7, Cambridge, MA, USA

Craighero L, Leo I, Umiltà C, Simion F. (2011). Newborns' Preference for Goal-Directed Actions. *Cognition*. [Epub ahead of print] PubMed PMID: 21388616, ISSN: 0010-0277

Džeroski, S., de Raedt,L., & Driessens, K. (2001). Relational Reinforcement Learning. *Machine Learning*, Vol. 43, No. 1-2 , pp. 7-52, ISSN 0885-6125

Elsner, B., & Hommel, B. (2001). Effect Anticipation and Action Control. *Journal of Experimental Psychology: Human Perception and Performance*, Vol. 27, No. 1, pp. 229-240, ISSN 0096-1523

Frensch, P. A., & Rünger, D. (2003). Implicit Learning. *Current Directions in Psychological Science*, Vol. 12, No. 1, pp. 13-18, ISSN 0963-7214

Gaissmaier, W. & Schooler, L. J. (2008). The Smart Potential Behind Probability Matching. *Cognition*, Vol. 109, pp. 416-422, ISSN: 0010-0277

Gaschler, R., & Frensch, P. A. (2007). Is Information Reduction an Item-Specific or an Item-General Process?. *International Journal of Psychology*, Vol. 42, No. 4, pp. 218-228, ISSN 0020-7594

Gaschler, R., & Frensch, P. A. (2009). When Vaccinating Against Information Reduction Works and When It Does Not Work. *Psychological Studies*, Vol. 54, No. 1, pp. 43-53, ISSN 0033-2968

Harnad, S. (1990). The Symbol Grounding Problem. *Physica D: Nonlinear Phenomena*, Vol. 42, No. 1-3, pp. 335-346, ISSN 0167-2789

Haider, H., & Frensch, P. A. (2002). Why Aggregated Learning Follows the Power Law of Practice When Individual Learning does not: Comment on Rickard (1997, 1999), Delaney et al. (1998), and Palmeri (1999). *Journal of Experimental Psychology: Learning, Memory and Cognition*, Vol. 28, pp. 392-406, ISSN: 0278-7393

Held, R., & Hein, A. (1963). Movement-Produced Stimulation in the Development of Visually Guided Behavior. *Journal of Comparative and Physiological Psychology*, Vol. 56, pp. 872-876, ISSN: 0021-9940

Kaelbling, L. (1993). *Learning in Embedded Systems*, MIT Press, ISBN 9780262512787, Cambridge, MA, USA

Katz, D., & Brock, O. (2008). Manipulating Articulated Objects with Interactive Perception, *Proceedings of the IEEE International Conference on Robotics and Automation 2008*, ISBN 978-1-4244-1646-2, Pasadena, CA, USA, May 2008

Katz, D., Orthey, A., & Brock, O. (2010). Interactive Perception of Articulated Objects. In: *The 12th International Symposium of Experimental Robotics (ISER) 2010*

Katz, D., Pyuro, Y., & Brock, O. (2008). Learning to Manipulate Articulated Objects in Unstructured Environments Using a Grounded Relational Representation, *Proceedings of Robotics: Science and Systems IV*, ISBN 978-0262513098, Zurich, Switzerland, June 2008

Logan, G. D. (1988). Toward an Instance Theory of Automatization. *Psychological Review*, Vol. 95, pp. 492-527, ISSN: 0033-295X

Luce, R. D. (1959). *Individual Choice Behavior: A Theoretical Analysis*. New York: Wiley. ISBN 0-486-44136-9.

Sun, R., Merrill, E., & Peterson, T. (2001). From Implicit Skills to Explicit Knowledge: A Bottom-up Model of Skill Learning. *Cognitive Science*, Vol. 25, pp. 203-244.

Sutton, R. S., & Barto, A. G. (1998). *Reinforcement learning: An introduction*, ISBN 978-0262193986, Cambridge, MA: MIT Press.

Tadepalli, P., Givan, R., & Driessens, K. (2004). Relational Reinforcement Learning: An Overview. *Proceedings of the Workshop on Relational Reinforcement Learning at ICML '04*, Banff, Canada, July 8, 2004

Thorndike, E. L. (1911). *Animal Intelligence: Experimental Studies*, Macmillan, New York, NY, USA

van Otterlo, M. (2005). A Survey of Reinforcement Learning in Relational Domains. *CTIT Technical Report series TR-CTIT-05-31*, Centre for Telematics and Information Technology University of Twente, Enschede, ISSN 1381-3625 [for more: http://eprints.eemcs.utwente.nl/1879/]

Weir, A. A. S., & Kacelnik, A. (2006). A New Caledonian Crow (Corvus Moneduloides) Creatively Re-designs Tools by Bending or Unbending Aluminium Strips. *Animal Cognition*, Vol. 9, No.4, pp. 317-334, ISSN 1435-9448